This collection of essays examines the struggles of the people of England with the collapse of civilisation as they knew it. As the country fell into civil war and near anarchy, the people sought out in word and action how to preserve what could still be preserved or to create new political, religious and social certainties. The authors discuss individuals or groups who were soldiers, writers or statesmen of the Civil Wars or the Interregnum, people who were at the centre of power or in more humble and localised circumstances.

All of the authors take their inspiration from the work of Austin Woolrych, whose own books and articles focus on these very questions. The volume is published in his honour, and presents the most up-to-date thinking of both leading scholars and keen younger voices on many of the central issues dominating the study of the 'English Revolution'.

Soldiers, writers and statesmen
of the English Revolution

Austin Woolrych

Soldiers, writers and statesmen
of the English Revolution

EDITED BY
IAN GENTLES
JOHN MORRILL
AND
BLAIR WORDEN

CAMBRIDGE
UNIVERSITY PRESS

CAMBRIDGE UNIVERSITY PRESS
Cambridge, New York, Melbourne, Madrid, Cape Town, Singapore, São Paulo

Cambridge University Press
The Edinburgh Building, Cambridge CB2 8RU, UK

Published in the United States of America by Cambridge University Press, New York

www.cambridge.org
Information on this title: www.cambridge.org/9780521591201

First published 1998
This digitally printed version 2007

A catalogue record for this publication is available from the British Library

Library of Congress Cataloguing in Publication data
Soldiers, writers, and statesmen of the English Revolution / edited by Ian Gentles,
John Morrill, and Blair Worden.
p.   cm.
Includes bibliographical references (p. 323) and index.
ISBN 0 521 59120 1 (hc)
1. Great Britain – History – Puritan Revolution, 1642–1660.
2. Great Britain – History – Puritan Revolution, 1642–1660 – Biography.
I. Gentles, I. J.   II. Morrill, J. S. (John Stephen)   III. Worden, Blair.
DA405.S65   1998
941.06′3–dc21   97–44329   CIP

ISBN 978-0-521-59120-1 hardback
ISBN 978-0-521-03875-1 paperback

Contents

Frontispiece photograph by Gerard Hearne

Preface

JOHN MORRILL

This book is a tribute to Austin Woolrych and its appearance is timed to coincide with his eightieth birthday. Lesley le Claire gives an account of Austin Woolrych's life and achievement in the essay that follows this preface; and Sarah Coombs has co-ordinated the preparation of a bibliography of his writings that appears at the end of the book. The essays themselves were commissioned to represent one principle above all: Austin's rare gift of friendship; his ability quickly to communicate his own fundamental decency and kindness and to evoke deep feelings of loyalty and affection. Lesley le Claire evokes that gift below, but it is one with which all the contributors would wish to be associated. He is a generous host, a grateful guest, a warm and concerned friend. He is someone we all admire both as a person and as a scholar, and we feel privileged to be able to offer this tribute to him. Some of us are his former pupils – notably Colin Phillips and John Sutton who were his research students; others – John Reeve, John Adamson and Sarah Barber – had their doctorates examined by him and found in him someone who not only offered wonderfully clear and helpful advice on their theses but who remained keenly interested in their subsequent careers. Austin is a great traveller and many of the essays in this volume reflect the friendships he has made on his travels around the globe: Colin Davis and Glenn Burgess during lecture-cum-vacation trips to New Zealand, Barbara Taft and Barbara Donagan during visits to research libraries on the East and West coasts of North America, for example. All three editors have been friends of Austin for more than a quarter of a century and all have benefited especially from his knowledge, precision of mind and strong encouragement.

Austin has an army of friends and what defined the group who were invited to contribute to this volume was an interest in the central concerns of Austin's scholarly career: with the English Revolution in general, and its military, political and intellectual dynamics in particular. The title evokes the title of perhaps his finest work – *Soldiers and Statesmen: the General*

Council of the Army and its Debates 1647–1648 (1987); but his other major
books are also about soldiers (*Battles of the English Civil War* (1961, 1991))
about soldiers who are statesmen (*Oliver Cromwell* (1964)) or about the
relations of soldiers and would-be statesmen (*Commonwealth to Protectorate*
(1982)). The title also evokes his love of literature and of the literary. His
study of the historical context of Milton's writings of 1659–1660, which
appeared as the 228-page introduction to volume 7 of the Yale Edition of
the *Complete Prose Works of John Milton* (1947, 1979) is effectively an
additional monograph in its own right; and he has written a series of
observant and shrewd essays on Milton's prose works. His essay on
'Political theory and political practice' in a volume entitled *The Age of
Milton: Backgrounds to Seventeenth-century Literature*, eds. C. A. Patrides and
R. B. Waddington (1980) is a model of lucidity and balance. And it
demonstrates one of Austin's great strengths – the desire to link fields of
scholarly endeavour too often hermetically sealed off from one another.
His first book, *Battles of the English Civil War*, manages, far better than
anyone else has done, to correlate the military history of the civil wars
with their political and social contexts – and to do so in both directions.
His decision to use three case studies – the battles of Marston Moor,
Naseby and Preston – to bring out the nature of the conflict and the
interconnections was a typically thoughtful and effective deep-planning
stratagem; and it worked. Similar searches for interconnection (of history
and literature, of political theory and practice) can be found throughout
his writings and we hope that this volume offers some comparably fruitful
searches. Certainly his interest in the Civil War as a military event which
was shaped not just by the technologies of war but by the cultural
expectations of the participants, is reflected in three essays: Barbara
Donagan writes about the care of sick, dying and dead soldiers; Ian
Gentles discusses the iconography of war to be found in the regimental
banners; and Sarah Barber recovers the history of bodies of irregular
troops raised in 1648. The broader set of problems raised by the need to
manage the war, and the political problems thrown up by warfare, are
examined in John Adamson's exploration of Robert Scawen's work as both
a public and private man of business for the tenth Earl of Northumberland;
and in Ian Roy's study of the stormy career of George Lord Digby, royalist
soldier and statesman. Austin was one of the first to recognise that the
English Revolution looks different through the prism of local history; and
he explored the local contexts of a number of important episodes from his
precocious study of the Yorkshire neutrality petition of 1642 via a
Historical Association Pamphlet of 1955 on Penruddock's Rising of 1655,
through to a study of the Restoration in Yorkshire. Many of his other
writings also reveal his strong sense of place and acute knowledge of and

feeling for landscape. It is therefore fitting that we should have two regional studies from his own former pupils, Colin Phillips' account of the political confrontations in Kendal and John Sutton's pioneering prosopographical study of the Major General's commissioners for Staffordshire.

Austin Woolrych is one of the few historians who is manifestly equally at home both in the 1640s as in the 1650s, and this volume seeks to do equal justice to the whole period. Above all there is a cluster of articles on that relationship of political theory and political practice that lies at the heart of his studies of 1647–8, 1653 and 1659–60 and which are his major contributions to scholarship. Blair Worden and Nicholas von Maltzahn focus on Milton's relations with Oliver Cromwell[1] and with early Restoration critics; Colin Davis and Glenn Burgess both examine problems in the thought of James Harrington (in the latter case coupled with a study of Hobbes); and Gerald Aylmer and Barbara Taft offer assessments of the Levellers from a Restoration perspective – through an analysis of their alleged influence on the political writings of John Locke and through a study of the later writings of Robert Overton.

Austin Woolrych's mind and interests therefore bind together this book. Austin is one of the most graceful of writers as well as one of the most gracious of reviewers (the bibliography of his writings shows that he has reviewed well over one hundred of the most important works on the period to have appeared over the past forty years), always courteous in tone and yet observant and firm about fundamentals. Austin never has to raise his voice, but his approval and disapproval can readily be discerned. But not once in his career has he resorted to personal attack or cheap jibe. In preparing this volume, the authors and editors have tried to ensure a tone and thoughtfulness of manner worthy of the man. They cannot hope to sustain writing of his pellucid quality or narrative clarity and vividness; but they hope that something of the calm authority he has taught them will come through.

Austin Woolrych is one of the best-loved and most widely respected of early modern historians. This book is written by those who count themselves amongst his friends to share with him and with others an enthusiasm for that Mount Everest of British History, the English Revolution of the seventeenth century, an enthusiasm that Austin has helped to nurture or sustain in each of us.

---

[1] It was intended that an essay specifically on Oliver Cromwell (and his uses of the Bible) would be written by the author of this preface. He deeply regrets that chronic ill-health in the second half of 1996 prevented the completion of that essay in time for its appearance in this volume.

Austin Woolrych: an appreciation

LESLEY LE CLAIRE

In the Michaelmas term of 1981 I well remember a lunch-time conversation in the Senior Common Room of Worcester College. My colleagues were gently teasing me because twenty years in Oxford had still not destroyed my inbred Scottish reverence for the title 'Professor'. I protested that the trepidation I was feeling about my meeting with the formidable and distinguished scholar who was to visit the College Library the next morning was fully justified and I added for good measure that he was a Visiting Fellow of All Souls. This gave everyone pause and then our elderly politics tutor chipped in. He frequently affected Bertie Wooster's style. 'Oh, I've met him', he said, 'and he *is* rather a swell, but a *very* good egg – a real gent – you'll like Austin Woolrych'. And, of course, he was quite right. Austin is all of those things and I was to like him very much indeed. As soon as I met him, he put me at ease and almost before I knew it, we were having great fun imagining C. H. Firth's dawning excitement as Henry Pottinger (the highly eccentric Librarian of Worcester in the latter half of the nineteenth century) showed him the Clarke manuscripts for the first time and he realised what a treasure trove he had stumbled on. Not quite Schliemann and the face of Agamemnon perhaps, but when he opened the folio volume bound in smooth brown leather that contains the *Putney Debates* Firth must have felt that he was hearing, not only the voice of Oliver Cromwell, but also that much more elusive and faint murmur, the voice of the common man. We agreed, Austin and I, that they dined well in Worcester that evening. Austin, as all his friends know, is a past master of the dying art of letter writing and, years after that first meeting, he was to write to me, 'what happier way could there be of forging a friendship than through a common enthusiasm for a great historical archive?' What happier way indeed! It is an enthusiasm that all the contributors to this volume share. The Clarke Papers have made Worcester College, Oxford, a place of pilgrimage for most of them and form a common link between us all.

His friends said of Sir Walter Scott that he was a man so sure of his own dignity that he never stood on it. It has always seemed to me that this statement could be applied with equal truth to Austin. He is the least self-important of men. So it is with a slight sense of shock that one enters the little church of St Andrew at Quatt, a tiny village lying just over the border into Shropshire. At first glance, the church appears a not particularly distinguished eighteenth-century building in red brick. In fact this is the restoration of a much earlier building: there is evidence in the chancel that previously there was a smaller church dating from the Saxon period. But the overwhelming impression of the interior is that this is the Wolryche (*sic*) family vault. In the first place the church was no doubt raised to the glory of God, but in the second, and a close second at that, it celebrates the Wolryches and their connections. From the seventeenth century onwards their marble tombs and gilded monuments abound. The finest perhaps is that of Mary Wolryche (1637–78). She is represented as a semi-recumbent figure with a lyre. A long epitaph reveals her as a lady of such awesome piety, virtue and accomplishments as to make Milton's 'late espousèd saint' seem frivolous by comparison. She was the daughter of Matthew Griffith, 'a reverend and learned man who served two of the best of Kings, Charles I and Charles II, as their private chaplain, in bad times as in good unshaken in his loyalty to King, liberty and true religion'. Her second husband was 'John Wolryche, the not unworthy son of a brave and faithful father, Thomas of Dudmaston, Shropshire Knight and Baronet'. It is this Sir Thomas Wolryche (1598–1668) who is of interest to us because his great-great-grandfather, Humphrey Wolryche of Dudmaston (1460–1533), had three sons and Austin is descended from the third of them. Sir Thomas was Charles I's governor of Bridgnorth. He is represented in the church as a kneeling boy in a group of his siblings round the monument dedicated to his parents and he has his own very handsome table tomb near the west aisle. Austin himself – and it is hard to imagine anyone more remote from all this funereal splendour – regards his interesting kinsmen with that mixture of amusement, embarrassment and pride most of us reserve for ancestors whose views we tend to deplore. Of Sir Thomas he always says, 'He only lies in the collateral, you know ... and anyway I'm sure he was a very *lukewarm* Royalist ...'

Austin is a natural countryman but Houseman's 'blue-remembered hills' were not the background of his early youth. He grew up in London. Born in 1918, he belongs precisely to the 'entre deux guerres' generation. His father was in the Intelligence Corps in World War I and he himself served for six years in World War II. He had a fairly typical middle-class childhood. He attended Westminster School, and, as one might expect, was a highly intelligent pupil, obviously destined for a successful professional career. But when he reached the sixth form the family found itself in straitened financial circumstances. These were the years of the Depression and there were two other bright children to educate. So further education was ruled out for Austin and for the next four years, improbable though it may sound, he worked as a clerk in Harrods. His starting salary was a princely £1 per week. It is hard to imagine a squarer peg in a rounder hole and in retrospect it is difficult not to feel a little angry. There cannot have been many young clerks in Harrods whose reading in the tube to and from work included Proust, Joyce and Hardy. Without in the least wishing to portray the young Austin as a latter-day Jude Fawley, he may well have found that the novel had its resonances. On the other hand, in the late thirties, young men everywhere, student and office-boy alike, were about to be swept up by the looming global crisis and their worries and frustrations about education and a professional future were to be displaced by the very real possibility that they might have no future at all. In the late summer of 1938, Austin burned off some of his physical energy by riding a push-bike to Venice. He covered eleven hundred miles in seventeen days, crossing four Swiss mountain passes. His life-long passion for travel and for mountains was expressed thus early. After four days in Venice (he had taken a third week's holiday without pay), he returned home by train. However this was the year of the Munich crisis; in the breathing space provided by Chamberlain's shabby and temporary peace the country prepared for war, and Austin, with many of his contemporaries, joined the Territorial Army.

> What will happen next. What will happen.
> We ask and waste the question on the air;
> Nelson is stone and Johnnie Walker moves his
> Legs like a cretin over Trafalgar Square.
> And in the Corner House the carpet sweepers
> Advance between the tables after crumbs
> Inexorably like a tank battalion
> In answer to the drums.[1]

What happened next to Austin *was* a tank battalion. When war was finally declared he was drafted immediately to RMC Sandhurst with his fellow-members of the Inns of Court Regiment. He was commissioned into the Royal Tank Regiment in March 1940. For the next six years he was to live the life of a soldier.

Austin insists that he had what is called, in a classic example of oxymoron, a 'good war'. Yet when one remembers that only nine months after he had married Muriel in September 1941 he was posted to the

---

[1] Louis MacNeice, *Autumn Journal* (London, 1939), Section v.

Middle East and that his first thought on being wounded at El Alamein was 'Perhaps I shall survive after all and see her again', one realises that he is making rather light of his experience. For a few years he thought quite seriously about becoming a professional soldier but Muriel, sensible woman, was against it and he gradually realised that this was not his true métier.

All the same, his time in the army was to prove an important part of his education. If Gibbon felt that even some gentle army manoeuvres in the home counties were a useful interlude for the future historian of the Roman Empire,[2] one can understand how Austin's more extensive military experience stood him in good stead later when he turned his attention to the battles of the English Civil War. Of course his study of the under-currents of that war was to go much wider and deeper but one feels that soldiers under the physical stress of battle or the psychological fret of religious and political dilemmas always engage his particular sympathy and fire his imagination. When he writes, 'the strain and excitement of battle play odd tricks with one's sense of time',[3] a man who has experienced the heat of action himself is speaking; when he describes the anger of Major General Lambert in 1652 because the Rump had just abolished the office of Lord Deputy of Ireland as he was about to take it up and explains, 'what moved him was the sort of distrust that clever young generals, fresh from active service, often feel toward prevaricating self-interested politicians',[4] one feels he knows this sort of young officer at first hand; when he describes the New Model as 'moved by the call of a cause rather than by the usual lures and rewards of the military profession',[5] one remembers that he too fought in an army similarly motivated, however much he and his fellow officers may have grinned at General Montgomery in his Cromwellian mood. Indeed, without wishing to push the analogy too far, the political awakening he was to analyse so acutely in the New Model had its parallel in the army he knew. In 1945, despite Churchill's general popularity, persuasive radical voices swung the ex-service vote to Labour. In the mid-nineteen-forties as in the mid-sixteen-forties, 'men who con-stantly risked their lives in what they were told was a war of ideals were bound sooner or later to start thinking about those ideals for them-selves ... [and] questioned every traditional assumption about political and

---

[2] C. V. Wedgwood, *History and Hope, Collected Essays* (London, 1987) p. 340.
[3] A. Woolrych, *Battles of the English Civil War* (London, 1961), p. 74.
[4] A. Woolrych, *England without a King, 1649–1660* (London and New York, Lancaster Pamphlets Series, 1983), p. 25.
[5] A. Woolrych, *Soldiers and Statesmen: The General Council of the Army and its Debates, 1647–1648* (Oxford, 1987), p. 14.

social hierarchy'.[6] Finally, I know no better setting of a scene before a battle than his simple prologue to Marston Moor. It bears repeating because of the way in which he takes that dangerous but necessary leap of the imagination from one epoch to another. It is not a romantic leap. His personal experience as a soldier in the twentieth century is fused with his accumulated knowledge of the mind-set of a soldier in the seventeenth and of the battle procedures under which he would be operating. None of his carefully inserted background details of sound and colour is super-fluous; all of them serve to heighten the reader's sympathetic awareness to a remarkable degree.

> By about five a quiet fell upon the two armies and the royalists could hear their opponents chanting their metrical psalms in Marston Field. It was a comfort to taut nerves and tired muscles to sing the songs of an earlier chosen people, for those soldiers had to stand a test which modern warfare has forgotten – that of watching for hours, without cover and at a range close enough to be seen, a whole enemy army poised rank on rank for battle, arms glinting, colours flying and all the panoply of death flaunting its gayest colours.[7]

Austin returned to civilian life in 1946. He was now twenty-eight and a married man of five years' standing. Quite rightly he saw that an ex-service grant would enable him to acquire the university education so sorely missed ten years earlier. He applied to read English at Pembroke College, Oxford, largely because an earlier Woolrych had preceded him there. Pembroke, 'that college so polite and shy',[8] is still one of the smaller colleges in Oxford but in 1945 the number of undergraduates had dwindled to twenty-three. During the war it had been partly requisitioned for service cadets and various service departments. There were nine tutorial fellows. The Master, the Reverend Frederick Homes Dudden, was already in his seventies. Having interviewed Austin, he assured him they would be delighted to admit him (it was all very gentlemanly), 'but', he added casually, 'I'm afraid we don't have an English tutor at the moment – can I interest you in History instead?' So, almost by accident, the future historian was born. Austin, viewing as he does the more eccentric manifestations of recent English studies with a sardonic eye, feels he had a lucky escape. All one can say is that English's loss was History's gain.

Austin's tutor was Ronald Buchanan McCallum who was later to

[6] C. A. Patrides and Raymond B. Waddington (eds.), *The Age of Milton: Backgrounds to Seventeenth Century Literature* (Manchester, 1980), p. 47.

[7] A. Woolrych, *Battles of the English Civil War*, p. 72.

[8] John Betjeman, *Summoned by Bells* (London, 1960), p. 105.

become Master of the College. His chief area of interest was nineteenth-
and twentieth-century politics and history. But since siren voices from the
Civil War period were calling Austin quite early on, it is perhaps sad that
he had not gone to Balliol where the events of the mid-seventeenth
century were inspiring yet another intellectual revolution spearheaded by
Christopher Hill and where Gerald Aylmer, albeit a year behind him,
would have been a fellow student.

But it was a war-weary Oxford that Austin found. There was a shortage
of teachers and a shortage of books. There is an account in the Pembroke
College Record that one winter's morning in 1947 when it became known
that a number of copies of Stenton's *Anglo-Saxon England* would be
available, there was a queue of more than a hundred people outside the
Oxford University Press showroom in the High before the doors opened at
9 a.m. Oxford in the immediate post-war years was probably a more
serious place than it had ever been. E. R. Dodds, who had succeeded
Gilbert Murray in the Regius Chair of Greek in 1936, was very struck by
the change of mood and by the steadying influence of this new, mature
generation of students, many of whom had seen active service. 'They were
not interested in preserving or restoring the more puerile Oxford traditions such as "sconcing" in Hall or learning long Latin graces by rote ...
What most of them wanted was to fulfil their educational commitments as
speedily as possible and get on with their professional careers.'[9]

Ex-servicemen were excused prelims, so it was possible to acquire a BA,
as Austin did, in seven terms – no mean feat when one considers the
punishing reading lists confronting undergraduates in History and remembers that his war wound had left him with a damaged eye. Another two
terms were spent in postgraduate work, after which he was appointed to a
history lectureship in Leeds University. There had not been much time for
long, lazy, sunny afternoons on the river.

If Austin at this stage in his life sounds a little like one of Cornford's
'Young Men in a Hurry',[10] it is not surprising. With a wife and family to
support, he had every reason to be in a hurry. It is, however, a false
impression; in fact he was far removed from the youthful prig of
Cornford's imagining. He had already discovered that 'the silent reasonable world',[11] and 'the company of clean humorous intellect'[12] were where
he belonged. Moreover, if the romantic idyll that layered memory often
makes of the initial Oxford experience had partially eluded him, it meant

[9] E. R. Dodds, *Missing Persons: An Autobiography* (Oxford, 1978), p. 168.
[10] F. M. Cornford, *Microcosmographia Academica: Being a Guide for the Young Academic Politician*,
   5th edn (Cambridge, 1953), p. 5.
[11] Ibid., p. 24.   [12] Ibid., p. 24.

that working in a very different academic setting did not come as so much of a shock. The transition from our older universities with their close communication between teacher and taught, their facilities for civilised discussion, their omnipresent beauty of buildings and gardens, to civic universities in ugly post-industrial towns, can seem very harsh. I remember hearing a talk in the sixties in Lady Margaret Hall by an ex-Principal of the College, Lynda Grier. She was a surviving member of that splendid, pioneering generation of Edwardian she-dons to whom modern women academics owe so much. She startled her Oxford audience by describing the thrill of going to Leeds in 1915 and finding herself, for the first time, a member of a great university! Ostensibly, of course, she was comparing her status as a woman in Leeds with what it had been in Oxford and Cambridge but, with a gleam of mischief, she was also reminding her old colleagues that the red brick of Leeds could bear comparison with the same building material at Lady Margaret Hall.

Thirty-five years later, the Leeds University that Austin found had developed considerably. The earlier emphasis on science and technology had diminished and there was a steady move towards the humanities. The student body was far less local in flavour than hitherto. In 1938–39 only twenty-five per cent of it was drawn from outside Yorkshire, but in 1950–51 this had increased to forty per cent. Student numbers rose from 3,000 to 9,000 between 1952 and 1972, more rapidly than in any other university except London. Partly thanks to the Brotherton bequest, it had the finest library in the North after Manchester. Famous names had headed the History department for some time – Grant, Turberville, Guy Chapman, Norman Gash, and in 1955 Asa Briggs. John Le Patourel was professor of medieval history when Austin arrived – a man he was to hold in great affection and to regard very much as one of his mentors. Austin's brief was largely to cover early modern history, the area to which in those days we referred, quite unabashed, as the 'Tudors and the Stuarts'. At a time when 'aids to students' were unknown and textbooks still in short supply, Austin's elegant, carefully presented and thought-provoking lectures were gratefully received. A younger colleague, Gordon Forster,[13] describes him as 'surely one of the most effective and well-liked teachers in his department and graduates encountered long afterwards often said how much they had enjoyed his lectures, tutorials and classes'. This one can well believe. He has that mark of the first-rate teacher of being able to draw out the best in the most tentative student without appearing to

---

[13] I am deeply grateful to Gordon Forster for the information he gave me about Austin's time in Leeds.

dominate or patronise. Moreover, he can achieve this at any stage. Anne
Laurence, Senior Lecturer at the Open University, tells me that when she
had reached that daunting moment in a young scholar's life of shaping her
doctoral thesis into a book, Austin was briefed by the editorial board of
'Studies in History' to advise her. She has always remembered with what
skill and care he helped to guide her through that particular rite of
passage. It was the beginning of yet another delightful friendship. Mr
Forster also remarks on how well Austin's earlier experience on military
selection boards had prepared him for the arduous task of admissions tutor:
'His interviewing technique was pleasant, polite and persistent, never
impatient or overbearing; it was a pleasure (as well as a help to a less
experienced colleague) to interview with him; and he recruited many very
able – and very agreeable – young men and women to the History
honours school.' It was at this stage in his career that Austin began to think
hard about the constitution of a university as a whole and of degree
courses in particular – thoughts to be translated much later into practice in
Lancaster. He was appointed to several important committees in the
Faculty of Arts and was instrumental in the reform of the unsatisfactory
General degree which was replaced by a slimmed-down and better-
balanced Combined Studies degree. 'He showed himself', says Mr Forster,
'a doughty, quietly determined, fighter for his reformist views, successfully
standing up to one or two overmighty professors who sought to defend
outmoded degree schemes'. He was also unsparing of his time when it
came to participating in University Extension courses on historical
subjects, lecturing to student historical societies and the Historical Association and working with adult students on short residential courses at
Grantley Hall near Fountains Abbey. These last involved really serious
study intermingled with jolly sessions at the local pub. In addition to all
this he was writing review articles and essays as well as his book on the
Civil War battles. It was in the Brotherton that he began his vast and
detailed research on Barebone's Parliament. His biographical index of the
members finally saw the light of day in his description of the social
composition of the House of Commons in Chapter VI of *Commonwealth to
Protectorate*. The delay in the completion of this work was largely due to
the fact that the most exciting and demanding task he had ever contemplated had presented itself. In 1963 fate threw down a challenge he simply
could not refuse.

In May 1962 Professor Bruce Williams, a member of the Academic
Planning Board for the proposed new university of Lancaster, wrote from
Australia that he 'was not convinced that history should be the central
discipline of the faculty … [it] would depend in some measure on getting
[in my experience the rather rare] historians who really understand what a

civilisation is ...'.[14] Professor Williams was in for a pleasant surprise. Eighteen months later Lancaster was to acquire just such a rare historian. Austin has no difficulty in remembering what he was doing the day President Kennedy was assassinated – he was being interviewed for the new chair of history in Lancaster. There followed a cliff-hanging period when it seemed that a rival candidate might be appointed and then, just before Christmas, he learned that he was to be offered the chair. It was a very happy Christmas.

Sussex – Essex – Norwich – Kent – Warwick – York – Lancaster; the roll call of the English post-Robbins universities has the noble thunder of the *dramatis personae* of a Shakespeare history play. It is a not inappropriate nobility. It was a time of high ideals and great excitement in the university world. The older 'new' universities of the late nineteenth and early twentieth centuries had served long apprenticeships as university colleges before achieving their autonomy but this newer group sprang into being, Athena-like, fully armed with complete university status from the beginning. However, before this stage was reached, an immense amount of planning and discussion was involved. The contrast with the recent rash of educational institutions upgraded to university ranking simply by wave of wand and gift of name could hardly be more stark.

At the end of 1961 Lancaster had finally defeated its rival Blackpool in the contest to be chosen as the site of the new university in the North. There followed a period of intense activity until the first students were admitted in 1964. During these three and a half years land was purchased, buildings designed, possible patrons, local and national, approached, the constitution of the university drafted, admission procedures decided on and, above all, degree courses discussed and planned. As one of the first sixteen heads of department who formed the Shadow Senate, Austin was sucked into this whirlpool of activity from the beginning of 1964.[15] Although the seven wise men (one, Kathleen Major, was a woman) who formed the original Academic Planning Board had strong Oxbridge connections – as also had the Shadow Senate – many of the members of both bodies had wide experience of provincial, Scottish, Commonwealth or American universities.[16] So there was a very real desire not to be hidebound by Oxbridge models. It is true that from the beginning it was largely accepted that a collegiate system was to be preferred to a non-collegiate (though there were some mutterings – Professor Williams again – about an out-of-date romanticised image of life in Oxford or Cambridge).[17] A modified collegiate system was finally adopted – with Austin

---

[14] Marion E. McClintock, *University of Lancaster: Quest for Innovation* (Lancaster, 1974), p. 130.
[15] Ibid., p. 138.   [16] Ibid., p. 24.

urging on more than one occasion the centralising of arts teaching in one
building rather than in the colleges. He felt that to group the arts
departments in one place would 'greatly facilitate the close consultation
and cooperation between them which our degree schemes, more than
most, will demand. If our business is the interlocking of subjects, are we
wise to start by physically separating them?'[18] He had a very real point
here. The desire to avoid the narrow specialisation of the Oxbridge degree
model and to create flexible cross-disciplinary courses had resulted in a
degree structure of almost Byzantine complexity. At one point there was a
rather pathetic *cri de coeur* from the Vice-Chancellor to the Board: 'Please
do not think of any more alternatives – there are too many here already!'[19]
In the end it seems to have been Austin who cut through the tangled skein
of argument by presenting a paper to the Shadow Senate which came
down on the side of a final degree based on nine units, a proposal which
was finally accepted without debate.[20] But it was a student joke in
Lancaster – just as it was when I was a student in Glasgow – that anyone
who could understand the course structure deserved a degree on that basis
alone. In fact, in many ways there was a distinctly Scottish flavour to the
degrees evolving in the new universities, partly because Keele, over which
Lord Lindsay had cast a long shadow, was often cited as a pattern and in
Lancaster's case because Sir Malcolm Knox, the Principal of St Andrews,
was a member of the original Academic Planning Board. It was he who had
suggested that the Faculty of Arts should be built round a central
discipline, not philosophy as in Scotland, but history.[21] Despite the
objections, already quoted, by Professor Williams, history was a key
subject from the beginning. The numbers speak for themselves: of the
three hundred original students, two thirds were studying history as one of
their three first-year subjects. The department expanded rapidly. In the
first year Austin had two lecturers and one assistant; ten years later he had
more than twenty on his staff, with six new appointments being made in
one year. Harold Perkin,[22] from 1965 his most valued lieutenant, bears
witness to his skill in attracting talent: 'we were able to recruit over two
dozen remarkable scholars in an extraordinary variety of fields ... who
combined to make it one of the largest and most productive history
departments in the country'. Austin aimed, almost from the start, to give
the department a special strength in social history; hence the early
appointment of Harold Perkin, through whose initiative the Social History

---

[17] Ibid., p. 329.   [18] Ibid., pp. 333–34, 337.
[19] Ibid., p. 137.   [20] Ibid., p. 108.   [21] Ibid., p. 130.
[22] My sincere thanks are due to Harold Perkin, from 1985 Professor of History and Higher
Education at Northwestern University, Illinois, for his very helpful account of his long
association with Austin at Lancaster.

Society of the United Kingdom was founded with Lancaster as its headquarters. Other early commitments which have since flourished were to the history of science and local history.

The workload was enormous. The preparation and teaching of the new degree courses would have been enough for most men – and Austin took on the same teaching duties as the rest of his staff – but, in addition, he and his fellow Senators sat through endless committees whose wide-ranging agenda covered every possible aspect of the new university. It is almost as though the zest generated by the new universities created a new breed of academics/administrators whose energy levels rose as the magnitude of the tasks confronting them demanded. Gerald Aylmer in York was one such, Asa Briggs in Sussex another. It was Lord Briggs who recognised the same quality in Austin; having found him one of the most effective members of his department in Leeds, he had warmly encouraged his move to Lancaster and helped him greatly with advice after his appointment.[23]

By 1971 Austin's department was securely established, but then he became even busier when he was elected Pro-Vice-Chancellor of the University (one of three), with special responsibility for student and college affairs. He held this office for the next five years. In 1970 he had two sabbatical terms, most of which he spent at the Folger Library in Washington where he formed a lasting friendship with one of the contributors to this volume, Barbara Taft. In 1981–82 he had an interlude in Oxford as a Visiting Fellow of All Souls – a time he greatly enjoyed. In the following year he was Commonwealth Visiting Fellow to Universities in Australia and New Zealand. His travels have taken him – literally – from China to Peru, sometimes for professional reasons, sometimes for pleasure, often for both. His Chinese connection has been particularly interesting. The slow loosening in the eighties of the suffocating political straitjacket imposed by Mao and the recent economic reforms have certainly given the 'poorest hee' that is in China a better life to live than heretofore. At last cultural exchanges with the West have become possible again. As early as 1982, Professor Wang Jue-fei, who was teaching British history in Nanjing, managed to visit Edinburgh and other British universities and to make contact with most of the important historians in his field. A quiet, gentle man who had suffered greatly in the dark years of the Cultural Revolution, he visited my house in Oxford and very much delighted my mother with his old fashioned oriental reverence for great age. Austin did not meet him on this occasion but I can see why they became friends later. As well as their mutual devotion to historical studies

---

[23] I am grateful to Lord Briggs for his comments to me about the high regard he had for Austin as a colleague.

they have much in common. Westerner though he is, Austin has the same
knack with old ladies – my husband's ninety-year-old stepmother has
never forgotten meeting him. But it has to be said that he is very good at
charming younger ladies too. Four years after Wang Jue-fei's visit, an
international conference of seventeenth-century historians, financed by
Cable and Wireless, Hong Kong, was arranged in Nanjing. Austin attended
it and has maintained contact ever since. All this, of course, was before
Tiananmen Square and its aftermath, that harsh reminder that even yet,
Chinese John Lilburnes land up in prison – with little or no chance of
smuggling out vindications, justifications or remonstrances. Yet if there is a
certain irony that in the history departments of Chinese universities the
implications of radical movements in England three and a half centuries
ago are seriously discussed with experts like Austin, there is also a ray of
hope.

All in all, Austin gave twenty years of his life to Lancaster. Harold
Perkin, who worked closely with him for almost the same length of time,
writes, 'When I think back to my nineteen years at Lancaster, Austin
Woolrych fills the foreground with his sunny and generous, proficient and
considerate personality.' Like Gordon Forster, he pays tribute to that rare
combination of tact and toughness which was his particular skill in
interview and negotiation, and, also like Forster, he points out that,
inevitably, the price paid for all this selfless administrative work was the
writing that was slowed down. All the same, glancing at his bibliography, it
is clear that his introduction to Milton's prose in the Yale edition of 1974
was written entirely while he was head of department (and was highly
regarded by critics who for the most part savaged the rest of this unhappy
enterprise): *Commonwealth to Protectorate* was also written while he was still
in full employment, not to mention various shorter pieces. But Harold
Perkin quite rightly points to his increased creativity of recent years:

> ... publications that had been gestating came flooding out, to the surprise of
> those who thought him too modest and self-effacing for his own academic
> good. He was delighted when, on retirement, he was deservedly elected a
> Fellow of the British Academy, crowning a career more distinguished than
> any other of Lancaster's founding fathers. More than that, he will always be
> remembered with affection, as one of those people whom it was an immense
> pleasure, as well as a privilege, to know.

It would be idle to pretend that, in common with most academics of his
generation, Austin is not dismayed to see what has been happening of late
to universities in general and to Lancaster in particular. Thirty-two years
after it was launched with such high hopes, Lancaster quite recently faced
grave financial problems. For a time, the expenditure on books for the

Library (one of Austin's chief concerns – he was Chairman of the Library Committee for two three-year stints) was cut to the bone. Fortunately, there are now signs of recovery. Austin can take comfort. Despite its difficulties, the University ranks in the British top ten for teaching and researching. The intellectual sparkle that marked it from the beginning is still there.

In both Leeds and Lancaster, there was a very pleasant backcloth to the scene of Austin's intensely busy life. I have said that he is a natural countryman; it would be more precise to say that, despite his love of the Mediterranean, he is a natural *North*-countryman. Writers often reveal themselves in a sudden, unexpected turn of phrase. When Austin describes Cromwell before Preston 'marching where the knotted muscles of the high Pennines relax into the pastoral slopes and fertile closes of the lower Ribble',[24] one realises that a man who describes that hill-country in those terms knows it and loves it and has walked it. In fact, the only trace of vanity I have been able to detect in Austin is his glee (fully justified) at being able to walk much younger friends and colleagues off their feet. And in the pursuit of this activity he is as fearless in confronting a feudal landowner as in facing a heavyweight academic. Professor Perkin has a good story of his meeting an irascible man with a shotgun in that lovely but inaccessible area, the Trough of Bowland. On being asked who he was and what he was doing there Austin said stoutly, 'I am Professor Woolrych of the University.' To which the man replied, 'And I'm the Earl Sefton and I own this land.' It is not quite clear how the conversation proceeded from this point, but it is typical of Austin that the two men parted friends. However, in this Northern countryside of their adoption he and Muriel found beautiful corners to call their own. For most of their time in Leeds they lived beyond the city on the edge of what is arguably the loveliest of all the Dales, Wharfedale. Gordon Forster has a delightful account of a hot summer's day when he and Austin had spent weary hours cross-checking the Finals papers of some seventy or eighty candidates. They managed to agree the marks in time to switch on the Test Match commentary, open a bottle of wine (College cellarers cannot compete with Austin), put their feet up and sit in the warm sun, contentedly gazing at the splendid views of Wharfedale. The exams were over and the long vacation (the phrase in those days still had some meaning) stretched blissfully ahead.

Yorkshire folk can become the most loyal of friends but initially they tend to look askance at the 'comer-in' and they deeply mistrust charm. On both counts Austin and Muriel were clearly at a considerable disadvantage. It is remarkable, therefore, how quickly they were accepted and their

---

[24] Woolrych, *Battles of the English Civil War*, p. 166.

reputation for hospitality established. Students and colleagues alike were invited for evenings of good talk, music, and excellent food and wine. 'One never heard', says Gordon Forster, 'of anyone refusing an invitation'. This tradition was continued when they crossed the Pennines to Lancaster, as I myself know very well. I remember driving down from Edinburgh to Oxford on a fearsomely hot day. The motorway was even more unpleasant than usual and as I turned off at Caton and drove up the lane to 'Patchetts', their lovely old house with its cool green garden, I felt I was entering a different world. This was one of many visits. Muriel was already very frail by the time I met her, but the flame of her hospitality still burned bright. Once I brought a friend, even frailer than her hostess because she was recovering from major surgery; after lunch, Muriel took one look at her and whisked her off to a quiet bedroom for a restoring siesta. Sadly, her own health steadily declined in the latter half of the eighties and we all watched, with aching admiration, the unobtrusive loving care with which Austin surrounded her. She died in 1991. They had been married for nearly fifty years. Austin no longer lives in the beautiful home they created together, but the welcome he extends to his guests is as heart-warming as ever.

The essays in this volume are devoted to soldiers, writers and statesmen in the period of English history Austin has made his own. It is a singularly appropriate title. In his time, he has been a soldier in a fierce conflict, a statesman in university politics and is still a writer. Long may he continue to be so; as he himself said of a fellow scholar, retirement is 'another term which historians understand differently from most other mortals'.[25] What is more, much of his life experience is woven into his writing. I have already touched on his empathy with fighting men in action, but his growing involvement with the emergence of a new order in the universities (which in some ways are the microcosms of larger constitutions) is reflected in his later studies on the outburst of creative political theory generated by the Civil War.

It would be impertinent for a layman like myself, who reads history simply for pleasure, to attempt anything like a critical evaluation of Austin's work. The reviews of his important works speak for themselves. What follows, therefore, are some random reflections on his writing as a whole and parts of it that I have particularly enjoyed.

The first thing that strikes me is the unselfish nature of the forms he chooses. '*Le style c'est l'homme*' is particularly apposite in his case. Just as he will take endless trouble in promoting the interests of some struggling

---

[25] J. Morrill, P. Slack and D. Woolf (eds.), *Public Duty and Private Conscience in Seventeenth Century England: Essays presented to G. E. Aylmer* (Oxford, 1993), p. 28.

research student, so he is meticulous in his writing of essays for collective volumes. His chapter in *The Age of Milton* ought to be required reading for any bewildered student of literature trying to understand the intellectual cross-currents behind the magnificent rhetoric of that most élitist of republicans, but pieces of this sort are easily overlooked. It would be good if all such essays by Austin were collected in one volume. Similarly his more profound, magisterial treatise on the same theme is buried deep in volume 7 of the Yale edition of Milton's prose when it deserves to be a book in its own right. So, too, he takes enormous care in the sometimes thankless task of reviewing other writers' books and the tone of his reviews frequently comes as a relief. The long and continuing debate on the nature of the English revolution can be both shrill and bitter. Young wolves sometimes snap hard on the heels of an ageing Akela. But in the middle of all this, Austin's is a sane voice, calmly and courteously avoiding the various brands of determinism.

The second noticeable element in the body of his writing is the number of articles appealing to a wider audience. He does not in the least despise sharing his enjoyment of his subject in articles for *History Today* or the late lamented *Listener*, especially in the days when it was edited by Maurice Ashley (himself a sometimes underestimated observer of the seventeenth-century scene). This lack of 'side' in Austin is one of his most endearing traits of which I myself have experienced a startling example. During the time I was getting to know him I had been revising a rash attempt I had made to dramatise the 'Putney Debates' and was discovering, like many another before me, that a dramatic moment in history is not necessarily easy to turn into good theatre. Austin was kind enough to read my dramatisation and to write me a long letter about it which I still have. He starts off with a charming and characteristic disclaimer: 'The detailed comments which follow are those of a nit-picking professional historian and they take little account of the simplification that faced you – inevitably!' He then proceeded to go through my script with a small tooth comb, correcting downright mistakes, arguing points of interpretation and showing me, very subtly, how to change an emphasis here, an aside there. He could not have paid me a greater compliment. It made me realise, not for the first time, that he will always respond to a genuine interest wherever he may find it and I wished very much that I had been one of his pupils in Leeds or in Lancaster. The truth is, he cares more about the subject for its own sake than for any acclaim for his own performance. At a time when one sees young scholars increasingly driven by the 'publish or perish' imperative, this is singularly refreshing.

I think, perhaps, the reason Austin was ready to take seriously even an indifferent dramatisation of 'Putney' is that, although his chief concern is the evolution of constitutional ideas, he never loses sight of the men enunciating those ideas. He hears their voices in his head. He is not a Clarendon, writing history in the form of a magnificent portrait gallery, but neither are the actors on his stage mere pawns at the mercy of social and economic forces. He has a 'snail's horn delicacy of perception' not only for the dramatic tensions between different groups and different individuals but also for those within the mind of a single individual; he is particularly good in this respect on the enigma of Cromwell. The characters that throng his pages live and breathe and have their being as he puts flesh on their bones in lucid, economical and illuminating phrases. His long research on Barebone's Parliament not only rescues it from the royalist myth that it was merely a fanatical rabble, but also gives us a remarkable series of portrait-sketches of its members.[26] Elsewhere, in a few words he gives us Major General Harrison – 'that flamboyant, God-intoxicated man'.[27] Rainborough is 'an impetuous man, generous in his sympathy with the underdog, undoubtedly brave, instinctively radical, but apt to keep his fiery temper on too short a fuse'.[28] Austin's own quick sympathy with the underdog, the 'meaner sort', can be seen in his moving description of Winstanley whose mystical, compassionate vision of a just society declined so tragically into harsh authoritarianism. Did Austin's Chinese friends wince when they read, 'He would not be the last apostle of a communist Paradise to realise that it would only be kept going by draconic laws'?[29] The more glamorous figures in the Pantheon are not neglected either; the poignancy of the encounter between Montrose and Prince Rupert does not escape him – 'a strange meeting between two young soldiers, the one bent on a crazy adventure that was to make a legend of him, the other fiercely casting off the temptation to despair over his shattering defeat'.[30] Of the Duke of Hamilton, that tortuous man of backstair intrigue whose wild dreams of succeeding Charles I came true – save that it was not to the throne he followed him, but to the scaffold – he writes: 'Hamilton was unlucky to live in a time and a land whose politics posed a choice between stark irreconcilables and his vain efforts to drive a path between them for himself and his master, gave his whole career its character of vacillation and subterfuge.'[31] This errs on the side of charity perhaps but then one hears an echo of Alison Wilson's kindly epitaph on Hamilton in *Old Mortality* – 'That was him that lost his heid at London.

[26] A. Woolrych, *Commonwealth to Protectorate* (Oxford, 1982), pp. 168–93.
[27] Woolrych, *England without a King,* p. 12.
[28] Woolrych, *Soldiers and Statesmen,* p. 227.
[29] Patrides and Waddington (eds.), *The Age of Milton,* pp. 53–55.
[30] Woolrych, *Battles of the English Civil War,* p. 79.   [31] Ibid., p. 157.

Folks said that it wasna a very guid ane, but it was aye a sair loss to him,
puir gentleman.'

And what, one asks oneself, would that 'lukewarm' royalist, Sir Thomas
Wolryche, lying in his splendid tomb at Quatt, have made of all this?
Would he have been shocked at Austin's description of Charles I as 'this
melancholy, thin-blooded, fastidious monarch ... finer in the grain than
either his father or his eldest son, he had the native indolence of both
without either the intelligence or the shrewd sense of realities which
pulled them up on the brink of real trouble'?[32] Would he have joined in
the *de haut en bas* sneers at Barebone's Parliament by Clarendon and his
chums? Perhaps; but Clarendon had better manners in his youth, and
better chums, so I like to think Sir Thomas' lukewarmness cast him more
in the mould of Lord Falkland, a royalist quite unblinded by the deadly
Stuart charm and far too perceptive not to sense at an early stage the
destructive potential of the personality he had chosen to serve – 'He had
not the Court in great reverence and had a presaging spirit that the King
would fall into great misfortune: and often said to his friends that he chose
to serve the King because honesty obliged him to it; but that he forsaw his
own ruin by doing it.'[33]

If ever there were a group of royalists whose company Austin would
have enjoyed, it must surely have been the Falkland circle at Great Tew.
Indeed, a recent biographer of Clarendon has pointed out that the
atmosphere at Tew had a touch of All Souls about it.[34] It is true that
Austin is too stalwart a character to have fallen into that wistful
melancholy which brought Falkland to the point of self-destruction at
Newbury but, in the halcyon days before the war, how well he would have
fitted into those delightful, leisurely house-parties. He would have found
there all the qualities that he himself embodies – the scrupulous pursuit of
learning, a deep tolerance for an opposing point of view, an immense
capacity for friendship, a delicate generosity and a princely hospitality to
match his own (though even he might blench at not knowing how many
guests he had until he came to table!). There must often have been music
at Tew and undoubtedly there would be excellent claret in the Falkland
cellars. What better place then to take our leave of him than in 'that
college situated in a purer air',[35] that 'university bound in a lesser
volume',[36] where serious talk was 'enlivened and refreshed with the

---

[32] Ibid., p. 24.
[33] Edward, Earl of Clarendon, *Life*, 3rd edn (Oxford, 1761), vol. II, p. 92.
[34] Richard Ollard, *Clarendon and his friends* (Oxford, 1988), p. 31.
[35] Edward, Earl of Clarendon, *The History of the Rebellion and Civil Wars in England*, ed. W. D.
Dunn Macray, 6 vols. (Oxford, 1888), vol. III, p. 180.
[36] Ibid.

facetiousness of wit, and good humour and pleasantness of discourse which made the very gravity of the argument (whatever it was) very delectable'?[37]

[37] Clarendon, *Life*, vol. II, p. 42.

I

Secret alliance and Protestant agitation in two kingdoms: the early Caroline background to the Irish rebellion of 1641*

JOHN REEVE

I

This is an essay in British[1] and to a lesser extent in European history. By exploring Anglo-Irish politics during the late 1620s and early 1630s it seeks to be doubly topical, shedding light on the British problem as well as on the background to the Irish rebellion of 1641. We have a growing awareness of the importance of British events, of the interplay of developments in the three kingdoms, in the coming of the crisis of the 1640s.[2] The Irish rebellion, for example, helped set the English political stage for civil war by preventing the dissolution of the Long Parliament.[3] Indeed the theory has recently been advanced that Ireland was the critical element in the British problem.[4] Moreover, amongst Irish historians, how far back to trace the causes of the 1641 rebellion is still a controversial question.

* I thank John Morrill and Conal Condren for discussion of this subject, Aidan Clarke and Nicholas Canny for information, Terence Ranger and Simon Adams for enabling me to cite their D.Phil. theses, the President and Fellows of Clare Hall, Cambridge, for electing me to a Visiting Fellowship and the University of Sydney for allowing a special study programme in the UK in 1996. Transcripts of Crown Copyright records appear by permission of the Controller of HM Stationery Office. I thank Olive, Countess Fitzwilliam's Wentworth settlement trustees for permission to cite the Strafford papers and the Director of Sheffield Libraries and Information Services for access to them, as well as the Keeper of Collections at Chatsworth House for permission to cite manuscripts held there.

[1] In this essay I use 'British' in the sense of the three kingdoms of England, Scotland and Ireland.
[2] See in particular C. Russell, *The Fall of the British Monarchies 1637–1642* (Oxford, 1991); J. S. Morrill, *The Nature of the English Revolution* (London, 1993).
[3] C. Russell, *The Causes of the English Civil War* (Oxford, 1990), pp. 129–30, 212–13; Russell, *The Fall of the British Monarchies*, pp. 379, 398–99, 415, 469. Clarendon understood this. Edward Hyde, earl of Clarendon, *The History of the Rebellion and Civil Wars in England*, ed. W. D. Macray, 6 vols. (Oxford, 1888), VI, pp. 2–3.
[4] N. Canny, 'The attempted Anglicisation of Ireland in the seventeenth century: an exemplar of "British history"' in J. F. Merritt (ed.), *The Political World of Thomas Wentworth, Earl of Strafford 1621–1641* (Cambridge, 1996).

These two dimensions, the British and the more particularly Irish, will be illuminated here by an investigation of a hitherto missing link in Irish political history.

The lords justices, Cork and Loftus, governed Ireland between 1629 and 1633. These years in Irish politics, between the departure of Falkland and the coming of Wentworth, have not received as much attention as they deserve. It is tempting to focus on the commencement of Wentworth's deputyship as a pivotal point. But the government of the lords justices had its own character and a wider historical significance. We can better understand both the character and the significance when we learn of a secret political player in London – an English and a European figure – and of his role in facilitating the aims of an ideological regime in Ireland. Placing this period of Irish politics in its British – and its European – contexts enables conclusions about the general dynamics of Anglo-Irish politics under Charles I and the background to the British crisis of the early 1640s to be drawn.[5]

Certain themes will recur in this story: race and religion, money and land, and political and military power. It is one episode in the evolution of Irish society from the days of the Elizabethan conquest, of English colonisation and Irish resistance, to the eighteenth-century era of Protestant ascendancy. An alliance between militant Protestant politicians in London and Dublin had progressively driven the Catholic Old English of Ireland into the political wilderness. There, in desperation, they sided with the Irish rebels in 1641, subverting royal authority in Ireland and indirectly in England. These events took place within the wider European context of the Thirty Years' War and of the options of peace and war that were available to the English government.[6]

II

Ireland had been low on James I's list of state-building priorities. His general approach there was pragmatic. In the wake of Tyrone's War (1594–1603), and of the flight of the earls in 1607, James sanctioned a policy of plantation out of a desire to secure his authority. His religious policy was conceived in moderation and was subject to the vagaries of international politics. Seeking an alignment with Spain, at a time of

[5] On the importance of the European context of British events see most recently S. Adams, 'England and the world 1485–1603' and J. Reeve, 'Britain and the world 1603–1689' in J. S. Morrill (ed.), *The Oxford Illustrated History of Tudor and Stuart Britain* (Oxford, 1996).

[6] On these options see L. J. Reeve, 'The politics of war finance in an age of confessional strife: a comparative Anglo-European view', *Parergon. Journal of the Australian and New Zealand Association for Medieval and Early Modern Studies*, new series, 14, 1996, 1.

reduced international tension, it suited his foreign policy, as well as his temperament, to treat Irish Catholics with patience. Recusancy proceedings continued (although they were suspended in 1623 to aid the Spanish match), but there was de facto toleration in private and no real action against the Catholic clergy. The Roman church penetrated Ireland successfully, achieving extensive influence. The kingdom (especially the army) was a drain on the English exchequer. An Irish fiscal crisis loomed in the early 1620s.[7] In absolute terms, Jacobean rule in Ireland was short of success. Relatively, however, it had – when looked at from London – not a bad record. A kingdom wracked by war and foreign invasion under Elizabeth had been stabilised so as to suit James's foreign agenda.

In Irish as in other areas of policy, Charles I's accession marked a new departure.[8] Insensitive politically, and blind to the dangers of conflict and innovation, he also failed to inspire trust.[9] These qualities found their way into Irish government under his rule. Two factors, broadly speaking, shaped the context for Irish politics under Charles, neither of them new: the elusive goal of Irish social reformation and considerations of foreign policy. Charles's Spanish war during the late 1620s renewed Ireland's strategic importance for England. With its geographical position, and unruly and mainly Catholic population, it was of course the part of the British Isles most vulnerable to Spanish invasion. The Irish Catholic exiles, including Tyrone, urged such an enterprise upon the government of Philip IV.[10] A Hispanophile and a residual admirer of the ways of his temporary enemy, Charles was receptive to the idea of a union of arms on the model of Spain.[11] The principle that each of his kingdoms should contribute to mutual defence meant the raising of more troops for Ireland and, necessarily, paying for them.

This policy aimed at avoiding the arming of the Old English. That ancient, wealthy social group, imbued with warrior values, were eager to prove their loyalty. But being predominantly Catholic in religion, they

[7] Canny, 'Attempted Anglicisation of Ireland', p. 184; N. Canny, 'Early modern Ireland, c. 1500–1700' in R. F. Foster (ed.), *The Oxford History of Ireland* (Oxford, 1992), pp. 101–2, 113; A Clarke, *The Old English in Ireland 1625–42* (London, 1966), p. 20; T. W. Moody, F. X. Martin and F. J. Byrne (eds.), *A New History of Ireland*, vol. III (Oxford, 1976), pp. 192–93, 208–9, 215ff.

[8] Clarke, *Old English*, p. 10.

[9] See L. J. Reeve, *Charles I and the Road to Personal Rule* (Cambridge, 1989), ch. 6.

[10] H. Lonchay and J. Cuvelier (eds.), *Correspondance de la cour d'Espagne sur les affaires du Pays-Bas du XVIIe siècle*, 6 vols. (Brussels, 1923–27), II, p. 547 and n; A. Clarke, 'Ireland and the general crisis', *Past and Present*, 48, 1970, p. 83. See also H. F. Kearney, 'Ecclesiastical politics and the counter-reformation in Ireland 1618–1648', *Journal of Ecclesiastical History*, 2, 1960, pp. 202–12.

[11] Russell, *Fall of the British Monarchies*, p. 380.

appeared unreliable in London and Dublin. In 1641 their reluctant resort
to force would be a critical moment in Ireland's descent into chaos and
bloodshed.[12] The Crown's policy during the Spanish war was to buy Old
English support with political concessions. The undertakings by Charles
(known as the 'graces') included effective security for Old English land
tenures.[13] The failure of Lord Deputy Falkland to comply with proper
legal procedure meant that the parliament called in 1628 never met. There
was no legislative guarantee of land titles. Yet the related subsidies
continued to be collected. The agreement with the Old English was,
essentially, betrayed. Charles's capitalising on the situation is entirely in
character, reminiscent of his simultaneous attitude towards the Petition of
Right.[14] The ending of his involvement in war abroad, after 1629, further
released the pressure to fulfil the bargain.

An ill omen compounded the bitterness of the Old English. The English
government was deeply concerned about the state of Ireland and the
danger of revolt by late 1628. As well as insolvency and conciliar
factiousness, there was indiscipline in the army (which had an Irish
contingent of dubious loyalty) and a relaxed atmosphere towards the
practice of Catholicism. Charles instructed Falkland to get a grip on the
situation.[15] The lord deputy began a campaign against Irish Catholicism,
aimed at ending the tacit Jacobean toleration which had accompanied the
war. A proclamation of 1 April 1629 forbade Roman jurisdiction and
ordered the dissolution of religious houses on pain of confiscation. The
circuit judges were to suppress recusancy and Catholicism. The oath of
supremacy was to be applied to all Catholic magistrates on threat of
dismissal. Falkland soon wrote to London claiming success, but the effect
of his measures was actually equivocal. His understandable failure to deal
with Irish problems in time of war, when combined with his avarice in
attempting to dispossess the O'Byrnes of their Wicklow lands, led to his
recall.[16] Falkland, we might say, had 'lost the plot'. But the de-escalation of
war and the weakened position of the Old English had enabled him to
alter the direction of government religious policy. This offensive was

---

[12] Ibid., p. 393; M. Perceval-Maxwell, *The Outbreak of the Irish Rebellion of 1641* (Montreal and
Kingston, 1994), p. 245.

[13] About two thousand Old English families owned approximately one third of Ireland's
profitable land, or two and a quarter million acres. The graces guaranteed legal immunity
to title older than sixty years. Clarke, *Old English*, pp. 25–26, 47ff, App. 2.

[14] Ibid., pp. 55–59; Moody *et al.*, *New History of Ireland*, III, p. 239; Reeve, *Charles I*, passim.

[15] Public Record Office, State Papers (SP) 63 (Ireland)/247/fos. 152–53.

[16] Falkland's position was also undermined by the assassination of his patron, the duke of
Buckingham. Moody *et al.*, *New History of Ireland*, III, pp. 239–41. Reeve, 'Secretaryship of
state of Viscount Dorchester, 1628–1632', University of Cambridge Ph.D. dissertation
(1984), pp. 228–30.

welcome to the Protestant New English in the Dublin government. They had advocated anti-Catholic measures in the 1620s despite the difficulty of implementing them in the climate of war.[17]

III

The most prominent of these men was Richard Boyle, first earl of Cork. With a query over Falkland's future, Cork and his factional opponent, Lord Chancellor Loftus, were appointed to govern as lords justices.[18] Cork's stake in the Irish Protestant status quo was enormous. The wealthiest man in Charles's three kingdoms, he had based his fortune largely on church lands.[19] His material interests dovetailed with his ideological convictions. These were both cultural and religious. To Cork the New English were an isolated group in an alien land, threatened by the Counter-Reformation. They had a religious mission to conquer and civilise the native Irish through the use of military force, laws against recusancy, and the apparatus of Protestant colonialism. Anti-episcopal, possessed of Puritan intensity, and convinced of his role as a tool of God's providence, the earl was a remarkable religious ideologue.[20]

Cork was a British political figure. Born in England, and the leading Protestant nobleman in Ireland, he pursued an Anglo-Irish political career (being admitted to the English Privy Council in 1640), and was covetous of advancement in English society. Yet despite a Boyle–Wentworth marriage alliance, he was short of political patronage at the English court.[21] Viscount Dorchester, secretary of state from 1628 to 1632, largely remedied this want during Cork's tenure as lord justice. The Cork–Dorchester alliance, which was vital in Anglo-Irish politics during this period, has long gone undetected.[22] We can unravel it here.

To do so we must set it within the framework of European politics and warfare, and of English attitudes to those conflicts, during the early seventeenth century. Despite the easing of international tensions at the beginning of this period,[23] serious fissures remained in European society. Religious antagonism between Catholic and Protestant communities

---

[17] Moody et al., New History of Ireland, III, pp. 235ff.

[18] Boyle's appointment was facilitated by an interest-free loan to the king of £15,000. N. Canny, The Upstart Earl (Cambridge, 1982), pp. 34, 62.

[19] Ibid., pp. 10–11, 16, 22, 35–36.   [20] Ibid., pp. 23ff, 129ff.

[21] Ibid., pp. 10, 35, 59ff; T. Ranger, 'Strafford in Ireland: a Revaluation' in T. Ashton (ed.), Crisis in Europe 1560–1660 (London, 1965), p. 292.

[22] Dorchester is identified in this connection in Reeve, 'Secretaryship of state of Viscount Dorchester', ch. 5.

[23] England had ended the Elizabethan war with Spain in 1604 and the Dutch had concluded a truce in 1609.

underlay relations between states. Spain's bid for mastery in Europe was
still a potent force which many rightly feared. These conflicts were
sharpened by economic rivalries in which trade was a form of war within
the context of overseas expansion. By the early 1620s, with the outbreak of
the Thirty Years' War and the resumption of open conflict between Spain
and the Dutch, James I's policy of mediation in Europe had collapsed. The
fact that his daughter Elizabeth was married to Frederick, Elector Palatine
and defeated king of Bohemia, meant that English interests were deeply
engaged on the Protestant side of the wars. A coalition of interests had
dragooned James into war with Spain before he died – an alliance of
expediency that drew together Prince Charles, the duke of Buckingham,
and the parliamentary war lobby which wanted to fight in the Protestant
cause. This coalition broke down at the end of the 1620s, with Charles's
willingness to deal with Spain deeply offending the English Protestant
supporters of war. This was the strife-torn Anglo-European political world
in which Dorchester had risen to power.

Who was Viscount Dorchester? Better known to history by his earlier
appellation of Sir Dudley Carleton, he was an English diplomat of some
European fame. His urbane and worldly exterior concealed a fiercely
ideological inner self. As secretary of state he fought a rearguard action at
court against innovatory Caroline policies. A devout and orthodox English
Calvinist, he opposed religious toleration and particularly hated the
Jesuits. Believing in European Catholic and Habsburg aggression, he was a
professional lobbyist for Protestant war. Close to Elizabeth of Bohemia,
pro-Palatine and pro-Dutch, he became a Buckingham man when the
duke made war against Spain. He was a court contact for Sir Thomas Roe
and other radical Protestant internationalists. His witnessing (as English
ambassador at the Hague) of the Dutch Calvinist revolution, and of a
decade of European war since 1618, had shaped his political views. To
Dorchester the critical need was for unity and conformity under a single
sovereign power. The state would otherwise fall prey to its enemies who
would exploit its internal weaknesses. This was the lesson of the Dutch
religious strife. Dorchester's thinking was in line with that of the English
House of Commons in 1628, which saw Arminianism as the fifth column of
Spain and of Rome. Likewise he sympathised with their attack on English
Arminianism in 1629.[24] Here was another active Protestant ideologue in
the upper reaches of the Caroline regime.

The parallels between Dorchester and Cork are striking. Sharing an
intense personal piety, they both saw themselves as belonging to isolated

---

[24] Reeve, 'Secretaryship of state of Viscount Dorchester', ch. 1; Reeve, *Charles I*, pp. 39–40,
107, 189.

godly communities. (Dorchester wrote to Elizabeth of Bohemia of the Winthrop generation of emigrants to New England, calling them 'our godly people, who weary of this wicked land are gone (man, woman and child) in great numbers to seek new worlds'.)[25] Both men saw themselves as players in a European drama in which the predator was Catholic aggression and the endangered species international Protestantism.[26] Both had a sense of militant religious mission and were willing to use force.[27] Both saw themselves locked in a struggle in which church and state were at risk of breakdown or, in Cork's case, at least erosion.[28] Perhaps above all, they shared a sense of political isolation under the Caroline regime. Both lacked allies at court. Both were opposed by Weston and Cottington.[29] Both had to conceal or understate their religious views.[30] Both experienced the difficulty involved in staying loyal to Charles I given his religious policies.[31] Both had the assets of impressive political skills picked up in tough schools (Cork in the wild Anglo-Irish politics of the late sixteenth century, Dorchester in the Europe of the Dutch revolt and the Thirty Years' War). For both men Ireland was an arena in which they could express the religious intensity within their souls.

Cork and Dorchester had personal connections which paved the way for their political alliance. Cork was the leader of the pro-Falkland group in the Irish Council; Falkland and Dorchester were old friends. Cork became closely associated with Dorchester in England in 1629, and the latter arranged the marriage of his relation the earl of Kildare to Cork's daughter, Joan Boyle. This match consolidated Cork's Irish interests considerably.[32] His efficient political antennae identified Dorchester as a like-minded figure who had access to the king. The secretary participated in policy-making as a member of the Irish Committee of Council, and through his control, on the king's behalf, of royal correspondence with the Dublin government. But he also had a confidential correspondence with Cork, in which matters were withheld from the Committee and apparently

---

[25] SP81 (Germany)/36/fo. 113v.
[26] Canny, *Upstart Earl*, pp. 29, 34. Cork's belief in English betrayal of European Protestantism echoes the use of covenant theology in English Calvinist views of foreign policy. S. L. Adams, 'The protestant cause: religious alliance with the West European Calvinist communities as a political issue in England, 1585–1630', Oxford University D.Phil. thesis, 1973.
[27] Reeve, *Charles I*, p. 268.   [28] Canny, *Upstart Earl*, p. 130.
[29] H. Kearney, *Strafford in Ireland 1633–41* (Cambridge, 1959, repr. 1989), pp. 24–25; Reeve, *Charles I*, passim.
[30] Canny, *Upstart Earl*, p. 31.   [31] Ibid., p. 36; Reeve, *Charles I*, passim.
[32] Reeve, 'Secretaryship of state of Viscount Dorchester', pp. 226, 230–31. See also PRONI, D.3078/3, 1/5, Leinster Papers, letter book of the 16th earl of Kildare, pp. 6–9, 11–14.

from the king.[33] Cork gave Dorchester information on Irish affairs, on the basis of which the secretary advocated and sanctioned Irish policies. He told Cork: 'nothing I assure you comes from your hands, whereof I make not the best use for advancement of his majesty's service and improvement of your merit in his good opinion'. He assured Cork that their correspondence remained secret. Cork expressed his gratitude for Dorchester's 'support and encouragement, by procuring me gracious returns upon all such propositions as I have humbly tendered unto you to be promoted to his majesty'.[34]

IV

The Dorchester–Cork agenda informed the proceedings of the Cork–Loftus administration. It favoured planter and Protestant interests and was aggressively anti-Catholic.[35] Dorchester and Cork shared a belief in the reformation of Irish society and of course wanted to preclude rebellion.[36] There was antagonism between Cork and Loftus, but they shared vested interests.[37] The lords justices had a purely New English platform. Falkland's religious measures had not been forcefully applied. The new regime had conviction, and was given a greater scope for action by an emerging climate of peace. The lords justices, like Falkland, stood in the broad Elizabethan colonising tradition, but gave it an aggressively Protestant form. The contrast with the relatively indulgent days of James I was, for the Old English, alarming. In the face of anti-Catholic measures, hopes of important concessions had given way, in a short space of time, to fears for land tenures.[38] The incompatibility of Old English religious and political allegiances was being painfully exposed.[39]

Charles I's attitude to these courses is fairly easy to deduce. He had other difficulties to contend with during these years, notably a constitutional crisis in England and dramatic events in foreign affairs (where he failed to capitalise on the Swedish victories of 1631–32).[40] Family life also distracted him. There was always something of a policy vacuum in early

---

[33] SP63/248/fos. 177–178r; SP63/249/fos. 261, 263; Historical Manuscripts Commission 23 (Cowper I), p. 408; Hardwicke MS 78 (Chatsworth), Cork Letter Book, pp. 381–84; A. B. Grosart (ed.), *Lismore Papers*, 10 vols. (London, 1886–88), 2nd series, III, pp. 174–75.

[34] Ibid., 2nd series, III, pp. 153–55, Dorchester to Cork, 15 March 1630; Chatsworth, Cork Letter Book, p. 273, Cork to Dorchester, 10 March 1631.

[35] SP63/249/fos. 6–10, 102–9, 261; Clarke, *Old English*, pp. 71–72.

[36] *Lismore Papers*, 2nd series, III, pp. 153–55, 176; SP63/250/fo. 103r; SP63/251/fos. 46r–v; SP63/252/fos. 99–101, 264; SP63/253/fos. 19–20; SP63/270/fos. 66v–79r.

[37] Kearney, *Strafford in Ireland*, p. 11.

[38] Moody *et al.*, *New History of Ireland*, III, p. 242; Clarke, *Old English*, p. 68.

[39] Canny, 'Early modern Ireland', pp. 102–3.   [40] Reeve, *Charles I*, passim.

seventeenth-century Irish affairs.[41] Officials beneath the monarchy tended to manoeuvre, picking up fragments of power. Here was a case in point. Dorchester's religious policy for Ireland represented for Charles an approach to pre-empting revolt – always a welcome theme for him, particularly at this time.[42] Whatever else one may say of him, he rarely shirked conflict within his realms.

Falkland's proclamation of 1629 authorised action against the public practice of Catholicism. The justices proceeded to enforce it. On St Stephen's Day, 1630, the archbishop and civil officers of Dublin tried to arrest the celebrant of a Mass in a Cook Street friary. The congregation resisted and there was public rioting. The government responded with harsher measures. Dorchester gained the king's support for the national-isation of the policy. There was confiscation of all known religious houses in Dublin, Cork, Drogheda and elsewhere. Cork reported to Dorchester: 'Your lordship's high favour in procuring this latter part to be commanded hath crowned the whole work. The example whereof done in this chief city hath extended itself into all other cities and towns in this kingdom ... and I hope by your good mediation we shall receive a comfortable command touching the countess of Kildare's house, which was converted to a college of Jesuits.'[43] The talk in London was that five hundred priests and friars had fled Ireland.[44] There were further anti-Catholic measures at Christmas, 1630, and by February 1631 it appeared that the government had successfully abolished the public practice of Catholicism. The religious life of the people retreated underground, however, and readily continued.[45]

The regime was aware that its religious offensive risked aggravating the danger of revolt. It increased the garrison of Dublin. Cork wrote to Dorchester that he suspected there were armed forces in the city capable of insurrection.[46] Despite the peace with Spain, the secretary warned the justices to be on guard 'against foreign practices ... the great engineers of that art, the friars and Jesuits (a poison Ireland rejects not) will give your lordships continual subject'.[47] Dorchester was concerned to combat a European threat, a 'work of darkness' in alliance with Irish disaffection.

[41] Canny, 'Attempted Anglicisation of Ireland', p. 184.
[42] Reeve, *Charles I*, chs. 3–5, 8.
[43] SP63/250/fos. 131r–v, Cork to Dorchester, 2 March 1630. The Kildare college was proceeded against; SP63/250/fos. 69–70. See also SP63/250/fos. 17–18; Clarke, *Old English*, p. 62.
[44] T. Birch (ed.), *The Court and Times of Charles I*, 2 vols. (London, 1848), ii, p. 69.
[45] *Lismore Papers*, 1st series, iii, p. 106; SP63/252/fo. 89r; SP63/253/fos. 19–20; Moody *et al.*, *New History of Ireland*, iii, pp. 241–42; Kearney, *Strafford in Ireland*, p. 23.
[46] SP63/250/fos. 69–70, Cork to Dorchester, early 1630. See also SP63/250/fos. 13–14.
[47] SP63/251/fo. 233, Dorchester to Lords Justices, 3 December 1630.

The attack on Irish Catholicism was the defence of the realm at the point where internal and external enemies were one. He called Ireland 'an outwork subject to danger', and feared that 'some party and intelligence before hand be made with the natives ... use your best industry in penetrating into foreign intelligences, wherein invasion from abroad must have the first foundation'.[48] Fear fed ambition. Dorchester wanted to purge Ireland of the religious orders, Cork to banish the Jesuits.[49]

The style, as well as the substance, of this regime is telling. Dorchester authorised ruthless military rule against Irish civilians where there was any danger of invasion or revolt. He ordered the prosecution 'by fire and sword, and by all means' of any traitor or rebel or those who aided them, and approved infliction of the death penalty under martial law.[50] Dorchester's commitment to war without mercy in Ireland came from the wellsprings of his being. It also reflected his frustration at Charles's and Laud's religious policies in England and at the king's developing dalliance with Spain abroad.[51] Sir Thomas Barrington – a pillar of the English Protestant parliamentary interest – rejoiced at the end of religious appeasement in Ireland.[52] The resumption of Irish plantation projects, which Dorchester (and naturally Cork) favoured, confirmed the worst fears of the Old English.[53]

By late 1630, Dorchester ventured to tell Cork that the Crown was settling and ordering the government of all three kingdoms. Both men saw Irish politics against a wider British background.[54] Here is a hint of the emerging seventeenth-century English imperial view of the Atlantic archipelago. Fuelled by Protestant anxiety in time of war, as well as missionary zeal, it echoed the anti-Irish fears of the English House of Commons in 1628.[55] The lessons which Dorchester had drawn from the

---

[48] SP63/251/fo. 228r, Dorchester to Lords Justices, 26 November 1630.

[49] *Lismore Papers*, 2nd series, III, p. 154; Chatsworth, Cork Letter Book, pp. 100–1.

[50] Dorchester's draft of Lord Conway's commission as governor of Londonderry and Coleraine. SP63/269/fos. 108v–115, c. 10 August 1629. See also Reeve, 'Secretaryship of state of Viscount Dorchester', pp. 237–38.

[51] Reeve, *Charles I*, p. 189.

[52] A. Searle (ed.), *Barrington Family Letters 1628–1632* (Camden Society, 4th ser., 28, London, 1983), p. 138. Bedell, bishop of Kilmore, dedicated a conservative Calvinist tract to the lords justices in 1631. P. Kilroy, 'Protestantism in Ulster, 1610–1641' in Mac Cuarta (ed.), *Ulster 1641: Aspects of the Rising* (Belfast, 1991), pp. 31–32.

[53] Reeve, 'Secretaryship of state of Viscount Dorchester', pp. 236–37; Clarke, *Old English*, pp. 63–64.

[54] Cork considered anti-Catholic measures in England and Ireland as part of one campaign. Reeve, *Charles I*, p. 169; Reeve, 'Secretaryship of state of Viscount Dorchester', pp. 233, 235.

[55] Reeve, *Charles I*, pp. 27–28.

Dutch crisis – on the need for unity and conformity under singular authority – also seem pertinent to his attitude here.[56]

V

Early Caroline Irish politics were fraught with fierce factional strife. The New English personalised issues to a remarkable degree. This has been attributed to the lack of an agreed focus of authority in Ireland, and to a tendency for individuals to take the moral high ground.[57] The Protestant planters also lived in a frontier society, hardened by racial conflict, in which the stakes were high. Webs of intrigue abounded in and about the Irish Council. We need to understand this acrid and vicious arena; its battles resolved major policy issues. During the late 1620s and early 1630s, a factional struggle decided the direction of Irish social policy until Wentworth's fall.[58] Exploiting this struggle, Wentworth wrested the initiative from the New English and temporarily ended their regime.

Falkland as lord deputy had had support from Cork and others, but a group had opposed him which included Loftus and Vice Treasurer Annesley (later Lord Mountnorris). After his political position in Ireland had collapsed, he preserved hopes of retrieving the deputyship and fought on from England. This was the background to the grudging character of the cooperation between Cork and Loftus. Falkland pursued a vendetta against Mountnorris, who had promoted the charges of corruption against him in Ireland. At court he planned a conspiracy against the vice-treasurer, against whom, it was intended, charges would be fabricated. Mountnorris gave Falkland his opportunity by slandering his government in a speech in Castle Chamber in February 1630. Cork, a born intriguer, joined the attack when Mountnorris opposed his plans for the Irish revenue. Charges were forwarded to England, giving Falkland ammunition. The former lord deputy had filed a Star Chamber action against Mountnorris, and had lobbied against him in the English Privy Council, in which he – Falkland – sat.

Dorchester, in a striking example of opposition to factionalism, intervened for Mountnorris. The secretary of state was opposed to such feuding

---

[56] Note also the words of Christopher Sherland in the Commons in 1628: 'Why are the Arminians who have sought the ruin of the Low Countries allowed here?' *The Commons Debates in 1628*, ed. M. F. Keeler, M. J. Cole and W. D. Bidwell, 4 vols. (New Haven and London, 1977), IV, p. 120.

[57] Canny, *Upstart Earl*, p. 136.

[58] The account which follows is based upon Kearney, *Strafford in Ireland*, pp. 13–14; Moody et al., *New History of Ireland*, III, pp. 238ff; Reeve, 'Secretaryship of state of Viscount Dorchester', pp. 241–49; T. Ranger, 'The career of Richard Boyle, first earl of Cork, in Ireland 1588–1643', Oxford University D.Phil. thesis, 1958, chs. 7, 8.

in principle: his Dutch experience had gone deep. Encouraged by Lord
Wilmot (an Irish conciliar opponent of the Falkland group), he interceded
personally with the king for Mountnorris, assured him that he had
Charles's confidence, and acted to protect him. He offered goodwill to
those threatened by Falkland, and reprimanded Cork severely. Dorchester,
a smooth operator, managed throughout to preserve his alliance with the
Falkland–Cork group. Mountnorris came to England to answer charges.
Dorchester was ill on 4 May 1631 when the Council appointed a
committee to examine the case. Wentworth, by this time in the running for
appointment to Ireland,[59] apparently became Mountnorris's main advocate, foiling Falkland's attempt to topple him.[60] We can rightly suspect
Wentworth's motives in doing this. They were deeply political. Cork,
Mountnorris's declared enemy, had a stake in the outcome of the case. He
also coveted the lord deputyship of Ireland. Certainly Wentworth, with his
own plans for Irish government, would have to deal with him in Dublin. It
was in his interests to weaken the earl and the planter regime. While
Wentworth threw in his lot with the Mountnorris–Loftus connection,
Cork attempted to force the royal hand. He threatened resignation,
claiming he could not work with Loftus. Dorchester faced him down.[61]
Cork's local position was strengthened by his appointment as Lord
Treasurer of Ireland from October 1631. With control over exchequer
patronage he had influence comparable to that of Loftus.[62] His ally
Dorchester, moreover, remained at court. News of Wentworth's appoint-
ment had been circulating since July,[63] but his departure for Dublin was
delayed. Who would sway policy at the outset of the new regime?
Financial necessity was forcing the issue.

VI

The coming of peace with Spain had made possible a reduction in the size
of the military force in Ireland. Cork and Dorchester took this opportunity
to cashier the Irish regiment. The Protestant character of the army was
thus restored. But the overall halving of the force, decided on in 1629,
meant that the payment of the 1628 subsidies could be extended over a
longer period. This suited Cork's policy of Irish financial solvency and
independence, and Dorchester's of the continuing defence of the

[59] Kearney, *Strafford in Ireland*, p. 31.
[60] The Star Chamber case against Mountnorris (in Easter term, 1631) was but a hollow
victory for Falkland. His name was cleared but the vice-treasurer was merely censured.
See Reeve, 'Secretaryship of state of Viscount Dorchester', pp. 246–48.
[61] Ibid., pp. 248–49; Ranger, 'Career of Richard Boyle', pp. 263–64.
[62] Ibid.   [63] Kearney, *Strafford in Ireland*, pp. 26–27.

country.[64] It did, however, point to a fiscal reckoning, which would come in the autumn of 1632 when the money ran out. Two competing policies emerged for the management of the Irish treasury after that time. These became inextricably bound up with the factional feud.

Cork and his New English conciliar followers, encouraged by Dorchester in London, favoured a scheme of recusancy fines. In short, the planter community would not be taxed to support a standing army to defend itself. Irish Catholics would pay for it in the form of the fines. There would be no need for statutory provisions at the price of concessions.[65] Within the framework of Anglo-Irish Protestant prejudice, this policy had a beautiful logic. There were, however, two obstacles to its being adopted as policy. One was the king's inclination to be patient of the religion of his Catholic subjects. This made him unhappy with the plan.[66] The other, more serious, was the fact that it cut clean across Wentworth's strategy for governing Ireland. Clearly Wentworth intended to play the competing Irish social groups off against each other. He disliked the New English, seeing them as self-interested and inferior colonials.[67] The recusancy scheme, moreover, would sever his line of communication with the Old English. His overall fiscal policy was the better management of the Irish customs. Much hung on this conflict of policies as it was played out between February and December 1632. Its implications, for the foreseeable future of Irish society and for Wentworth's career, were profound. Aided by royal sympathy, Dorchester's death and his own manipulative skills, Wentworth would win.

The recusancy project had its genesis in England. Captain John Butler, a suitor to the king, first mooted it in official circles in the summer of 1631. Dorchester seized on the idea. He put it to Cork and Loftus, eliciting a positive response.[68] Cork in turn pushed for the project at the beginning of 1632. He intended to present it as the only financial solution, and as the Irish Council's advice to the English authorities. On 2 January he wrote to Dorchester, as was his practice with such initiatives. He requested that the secretary procure a royal injunction for its formal consideration in Ireland.[69] Dorchester, however, fell ill at just this time and died in February. As in foreign, so in Irish policy, his demise facilitated the control of Lord Treasurer Weston over government paperwork: a development fortuitous for Wentworth. Weston was Dorchester's rival, utterly out of

[64] Reeve, 'Secretaryship of state of Viscount Dorchester', pp. 239–41.
[65] Ibid., p. 250; Ranger, 'Career of Richard Boyle', pp. 270–71.
[66] Clarke, *Old English*, p. 66.   [67] Canny, *Upstart Earl*, p. 11.
[68] Reeve, 'Secretaryship of state of Viscount Dorchester', pp. 250–51; Sheffield City Archives, Strafford Papers, vol. I, fos. 26r–v.
[69] Chatsworth, Cork Letter Book, pp. 381–84.

sympathy with his Protestant, hawkish views, in favour of peace at home and abroad and its attendant commercial prosperity, and wishing to smooth Wentworth's way to Ireland.[70]

Weston and Wentworth had little trouble in enlisting the support of the king. The tactic of the lord deputy elect was to exploit Irish conciliar division and the friction between the Irish social groups. Maintaining his connection with Cork, and using the recusancy project for leverage, he pressured the Old English while having Mountnorris negotiate with them. Within the Council, Mountnorris (joined by Loftus) opposed Cork and acted for Wentworth. The aim was the sabotage of the Dorchester–Cork recusancy scheme. An agreement with the Old English would be substituted, and a promise to implement the graces exchanged for further subsidies.[71] Wentworth's view, as he frankly told Cottington, was that it was safer to upset the Irish Protestants in this than the Irish Catholics. The political battle raged, and Wentworth was desperate to know the outcome. But Mountnorris and the Old English had their way. In December the king ordered the suspension of the proceedings against recusancy.[72] Cheated once under Falkland, and with their hopes now raised again, the Old English were eligible for even worse disappointment. This duly came their way in 1634 with Wentworth's manipulation of the Irish parliament.

We must view Wentworth's rule in Ireland in its international, as well as its British context, and contrast it with the zealously Protestant regime which preceded it. Dorchester and Cork had put the Irish government on a war footing, both physically and psychologically. This was consistent with Dorchester's working to sustain English involvement with the Protestant cause.[73] Wentworth was in many ways a pragmatist, and was disinclined to enter into conflict with Spain; he predicated his rule on the new English outlook of peace. A changing foreign policy had enabled his entry into royal service. In 1632 he lectured Cork on the benefits of peace under Charles I, in comparison with the rest of Christendom. This was the party line of the personal rule.[74] As in England, so in Ireland, the great

---

[70] Sheffield City Archives, Strafford Papers, I, fos. 22r, 26r–v, 27r–v; *The Earl of Strafford's Letters and Dispatches*, ed. W. Knowler, 2 vols. (1739), I, pp. 66, 68–69; Reeve, *Charles I*, pp. 284ff; Reeve, 'Secretaryship of state of Viscount Dorchester', pp. 251–53.

[71] Wentworth also used an agent, Michael Hopwood, to approach the Old English. Clarke, *Old English*, pp. 65ff. See also Sheffield City Archives, Strafford Papers, I, fos. 41v, 53r, 63r–v; Knowler (ed.), *Strafford Letters*, I, pp. 70–72, 78–79; Kearney, *Strafford in Ireland*, pp. 37–38; J. F. Merritt, 'Power and communication: Thomas Wentworth and government at a distance during the personal rule, 1629–1635' in Merritt (ed.), *Political World of Thomas Wentworth*, p. 115.

[72] Knowler (ed.), *Strafford Letters*, I, pp. 74–77, Wentworth to Cottington, I October 1632. See also Sheffield City Archives, Strafford Papers, I, fos. 63r–v; Clarke, *Old English*, pp. 71–73.

[73] Reeve. *Charles I*, passim.

[74] Sheffield City Archives, Strafford Papers, I, fo. 62v, Wentworth to Cork, 29 August 1632.

fiscal opportunity of peace was trade and hence customs revenues. Wentworth saw the Irish government as a vehicle for subsidising the English Crown and obviating the need for another English parliament.[75] Foreign and commercial policies were linked to religion. A new patience of Irish Catholicism, consistent with Charles's position in England, was less offensive to Continental Catholic powers.[76] Laud encouraged this policy, sharing Wentworth's fundamental plans for Irish conformity, Anglicisation, and the recovery of church property.[77]

Religion and property were the obvious sticking points for the earl of Cork. The power struggle between the earl and the lord deputy, with Cork's eventual testimony at Wentworth's trial in 1641,[78] was inseparable from a conflict of ideas about Irish society and the world. That conflict throws the views and vested interests of the New English into sharp relief: Protestant militancy, landed wealth guarded by common law, and the unthinkability of reversing the economic consequences of the Reformation – positions they essentially shared with the English parliamentary interest. Wentworth, ruthless political animal that he was, understood this well.[79] Ironically, perhaps, this political axis was critical in his fall at the hands of the Long Parliament – or, more precisely, of the alliance between the Protestant New English and the Pym clique. Thus was Ireland the graveyard of another English politician, and the design of Weston and Cottington against Wentworth – by removing him to Ireland – spectacularly fulfilled.[80]

VII

There was then a dynamic interaction of radical Anglo-Irish Protestant politics under Charles I. Exemplified in the Dorchester–Cork alliance and

See also ibid., I, fo. 50r; Reeve, *Charles I*, pp. 185, 258; Kearney, *Strafford in Ireland*, pp. 27–28.

[75] Ibid., p. 37; Reeve, *Charles I*, pp. 204ff; Moody *et al.*, *New History of Ireland*, III, pp. 243, 246.

[76] Canny, 'Attempted Anglicisation of Ireland', p. 169.

[77] Ibid., pp. 171ff; W. Laud, *Works*, ed. W. Scott and J. Bliss, 7 vols. (Oxford, 1847–60), VI, pt 1, pp. 307–9; W. Hutton, *William Laud* (1896), pp. 61, 168; G. A. Ford, *The Protestant Reformation in Ireland, 1590–1641* (Frankfurt, 1985), pp. 269ff.

[78] Canny, *Upstart Earl*, pp. 7, 24. See also P. Little, 'The earl of Cork and the fall of the earl of Strafford, 1638–41', *The Historical Journal*, 39, 1996, 3.

[79] Ranger, 'Strafford in Ireland', pp. 278ff.

[80] M. Perceval-Maxwell, 'Ulster 1641 in the context of political developments in the three kingdom', in Mac Cuarta (ed.), *Ulster 1641*, p. 100; Canny, *Upstart Earl*, pp. 36–37; Reeve, 'Secretaryship of state of Viscount Dorchester', p. 253; P. Zagorin, 'Sir Edward Stanhope's advice to Thomas Wentworth, Viscount Wentworth, concerning the deputyship of Ireland: an unpublished letter of 1631', *The Historical Journal*, 7, 1964, 2; Kearney, *Strafford in Ireland*, pp. 30–31, 199ff. The tenor of the vital Irish articles of impeachment against Wentworth was the grievances of the New English. One article specifically mentioned his mistreatment of Cork. Ibid., p. 200.

the Cork–Loftus government, manifested in the campaign against Wentworth (in which Cork played a vital role), it was a dangerous and
increasingly provocative force in British politics from the 1620s to the
early 1640s. Compounded by Scottish involvement, and by fear of
Wentworth's Irish (largely Catholic) army, it was finally lethal for the
peace of Ireland (and deeply contributory to civil war in England) in
1641–42. The radical Protestant agenda of the Long Parliament inflamed
Irish politics. In particular, the circulation of root-and-branch petitions in
Ulster, the news that Wentworth's successor in Dublin would be Leicester,
Pym's objection in principle to religious toleration for Irish Catholics, and
the English parliamentary scheme to pay off Irish adventurers by land
confiscation – together with Charles's regranting and withdrawal of the
graces – had tipped Ireland into the abyss of rebellion by early 1642.[81]

The defection of the Old English in December 1641 was the vital event
in the loss of royal authority over the kingdom.[82] Wentworth's rule and
Charles's latest betrayal had extended the sorry tale of the campaign for
the graces. The Old English held the English parliament finally responsible.[83] Their general fear of the alliance between the Pym clique and the
Dublin government, backed up by the Covenanters, led them into armed
resistance and constitutional limbo. They were inspired, ironically, by
Scotland's example of revolt.[84] Their confused ideology of loyalty,
ultimately running up against the impasse created by the Reformation, was
the fruit of a long search in which the reign of Charles I was the critical
phase.[85] Aggressive, powerful Protestant interests in two (and finally three)
kingdoms, and an untrustworthy monarch, had boxed the Old English into
an intellectual and political corner since 1625.[86] The result was the Irish
rebellion – a critical link in the chain of circumstances leading to the

---

[81] Russell, *Causes of the English Civil War*, pp. 128–30; Russell, *Fall of the British Monarchies*,
pp. 388ff, 397–98; Perceval-Maxwell, *Outbreak of the Irish Rebellion*, pp. 201, 290; J. S.
Morrill, 'Three kingdoms and one commonwealth? The enigma of mid-seventeenth
century Britain and Ireland' in A. Grant and K. Stringer (eds.), *Uniting the Kingdom? The
Making of British History* (London, 1995), p. 176.

[82] Russell, *Fall of the British Monarchies*, p. 393; Perceval-Maxwell, *Outbreak of the Irish
Rebellion*, p. 245. See also N. Canny, 'Irish, Scottish and Welsh responses to centralisation,
c. 1530–c. 1640: a comparative perspective' in Grant and Stringer (eds.), *Uniting the
Kingdom?*, pp. 167–68; N. Canny, 'What really happened in Ireland in 1641?' in J. H.
Ohlmeyer (ed.), *Ireland. From Independence to Occupation 1641–1660* (Cambridge, 1995), pp.
41–42; Moody *et al.*, *New History of Ireland*, III, pp. 290, 293, 296.

[83] Russell, *Fall of the British Monarchies*, p. 392.

[84] Ibid., pp. 379–80, 392ff, 398; Canny, 'Early modern Ireland', p. 120; Canny, 'Irish, Scottish
and Welsh responses to centralisation', pp. 165–66; Perceval-Maxwell, 'Ulster 1641',
p. 102.

[85] Clarke, *Old English*, pp. 9–11, 233–4; Canny, 'What really happened in Ireland in 1641?',
pp. 28–30.

[86] On conflicting conceptions of the early modern Irish constitution see Morrill, 'Three
kingdoms and one commonwealth?', pp. 174–76.

English Civil War.[87] The outcome was civil war in Ireland, Cromwellian conquest, the divisive scarring of Irish memory, and the end of a proud and ancient race.

The significance of the Cork–Loftus administration, supported by Dorchester in England, is not its immediate lack of missionary and repressive success, but its wider historical context. It was the initial stage in the emergence of a very destructive Anglo-Irish Protestant politics under Charles. It would, moreover, win in Ireland in the end – in political and military (if not in religious) terms.[88] Within this picture, the connections between the militant Protestant lobbying of the 1620s and the early 1640s are very significant, on both sides of the Irish Sea. Cork is clearly a salient link, but so too is Dorchester, despite his death in 1632. Sympathetic to parliamentary ways, and subscribing to the ideological agenda of international Protestantism, he was the servant of the Palatines, the relative of the Barringtons and the friend of Sir Thomas Roe. He was also the advocate (like Pym and the Providence Island Company) of war in the West Indies: an issue which provides an excellent test of potential hostility to the Caroline regime.[89] Charles's court progressively excluded such persons and views, which became politically marginalised and were galvanised in England. With the Scottish revolt, the failure of Spanish aid to Charles and the calling of the Long Parliament, they had their chance.[90] Their natural allies were the Covenanters, but also – once again – the New English in Dublin. Conversely, their difficulty in believing in their king is comparable to that of the Old English and their troubled loyalty.[91] Ireland indeed had a tendency, as Conrad Russell has observed, to turn the reference points of English politics upside down.[92]

The roles of Cork and Dorchester in Irish affairs before 1633 prefigured the issues (particularly religion and land) and the very sensitive political atmosphere of 1640–42. This fact underlines the Caroline nature of the Irish crisis and the coming of rebellion. It also suggests their deeply British (and international) nature, which are traceable back in time as well as across sea and land. The Cork–Loftus administration was at the same time an important connecting episode in the failed search for compromise by the Old English in Ireland. It was part of a tragic chapter in the story of that tragic country, and part of the essential background to the British civil wars.

[87] Russell, *Fall of the British Monarchies*, pp. 398–99.
[88] Kearney, *Strafford in Ireland*, p. 221.
[89] Reeve, *Charles I*, pp. 106ff, 157, 189, 191–93, 211, 242, et passim.
[90] Ibid., ch. 6; Russell, *Fall of the British Monarchies*, pp. 80, 129.
[91] Reeve, *Charles I*, pp. 217–18.
[92] Russell, *Causes of the English Civil War*, pp. 129–30.

2

Of armies and architecture:
the employments of Robert Scawen

JOHN ADAMSON

When the New Model Army won the Civil War for Parliament in 1646, a relatively obscure Cornishman was singled out for particular reward.[1] 'Some considerable recompense' was to be bestowed on Robert Scawen, a grateful House of Commons decreed, to 'remain to posterity as a mark of the favour and acknowledgement of this House to him, for the great pains and the faithful and extraordinary service he hath performed in the affairs of the army'.[2] From the 'new modelling' of Parliament's forces in the spring of 1645, Scawen served as chairman of the parliamentary body most intimately involved in the war-effort, the 'Committee of Lords and Commons for the Army' – a post he held continuously for over four years, to within a few weeks of the king's trial in January 1649. His committee was the principal agency through which the English Parliament saw to its army's recruitment, pay and provisioning. No other civilian MP dealt more directly or frequently with the New Model's senior officers than he.[3] And in purely financial terms, all this 'extraordinary service' at the head of the Army Committee was well rewarded: £2,000 was assigned to him in cash, all of which was actually paid – making him one of the most generously recompensed of all the Long Parliament's MPs.[4]

[1] I am indebted to Professor Ian Gentles, Professor the Earl Russell, Dr David Scott and Professor Blair Worden for commenting upon an early draft of this essay. Part of this essay draws upon research undertaken in the course of preparing a draft biography of Robert Scawen and a study of the Army Committee for the History of Parliament Trust; the author gratefully acknowledges the permission of the Trust, in which copyright rests, to draw upon this work here.

[2] *Commons' Journal* (*CJ*), IV, 414b; M. F. Stieg (ed.), *The Diary of John Harington, MP, 1646–53* (Somerset Rec. Soc., 1977), p. 26.

[3] E.g. SP 28/56/3, fo. 433: Fairfax to Scawen, 27 July 1648; SP 28/56/1, fo. 144: Fairfax to Scawen, 19 August 1648; SP 28/55/3, fo. 522: Fairfax to Scawen, 19 August 1648; Charles Hoover, 'Cromwell's status and pay in 1646–47', *Historical Journal*, 23, 1980, 710.

[4] *CJ*, IV, 539a; Bodl. Lib., MS Nalson XIV/1, fo. 222v: list of payments and offices conferred on MPs [1646]. For the payments to Scawen, see PRO, E 407/8/167 (Accounts of Thomas Fauconberge, receiver-general of the king's revenues), fo. 9.

Not all contemporary notices, however, were quite so laudatory. To his critics – particularly those who had opposed the military reforms of 1645 and who resented Scawen's hand in their success – the chairman of the Army Committee was a man of faction; a back-room figure whose influence could be decisive, at critical moments, in determining the outcome of events. To Denzell Holles, it was collusion between Scawen and the army treasurer, Francis Allein, that left the Presbyterians powerless to avert the New Model's march on London in August 1647.[5] To Clement Walker, Scawen was yet another wartime profiteer; a placeman and lackey of the 'Independent Junto'.[6] Yet despite the Commons' plaudits, and the brickbats of vanquished Presbyterians, Scawen's 'extraordinary service in the affairs of the army has gone virtually unnoticed in the historiography of the Civil War.[7] The nineteenth-century editors of the *Dictionary of National Biography* declined to offer him a place in the national pantheon; and in the four volumes of S. R. Gardiner's great study of the Civil War – a work which continues to be highly influential in defining the *dramatis personae* of the 1640s – he rates not a single mention.[8] Nor is it hard to see why. The creation of the New Model has traditionally been seen as marking a decisive break between the 'aristocratic' management of the war-effort of 1642–44, and a general curtailment of the nobility's political influence that reached its nadir in 1649. From this Whig perspective, Scawen is an anomalous figure to cast as a leading actor in the affairs of the New Model Army. For of all the Long Parliament's MPs there is probably none who merits more unambiguously the label of an aristocratic 'client',[9] his entire adult life – from the age of twenty-two until sixty-five – was spent successively as a senior member of the households of two great peers: Francis Russell, 4th earl of Bedford, the patron of Pym and a leading critic of Charles's Personal Rule; and Algernon Percy, 10th earl of Northumberland, by turns lord high admiral of England, general, governor of the king's children and parliamentarian grandee. To use the

---

[5] 'Memoirs of Denzil, Lord Holles [printed 1699]', reprinted in Francis Maseres (ed.), *Select Tracts Relating to the Civil Wars in England*, 2 vols. (1815), i, pp. 253, 270, 283.

[6] [Clement Walker], *Anarchia Anglicana: or, The History of Independency* (1648), pp. 105–6.

[7] The recent exceptions are M. A. Kishlansky, *The Rise of the New Model Army* (Cambridge, 1979), which briefly notes the importance of his role and that of the Army Committee in the war-effort; and Ian Gentles, *The New Model Army in England, Ireland, and Scotland, 1645–53* (Oxford, 1992), pp. 226, 268.

[8] S. R. Gardiner, *History of the Great Civil War, 1642–49*, 4 vols. (1893; repr. 1987). Nor is he mentioned in Sir Charles Firth and Godfrey Davies, *The Regimental History of Cromwell's Army*, 2 vols. (Oxford, 1940; rep. 1991).

[9] Conrad Russell, *The Fall of the British Monarchies, 1637–42* (Oxford, 1991), p. 149n.

vocabulary current in Northumberland's household, Scawen was a peer's 'gentleman servant', and (as we will see) he was that to his fingertips.[10]

In some respects, Scawen is even an unlikely parliamentarian. In the Bishops' Wars, he served as a military secretary in the campaign to suppress the Covenanter revolt and defend Charles I's non-parliamentary regime. In religion, he showed no enthusiasm for the reformist zeal of the godly. And during the first year of the Long Parliament, when other MPs chorused their denunciations of the Personal Rule, he ventured not a word of public criticism of the Caroline regime. Indeed, he was one of the small group of MPs (almost all of them future royalists) who voted *in favour* of the earl of Strafford.[11] It is not the most obvious apprenticeship for the MP who was to become perhaps the most influential civilian in the parliamentarian war-effort in the period between the Self-Denying Ordinance and Pride's Purge. Scawen fits uneasily into the world of the 'Puritan Revolution'. In a Parliament which contained many Puritans and a few revolutionaries, he was neither.

His career poses a series of questions. How did Scawen come to occupy his place as one of the major figures in the parliamentarian war-effort? Was this highly public role he played during the years 1644–48 an aberration from – or in some sense a complement to – his much longer career as a nobleman's gentleman-servant; a career which ran continuously, in Northumberland's employ, for twenty-seven years? And was there a relation between his activities in the public sphere and the wider political and dynastic strategies of the noble household in which he served? The ramifications of these questions affect not merely our assessment of his singular career, but also the wider issue of the relation between Parliament and the New Model during the 'Puritan Revolution'. To venture answers to them, we must first retrace the circuitous route which had brought this apparently improbable figure, by the spring of 1645, to the chairmanship of Parliament's major standing committee responsible for the New Model Army.

I

Born in 1602, Robert Scawen was the second son of a moderately prosperous Cornish gentry family, which had been seated at Molinick,

---

[10] Alnwick Castle, Northumberland MS u. i. 5: Peter Dodesworth's account as steward of the household, to 16 January 1635. (I am grateful to His Grace the Duke of Northumberland for permission to cite from manuscripts in his collection.)

[11] John Bruce (ed.), *Verney Papers: Notes of Proceedings in the Long Parliament* (Camden Soc., 1845), p. 58.

near St Germans, since the reign of Edward I.[12] But it was his mother's family, the Nicolls of St Tudy, which provided the connections that gave him the *entrée* into the world of Westminster and the court. John Pym, another west-country man, was his mother's uncle and eighteen years Scawen's senior; and it was probably Pym who in 1624 recommended the bright, twenty-two year-old Scawen to his own patron, Lord Russell – the future 4th earl of Bedford. Godly, bossy and litigious, Russell took Scawen on (notwithstanding his lack of a formal legal education) as one of his fee'd solicitors in the Westminster courts, with an annual retainer of 20 marks. By 1626, Russell's litigation was occupying him to the exclusion of all others'; and so, by mutual agreement, Scawen ceased to be a casually employed solicitor and entered Russell's household, as a member of the peer's 'family' (as the household was termed).[13] Scawen's responsibilities multiplied rapidly – particularly after Russell's accession to the earldom of Bedford in 1627. The volume of business with which he dealt was frenetic: schemes to drain the Fens,[14] to create a new Italianate church and piazza, north of Bedford House, to designs by Inigo Jones; suits in Star Chamber and the Westminster courts. For almost a decade, Bedford House, the earl's rambling late-Tudor palace between the Strand and Covent Garden, became the centre of Scawen's life. As Scawen admitted, Bedford even seems to have arranged his marriage, to Katherine Alsopp, whose parents, in their day, had also been servants brought up 'in the said Earle's family'. At Bedford House, Scawen regularly encountered not only Pym, but also Bedford's 'counsel', Oliver St John – who, a decade later, was to serve beside him on the Army Committee of 1645–48.[15]

But then, in the mid-1630s, Scawen's relations with Bedford soured. Scawen demanded more money, in line with his ever increasing responsibilities. Bedford hedged: making promises, then reneging, then alternating between blandishments and intimidation – which included breaking down Scawen's study door – when his servant threatened to leave. But Scawen was too good to lose, and on 18 February 1636 the earl invited him to Bedford House for a meeting with himself and Pym, in a bid to effect a reconciliation. St John was brought in to draft the terms of Scawen's future employment. But despite the negotiations, and Pym's efforts to retain his great-nephew within the Bedford fold, Scawen left the earl's service not

[12] Cornwall RO, P/68/I/I St Germans parish register, entry for 16 May 1602; G. C. Boase and W. P. Courtney, *Bibliotheca Cornubiensis*, 3 vols. (1874–82), II, p. 628.

[13] Alnwick Castle, Northumberland, Northumberland MS, Box Y. III. 2 (4) 7 (Misc. legal papers), fos. 4–6.

[14] Alnwick Castle, Northumberland MS, Box Y. III. 2 (4) 6, unfol., 8 October 1631.

[15] Alnwick Castle, Northumberland MS, Box Y. III. 2 (4) 7. By 1636, Scawen had personally stood surety to Bedford for bonds amounting to over £20,000; ibid., fos. 48–49.

long before the autumn of 1636 – acrimoniously, and taking a large cache
of deeds and papers relating to the earl's Covent Garden project with him
as he went.[16] In the Michaelmas term that year he began a suit against his
former employer in Chancery, beginning with a petition which portrayed
the earl as a capricious and exploitative martinet.[17]

An experienced and able man-of-affairs, still in his early thirties,
Scawen did not remain unemployed for long. He turned, successfully, to
the royal administration and the court. First, he acquired, shortly after
1636, the receivership of the crown lands in Gloucestershire, Wiltshire
and Hampshire, in succession to his great-uncle Pym – almost certainly a
literal instance of nepotism.[18] And then, around the end of 1639, he
entered the household of the earl of Northumberland, who, as lord
general, was making preparations for the 1640 campaign against the Scots.
At the time, Northumberland seemed the Caroline courtier *par excellence*.[19]

Scawen's entry into Northumberland's household looks like something
more than a simple re-start to his stalled career. By 1639, the households
of Bedford and Northumberland represented polar opposites in British
politics. The Bedford House circle – Bedford himself, Pym, St John,
Warwick and Mandeville – were in the vanguard of opposition to Charles
I's Personal Rule, and the house itself was a notorious gathering point for
Covenanter-sympathizers and English Fifth Columnists.[20] Northumberland, on the other hand, was its antithesis; not only was he the general
directing preparations to suppress the Scots' revolt in 1640, but he was also
one of the closest friends of the earl of Strafford, the lord lieutenant of
Ireland and *bête noire* of the Bedford House clique. While Northumberland
was himself far from uncritical of Charles's regime, he was a passionate
opponent of the 'beggarly' Scots,[21] and intimately involved in planning the
two campaigns to defeat them. Scawen served as a member of his military
secretariat: overseeing the budget for the purchase of arms for the
campaign; dealing with moneys advanced by the treasurer-at-war; liaising

---

[16] Alnwick Castle, Northumberland MS, Box y. iii.

[17] Alnwick Castle, Northumberland MS, Box y. iii. 2 (4) 7, fos. 33–4. After the meeting on
18 February 1636 at Bedford House, Scawen recalled, 'Mr Pyme came to [me] from the
said Earle, and told [me] from him that the said Earle was very willing to have [me]
continewe [as] his servant.'

[18] Pym held the office at least until Michaelmas 1636: PRO, SC 6/CHASI/370 (Receiver-
general's account for Glos. for year to Michaelmas 1636); Bristol RO, Bristol Corporation
MSS, Audit Book 20, entries for 1636; BL, Add. MS 31116 (Laurence Whittaker's diary),
fo. 100v; *CJ*, iii, 283b.

[19] Northumberland, born on 29 September 1602, was some five months Scawen's junior.

[20] Russell, *The Fall of the British Monarchies*, pp. 149–51.

[21] William Knowler (ed.), *The Earl of Strafforde's Letters and Dispatches*, 2 vols. (1739), ii,
p. 186.

with other court officials.[22] Scawen's transference of allegiance could hardly have been more extreme. After his fraught relations with his previous employer, it is hard not to see this as a deliberate snub to Bedford and his retinue of godly hangers-on; certainly, after joining Northumberland's staff, his relations with Pym seem to have been singularly cool. And when he entered Parliament in December 1640, as a 'carpet-bagger' in a by-election at the northern garrison town of Berwick-upon-Tweed, he did so as Northumberland's nominee.[23]

Thus, by the beginning of 1641, Robert Scawen had entered the Commons as a member firmly identified with the anti-Scottish cause; to all appearances a 'creature of the court'; and – as he was soon to be denounced in placards posted up around Westminster – a loyal Straffordian.[24] Few MPs were more distanced from the reformist activities of 'Pym's junto'; perhaps the closest he came to being associated with the court's opponents in the years before the outbreak of the Civil War was membership of a committee set up to investigate the patent for payment of 40s. per tun on wine.[25] For the figure who was to be the parliamentary champion of the New Model Army, it was an interesting start.

II

Charting Scawen's parliamentary career during the first phases of the Civil War compounds these paradoxes rather than resolving them. In the three years between the descent into war in the summer of 1642, and Naseby in the summer of 1645, his career veers – apparently erratically – between periods of close involvement in the parliamentarian war-effort and periods of disengagement and withdrawal. Almost alone among the Straffordians of May 1641, Scawen sided with Parliament in 1642, staying on at Westminster and devoting himself to the parliamentarian cause.[26] His

---

[22] PRO, SP 16/452/93: Scawen to Edward Nicholas, 9 May 1640; *Calendar of State Papers Domestic, 1640–41*, p. 241.

[23] Scawen, being a newcomer to the household and relatively low in its pecking order, appears not to have been proposed for a seat in the general elections to the Long Parliament; only in December 1640, when a vacancy occurred at Berwick – the result of the House's voiding the election of Sir Edward Osborne, Strafford's deputy as president of the council of the north – did Scawen find an opening. Berwick RO, B1/9 (Berwick Guild Book, 1627–43), fo. 201v (a reference I owe to Dr David Scott). Wallace Notestein (ed.), *The Journal of Sir Simonds D'Ewes from the Beginning of the Long Parliament to the Opening of the Trial of the Earl of Strafford* (New Haven, 1923), p. 119n; M. F. Keeler, *The Long Parliament, 1640–41: A Biographical Study of its Members* (Philadelphia, 1954), p. 58; PRO, C 219/43/2: election indenture for Berwick-upon-Tweed, 22 December 1640.

[24] Bruce (ed.), *Verney Papers*, p. 58.   [25] *CJ*, II, 157a.

[26] *CJ*, II, 474a: his first major appointment, to the committee set up to examine the public accounts, and the state's debts.

expertise as a military administrator, acquired on Northumberland's staff during the Bishops' Wars, made him a particularly useful member of the Commons' military committees. And in April 1643, when the House at last tried to formulate procedures to regularise the pay and musters of Essex's army, Scawen's name topped the list of those nominated to the committee.[27] After having kept a relatively low profile – notwithstanding, or perhaps because of, his loyalty to Strafford – in the Long Parliament's first year, he was involved consistently, from around May 1642 until May 1643, in the campaign to defeat the king.

Then suddenly, in the spring of 1643, all these efforts cease. For six months, from the end of May to mid-November 1643, he virtually disappears from the parliamentary record: a single committee appointment (to investigate a challenge to a duel),[28] then – during the summer of 1643, with Parliament's fortunes at their lowest ebb – nothing. Not until November, in response to a summons to take the Covenant, did he return to the business of the House.[29] But from that point, in sharp contrast to the distance he kept from matters parliamentary during most of 1643, he again applied himself with gusto to the 'cause'. Within a matter of a couple of months of his return to parliamentary business in November 1643, Scawen had been appointed to chair an important new standing committee, responsible for the armies' pay, mustering and audit.[30] Over the winter of 1643–44, Scawen was transformed from an obscure and retiring backbencher into the one MP who was probably the most active figure in the organisation of the parliamentarian war-effort, working with a zeal and energy which continued unabated until the end of December 1648. During this period of extraordinary activity, his name recurs in the *Journals* and the committee papers – drafting, recruiting, reporting, chairing – every few days.[31]

The veerings of this on-again off-again career demand explanation. Its sudden switches between close involvement and disengagement, at first sight, appear *sui generis*. In fact, it is less idiosyncratic than it seems. One career, at least, replicates Scawen's shifts of direction and their timing with almost exact precision: that of his employer, Northumberland. It seems

[27] *CJ*, III, 30b.   [28] *CJ*, III, 107a.

[29] *CJ*, III, 297b, 299a. On 10 May 1643, Scawen had been named to the committee for Irish affairs; *CJ*, III, 78b. But he did not take his seat until 13 January 1644: BL, Add. MS 4771 (Cttee for Irish Affairs minute book), fo. 10v. (I owe this reference to Mr Patrick Little.)

[30] *CJ*, III, 375b; (not to be confused with the committee established on 25 March 1644, also chaired by Scawen, to consider the establishment of pay for the armies; *CJ*, III, 437a–b).

[31] For Scawen's activities in 1644 in relation to the war-effort: *CJ*, III, 426a, 430a, 431b, 432a, 432b–33a, 437a–b, 461b, 473a, 475a, 481b, 488b, 502b, 503b, 509b, 544b, 565b–66a, 567b, 597b, 602b, 606a, 609a, 660a, 681a, 682a, 698b, 709b, 717b, 722b; BL, Add. MS 31116 (Whittaker diary), fos. 127v, 139v–40.

reasonable to ask whether there was a connection between Scawen's 'public career' in the Commons and his contemporaneous (and, in the event, far longer) career within the household. For the early 1640s were a period when Scawen was making his mark as a member of Northumberland's 'family', and making it well. There seems to have been a growing rapport between master and 'gentleman servant' – a regard which, on Northumberland's side, manifested itself in the growing list of responsibilities he entrusted to Scawen. Scawen's rise up the domestic *cursus honorum* culminated in 1645 when he was appointed to a series of major household offices which he subsequently held continuously for almost a quarter of a century.[32] His place within the household will be examined in detail later; for the moment we need to turn, first, to Northumberland's own political conduct. Given the obvious connection between master and servant in the domestic sphere, it seems unlikely that their activities in the public sphere were wholly unrelated.

In fact, the parallels are striking. During 1640–41, Scawen's reticence in criticising the politics of the Personal Rule closely mirrors that of his employer, who, as a senior Privy Councillor during the 1630s, had been intimately involved in the enforcement of Charles's 'imperial designs' against the Scots and the policies of the Personal Rule. Northumberland opposed the attainder of his old friend, Strafford, in 1641; and, when Scawen did likewise, it seems (as Professor Keeler suggested as long ago as 1954) that he was voting at his master's behest.[33] By the autumn of 1641, however, Northumberland was diverging ever more sharply from the court party, coming round to the view, by early 1642, that the king could only be rescued from his 'evil counsellors', and permanent reforms effected, by military force. Throughout 1642, Northumberland was a pillar of the 'war party' at Westminster, strongly backing the creation of a parliamentarian army under Essex (his own first cousin). But when the war in England had failed to produce a definitive parliamentarian victory by early 1643, Northumberland put his influence behind a negotiated settlement[34] – not out of a supine acceptance of 'peace at any price', but from an abhorrence of what a further escalation of the conflict would entail: a shift from a relatively limited war between Englishmen in England, to a war in which all three nations under Stuart rule were fighting on English soil. Northumberland detested Pym's proposals that Scottish

---

[32] Alnwick Castle, Northumberland MS υ. 1. 6. (Peter Dodesworth's acc. to 17 January 1643); Petworth House Archives, MS 645; Northumberland MS υ. 1. 6. (Edward Payler's acc. to 17 January 1644). For the continuity of Scawen's service: F. W. Steer and N. H. Osborne (ed.), *The Petworth House Archives: A Catalogue*, 2 vols. (Chichester, 1968–79), II, pp. 1–4.

[33] Keeler, *The Long Parliament*, p. 58n.   [34] *Lords' Journals (LJ)*, VI, 163a, 171a.

Covenanters should be hired to fight for Parliament almost as much as he loathed the prospect that royalists might recruit Irish Catholic rebels to fight for the king. Thus he opposed the proposal, current throughout the summer of 1643, for a new 'League and Covenant' between Parliament and the Scots. And when, in August 1643, the Commons narrowly rejected the Lords' demands for a negotiated settlement – and turned instead to concluding the military alliance with the Scots – Northumberland boy-cotted Parliament and withdrew to Petworth, his Sussex seat,[35] where he almost certainly considered the possibility of throwing in his lot with the king. Northumberland's alternating phases of involvement in, and with-drawal from, the parliamentarian cause between 1641 and October 1643 correspond with Scawen's parliamentary record almost exactly: active support for the war-effort until May 1643, then a distinct cooling in his enthusiasm for the cause as Pym pressed ahead with the Scottish alliance, culminating in his withdrawal from Westminster in August of that year.

The turning-point in Northumberland's attitude to the conduct of the war – and the moment from which Scawen also assumed a major role in Parliament's military affairs – came in the late autumn of 1643, with the Irish Cessation: the agreement, brokered between Ormond and the Catholic 'rebels', which, it was believed, was likely to bring some 10,000 Irish troops to intervene in England on the royalist side.[36] Faced with that threat, a negotiated settlement with the king was no longer an option, and Northumberland's hostility to the Covenanter alliance dissolved. The 'war of the three kingdoms' which he had worked so hard to avoid now became inevitable. Within days of news of the Cessation reaching London, North-umberland had returned to his place in the Lords,[37] and was soon paying court to the Scottish commissioners, encouraging the Covenanter army's rapid advance. From that moment, Northumberland was among the parliamentarian hawks, intent on a vigorous prosecution of the war, and prepared to swallow his antipathy to the Scots in order to achieve it.[38]

Scawen's career followed an almost identical trajectory. In the six months before the Irish Cessation in October 1643, he had been named to not a single committee dealing with the conduct of the war,[39] and he seems to have followed Northumberland in flirting with royalism when

---

[35] Bodl. Lib., MS Eng. hist. c. 53 (Letters to Sir Samuel Luke), fo. 59v: intelligence report, 26 July 1643; BL, Add. MS 37343 (Bulstrode Whitelocke's Annals), fo. 272.

[36] BL, Add. MS 18778 (Yonge's diary), fos. 70, 74.

[37] Claydon House, Bucks., Verney MS: Sir Roger Burgoyne to Sir Ralph Verney, 17 October 1643; *LJ*, VI, 260a.

[38] David Laing (ed.), *The Letters and Journals of Robert Baillie*, 3 vols. (Bannatyne Club, Edinburgh, 1841–42), II, pp. 107, 115, 141.

[39] For the handful of *Commons Journals* references to Scawen during the period May–October 1643: *CJ*, III, 78b, 107a, 118a. He was given leave of absence in August (*CJ*, III, 222b),

the Commons threw out the peers' proposals for a negotiated peace in August. On 1 August, Scawen stood surety for a loan of £2,000 taken out by Northumberland from Adrian May, a notorious royalist to whom Charles I had recently entrusted the pawning of the crown jewels.[40] In sharp contrast, in the six months after the Cessation, and Northumberland's return to Westminster, Scawen was named to a series of major committees dealing with the war-effort, and was called upon to draft legislation or to report to the House, on average, once a week[41] – not counting the many more meetings with fellow MPs dealing with the armies' recruitment, logistics and pay which necessarily went unnoticed in the *Journals*.[42] The 'fiery spirits' had a convert. Scawen, 'who, formerly, had not very well liked of their ways', had suddenly become a zealous war-party man.[43]

So, with happy simultaneity, Scawen and Northumberland both came round from tentative royalism to support for a vigorous prosecution of the war. The casualty of this new-found insistence on a decisive victory was Essex, Parliament's dilatory and politically ambitious lord general. Thus, Northumberland supported efforts between February and May 1644 to curb Essex's powers by subordinating him to a new bicameral executive, the Committee of Both Kingdoms[44] – a body which superseded the far larger Committee of Safety that had been dominated by 'peace-party' peers.[45] With the Committee of Safety defunct, an entirely new series of specialist committees was established to oversee the armies' structure, pay and supply. The most important of these, a Commons-only body established on 25 March, was entrusted to Scawen, the Committee for the Lord General's Establishment (often simply known eponymously as 'the committee where Mr Scawen has the chair'), responsible for determining the size and organization of all the parliamentary armies. From this base, Scawen waged an effective campaign to demote the lord general's force to the status of the Parliament's second field army – the larger force going to

and evidently delayed his return, as he was repeatedly summoned to attend in September and early October (*CJ*, III, 253a, 264b, 283b).

[40] Petworth House Archives, MS 645; for May: BL, Add. MS 31116 (Whittaker diary), fo. 169v. (I am grateful to Dr Jason Peacey for information concerning May.)

[41] See, for a representative series of examples, his activities in February and March 1644: *CJ*, III, 384a, 389a–b, 390a, 402a, 403a, 405a, 419b, 426, 430a, 431b, 432a, 433a, 437a–b; BL, Add. MS 31116 (Whittaker diary), fo. 127v.

[42] PRO, WO 47/1 (Ordnance office, papers of Scawen's Committee for the Establishment of the Army), 211–345.

[43] Maseres (ed.), 'Memoirs of Denzil Lord Holles', I, p. 270.

[44] Laing (ed.), *The Letters and Journals of Robert Baillie*, II, p. 141.

[45] L. Glow [Mulligan], 'The Committee of Safety', *English Historical Review*, 80, 1965, 289–313.

Essex's arch-rival, Sir William Waller.[46] And in June, when the Commons established a committee with an extensive brief to manage the recruitment, pay and provisioning of Waller's army, this too came under Scawen's chairmanship.[47]

But it was after the *débâcle* of Essex's western campaign, in the autumn of 1644, that Northumberland and Scawen placed themselves in the vanguard of the movement to oust Essex from his command, and to undertake a 'new-modelling' of all the parliamentary forces.[48] As Essex's ally in the Lords, Lord Robartes, noted of that autumn, it was 'The earl of Northumberland who was the great instrument of the New Model, and complied wholly with the Independent party about this time' – a development which he dated to as early as October 1644.[49] As Northumberland took a prominent part in promoting the cause of military reform within the Committee of Both Kingdoms and in the House of Lords – in the teeth of Essex's opposition – Scawen's committee got on with the practical task of bringing the new force into being, drawing up plans for its musters, accounts, debentures[50] and 'instructions' (or military regulations).[51] In February he headed another *ad hoc* committee to deal with the army's recruitment 'according to the new model'.[52] Thus during the period from December 1644 to March 1645, Scawen chaired deliberations on almost every aspect of the new army's organization – from the raising of revenue through to the size and cost of the New Model's artillery train.[53]

[46] For Scawen's principal chairmanships: *CJ*, III, 375b (committee to consider the state, musters, and pay of the army, 24 January 1644), and III, 437a–b (committee to consider the establishment for all the parliamentary armies, 25 March 1644). Although this latter body became known as the 'committee for the establishment of the lord general's army' (or the 'committee where Mr Scawen has the chair' – *CJ*, III, 563b, 583a), its original brief gave it power to consider the establishments of all the parliamentary forces. Cf. *CJ*, III, 544b.

[47] *CJ*, III, 544b; for Scawen's efforts to support Waller's army, see also *CJ*, III, 563b, 567b, 597b, 602b.

[48] For Northumberland's involvement in the military re-organisation during the autumn of 1644: PRO, SP 21/8 (Committee of Both Kingdoms minute book), p. 20; John Adamson, 'The baronial context of the English Civil War', *Transactions of the Royal Historical Society*, 5th series, 40, 1990, 110–15.

[49] BL, Harl. MS 2224 (Lord Robartes's notes of the Long Parliament), printed in J. L. Sanford, *Studies and Illustrations of the Great Rebellion* (1858), pp. 291n–92n; cf. PRO, SP 21/7 (Committee of Both Kingdoms minute book), p. 214: Northumberland's appointment to the committee to draw up new instructions to the remaining field armies, 30 September 1644 – with Saye, William Pierrepont, John Crewe and Oliver St John; *LJ*, VII, 83.

[50] *CJ*, III, 717b; cf. *CJ*, IV, 13a, 23b, 31b, 39a, 52b, 56b, 59a.

[51] *CJ*, IV, 31b.   [52] *CJ*, IV, 51a.

[53] *CJ*, IV, 59a, 31b, 73a. Another army committee, chaired by Zouche Tate, assisted in preparing for the forthcoming campaign; but this ceased to sit after the end of March 1645.

However, it is the commission defining Sir Thomas Fairfax's powers as commander of the new army which provides perhaps the clearest instance of the parallelism between Scawen's and Northumberland's respective parliamentary roles. Reported by Scawen on 24 March, this bill effectively dismantled the few remaining powers left to Essex by his original 1642 commission. Under the terms of the proposed new commission, Fairfax's authority was to be extended to permit him to execute martial law within the army, to command all 'garrisons, forts, castles and towns' in England, and, in its final form, the commission notoriously omitted any reference to preserving 'the safety of the king's person' (such as had been contained in Essex's commission as lord general).[54] In the upper House, Scawen's bill immediately won the support not only of Northumberland, but of a cohort of like-minded peers who were to vote *en bloc* with a high degree of consistency in the years ahead: the earls of Kent, Pembroke, Nottingham and Salisbury, and Lords Howard of Escrick, North and Wharton, and Viscount Saye (brandishing the proxy of Fairfax's grandfather, the aged earl of Mulgrave). It was these peers (joined belatedly by the earl of Bolingbroke) who ensured that the commission Scawen had reported to the Commons was passed in the Lords – notwithstanding the fierce opposition of 'Essex's party' and perhaps the most acrimoniously fought division in the upper House since the outbreak of the Civil War.[55]

'New-modelling' the armies required, in turn, a streamlined parliamentary bureaucracy. The pre-1645 army committees, with their tangle of duplicated responsibilities, were set aside. A new 'Committee for Sir Thomas Fairfax's Army' was established on 31 March 1645 – the eve of Essex's resignation as commander-in-chief – with its principal task to oversee the raising and disbursing of funds.[56] Piecemeal and unobtrusively, however, over the next twelve months, it accumulated a wide jurisdiction over military affairs. What has gone unnoticed hitherto is that, unlike its predecessor (Scawen's Committee for the Establishment of 25 March 1644) which had been a Commons-only body,[57] this new standing committee was a joint-committee of the two Houses.[58] Scawen was once

---

[54] *CJ*, IV, 87b–88b; *LJ*, VII, 297b–99a. For Essex's commission, C. H. Firth and R. S. Rait (ed.), *Acts and Ordinances of the Interregnum, 1642–60* 3 vols. (1911), I, pp. 14–16.

[55] For this list – recorded on 31 March when, at its first presentation, the commission failed to pass the Lords – see *LJ*, VII, 297b; for Bolingbroke's last-minute defection from Essex's party to Northumberland's, BL, Harl. MS 166 (Sir Simonds D'Ewes diary, 1644–45), fos. 196v–97.

[56] *Acts and Ordinances* (*A&O*), I, 656–60.   [57] *CJ*, III, 437a–b (25 March 1644).

[58] *LJ*, VII, 293b–95a; *A&O*, I, 656–60. Professor Gentles identifies the Army Committee as the (Commons-only) body established on 17 February 1645 to deal with the recruitment of the New Model, which included the Essex-supporters, Sir William Lewis and Sir Philip Stapilton (*CJ*, IV, 51a); but this body was distinct from, and superseded by, the

again appointed chairman, but he now sat with ten lords. The list of lords on the committee corresponds almost line for line with the list of peers who supported Scawen's legislation for Fairfax's commission – Northumberland himself, Kent, Pembroke, Salisbury, Bolingbroke, Saye and Sele, Wharton, and Howard of Escrick.[59] In effect, the new committee gave institutional form to the informal bicameral interest which had been supporting the cause of military reform since at least the previous October.

Appropriately then, Scawen's public elevation to the chairmanship of this new bicameral Army Committee was paralleled by promotion within the private commonwealth of Northumberland House. On 24 May 1645, just as the new Army Committee was establishing itself, Northumberland demonstrated the high esteem in which he held Scawen by promoting him to one of the senior offices within his household, 'paymaster' (in effect, project manager) of Northumberland's ambitious series of architectural schemes, and steward of his Syon estate.[60] At least in terms of length of tenure, the paymaster was the major appointment of Scawen's life; he held it continuously for the next twenty-two years, directing a series of major enterprises at Syon, York House and Suffolk (soon to be Northumberland) House, the great Jacobean town house at Charing Cross that Northumberland had bought in 1642.[61]

It is all very well to identify parallels between the courses pursued by peers and commoners; but might these not be merely chance congruities? And, even if they are not purely accidental, where do they leave our assessment of Scawen's place in the public realm? Several caveats need to be entered. It was relatively rare for an actual household servant of a nobleman to take on such a prominent public role; most MPs who served as peers' stewards were far more actively engaged running their masters' estates than in running the affairs of the realm.[62] To this extent, the relationship between Northumberland and Scawen was probably so much

---

bicameral Army Committee which came into existence at the end of March – in the process excluding all Essex-supporters from its ranks; cf. Gentles, *New Model Army*, p. 31 and p. 454 n. 21.

[59] Only two out of the ten Lords' nominees were less than wholehearted in their support for the New Model: Denbigh (who shortly underwent a change of heart and emerged as a firm ally of Northumberland's party in the Lords), and the fence-sitting 8th earl of Rutland – who, like Glynne, seems never to have set foot in the committee's meeting-room.

[60] Alnwick Castle, Northumberland MS v. 1. 6: Scawen's account as paymaster, 24 May 1645–14 March 1646; general account for 1646.

[61] Petworth House Archives, MS 5817: Scawen's account for Syon and Northumberland House, 1667; Alnwick Castle, Northumberland MS v. 1. 6/36.

[62] For other examples, J. S. A. Adamson, 'Parliamentary management, men-of business, and the House of Lords, 1640–49', in Clyve Jones (ed.), *A Pillar of the Constitution: The House of Lords in British Politics, 1640–1784* (1989), pp. 45–46.

sui generis that it would be unwise to generalise from it, even in other cases where MPs were formally fee'd or retained by a nobleman. Still less do I wish to imply that so complex a process as the new-modelling of Parliament's armies was the achievement of any one pairing of commoner and peer, however closely they may have been working in tandem.[63] On the other hand, to see Scawen as a wholly independent figure in this process, merely *coincidentally* turning up as the public advocate of policies which just happened to be the same as those supported by an aristocratic grandee who was his master, would be to imagine a world which bears little relation to the realities of early-modern noble households in general, or to Northumberland's in particular – 'where', as Clarendon observed, 'no man was more absolutely obeyed'.[64]

Scawen may well have played an important part in advising and counselling Northumberland. But when he spoke in the Commons – often on matters controversial – there could have been few who heard him who imagined that he ever pursued a course, be it saving Strafford or ousting Essex, other than with his master's approbation. It could hardly have been otherwise. Scawen ate with the officers of the household when Northumberland dined in state; and on ceremonial occasions would probably have worn the 'blew coates taffetie', embroidered with the half-moon badge of the Percys, which Northumberland had assigned as a livery to his 'gentlemen servants' in 1635.[65] He had rooms in Northumberland House; and by the late 1640s these were located in 'the Lower Lodgings on the right hand of the Courte': that is, at the ground-floor level in the house's western range, looking onto the central courtyard.[66] And when the Commons' business of the day was done, it was to these lodgings in Northumberland's household that he returned; to deal – as we shall see – with architects and masons, carvers and gilders, gardeners and glaziers, a series of responsibilities which, at first sight, may seem wholly unrelated to his preoccupations in the public realm.

This courtly milieu of Northumberland House is not, perhaps, one usually associated with Cromwell's 'russet-coated captains' and the New Model's godly grandees. But for the next four years, these very different worlds converged in the person of Robert Scawen. Warrants for muskets

---

[63] The discussion in Adamson, 'The baronial context' (at p. 113), fails to notice sufficiently Northumberland's active role in promoting these reforms.

[64] Edward Hyde, earl of Clarendon, *The History of the Rebellion and Civil Wars in England*, ed. W. D. Macray, 6 vols. (Oxford, 1888), II, p. 538.

[65] Alnwick Castle, Northumberland MS U. I. 5: Peter Dodesworth's account as steward of the household, to 16 January 1635. (I owe this reference to Mr Jeremy Wood.)

[66] Alnwick Castle, Northumberland MS U. III. 2: Scawen's account as paymaster of Northumberland House, 1642–9.

and the payment of Cromwell's arrears jostled for space on his desk with plans for Northumberland House's new Classical staircases, the details of Ionic volutes, and the arrangements for catching moles in the gardens of Syon House.[67] It is time we considered Scawen's work as chairman of the Army Committee, and the broader significance that attached to this convergence of domestic and public roles.

III

As committees went during the 1640s, none was more overtly partisan than that 'where Mr Scawen has the chair'.[68] It was dominated by those who would soon be dubbed 'Independents' in politics.[69] Only one out of this cohort of twenty was later to emerge as a political Presbyterian, the recorder of London, John Glynne; and he evidently felt so ill at ease in such partisan company that he failed to attend a single meeting.[70] Similarly, the Lords' contingent, as we have noted, was virtually identical

[67] Alnwick Castle, Northumberland MS u. 1. 6: Scawen's account, 24 May 1645–14 March 1646 ('to Andrew Barton for catching moles in the grounds about Syon and in the gardens for one year ended at Christmas last', 53s. 4d.). For Northumberland's architectural patronage, F. Allardyce, 'The patronage of the 9th and 10th earls of Northumberland' (unpublished MA dissertation, Courtauld Institute of Art, University of London, 1987); Jeremy Wood, 'The architectural patronage of Algernon Percy, 10th earl of Northumberland: a comparison', in John Bold and Edward Chaney (ed.), *English Architecture Public and Private: Essays for Kerry Downes* (London and Rio Grande, 1993), pp. 55–80.

[68] Limitations of space preclude a detailed examination in this essay of the work of the Army Committee; I will attempt to provide this in a forthcoming paper.

[69] Of the twenty members of the Commons who found places on the new body, almost all had been prominently associated with the campaign to 'new-model' the army. Most of the committee which had been appointed back in December 1644 to draft the first ordinance for Self-Denial, for instance (six out of that committee's eight members), were named to the new Army Committee: John Crewe, William Ellys, John Glynne, Oliver St John, William Pierrepont and Robert Reynolds. Of the remaining fourteen Commons-men on the Army Committee, another ten can be identified as supporters of the creation of the New Model, including some of the most trenchant critics of Essex's conduct of the war: the younger Sir Henry Vane, William Strode of Devon (D'Ewes's archetypal 'fiery spirit'), Sir Arthur Hesilrige, the radical London Alderman John Venn, Edmund Prideaux, the older Thomas Pury, Denis Bond, Thomas Hodges, Sir John Evelyn of Wiltshire and Scawen himself. The four remaining Commons-men – Sir Thomas Soame, Robert Jenner, Anthony Bedingfield and Sir Gilbert Gerard – are harder to place; but only Gerard, Essex's former treasurer-at-war, was identified at this time with the Presbyterian interest, and even he strove hard to '[keep] himself levell betwixt the Factions'. *A&O*, 1, pp. 656–60; for Gerard: *Mercurius Pragmaticus*, no. 11 (6–13 June 1648), sig. M2[1].

[70] As the committee's order (or minute) books do not appear to have survived, attendances have been reconstructed by collating the signatures on all of the several thousand surviving warrants issued by the committee between March 1645 and January 1649. These are principally to be found in PRO, SP 28/29–58.

to the bloc which supported Scawen's bill to commission Fairfax and extend his powers. There was nothing balanced or consensual about this line-up; it was a committee composed of those who had backed the movement for radical reform of Parliament's military organisation, at least since Essex's disaster at Lostwithiel, and in some cases well before.

The duties were onerous. From its initial brief to oversee the collection of the assessment, the Army Committee gradually acquired extensive powers: over the delivery of arms, ammunition and clothing for the New Model;[71] the collection of arrears; dealing with recruitment for the New Model;[72] paying off demobilised officers and troops;[73] funding Fairfax's network of scouts (intelligence officers) and spies.[74] The bulk of the Army Committee's work was shouldered by a relatively small, highly motivated inner clique: no more than some six or seven members. Scawen (whose attendance record is virtually faultless), was by far the most assiduous member throughout the period from March 1645 to December 1648. All Scawen's most active colleagues were prominent anti-Essexians: Venn, Hesilrige, Evelyn of Wiltshire, Hodges, and (from October 1645), the former New Model officer, Colonel Edward Mountagu (the future earl of Sandwich). So too was Scawen's deputy, Thomas Pury, the Gloucester alderman who served intermittently as man-of-affairs and, later, executor to the earl of Pembroke (who was himself a member of the Army Committee).[75] These 'few', as the *Moderate Intelligencer* reported in August 1645, 'attend so constantly that the Kingdom owes them very much',[76] and although the peers were only rarely part of the 'few', the bicameral aspect of the committee was not merely notional, with Kent, Denbigh, Saye and Sele, Howard of Escrick and Wharton all recorded as having attended meetings.[77]

Their principal task, as defined by the ordinance which brought the

---

[71] *CJ*, IV, 99b.   [72] *CJ*, IV, 101b, 104b, 163b, 187a.

[73] *CJ*, IV, 121b, 129b, 159a, 164b, 231b.

[74] *CJ*, IV, 130b. Similarly, in December 1645, Scawen's committee took on the responsibility for the impressment of men to bring the New Model up to strength for the forthcoming 1646 campaign; *CJ*, IV, 388a; BL, Add. MS 19398 (Misc. autographs), fo. 179: Scawen to Committee at Norwich, 26 January 1646.

[75] Sheffield Central Lib., Elmhirst MS 1352/11; Elmhirst MS 1360, fo. 6; Hatfield, Accounts 127/9 (Pembroke's privy purse accounts, April 1647–February 1650), unfol., entries for February 1648.

[76] *Moderate Intelligencer*, no. 23 (31 July–7 August 1645), p. 183 [*recte* 182] (BL, E 295/7).

[77] E.g., PRO, SP 28/38/3, fo. 277; SP 28/38/4, fo. 308; SP 28/50/1, fos. 24, 144; SP 28/55/1, fos. 35, 47, 87; SP 28/55/2, fo. 263. In the absence of the committee's minute books, it is impossible to give an accurate picture of the peers' attendance, and it is clear that peers rarely signed warrants, even when they were present at meetings; see, e.g., the warrants for 3 May 1648: SP 28/54/2, fos. 228, 230 (warrants of the day signed by Kent); SP 28/54/2, fos. 232, 234, 238, 283 (warrants of the day which Kent did not sign).

committee into being, was to administer the system of assessments levied on each county to meet the cost of Fairfax's army. 'Money ... is the Sinews of the Warr', Scawen and his fellow-committeemen declared as they got down to work in April 1645,[78] and it is this responsibility for the raising and disbursing of money which made the committee's role so critical to the success or failure of the New Model. Its procedures were brisk and businesslike. Funds collected were paid into a central treasury-at-war in Guildhall, administered by eight treasurers-at-war; payments were issued on the committee's warrant to the treasurers, usually signed by the chairman and at least four other members. Cash was then issued, either to the officers of the New Model, for their own and their troops' pay, or to the numerous contractors who provided everything from boots to bando-leers. The treasurers-at-war were themselves a no less partisan group; like the committee they served, all but one or two were political Independ-ents.[79] And by far the most active of the treasurers was the London goldsmith, Francis Allein, a staunch critic within the City's Common Council of the political and religious pretensions of the Scots.[80]

Like Scawen, Allein owed more than a little of his prominence in public affairs to Northumberland's support. Although Allein's connections with the earl were not as close as Scawen's – he was never a member of the household, nor in receipt of an annuity – he was clearly known to Northumberland as early as 1642, well before he achieved prominence in the wartime administration. Early that year, Northumberland had put Allein forward as his candidate for the Cumberland seat of Cockermouth, where, as lord of the honor, he had been responsible for the borough's recent re-enfranchisement.[81]

It was as the earl's carpet-bagging nominee that Allein, a Londoner who had no known connections with the remote northern borough, was elected, finally taking his seat (after a protracted tussle before various Commons committees) in 1645.[82] Although Allein seems not to have been a North-umberland client in any formal sense, the political course he took, at least until the break-up of the Independent interest in 1648, was almost identical to Scawen's. He was Scawen's closest colleague among the

---

[78] BL, Add. MS 19398 (Misc. autographs), fo. 189: Army Committee to the Norfolk Committee, 9 April 1645.

[79] A&O, 1, 656; Hoover, 'Cromwell's status and pay', p. 711.

[80] For Allein's hostility to the Scots: Corporation of London RO, Common Council Journal 40, fos. 171r–v; Dr Williams' Lib., MS 24.50 (Juxon diary), fos. 61, 62.

[81] Centre for Kentish Studies, De L'Isle MS u1475/A98: Cartwright's acc. (for the earl of Northumberland) to January 1641; Cumbria RO (Carlisle), D/Lec/107, unfol.: notes [after 15 February 1641].

[82] Cumbria RO (Carlisle), D/Lec/107, unfol.: freeholders and burgesses to Northumberland [c. February–March 1641]; CJ, IV, 260a, 264a, 300a, 364b.

treasurers-at-war, and the one who was invariably the recipient of anything Scawen addressed personally from the committee.[83] As we shall see, the political consequences of this cooperation between Allein and Scawen were to be strikingly evident during the crisis of 1647.

With its politically cohesive membership and its extensive responsibilities, the Army Committee enjoyed extensive opportunities for the dispensing of patronage and favour. Denzell Holles later cited Allein's and White's appointments as treasurers-at-war as clear instances of factional patronage, part of a series of 'places of great profit' that were parcelled out to the Independents' friends.[84] And the records of the committee suggest that his charges were not without foundation. In December 1646, for example, the Army Committee ordered that the vast horde of silver and silver-gilt plate, confiscated from the royalist marquess of Worcester after the fall of Raglan Castle, should be made over in its entirety to Allein, rather than being deposited in the war-chest at Goldsmith's Hall. Allein, himself a goldsmith by trade,[85] was enjoined to dispose of the plate only as ordered by the committee or the Commons; but such arrangements tended to blur the distinction between public and private funds, creating what was in effect a private store on which Allein could draw without reference to his fellow treasurers-at-war.[86] The unusually large meeting on 14 December 1646 which gave its approval to this questionable arrangement was a roll-call of leading supporters of the New Model: Scawen, Pury, Hesilrige, Evelyn of Wiltshire, Venn, Mountagu and Lord Wharton; of those attending, only Sir Gilbert Gerard was anything less than a wholehearted adherent of the 'army interest' at Westminster and beyond.[87]

Similarly, as the body responsible for authorising payments from the treasury-at-war at Guildhall, the Army Committee exercised considerable discretionary powers, particularly when it came to determining whose financial claims should receive priority at times when, as was almost invariably the case, ready cash was in chronically short supply. With most army pay in arrears, often by as much as eight weeks, the committee could, where it chose, short-circuit the usual procedures for officers' pay, and issue *ad hominem* 'advances' of ready cash (drawn against future pay or current arrears). Henry Ireton, for example, received a series of grants

---

[83] E.g., SP 28/31/6, fo. 572v: apostil, on a petition, by Scawen to Allein, 1 August 1645; SP 28/31/6, fo. 610v: Scawen to Allein, 15 August 1645.

[84] Maseres (ed.), 'Memoirs of Denzil, Lord Holles', 1, p. 253.

[85] Goldsmiths' Company Library, London, Court Book Q, fo. 92; Court Book W, fos. 267v–68v; Court Book Y, fos. 89, 146, 165.

[86] SP 28/41/2, fo. 160: indenture, 18 December 1646.

[87] For the warrants on which these attendance records are based, see SP 28/41/2, fos. 160, 169, and the series between fos. 171–216.

from the committee, between 12 December 1646 and 27 May 1647, totalling £450.[88] Yet, by far the most spectacular recipient of the committee's favour was Oliver Cromwell. On 26 November 1646, a meeting chaired as usual by Scawen, and attended by Pury, Hodges, Mountagu and Venn, ordered the immediate issue of £500 to Cromwell – a payment of a magnitude unique in the committee's surviving records.[89] As Gerald Aylmer has observed, it is hard to find any parallel for 'so large an advance being made in this way'.[90] But even this payment pales into insignificance when compared to the issue of £1,976 – Cromwell's full pay and arrears to date – authorised by Scawen and four other colleagues on 27 May 1647,[91] and promptly issued by the treasurers-at-war the following day.[92] In one sense, this was no more than what Cromwell was properly entitled to receive; what makes this treatment exceptional is both the size of the payment and the promptness with which it was disbursed. At a time when many officers' salaries were extensively in arrears, Cromwell was clearly the recipient of exceptional favour from the committee.[93] And though this instance went undetected by the committee's Presbyterian critics, it was precisely the type of action which gave substance to more generalised complaints that the Independents dispensed favour on highly partisan lines.

Through the Army Committee, Scawen became one of the principal points of contact between the New Model's senior officers and Parliament. It was to him that Fairfax or his secretaries wrote when there were matters requiring the Commons' or the Army Committee's attention. And throughout 1645 and 1646, Scawen was the MP who pressed the case most persistently for the New Model's pay and recruitment: drafting letters to hasten the collection of assessments for the army,[94] and recommending that royalists' composition fines should be diverted to army pay to meet a shortfall in revenues assigned to the army from delinquents' lands.[95] It was a role which required patience and ingenuity; 'the more Victories wee

---

[88] SP 28/41/2, fo. 177: Army Cttee warrant, 12 December 1646; SP 28/303, fo. 769: receipt by Ireton, 28 May 1647; receipted by Ireton, 1 June.

[89] SP 28/41/4, fo. 377v. As Cromwell noted in his receipt, when he collected the money a week later, this payment was 'uppon accompt, to be Abated out of my next pay in the Army'.

[90] Gerald Aylmer, 'Was Cromwell a member of the army in 1646–7 or not?', History, 56, 1971, 185; see also Hoover, 'Cromwell's status and pay', 703–15.

[91] SP 28/49/4, fo. 498: Army Committee warrant, 27 May 1647 (signed by Scawen, Evelyn, Hodges, Hesilrige and the younger Vane).

[92] SP 28/303/3, fo. 765: receipt by Cromwell, 28 May 1647. (I owe my knowledge of this document to Dr Hoover.)

[93] For further payments, see SP 28/50/2, fo. 191: statement of Cromwell's accounts at 17 December 1647.

[94] CJ, IV, 146b. [95] CJ, IV, 342b.

have', Scawen wrote to Sir John Potts in the month after Naseby, 'the more troubles to us, how to get supplies'.[96] At the end of December 1645, Scawen spent almost three days on his feet in the Commons, reviewing the state of the army's funding during the past year, and presenting estimates for the arms and recruits that would be required for the forthcoming campaigns.[97] And when the king abandoned Oxford in April 1646 – his symbolic admission that he had lost the war – Scawen and Evelyn took the lead in managing (and no doubt drawing up) the contingency plans that were to be put into effect should the king appear in the capital.[98] All this virtue did not go unrewarded. In the spring of 1646, the Commons voted him the fulsome tribute that was the starting-point of this essay; and – more tangibly – the grant of £2,000 which came close to doubling his net worth.

IV

But there was more to Scawen's role as chairman of the Army Committee than doling out arrears and ensuring adequate supplies of hobnailed boots. The military reforms of which the Army Committee was part had been bitterly fought; and it was clear that by no means all MPs wished to see the new army prosper. Partisan sniping regularly frustrated Scawen's efforts. 'Could wee [but] agree heere, and attend the Publique', Scawen had written in July 1645, 'wee might hope – God blessinge us – to see an end of much of our miseries before October bee att an end'.[99] The end of the war, however, only intensified factional rivalries. With a large Scottish army still in England, and the Covenanter leadership clearly supporting Presbyterian plans for a lenient settlement with the king, Commons' Independents and Northumberland's party in the Lords looked to the New Model as an insurance policy against a royalist coup or, worse, a Scottish-backed restoration of the king. The role of the Army Committee changed accordingly: from providing men and matériel with which to win the war, to seeking to preserve the army in being, at least until such time as the Scots had been sent home and there was a secure peace. The partisan aspect of the committee became ever more overt. From 6 May

---

[96] Bodl. Lib., MS Tanner 60, fo. 214: Scawen to Sir John Potts, 17 July 1645.

[97] *CJ*, IV, 386b–88a; BL, Add. MS 31116 (Whittaker's diary), fo. 251r–v (27–29 December 1645). As a result of Scawen's report, legislation was passed to give effect to his recommendations and to renew the Army Committee's brief until September 1646. Similarly, in March 1646, when legislation was required to continue the New Model Army on foot for another six months, Scawen was the draftsman of the bill; *CJ*, IV, 484a; *CJ*, IV, 537a.

[98] *CJ*, IV, 498b–99a; BL, Add. MS 31116 (Whittaker diary), fo. 263v.

[99] Bodl. Lib., MS Tanner 60, fo. 214: Scawen to Sir John Potts, 17 July 1645.

1646, the day Parliament learnt that the king had given himself up to the
Scots army at Newark, Scawen's committee was given extensive powers of
interrogation and investigation into clandestine negotiations with the
court[100] – a move prompted by rumours that Essex and the Presbyterian
party in Parliament and the City were already well advanced towards a
private treaty, abetted by the Scots commissioners, about terms for the
restoration of the king.[101]

This clear factional identification between the Army Committee and
the anti-Scottish, anti-Presbyterian 'interest' in the two Houses came at a
price. With the Presbyterians in the ascendant in the Lords from the
spring of 1646, and in the Commons as well from early in 1647, Scawen's
advocacy of the army's interests encountered ever more formidable
parliamentary opposition. The committee's attempts to keep the New
Model in funds were repeatedly frustrated, and by the autumn of 1646 it
was clear that there was a strong body of opinion in Parliament intent on
suppressing the committee – and disbanding the army. When the committee's empowering ordinance expired in September 1646, the order to
instruct Scawen to bring in a new bill, continuing the Army Committee for
a further ten months, passed by a single vote in the Commons;[102] and once
in the Lords, the bill was deferred by the Presbyterian majority indefinitely.[103]

Although the Army Committee retained its coherence as a bicameral
group throughout the period of Presbyterian ascendancy, it was fighting a
losing battle. Its rearguard action in both Houses against attempts to
disband the army prematurely and without satisfaction of its arrears met
with meagre success. In the major conference between the two Houses on
18 January 1647 about the Lords' refusal to pass the army assessment bill,
it was Scawen and his Army Committee colleague, Robert Reynolds,[104]
who urged the Lords to pass the bill at once. As so often, this impasse

[100] *CJ*, iv, 537a–b: 'any treaties of intelligences whatsoever, either with the king, or with any
     other person or persons, which may any way tend to the prejudice of the Parliament or
     of their proceedings'. From that day it also became a 'close committee' – like the
     Committee of Both Kingdoms – enjoined to conduct its proceedings in secrecy.
[101] Dr Williams' Lib., MS 24.50 (Juxon diary), fo. 71; Robert Brenner, *Merchants and
     Revolution: Commercial Change, Political Conflict, and London's Overseas Traders, 1550–1653*
     (Cambridge, 1993), p. 475.
[102] *CJ*, iv, 713b (3 November 1646).
[103] *CJ*, iv, 737b; for a case of contempt of the committee's jurisdiction after its empowering
     ordinances expired, see PRO, SP 28/41/1, fo. 60: warrant (signed by Scawen alone), 29
     December 1646.
[104] *CJ*, v, 55a–b, 56b–57a. Reynolds had a personal interest, as his brother, Captain John
     Reynolds, was serving in Cromwell's own regiment: PRO, SP 28/41/2, fo. 197r–v: Army
     Committee warrant, 21 December 1646. For the relationship, see *Notes and Queries*
     (1876), p. 307. (I am grateful to Professor Ian Gentles for this last reference.)

between the Houses was not a straightforward Lords–Commons divide, but the result of opposing alignments which transcended the division between peers and the lower House. Thus, in pressing the case for the army's pay, Scawen could at least be confident of the support of 'Northumberland's party' in the upper House. When, after weeks of delay, the Presbyterian majority in the House of Lords took the provocative step of rejecting outright the New Model's assessment bill, the lords of the Army Committee constituted the core of those who entered their dissents – Northumberland's signature, in order of precedence, again heading the list.[105]

The survival of the New Model and the fortunes of Scawen's committee were intimately linked. On the eve of the notorious Declaration of Dislike – Holles's denunciation of the New Model's attempts to seek redress of its grievances[106] – Scawen delivered a powerful endorsement of the legitimacy of the army's claims.[107] But from the moment the Presbyterians' 'junto' gained control of the Derby House Committee at the beginning of April 1647, both Scawen and the committee he chaired went into eclipse. He is mentioned only once in the *Commons Journals* between 9 April and the beginning of June. In the interim, the Army Committee was ignored.[108] Similarly, from the beginning of April, Northumberland boycotted the proceedings of the Committee at Derby House (which had become, under the Presbyterians, Parliament's major executive committee).[109] Only in June 1647 – when the New Model's refusal to disband, and the seizure of the king by Cornet Joyce, had initiated an entirely new phase in the relations between the army and Westminster – did the Presbyterian junto begin to crumble, and Scawen to regain his former prominence at

[105] *LJ*, IX, 57a. The dissenters (with the names of Army Committee members italicised) were *Northumberland*, *Kent*, Nottingham, *Salisbury*, *Saye*, *Wharton*, Grey of Warke, *Howard of Escrick*, de la Warr and North (4 March 1647).

[106] *CJ*, v, 129a (29 March 1647); Austin Woolrych, *Soldiers and Statesmen: The General Council of the Army and its Debates, 1647–48* (Oxford, 1987), pp. 24–41.

[107] Scawen's report, delivered on 26 March, revealed that the horse and dragoons were owed forty-three weeks' pay (estimated at £252,750); the infantry and the artillery eighteen weeks' (or £78,250); collections were in arrears by £310,360; *CJ*, v, 126b.

[108] During this period (January–July 1647), the Army Committee met by virtue of a Commons order of 16 January 1647 (passed as an emergency measure when it became evident that the Lords were unlikely to agree to an extension of its mandate); PRO, SP 28/46/2, fo. 147. The frequency of meetings was: February, 4 meetings; March, 6; April, 4; May, 7; June, 3; July (to 22nd), 3; (in chronological order) PRO, SP 28/49/4; SP 28/49/2; SP 28/46/2, fo. 147; SP 28/47/1.

[109] For the highly influential position Northumberland had exercised at Derby House since the committee's establishment in October 1646: John Adamson, 'Strafford's ghost: the British context of Viscount Lisle's lieutenancy of Ireland', in Jane H. Ohlmeyer, *Ireland from Independence to Occupation, 1641–60* (Cambridge, 1995), pp. 135–36, 143–55.

Westminster. Indeed, from the moment Parliament began negotiations with the New Model (in the week following Joyce's seizure of the king), Scawen became an apparently indispensable broker between Fairfax's headquarters and Westminster. His first parliamentary appointment since the end of March came on 7 June, when he was named to serve as one of the commissioners 'to go down to the army';[110] and he spent much of the next six months acting as the principal negotiator in Parliament's dealings with Fairfax and the army's officer corps. So too with the Army Committee. Once the Eleven Members (the leading Presbyterians who had been impeached by the army) had withdrawn from the Commons at the end of June, the Army Committee was revived on the next full sitting day, and immediately charged with drawing up plans to deal with the whole question of army pay, the first public acknowledgement of the committee's existence since the beginning of the Presbyterian ascendancy at the end of March.[111] Formal renewal of its authority by both Houses came three weeks later, on 22 July.[112]

In the eyes of his critics, Scawen's conduct of these negotiations with the New Model was outrageously *parti pris*. He was not so much a broker *between* the army and the two Houses as one who identified himself overtly with the army interest and its supporters at Westminster. Holles gives a vivid account of Scawen's return from the army's rendezvous at Triploe Heath on 11 June 1647 – bringing with him the army's *Solemn Engagement* not to disband until its grievances were met.[113]

> Mr Scawen ... reported back to the House in such a ghastly, fearful manner (only to terrify us and make us more supple), he saying [that] the army was so strong, so unanimous, so resolved, as the poor Presbyterians' hearts fell an inch lower, and the Independents made themselves merry with it.[114]

But Scawen's rhetoric struck home. The following day, Parliament effectively abandoned the terms it had offered the army hitherto, and he and Povey were instructed to return to headquarters with a new and far more extensive negotiating brief;[115] indeed, Holles claimed, the authority

---

[110] *CJ*, v, 202a.   [111] *CJ*, v, 228b (1 July 1647).

[112] The bill had lain unpassed in the House of Lords since October 1646; *CJ*, IV, 687a (7 October 1646); *CJ*, v, 234a (reminder to the House of Lords, 6 July 1647); *LJ*, IX, 344a–b (22 July 1647). By 25 July, however, Scawen's fellow commissioners were requesting that Scawen return to army headquarters (now at Bedford), where negotiations with the ten-man committee of the council of war had been proceeding intermittently throughout July; *CJ*, v, 258b.

[113] *CJ*, v, 206b.   [114] Maseres (ed.), 'Memoirs of Denzil, Lord Holles', I, p. 253.

[115] *CJ*, v, 208b. For other references to Scawen as a commissioner, see *LJ*, IX, 308b: commissioners with the army to the Speakers, 30 June 1647. At the first formal meeting between the parliamentary commissioners and the army commissioners, headed by

given to Scawen and his fellow commissioners amounted to 'a power independent' that made them a virtual 'third Estate'.[116] Characteristically, it was Scawen who controlled the commissioner's purse-strings,[117] and whose own servant, George Pyke, acted as the delegation's secretary.[118]

Scawen's re-emergence as a broker between Fairfax and Westminster and the resuscitation of the Army Committee during July were part of the series of tactical victories by Independents which provoked the short-lived Presbyterian *putsch* of 26 July to 4 August – that last-ditch attempt by Holles and his cronies to recoup their fading power. Looking back on the coup, and the reasons why it failed, Holles singled out the roles of Scawen and Francis Allein, Scawen's principal ally among the treasurers-at-war. One incident in particular during the coup, he thought, had been decisive. By 2 August, the London Common Council had decided to abandon any attempt to raise an army, and the City fathers had dispatched a delegation to Fairfax to signal that their resistance to the New Model was at an end. But as late as 3 August, the Presbyterian leadership still hoped to avert a full-scale military occupation of London by immediately sending upwards of £40,000 to the general's headquarters. But the money was never dispatched by the treasurers-at-war. The grant had been intended by the coup's leaders as a conciliatory gesture towards the army; instead, the resentments of the soldiery intensified. It was this, Holles believed, which acted as the catalyst for the army's advance on London; and he placed the blame squarely with Scawen and Allein. 'Insomuch', Holles wrote,

> that at that very time, when the army was marching up for [the Presbyterians'] destruction, about £49,000 (which had formerly been ordered to be sent down for the army's drawing off farther from the City) could not be privily conveyed out of town by Sir John Wollaston [the senior treasurer-at-war] and some others, in which Mr Scawen and Mr Allen, Members of the House, had a principal hand; which was as great a blow to Parliament and City as could be given; for it served to keep the soldiers together, and unite them for marching up; whereas, before, there were high discontents amongst them; and it weakened us, even taking away so much (as it were)

Ireton, on 2 July, Scawen is recorded as being the opening speaker; C. H. Firth (ed.), *The Clarke Papers*, 4 vols. (Camden Soc., 1891–1901), i, pp. 148–49; *LJ*, ix, 314a. Similarly, it was upon Scawen's report of 6 July that the House finally decided to act to place the New Model's pay (which had hitherto been secured by a makeshift series of *ad hoc* grants) on a secure basis; *CJ*, v, 234a.

116 Maseres (ed.), 'Memoirs of Denzil, Lord Holles', i, p. 253.

117 PRO, E 351/1272 (Scawen's accounts for the commissioners to the army, June–September 1647); *CJ*, v, 239a.

118 PRO, PROB 11/332, fo. 321v (Scawen's will); *LJ*, 9, 314a; PRO, E 351/1272; SP 28/49/4, fo. 534: Army Committee warrant for payment to Pyke, 22 July 1647.

of our blood, being that which, at that time, we principally stood in need of.[119]

It is perhaps doubtful whether this intended sweetener could have prevented the army's intervention, even had it arrived as soon as Holles had hoped. His account is nevertheless illuminating for what it reveals of his image of Robert Scawen: Holles was convinced that the Army Committee's chairman (who would have had to sign the warrant for the payment) and Allein (who was in a position to control its issuing) were working in partnership; and that, in their desire to encourage the New Model's intervention at Westminster, they had deliberately supplied the army with a provocation (or pretext) for its advance.[120]

The failure of the coup and the New Model's march on London initiated a period which saw the apogee of the Army Committee's influence, and of Scawen's importance as the conduit between Fairfax's headquarters and Westminster. The bicameral subcommittee (which included Scawen and Allein, Northumberland and Saye) established in August 1647 to confer with Fairfax about the future security of Parliament was, in fact, simply the Army Committee meeting under another name: ten of its twelve members were Army Committee men.[121] Similarly, on 9 October – just as Northumberland's party in the Lords was moving to give statutory effect to the settlement approved by the army as the *Heads of the Proposals* – Scawen resumed the interrupted negotiations about the terms for the army's service and partial disbandment that he had begun in June.[122] Of course, Scawen was only one of several commissioners; but it was he who, after a fortnight's deliberation, reported the results of the commissioners' dealings with Fairfax and his officers.[123] By the autumn of 1647, Scawen had become – both through his chairmanship of the Army

---

[119] Maseres (ed.), 'Memoirs of Denzil, Lord Holles', I, p. 283; Corporation of London RO, Common Council Journal 40, fos. 219–22v; *CJ*, v, 214a, 217b, 219a, 223b, 224b, 226b, 229a, 234a.

[120] Scawen was given leave to go to the army on the day of the riots, 26 July; *CJ*, v, 258b. He was at Fairfax's headquarters on or before 1 August 1647; *CJ*, v, 264a.

[121] *LJ*, IX, 415b. Army Committee members: Northumberland, Kent, Saye, Wharton, St John, Hesilrige, Vane junior, Scawen, Francis Allein (the treasurer-at-wars and MP), and Venn; non-Army Committee members: the Buckinghamshire Thomas Scott and 'Mr [probably Humphrey] Edwardes' (who also became a member of the Army Committee, in January 1649; PRO, SP 28/58/1–2, warrants for 17–19 January).

[122] *CJ*, v, 320b; the commissioners were again entrusted with a wide-ranging brief 'to confer with the general, or such as he shall appoint ... [and] to perfect those matters' which the former commissioners had left unfinished.

[123] The upshot was a series of resolutions, greatly enhancing the Army Committee's responsibilities, and reaffirming its place in charge of virtually all aspects of the army's pay, debentures and the auditing of its accounts; *CJ*, v, 340b–41a (23 October 1647); cf. *CJ*, v, 470a.

Committee and what was (at the very least) a close working relationship with Fairfax – one of the most influential members at Westminster,[124] the servant, not merely of the New Model, but also of the wider parliamentary interest that had championed Fairfax's army since its creation in March 1645.

V

Yet, at the moment when Scawen was at the height of his influence – over the winter of 1647–48 – he virtually disappears from view. His role as intermediary between Parliament and the army grandees all but ceased. The last time Scawen is recorded as reporting directly on behalf of Fairfax or the army's councils is on 9 February 1648, when he presented a series of alterations to the army establishment which had been 'offered from the general ... and his council of war'.[125] But these were purely organisational reforms, connected with the contemporaneous disbandment of large sections of the New Model, in which Scawen took an active part.[126] Although Scawen continued to be involved in military affairs – drafting a new assessment ordinance in February,[127] and dealing with a series of minor orders and letters between March and July[128] – most of his work for the New Model was thenceforth in private. True, his work for the Army Committee went on unabated;[129] during 1648 the Army Committee met, on average, every second day – with Scawen almost invariably presiding.[130] Even after Pride's Purge (6 December 1648), he continued to go

---

[124] It was to Scawen, for example, rather than to the Speaker of the House, that Fairfax wrote on 19 November announcing that a regiment of the New Model under Colonel John Hewson had been sent to quarter in London – to 'be directed by the Committee of the Army' – to assist in the collection of arrears due from the City; *CJ*, v, 364b. And it was Scawen who headed a four-man committee, dispatched to consult with the army on 23 December 1647, which discussed the terms for the disbandment; *CJ*, v, 396a, 400a, 414b; Hull RO, BRL (Hull corporation letters), 484: Francis Thorpe to the corporation of Hull, 28 December 1647. (I owe this last reference to the kindness of Dr David Scott.) See also, Gentles, *New Model Army*, pp. 268–69.

[125] *CJ*, v, 459b.　　[126] *CJ*, v, 459b.　　[127] *CJ*, v, 466b (17 February 1648).

[128] *CJ*, v, 477a (2 March), 535a (18 April), 581b (1 June).

[129] The committee's schedule speaks for itself: in April, Scawen chaired seventeen of the committee's eighteen meetings (PRO, SP 28/53/1–3); all but one of its twenty-two meetings in May (SP 28/54/1–4).

[130] For June (thirteen meetings): PRO, SP 28/53/1, fo. 109v; SP 28/54/4–5; SP 28/55/2, fo. 261; for July (sixteen meetings): SP 28/55/1; for August (eighteen meetings): SP 28/55/2; BL, Add. MS 21417 (Baynes corr.), fo. 16; for September (sixteen meetings): SP 8/54/2, fo. 208; SP 28/55/2, fos. 82–414; SP 28/55/3; SP 28/56/3, fos. 328, 387, 435; for October (twelve meetings): SP 28/55/3, fo. 558; SP 28/56/3; for November (sixteen meetings): SP 28/56/1–2. Scawen was away from Westminster in mid-July, in Suffolk with Allein and two other colleagues, trying to galvanise local collectors to fund

about his duties at the Army Committee, chairing meetings as usual. But the chairman was no longer used by Fairfax as an advocate for the army's interests in the House of Commons. After 9 February 1648, there is not a single communication from the army recorded in the *Journals* as presented to the House by Scawen. And while Scawen was not one of Colonel Pride's victims in December, the radical turn of politics which followed the army's *coup d'état*, brought to a self-imposed end his public career. When the Army Committee convened on 29 December, Scawen suddenly absented himself, never to return.

This final phase of Scawen's Civil-War career, like the earlier, seems to have been intimately connected to the broader strategies of Northumberland and his political allies. On 17 January 1648, the earl had made a powerful speech in the Lords declaring his opposition to the 'vote of no addresses': the resolution, strongly insisted upon by the army, that the Parliament should not hold any further discussions of a negotiated settlement with the king.[131] From that point almost until the eve of the regicide, Northumberland remained a steadfast proponent of a negotiated peace with the king – a course of action which was anathema to an increasingly powerful strain of radical opinion in the army.[132] Thenceforth, there was an obvious tension, though not an open breach, in relations between the 'Independent peers' and the more hard-line of the army grandees – sufficient at least to make the earl's steward an inappropriate, or possibly embarrassing, public advocate for Fairfax within the House of Commons. Even so, this was an adjustment of appearances more than of substance. Northumberland's 'interest' – in particular, Saye, Wharton, Denbigh and Salisbury – maintained close links with Fairfax throughout 1648, even after Pride's Purge; just as Scawen himself continued to receive private letters from Fairfax and to work behind the scenes on the army's recruitment, pay and supply.[133]

By the same token, Scawen's break with the Army Committee at the end of December 1648 coincides exactly with Northumberland's breach in relations with the army grandees over the issue of the trial of the king. During the last two weeks of December, four of the Army Committee's members – Northumberland, Salisbury, Pembroke and Denbigh (all peers

---

Fairfax's campaign against the Essex royalists and the siege of Colchester; Bodl. Lib., MS Nalson vii, fo. 146: Scawen and others to Lenthall, 11 July 1648; *CJ*, v, 619.

[131] *Mercurius Pragmaticus*, no. 19 (18–25 January 1648), sigg. T2–T2[v] (BL, E 423/21); Bodl. Lib., MS Clarendon 30, fo. 273: letter of intelligence, 24–27 January 1648.

[132] [Walker], *Anarchia Anglicana*, pp. 112–13.

[133] *Mercurius Pragmaticus*, no. 17 (18–25 July 1648), last page; PRO, SP 28/56/3, fo. 433: Fairfax to Scawen, 27 July 1648; SP 28/56/1, fo. 144: Fairfax to Scawen, 19 August 1648; SP 28/55/3, fo. 522: Fairfax to Scawen, 19 August 1648.

who had continued to attend Parliament after the Purge) – made a private overture to the army's leadership in a final bid to prevent the king's trial or deposition, a venture which collapsed at some point in the week after 22 December.[134] Confronted with the radicals' insistence that Charles I should be 'brought to account', Northumberland severed his links with the army, delivering a passionate speech in the Lords against the ordinance for the king's trial. Scawen's definitive break with the Army Committee coincides precisely with the failure of these efforts to avert the trial. He made his last appearance at the Army Committee on 26 December – probably the last moment at which the trial could have been prevented – and absented himself from its meetings on 29 and 30 December.[135] After Northumberland's public denunciation of the trial on 2 January 1649, there was probably no going back. Scawen's 'extraordinary service ... in the affairs of the army'[136] had come to an end.

VI

For the greater part of this essay, we have been primarily concerned with Scawen's 'public employments'. But to view these in isolation would be to impose a false perspective. Like many MPs of modest means, Scawen's largely unpaid attentions to 'the Publique' (as he termed it) had to run in tandem with the salaried employments that provided his daily bread.[137] His role as the coadjutor of Fairfax's army ran concurrently with his place – an increasingly active and prestigious place – within Northumberland's household. And by far the most important of his duties there was another sort of 'new-modelling': the great series of building projects that North-umberland undertook during the 1640s in or near the capital: at Syon House, Suffolk House (soon to be renamed Northumberland House) and York House (the large palace on the Thames, rented for Northumberland – at public expense – from the duchess of Buckingham). From 24 May 1645, when Scawen took on the supervision of these projects as 'paymaster of the works' (within weeks of his appointment as chairman of the Army Committee), he became responsible for the earl's single largest item of annual expenditure. Indeed, Northumberland has been described as 'one of the most lavish architectural patrons during the Civil War and Commonwealth', spending some £15,000 on building. Almost all of this

---

[134] Bodl. Lib., MS Clarendon 34, fo. 12: 'Lawrans' [Marchamont Nedham] to Sir Edward Nicholas, 21 December 1648.

[135] PRO, SP 28/57/2 (Army Cttee warrants, December 1648); SP 28/58/2 (Army Cttee warrants, January 1649).

[136] *CJ*, v, 414b.

[137] Bodl. Lib., MS Tanner 60, fo. 214: Scawen to Sir John Potts, 17 July 1645.

expenditure was under Scawen's direction, with more than half of the total
going on a single project in the heart of the capital, the 'new modelling' of
Northumberland House – the conversion of the large but old-fashioned
Jacobean mansion, formerly Suffolk House, with most of the work being
concentrated between 1645 and 1648.[138]

This, the centre-piece of the earl's grand schemes, was as much a
political as an architectural statement: the creation of a new urban palace
worthy of its owner's place in the post-Civil War political order.[139] It was
in a tradition of the use of metropolitan architecture to assert political
status which went back to Buckingham's York House in the 1620s, Cecil's
Salisbury House in the 1600s, and the palace of an earlier guardian of the
king's children, Somerset House, in the 1550s – all of which, like Northumberland House, fronted ostentatiously onto the Thames. Northumberland's architect was the surveyor of the king's works, Edward Carter, Inigo
Jones's deputy in the rebuilding of St Paul's, and successor (in 1643) as
surveyor – and a figure whom Scawen would have known from their
earlier joint involvement in Bedford's Covent Garden development in the
1630s.[140] Under Scawen's direction, a new range of state apartments was
created on the south range of the new Northumberland House, including a
new state dining-room and presence chamber, richly decorated with
carvings by Zachary Taylor (who had executed the decorative work in the
queen's chapel at Somerset House during the 1630s, as well as commissions for Charles I). By 1648, most of this new principal façade, to the
south, fronting towards the river, London's principal thoroughfare, had
been completed. The old Jacobean front had been replaced by a new nine-
bayed stone façade 'in Inigo Jones's manner', probably the major commission completed by the surveyor of the king's works in London during the
1640s;[141] its regular Palladian lines in unflattering contrast to the dis-
orderly skyline of the royal palace of Whitehall with which it was
immediately juxtaposed. The extent of Scawen's involvement in aesthetic

[138]   Wood, 'Architectural patronage', p. 55n.
[139]   Collating the accounts at Alnwick and Petworth, Northumberland spent £12,413 18s.
        8d. in the period 1640–49; over £7,000 of this was expended on Northumberland House
        between 1643 and 1649. (I am grateful to Mr Jeremy Wood for his assistance with these
        computations.)
[140]   H. M. Colvin (ed.), *The History of the King's Works*, III, *1485–1660: Part I* (1975), p. 156;
        Wood, 'Architectural patronage', p. 59; Alnwick Castle, Northumberland MS Box y. III.
        For Carter's commissions in the 1630s and 1640s, see also, Timothy Mowl and Brian
        Earnshaw, *Architecture without Kings: The Rise of Puritan Classicism under Cromwell*
        (Manchester, 1995), pp. 60–1, 136–37, though Northumberland's patronage of Carter is
        not noticed.
[141]   Petworth House Archives, MS 5848: Scawen's account for 1649; Wood, 'Architectural
        patronage', pp. 68–71.

decisions is uncertain; but he was intimately involved in the execution of the work, commissioning carvers, painters and masons; vetting bills, monitoring expenditure and drawing up the final accounts for Northumberland's approval. Ironically, much of the disposable income necessary to complete such a lavish project, and others like it at Petworth and Syon, came from public funds – in the form of a grant of £10,000, authorised by the Commons in January 1647, out of the composition revenues at Goldsmiths' Hall, to recompense Northumberland for his 'losses'. Appropriately, Scawen was the household officer who saw to the collection of this vast sum (the largest awarded to any individual during the 1640s), and to the payment of the clerks of Parliament and Goldsmiths' Hall.[142]

It was engaged in this project, and in others like it, that Scawen spent the greater part of his adult life. After his rancorous parting with Bedford, he evidently found stability in Northumberland's 'family', and perhaps, too, a measure of contentment. Certainly, once he had joined it, he showed no desire to leave, even when he had long since accumulated the financial means to do so. He had enough capital to buy a modest Cornish estate near his birthplace for £1,380 in 1641;[143] and he bought a far more substantial estate at Horton, in Buckinghamshire, in 1658.[144] But the figure who had spent almost forty years in the households of aristocratic grandees showed no desire to set himself up as a rustic squire. He was an absentee landlord for most of the time,[145] and only retired from Northumberland's employment to take up permanent residence at Horton in 1667 – when he was sixty-five, and three years away from death.[146] For the previous twenty-seven years, Northumberland's 'family' was his point of fixity and stability in the uncertain world of mid-seventeenth-century England. By the most sceptical reckoning, during the 1640s Robert Scawen was Northumberland's man first; a 'Parliament man' only second.

If even this minimal estimate of the extent to which Scawen was beholden to Northumberland pertained, then it is difficult to view him as just another hardworking MP, pursuing 'a career of his own'.[147] As far as Northumberland was concerned, there could be few more public demon-

---

[142] CJ, v, 57a–b; Alnwick, Northumberland MS u. 1. 6/44: Scawen's account to 30 March 1647.

[143] Woburn Abbey, Beds., Account book of the 5th Earl of Bedford, 1641–42, entries for 10 August and 7 September 1641.

[144] PRO, C 54/3995/6.

[145] Anthony House, Cornwall, Carew-Pole MSS, I Carew CD/OO/1–12 (manor of West Anthony estate papers). As late as June 1658, he was being described as 'Robert Scawen of Isleworth Syon, Middlesex'; PRO, C 54/3995/6.

[146] Scawen's last account as paymaster is for 1667: Petworth House Archives, MS 5817.

[147] David Underdown, A Freeborn People: Politics and the Nation in Seventeenth-Century England (Oxford, 1996), p. 76. Underdown's remark refers specifically to Scawen.

strations of support for Fairfax's army than to permit a busy and able officer of his household to take on the chairmanship of the body responsible for the New Model's pay, recruitment and supply. In modern parlance, Scawen was 'on secondment' from Northumberland House; and his prominence in serving, and acting as a public defender of, Fairfax's army – at least until January 1648 – also had an obvious symbolic, as well as practical, utility. This operated at two levels. First, simply by being who he was, engaged in the type of work he undertook, Scawen's very public role as chairman of the Army Committee was a daily reminder of the impeccably blue-blooded political 'interest' that had championed the New Model from the outset, an interest which held Fairfax in high regard. In a political culture obsessed with law and legitimacy, the involvement of Northumberland (who had been a lord general appointed by the king), and of his household, in supporting and promoting the New Model Army, linked Parliament's forces and their lord general to a tradition of pre-Civil War military authority of unimpeachable legality. Second, as the New Model came to be cast by its detractors as a seminary of heresy and social subversion – most notoriously in Thomas Edwards's *Gangræna* of 1646 – there were probably few more effective rebuttals to this characterisation than the prominence of the 10th earl of Northumberland's steward in the management of its affairs.[148]

After the regicide, of course, it was men like Edwards who had the last, bitter laugh. By 1649, the political capital which peers like Northumberland had invested in the New Model's success seemed at best a naive miscalculation, at worst ruthless ambition. More charitably, Sir Edward Walker, the royalist secretary-at-war who had known Northumberland since the Bishops' Wars, came close to the truth when he wrote in 1653: 'I believe that hardly one of [the parliamentarian nobility] had ever a design to destroy the King, or totally to alter that Power and Government, but to be Petty Kings themselves; but they were mistaken, fancying to frame an Aristocratical Monarchy by the Hands of the Popular Anarchy.'[149] That assessment probably came as close as any to describing the milieu in which, during the 1640s, Scawen had served.

Ironically, the monument Northumberland had planned to his own central place in the post-Civil War government of the realm reached completion just as any possibility of such an 'aristocratical monarchy' was ended definitively by the regicide in January 1649. Under Scawen's direction, within a stone's throw of Inigo Jones's Banqueting House, a team

[148] Thomas Edwards, *Gangræna* (2nd edn, 1646), however, Edwards exonerated Fairfax himself of the charge of 'sectarisme'; ibid., p. 50.

[149] Sir Edward Walker, 'Observations upon the inconveniences that have attended the frequent promotions to titles of honour' [1653], in his *Historical Discourses* (1705), p. 304.

of carpenters and masons was putting the finishing touches to another Jonesian façade: Edward Carter's great new south front of Northumberland House, overlooking the river at Charing Cross, with its impressive sequence of gilded and panelled state rooms within, emblazoned with the Percy arms. To an age accustomed to reading in buildings what Sir Christopher Wren called the 'political use' of architecture,[150] Robert Scawen's dual roles in Civil-War England were not, perhaps, as divergent as at first they seem.

[150] Stephen Wren (ed.), *Parentalia: Or Memoirs of the Family of the Wrens* (1750), p. 351.

3

George Digby, Royalist intrigue and the collapse of the cause

IAN ROY

On Sunday 26 October 1645 the king was at dinner in Newark garrison, where twelve days earlier he had sought security with what remained of his army. At this moment some very aggrieved senior officers, who had recently lost their posts in his service, burst into his presence. They were led by Prince Rupert, the king's nephew and former commander-in-chief, his brother Maurice, and Charles Gerard, lately sacked from his command of South Wales. They had come to protest that the king had replaced one of their followers, Sir Richard Willys, as governor of Newark. They knew whom to blame for this dismissal, and for their own. The exchange between them was recorded in a London newsbook:

PRINCE: By God the cause of all this is Digby.

KING: Tis false.

GER.: I am sure, and can prove that Digby was the cause that I was outed of my command in Wales.

KING: Whosoever saies it [,] lyes. Gentlemen I am but a child so you esteem of me: Digby can leade me by the nose, but you shall find ...

PRINCE: I wish that Digby prove not a traytor at the last.

KING: By God Digby is an honest man, and they that say otherwise are in effect traytors.

GER.: Then we must be all traitors.[1]

The king's cause, after Naseby and the surrender of Bristol, was collapsing about him, and the generals were looking for scapegoats. Digby, one of the secretaries of state since the death of Lord Falkland at the first

---

[1] *The Bloody Treatie* (London, December 1645), BL, TT: E 311 (27). Normally London propaganda sheets are not to be trusted; but in this case there are good grounds, which Gardiner accepted, for the authenticity of the report. S. R. Gardiner, *History of the Great Civil War* (London, 1893), II, pp. 373–75. Several of Rupert's followers were in London negotiating for their passes to go abroad, and the essentials are in E. Walker, *Historical Discourses* (London, 1705), p. 147.

battle of Newbury in September 1643, had been at the centre of affairs for two years. Was he the man to blame for the failure of the royalist war effort and for their own plight? Was the king right in believing that he was an honest man, and a loyal servant? Who, if anyone, was a traitor to the royalist cause?

George, Lord Digby, later second earl of Bristol, has featured largely in royalist historiography. The best, and best-known, description is by his near contemporary, sometime close friend and longer-term political enemy, Edward Hyde, earl of Clarendon. The great royalist historian had much to say about Digby throughout his *History*, as befitted his importance; but it was in a less well-known 'character' of him, written in exile in 1669, that Clarendon fully realised his aim of setting down in memorable prose his remarkable career. Recently a sympathetic modern editor has given greater currency to what he calls Clarendon's 'comic masterpiece'.[2]

Digby's father, the first earl of Bristol, had risen in the service of the crown to be ambassador to Madrid, but had taken the blame in 1624–25 for the failure of the Spanish match. After brief imprisonment in the Tower he had retired to the family seat of Sherborne castle, Dorset. In Spain Bristol had introduced his sons, George and John, and Lewis Dyve, his wife's son by a previous marriage, to their talented kinsman Sir Kenelm Digby, son of one of the Gunpowder Plotters. Kenelm was a large man and an important figure, one of the most celebrated *virtuosi* and Catholic apologists of the age. He no doubt exerted some influence on the young George, eight years his junior.[3]

George was brought up in diplomatic, political and intellectual circles, which were wide enough to admit Catholic recusants. He was exceptionally talented; a good classical scholar, he thought at first of an academic career. His tutor at Magdalen College, Oxford, was the rising young Laudian divine, Dr Peter Heylin. He spoke Spanish like a native, and acquired a good knowledge of other languages in travel abroad. Extra-

---

[2] *Clarendon's Four Portraits*, ed. R. Ollard (London, 1989), p. 8. The editor reprints, pp. 51–105, the 'character' of Digby from the supplement to the third volume of the folio edition of the *Clarendon State Papers* (1786). He provides an admirable introduction and persuasively identifies one of the 'characters', hitherto confused with that of Henry Bennett, earl of Arlington, as in fact a separate, brief (and hostile) account of Henry Jermyn.

[3] The older authorities on Bristol and his son (*Dictionary of National Biography* (*DNB*), and D. Townshend, *George Digby, Second Earl of Bristol* (London, 1924)) are inadequate. See M. F. Keeler, *The Long Parliament* (Philadelphia, 1954), p. 157; *Death, Passion and Politics. Van Dyck's Portraits of Venetia Stanley and George Digby*, ed. A. Sumner (London, 1995); A. Sumner, 'The political career of Lord George Digby until the end of the First Civil War', Cambridge University Ph.D. thesis, 1985; R. T. Petersson, *Sir Kenelm Digby, the Ornament of England, 1603–1665* (London, 1956); *The Life and Letters of Sir Lewis Dyve, 1599–1669*, ed. H. G. Tibbutt (Beds. Hist. Rec. Soc., 27, 1948), pp. 11–12.

ordinarily handsome and charming he was, wrote Clarendon, 'the most accomplished person that that nation, or it may be, that any other at that time could present to the world'. The young Mr Hyde, so much his opposite, must have been entranced; he later admitted that 'in truth he loved him very heartily'. When, in 1634, Digby married Anne Russell, he was allying with a powerful oppositionist family, that of the earl of Bedford, and also with those of Lord Brooke and the earl of Manchester, whose wives were Anne's sisters. He was also connected with the 'New English' planters in Ireland. The Digbys had lands and title in Galway.[4]

Digby's intellectual brilliance was matched by a strong imagination. It was a characteristic noted in other members of his family. Dyve was said to be 'not a little given to romance', in his account of his escapades. His cousin Kenelm wrote his autobiography as an allegorical romance, and was famous for his semi-magical recipes and potions. According to his perhaps rather jealous younger brother, George was improvident, highly sanguine, and too inclined to astrological speculation. He certainly enjoyed role-playing, which would show off his many talents. Some of his adventures involved ladies. 'He was', wrote Clarendon, 'in his nature, very amorous'.[5]

The Digbys were among the most prominent families in Dorset and George sat as knight of the shire in both the Short and Long Parliaments. His connection with leading members of the popular party smoothed his entry into its higher echelons. His ability was obvious. In the Short Parliament, he made the case for redress of grievance before supply with exceptional skill and a wealth of memorable images. At the start of the next assembly he needed no written list of complaints from his county community to make a telling speech on the defects of the personal rule. He was appointed to important committees investigating the culpability of the king's ministers.[6]

If Digby, no doubt relishing the opportunity to get his own back on the court, was one of the first in to the business of criticising the government, he was notoriously the first out. After being adored at Christmas, he was hated at Easter. By the time of the presentation of the Root and Branch Petition from London, February 1641, he was the earliest convert to the court. 'Bold and waspish' in debate, he subjected the sacred documents of

---

[4] See authorities at Footnote 3 above; Ollard (ed.), *Clarendon's Four Portraits*, pp. 51–52, 60, 62; Clarendon, *History of the Rebellion*, ed. W. D. Macray (Oxford, 1888), I, pp. 461–63; *Letter-book of the Earl of Clanricarde, 1643–47*, ed. J. Lowe (Irish MSS Commission, Dublin, 1983), pp. 151–52.

[5] *Death, Passion and Politics*, pp. 45–53; Ollard (ed.), *Clarendon's Four Portraits*, pp. 13, 52–53; *Life of Dyve*, pp. 109, 123, 127, 129.

[6] *Proceedings of the Short Parliament of 1640*, ed. E. Cope (Camden Soc., 4th series, 19, 1977), p. 223; J. Rushworth, *Historical Collections of Private Passages of State …*, 7 vols. (London, 1659–1701), IV, pp. 30–32, 37.

the popular party to an equally merciless treatment, defended Strafford and mocked the Scots' influence on English affairs. These were acts of foolhardy courage. He became the target for popular fury; his name headed the list, which included his younger brother, of those placarded as Straffordians. He and his father drew close to the court. In June 1641 he was raised to the peerage in his own right; his father entered the Privy Council and became a valued counsellor. Digby persuaded Edward Hyde, another important convert, to work for the king, and intrigued with the queen during the absence of Charles in Scotland.[7]

With public order threatened at the end of the year, it may have been Digby who suggested the unpopular Colonel Lunsford for the command of the Tower, having failed to get his half-brother, Sir Lewis Dyve, an experienced soldier, nominated. The 'December days' of rioting in White-hall followed. Clarendon was definite in attributing the attempt on the five members to Digby's advice. The 'hurly-burly' a few days later at King-ston-on-Thames, the strategic bridge over the river, when he appeared with Lunsford and the armed men used at Westminster, caused great alarm. His flight immediately afterwards appeared to confirm his guilt. He was identified as a political extremist, and impeachment proceedings were started against him.[8]

He joined the queen in the Netherlands and was involved in the lengthy business of pawning her jewels and buying arms for the coming conflict. He must have acquired a good knowledge of weapons, munitions and all the implements of war, and of their cost, in the cockpit of Europe, as a result. The letter from Rotterdam, intercepted by Parliament in February 1642, shows the extent and expense of the royalist shopping list. A network of royal agents and suppliers was built up at that time, which was to be extended and further activated when the shooting started and the Cavaliers' military demands increased. Digby and Dyve must have met and planned their future moves with several exiled Army Plotters, and with some of the British officers released from the German wars, including the Princes Rupert and Maurice, the king's nephews, while waiting for the opportunity to return to aid the royal cause.[9]

[7] Ollard (ed.), *Clarendon's Four Portraits*, pp. 58–59; Rushworth, *Historical Collections*, IV, pp. 170–74; *The Journal of Sir Simonds D'Ewes*, ed. W. Notestein (New Haven, 1923), p. 335n; *The Life of Edward Earl of Clarendon* (Oxford, 1760), I, pp. 67–69.

[8] Clarendon, *History*, I, p. 478; Ollard (ed.), *Clarendon's Four Portraits*, pp. 62–63; *A True Relation of the Late Hurliburly at Kingston upon Thames* (London, 1642), BL, TT: E 131(15); Rushworth, *Historical Collections*, IV, pp. 554–55, reprints the intercepted letter from Digby, January 1642, in which he described his opponents as 'traitors'.

[9] *Letters of Henrietta Maria*, ed. M. Green (London, 1857), pp. 47, 53–65, 83–85; *Two Letters from Rotterdam ...* (London, 1642), BL, TT: E 154(26); *Two letters the One from the Lord Digby ...* (London, 1642), BL, 100.c.64. *The Lord George Digbie's Apologie For Himselfe* (London,

Digby had acquired a reputation as a political chameleon. There were few roles he could not play: he masqueraded as a travelling Frenchman when he was captured at sea and was brought before the governor of Hull on his journey back to England in the summer of 1642. He had made himself an expert in military matters.[10] He was among those eager young men on the king's side who gravitated to the brightest star in the Cavalier firmament, Prince Rupert. Digby's brother Dyve and another of his intimates, the rich and well-connected Irishman Daniel O'Neill, became two of the prince's chief officers. But good relations with the king's youngest general, who had been suddenly thrust into the limelight as commander of the Horse, and given almost free rein in that post, were difficult to establish. Digby flattered him as 'a gallant and generous Prince'. But it needed the mediation of O'Neill to overcome a slight that Rupert, prickly and impatient, had detected behind this show of affection and of high regard by a man eight years his senior.[11]

Despite his delayed arrival at court Digby was given command of a regiment of Horse, the last raised before the first major encounter (Edge-hill, October 1642). He displayed sufficient competence and energy as Colonel to be promoted by the prince to be second to Henry Wilmot, Lieutenant General of the Horse, and so commander of the left wing of cavalry at the battle. He performed admirably in this role. There was no doubt that, whatever his background and his pre-war career intentions, he made a dashing cavalryman, in the Rupertian mould. His regiment was officered by well-connected gentlemen and experienced soldiers.[12]

Digby took quarters with his father and a large retinue in Magdalen College at the east end of the new royal headquarters. During the royalist occupation of Oxford many Cavaliers lodged with their old colleges. His relations with the university had always been close; he was to be rewarded with the entirely honorific post of High Steward. He recruited under-graduates to his regiment, no mean feat as the student body was so much reduced in number. He was given command of Dragoons, the better to patrol the eastern approaches to the royal headquarters, the key area in any attack by forces from London.[13]

1643), BL, 101.a.2, is probably a forgery. *Life of Dyve*, pp. 21–23. For money raised at Rotterdam, see *The Lord George Digby's Cabinet and Dr Goff's Negotiations* ... (London, 1646), BL, TT: E 329(15), p. 44.

[10] Sumner, 'Digby', p. 163, corrects the view that he had no knowledge of arms. Although he did not participate in the Scottish wars, he was active in Dorset in 1640; he, his younger brother and his half brother were all quickly promoted in the Civil War.

[11] E. Warburton, *Prince Rupert and the Cavaliers* (London, 1849), I, pp. 368–69.

[12] P. Young, *Edgehill 1642. The Campaign and the Battle* (Kineton, 1967), pp. 211–12.

[13] *Journal of Sir Samuel Luke*, ed. I. G. Philip (Oxfordshire Record Society, 29, 31, 33,

He showed his mettle alongside Rupert in many of the early expeditions of the royalist Horse, the most active and successful element in the army. He sought excitement and fulfilment in battle, going where the fighting was fiercest; no one could deny his dauntless courage. At Rupert's investment of Lichfield he led dismounted cavalry officers into the moat, 'Himself being in the mud to the middle', and was there 'shot through the thigh with a musquet bullet'. In a cavalry action just before the first battle of Newbury, he was lucky to escape with his life. Charging with his troop alongside the French Horse brought by the queen and commanded by her chamberlain, Lord Jermyn, he was pistolled at close quarters by an opponent who had first pried 'into their countenances' to make sure, presumably, that he had the right target. Digby was stunned, burned and blinded by the shot, but saved by Jermyn.[14]

He must thereafter have borne some honourable scars. The soldiers in the royal camp could not accuse Digby of being a politician and penpusher ignorant of life at the front. As secretary with the king, on campaign, he wrote clear, perceptive and informative letters to a wide range of correspondents. The official account of Newbury, immediately printed as a supplement to the main royalist newsletter, was most likely by Digby. It includes the episode of his wounding; the temporary editor was his old tutor, Heylin. If he was the author, he had, among his other skills, a gift for publicity.[15]

Oxford politics would soon complicate the military picture. Divisions in the high command, and some disillusionment among the younger military men and courtiers with Rupert, are apparent in a letter of July 1643 from someone at Oxford, probably, but not certainly, Digby himself. He 'is not that gallant man we tooke him for; you may judge it by Percy's being his cheef favorite'.[16] Henry Percy, like Henry Wilmot, Digby's superior, had been an Army Plotter, exiled with the queen to Holland, and active there in recruiting men. She had sent him in advance to Oxford and had intrigued successfully to obtain the command of the artillery for him. In spite of this background, shared with Digby, he was not one of his friends. Digby was clearly disappointed that Rupert showed him favour. It was

1950–53), pp. 11, 14; *The Royalist Ordnance Papers, 1642–1646*, ed. I. Roy (Oxfordshire Rec. Soc., 42, 49, 1964, 1975), p. 183.

[14] Ollard (ed.), *Clarendon's Four Portraits*, p. 64; *A True and Impartiall Relation of the Battaile* ... (Oxford, 1643), BL, TT: E 69(50); F. Madan, *Oxford Books* (Oxford, 1912), ii, nos. 1453–54.

[15] P. W. Thomas, *Sir John Berkenhead 1617–1679. A Royalist Career in Politics and Polemics* (Oxford, 1969), pp. 34–35. The author is less complimentary about Digby's style.

[16] Historical Manuscripts Commission (HMC), *Portland*, i, p. 124. The letter is anonymous, but the breezy style, intimate knowledge of events and personalities at Oxford, and in the West Country, and promises of friendly coverage in the press, all suggest Digby, a close friend of the recipient, Sir John Berkeley.

probably a few months later that he gave up his cavalry command, 'not finding that respect from the Prince which he had promised himself'.[17]

He began instead to make his mark at the Oxford court, as he had done in Whitehall. Before the war, according to Clarendon, 'he had been instrumental in promoting' Falkland, Hyde and Culpepper, 'and was of great familiarity and friendship with the other three'. He had already helped others, such as Falkland, one of the secretaries of state, to persuade the greedy Culpepper to shed one of the posts he aspired to hold.[18] Hyde himself benefited from the absence of the queen from court at this juncture (February 1643), and the friendship of Digby, to obtain the chancellorship of the exchequer, which Culpepper had reluctantly given up.

The arrival of the queen altered the situation again. The fall of Laud and Strafford and the unfolding pre-war crisis had brought her into a position of influence, which contrasted with her role during the personal rule. The march from Yorkshire was a triumphant progress, led by 'her She-Majesty, generalissima', as she styled herself, with the arms and men she had brought from the Netherlands. She even had her stores reserved for her own use, and her troops, French and Lorrainer but also recruited in the north, kept semi-separate. She brought the full weight of her personal influence on the king, easily led by the wife he adored, to promote her own servants to high office. Charles at this time, as Clarendon said, 'saw with her eyes, and determined by her judgment'.[19] She wanted to play an active part in the direction of policy and the selection of councillors, and she backed Digby, with whom she had worked closely for several months in 1641 and 1642, for the vacant secretaryship on the death of Falkland. The other secretary, Sir Edward Nicholas, soon complained to the royal envoy in Paris: 'Since Digby hath been Secretary your Nicholas is not so much in esteem with the queen as he was ... I assure you the Queen hath as much power as ever.'[20]

A factor in the choice of Digby was his linguistic fluency. The imminent arrival of the French ambassador, the comte de Harcourt, made it imperative that a French speaker be appointed.[21] In the general exchange of offices at this time (with the queen and the refugee 'peace lords' at Oxford, and the royalists prospering in the field) the flamboyant Digby was always likely to be preferred to the strait-laced Hyde, and the devious and

---

[17] *Royalist Ordnance Papers*, pp. 20–21; Ollard (ed.), *Clarendon's Four Portraits*, p. 64; *Letters of Henrietta Maria*, pp. 211–13.

[18] Clarendon, *History*, I, pp. 461–62; Clarendon, *Life*, I, p. 112.

[19] *Letters of Henrietta Maria*, p. 222; Clarendon, *Life*, I, p. 112; *Royalist Ordnance Papers*, pp. 40–41, 50, 313, 496.

[20] Nicholas to Goring (Oxford, 1 November 1643), HMC, *Portland*, I, pp. 147–48.

[21] Clarendon, *Life*, I, pp. 130–31.

grumpy Culpepper. He could not fail to be a more dominant influence, a harder worker and more useful servant than his predecessor had been. His charming, attractive presence, and his positive attitude, would be a welcome contrast for the king, and the queen, to the short-of-stature, downcast, squeaky-voiced Falkland, who notoriously hated the war. He was a man who, to adopt Mrs Thatcher's words, brought solutions, not problems, and could be assured of a good reception wherever he went.

Digby, as secretary, was appointed to the Privy Council. He was made one of the 'junto', as Clarendon called it, which determined policy before it was brought to the council board. The others were Hyde himself, also newly admitted at this time, Richmond, Cottington, Nicholas and Culpepper. For the negotiations with Irish representatives in early 1644 Richmond was dropped and the earls of Bristol and Portland added.[22] The council itself was not consulted in the negotiations with Harcourt at Oxford. Only the queen, Digby and Jermyn, her head of household and not a Privy Councillor, were involved. The queen was confident that she could handle Harcourt, the younger son of the duc d'Elbeuf (of the house of Lorraine), and exploit the new circumstances, more favourable to herself as a Daughter of France, that had arisen with the deaths, in quick succession, of Richelieu and her brother Louis XIII.[23] She had written earlier that her friend, the duchesse de Chevreuse, ruled all at the French court;[24] and indeed the so-called 'Importants' had recovered their influence, once the strong hand of the cardinal was removed. The queen, with the able assistance of her two trustiest courtiers, had much to hope for.

Whether coincidentally or not, Oxford administration was tightened up at Digby's appointment; all royal orders were to be countersigned by the secretary. With Nicholas, Digby headed the intelligence and new postal services. It was soon reported to Ormond, the king's viceroy in Dublin, that: 'the Lord Digby is like to be the only man of affairs upon whom your Excellency can place your rule. He is a man of good fortunes, parts, industry and honour.' The new secretary was to take, as he claimed, most of the official Irish business into his own hands. He was used by the king to correspond with other heads of state, where his knowledge of languages, and his classical education, were helpful.[25] He was the administrator, with his military knowledge and experience, who went on campaign with his

---

[22] Ibid., I, p. 131; J. Lowe, 'The negotiations between Charles I and the Confederation of Kilkenny, 1642–1649', London University Ph.D. thesis, 1960, ch. 4.

[23] Clarendon, *Life*, I, p. 132. [24] HMC, First *Report*, Appendix, p. 5.

[25] *Calendar of State Papers Domestic*, 1644, pp. 6–7; T. Carte, *Collection of Letters* (London, 1735), I, pp. 44–46; S. Groenveld, *Verlopend Getij [The turning tide]. The Dutch Republic and the English Civil War, 1640–1646* (Leiden, 1984), p. 304. The official line to the Irish Confederates, that the king would not, under any circumstances, abandon his religion, was penned by Digby: HMC, *Franciscan MSS*, pp. 246–47.

sovereign, the commander-in-chief. Nicholas remained at Oxford and, as he complained, was 'none of the close committee at court'. The councillors there were rebuked by the king for offering advice on the movements of the army when he was at its head. In general the commanders and the war council in the field considered the royal capital, dominated by ladies of the court, to be too susceptible to exaggerated fears, and to be a hotbed of unfounded rumours and damaging scandals. It could take up to three weeks for news from the front to reach Oxford, while London gossip was fresh there every day. Digby was close to both the king and his wife, and trusted, at this time, by both.[26]

The new secretary had another, clandestine, role. As head of intelligence, in contact with agents and spies at home and abroad, he was paid secret-service money. He was soon at the centre of a web of secret intrigue. Parliament was to preface the publication of Digby's cipher correspondence with the adage: 'War can be won by policy as well as force.'[27] It was in keeping with Digby's character and role that he sought to assist the military effort in this way. As a former adherent of the popular party, connected by marriage with leading peers on the other side, and recently brought up to date about Westminster and London politics, he was well placed to employ his political skills to make converts. To win the war without using force was, for an incorrigible optimist, an irresistible challenge. It was, of course, a touchstone of royalist belief that the majority of Parliamentary supporters were basically loyal and simply misled by the conspiracy of a handful of wicked men, such as the puritan 'faction' ruling London. They could therefore be persuaded, with the correct mix of threats, bribes and propaganda, to switch sides. Much as Digby enjoyed fighting, he relished even more the cloak-and-dagger world of espionage, secret messages, ciphers and codes. It was more of an intellectual challenge for a clever man.[28]

The Waller Plot in London, exposed in May 1643, had been an attempt to exploit discontent in the capital to overthrow the city government by making use of prominent citizens now in the royal camp. The authority for the conspirators' actions was a secret commission, drawn up in March 1643 by the king alone, with the assistance of a few of his personal servants. It was carried to London by a lady of the court and hidden in a cellar. The

---

[26] Warburton, *Prince Rupert*, ii, pp. 188–89; Clarendon, *History*, iii, p. 525, iv, p. 40, on the nature of the court. The earl of Newcastle in 1643 was advised that he could 'expect nothing at court, truly the women rule all': HMC, *Portland*, i, pp. 701–2. W. Bray (ed.), *Evelyn's Diary*, ed. H. B. Wheatley (London, 1906), iv, p. 161; Carte, *Letters*, i, p. 62.

[27] *Digby's Cabinet.*

[28] On this attitude, shared by the king, see I. Roy, '"This proud unthankefull city": a Cavalier view of London in the Civil War', in *London and the Civil War*, ed. S. Porter (London, 1996), pp. 149–74.

document was discovered there, however, before the plotters were ready. That the king was quite capable of acting on his own in this way is, in the light of later events, noteworthy. Clarendon's story of the plot is distinctly that of an outsider not privy to the murky details. Nor was Digby – at this time busy soldiering – involved.[29]

In the winter of 1643–44, however, he and his father, based at Magdalen College, close to the London road, seriously entered the business of such secret operations. London was again targeted, but an outlying garrison, Aylesbury, and also Gloucester – a great prize if it could be bloodlessly taken – were the objectives of much clandestine activity. A leading recusant in the city was known to the Digbys through Sir Kenelm; another agent was sprung from a city prison to be briefed at Oxford. One of the Gloucester garrison exchanged letters with a royalist officer in the surrounding forces, who claimed that Digby, the 'best friend I have in the world', would expedite the matter in the utmost secrecy. The secretary wrote promising a pardon and £2,000 if the city were successfully yielded. He drew out the advance payment from the royal war chest. At Aylesbury it was rumoured that the same sum was offered.[30]

But in each case the Digbys were being duped. Parliament had been employing double agents and had penetrated all the conspiracies. Discontent with Parliament in London and elsewhere did not extend to open espousal of the royalist cause, far less to the betrayal of strongholds. The threatening Cavalier troop movements around Gloucester, and the arrival of Rupert's Horse in January 1644 before Aylesbury, had no result. The garrisons were forewarned, and at Aylesbury the cavalry were repulsed with severe loss. Rupert was humiliated and angry: he would have had to possess more patience than we know he had not to blame the secretary and his father for the disaster.[31]

The conquest by the royalists of much of the west, opening the ports there to supplies from Ireland and the continent, gave them new hope of military aid from overseas, which they had been seeking since before the war. The Cessation of hostilities achieved by Ormond, with the confederate Irish, meant that the English army in Ireland was available. It could not be supplied by the king, and faced starvation if it remained. Parliament's navy controlled the Irish Sea. In spite of these handicaps it

[29] Roy, 'Cavalier view of London', pp. 160–62; Clarendon, *History*, III, pp. 38–53.
[30] 'A secret negotiation with Charles I, 1643–4', ed. B. M. Gardiner, *Camden Miscellany*, 8 (Camden Soc. new series, 1883); *Bibliotheca Gloucestrensis*, ed. J. Washbourn (Gloucester, 1820), pp. 283–324; *Calendar of State Papers Domestic (CSPD)*, 1644, p. 22; *Journal of Luke*, ed. Philip, pp. 162, 238.
[31] Gardiner, *History of the Great Civil War* (London, 1893), I, pp. 264–70, 275; 'A secret negotiation'; HMC, *Portland*, I, p. 166; *Bibliotheca Gloucestrensis*, pp. 283–324.

was brought over to recruit the royal forces in the winter months 1643–44. Delegates from both the Protestants and the Catholic Confederacy came to Oxford, and had entered talks with the 'junto' as we have seen. But councillors such as Hyde and Nicholas were deeply suspicious of any concessions to Irish Catholics; and the king, though willing to treat, was fearful of public opinion. They went away empty-handed.[32]

Official negotiations were only half the story. Charles no longer viewed the Irish as rebels – as he consistently did the Parliamentarians – and his commanders in the field preferred native Irish troops to the returning, and often mutinous, government forces. The king therefore sought ways to make use of them. The most important was the most secret. Charles had been impressed by the efforts of the marquess of Worcester and his son, at Raglan Castle, in raising money and men on his behalf, both before the war and during the first part of the conflict. In April 1644, while the official talks were progressing, and later (March 1645), he commissioned the son, known to history as the earl of Glamorgan, in return for further advancements in the peerage, to go to Ireland, raise an army of 10,000 and bring it to Wales.[33]

The king bypassed the usual authorities to seal these documents, employing, it is believed, only his household servants. It is instructive that he had done the same with the commission of array which authorised the Waller Plot against London; and it is clear that Digby, surely his most intimate adviser after the queen, was ignorant of it. There is no mention, among Digby's forty-eight captured ciphers, of one designed for the earl of Glamorgan. Although the official correspondence to Ireland went through his hands, and he regularly kept in close touch with Ormond, he was no more trusted with such very secret matters than Hyde or Nicholas. This may be why, in the summer of 1644, when the queen was about to depart after a year at Oxford, he wrote that he was 'but a second instrument' to her in some Irish affairs.[34]

He did attempt to keep another initiative in his hands, however. The earl of Antrim, with his strong Scottish Highland and Ulster connections, also believed he could persuade the Confederate council at Kilkenny to

[32] Lowe, 'Charles I and Kilkenny', ch. 4; Hyde later wrote to Nicholas: 'You and I were never thought wise enough to be advised in [Irish affairs]', *Clarendon State Papers*, ed. R. Scrope and T. Monkhouse (Oxford, 1767–86), II, p. 337.

[33] The status of Glamorgan's commissions has been much debated; in addition to Gardiner, see J. H. Round, *Studies in Peerage and Family History* (London, 1901), ch. 9, and Lowe, 'Charles I and Kilkenny', ch. 5.

[34] *Clarendon State Papers*, II, p. 201; BL, Trumbull MSS Add. 43, bundle of ciphers; Bodl., Tanner MSS 60, fos. 327–29, list of captured Digby letters, read in the House of Commons, 22 October 1645; [T. Carte], *The Life of James Duke of Ormond* (Oxford, 1851), VI, pp. 118, 262, 301–3 et passim; *CSPD*, 1644, pp. 317–18.

provide men for Charles I. At court his wife, the widow of the great duke of Buckingham, was equally persuasive with the king. Digby assisted this process, and in a long passage of great comedy Clarendon explained how skilfully he gained the consent of both the king and Antrim to his 'special, dear and intimate friend', Daniel O'Neill, joining the expedition. Daniel was the Protestant nephew of the Confederate general in Ulster, Owen Roe O'Neill, and much was expected of him. At the same time Digby secretly treated with other Catholic Irish commanders to bring troops, no longer needed after the truce, to aid the king.[35]

Few of these elaborate plans materialised. Glamorgan was an amiable poltroon, who had already lost one army in South Wales. While he had some success in recruiting troops, his treaty with the Confederate council was undermined, as we shall see, by other Catholic interests. O'Neill stayed but a short time, and his only known report to Digby was intercepted. It was lengthy and over-optimistic, promising a 10,000-strong Confederate army. As the truce did not extend to Ulster, there could be no question of his uncle supplying men. After returning to England by July 1644 he was caught up in the quarrels of the court. Despite the promotion to the king's bedchamber that Digby had arranged, he fell heavily from grace. It quickly became apparent to the Irish that Antrim was a fool, and he was allowed to transport troops only to the west of Scotland, which became the nucleus of Montrose's forces in 1644–45. None of his, Glamorgan's, nor any of the Confederate generals' troops landed in England.[36]

All Europe was searched for military assistance. In 1642 it had been proposed that Digby be sent to Denmark, to get help from Charles I's uncle, Christian IV. Instead Colonel Cochrane, a much-travelled Scots aristocrat and soldier of fortune, was given the task. The king offered to cede the Orkneys and Shetland to Christian in exchange for arms and men. The queen cautioned her husband to keep this secret, lest 'the Scots … take offence'. The outbreak of war between Denmark and Sweden interrupted this mission, but it was resumed in 1645.[37] Like Cochrane, Sir

[35] Clarendon, *History*, III, pp. 513–24; J. Ohlmeyer, *Civil War and Restoration in the Three Stuart Kingdoms. The Career of Randal McDonnell, 1st Marquis of Antrim, 1609–1683* (Cambridge, 1993); BL, Trumbull MSS Add. 43, ciphers for Lord Taafe, Col. Barry etc.; *DNB*, 'Daniel O'Neill'; Carte, *Ormond*, v, p. 543, VI, pp. 21–22.

[36] O'Neill's letter is noticed in *The Letter Books of Sir William Brereton*, ed. R. N. Dore (Record Soc. of Lancs. and Chesh., 123, 1983–84), I, pp. 515–16. Carte, *Letters*, I, pp. 63, 76–83. O'Neill was sent back to Ireland in July 1645; at the same time another Irish officer, Colonel Fitzwilliam, contracted by the queen to bring 10,000 men to England, reported pessimistically to Digby: *Digby's Cabinet*, pp. 48–51, 56.

[37] S. R. Gardiner, *The History of England from the Accession of James I to the Civil War 1603–1642*, 10 vols., 1883–84, X, pp. 153, 188–89; *History of the Great Civil War*, I, pp. 39,

Kenelm Digby, the queen's chancellor, had important contacts in European courts. He was dispatched to Rome and spent several months negotiating at the papal court. As late as August 1645, George Digby wrote to Jermyn at Paris that his main hope remained 'Denmark for men, Rome for money'. Digby possessed the keys to Cochrane's and Sir Kenelm's cipher correspondence, and was fully informed by Jermyn of their progress. But these initiatives, like some of those for Irish aid, were largely in the hands of the court at St Germain.[38]

Neither move came to anything. Christian reminded his nephew that Charles had not come to *his* rescue when he was in trouble during the German wars. The new pope, Innocent X, was anti-French and equally uncooperative. He formed a low opinion of the royal emissary. Instead of assisting the king he sent a nuncio to Kilkenny, who persuaded the Gaelic lords and the clergy to reject, as not good enough, the treaties the Confederate Council had agreed with Glamorgan in 1645, and the war was resumed.[39]

France remained the most likely source of aid for the king. When the queen returned to the Continent with Jermyn, having given birth to Charles's daughter in Exeter in June 1644, she was very ill, but at least she was able to set foot there, a thing impossible so long as Richelieu were alive. In spite of the hopes of the previous October, however, the influence of her friends the 'Importants' had waned over the winter of 1643–44 as the queen mother and regent, Anne of Austria, came to depend more and more on Cardinal Mazarin. He was cautious in his approach to the English problem, and was not going to be hasty in any move to assist his late master's troublesome, meddling and opinionated sister. By the time of the queen's arrival, July 1644, English agents reported sadly that the old policies of Cardinal Richelieu seemed again to be in place.[40] The new cardinal had decided that he would not take sides in the English conflict, lest he be drawn in with no escape route open; and Parliament's control of the navy was a deterrent. As the king's powers declined it became clearer that France would have to find a *modus vivendi* with whatever regime emerged following his defeat.

The queen's agents in France remained busy however. The major part of Digby's correspondence was with Jermyn, his old comrade-in-arms.

140–41; *Letters of Henrietta Maria*, pp. 208–9; *Digby's Cabinet*, pp. 41–43; BL, Trumbull MSS Add. 43, ciphers.

[38] *Digby's Cabinet*, pp. 40–43, 52–55; BL, Trumbull MSS Add. 43, ciphers; *Secret Writing in the Public Records. Henry VIII to George II*, ed. S. R. Richards (London, 1974), pp. 128–30.

[39] Gardiner, *History of the Great Civil War*, III, pp. 30–57; *CSPD*, 1645–47, pp. 113, 393, 463; Lowe, 'Charles I and Kilkenny', chs. 7, 8; *A Military History of Ireland*, ed. T. Bartlett and K. Jeffery (Cambridge, 1996), ch. 8.

[40] Clarendon, *Life*, I, p. 132; *CSPD*, 1644, pp. 259–61.

Despatches from Paris (the queen's court at St Germain) were sent to him every week. Most for 1645 have survived among the state papers, either intercepted by Parliamentary forces, or found in his coach after his defeat at Sherburn in Elmet, North Yorkshire, in October 1645. They were read in the House of Commons a few days later, and a selection published, as *Lord George Digby's Cabinet Opened*, in March 1646. They throw light not only on the progress of negotiations for military aid from France but also on the embassy to the Hague of Dr Stephen Goffe, the ex-chaplain of a regiment in the Anglo-Dutch brigade, and brother of the Cromwellian general and regicide, William Goffe. Occasionally Goffe's letters to Jermyn were included in the package sent to Oxford. At the same time Digby had the key to the main cipher used by the king and queen in the years 1643–45. But the royal pair kept much completely secret from even their most trusted servants, themselves enciphering and deciphering the letters to each other. The king kept her letters and keys under his pillow.[41]

When official backing for intervention and authorisation for military supplies could not be obtained, private initiatives were not prohibited. The queen raised more money from her own resources and sold tin from Cornwall. She, Jermyn and their allies, mainly resident English merchants and wealthy recusants in exile, arranged shipping from ports in northern France. As long as the Cavaliers retained control of Bristol (taken in July 1643) and most western ports, especially Weymouth (until its loss in June 1644), Dartmouth and Falmouth, a brisk trade in gun running defied the Parliamentary blockade. There was much for Digby to do in this business. The owners of Sherborne castle probably had commercial contacts and interests in Dorset ports. When Weymouth was briefly recaptured by the royalists in 1645, it was Digby's brother, Dyve, a former MP for the town, who led the attack and was appointed governor. The Digbys, father and son, bought, or arranged credit for, some of the cargoes available. It could not be claimed by his enemies that the secretary kept aloof from practical affairs. No business was more hazardous than the trade in arms.[42]

There was equally limited success for Goffe's mission to the Netherlands. The Stadtholder, Frederick Henry, was allied to the Stuarts by the recent marriage of his son to the daughter of Charles and Henrietta. In 1642 he had been active, despite the opposition of the States of Holland

---

[41] *Digby's Cabinet*, pp. 10–18, 19–22, 25–26, 27–28, 31–37, 40–43, 44–47, 57–60; other letters from Jermyn, taken at Sherburn, are PRO, SP 16/506, fos. 193–94, 199–200, and 507, fos. 156–7; and BL, Add. MSS 33, 596, fos. 7–8. BL, Trumbull MSS Add. 43, ciphers; *Charles I in 1646*, ed. J. Bruce (Camden Soc. 63, 1856), p. 50.

[42] *Digby's Cabinet*, pp. 19–22, 25–26, 31–33, 44–47, 48–49; *Royalist Ordnance Papers*, pp. 40–45, 407, 410–11, 419; *CSPD*, Add. 1625–59, pp. 676–67; *Life of Dyve*, pp. 58–59; *Lords Journals*, VII, 260. More light will be shed on this subject when the researches of Dr Peter Edwards in foreign archives are completed.

and most of the regent class, in finding arms and men for the queen at the Hague. Now in 1644 Goffe had a new deal to offer. This was the marriage of the Prince of Wales to Frederick Henry's daughter, in return for a large dowry, which would be spent on arms. The negotiations lasted for months, but were inconclusive. Parliament sent over a capable agent, William Strickland, to oppose the deal, who was able to persuade the States not to cooperate. They remained suspicious of the Stadtholder's dynastic ambitions. His health and prestige were in decline. In any case the queen soon thought she had a better deal for the young Charles in the person of her wealthy niece, daughter of the duc d'Orléans. She withdrew her earlier offer, much to the Stadtholder's disgust.[43]

The Dutch were keen, however, to trade in arms with any powers not actually at war with themselves, whatever the political situation. Their ports, and those in the Spanish Netherlands, became marts for naval and military supplies, exploiting the needs of all combatants in the British Isles. Dunkirk, especially, was a great centre of privateering and piracy. Digby himself concluded agreements for supply with, and issued letters of marque for, the best known of these entrepreneurs, the Fleming Jan van Haesdonck. Royalist success in the arms trade was restricted, however, by the naval blockade, the lack of money, credit and goods for export, and the poor quality of the munitions offered.[44]

Although foreign affairs took up much of his time, his influence there was limited. The main lines of policy had been agreed before he was appointed, and the queen presided over a separate, alternative court in Paris. Her power over the king waned, and their previous good relations, while at Oxford, deteriorated in the course of 1645, with the distance between them and the conflicting influences upon them. Digby and Jermyn also grew apart under the impact of the 'torrent of misfortunes', as the former, in a rare moment of candour, described the succession of royalist defeats. He blamed Jermyn for undermining the Ormond treaties with the Confederates, by dangling before them the hope of better offers from the queen and from Catholic interests. Jermyn chided Digby for falling out with Rupert, and over some 'foolish scandall' that he had spread. Not surprisingly, Jermyn must have come to disbelieve the over-optimistic despatches Digby sent him, where losses were scarcely mentioned, and where hope sprang eternal – of Montrose in Scotland, of hosts of Irish veterans, of 10,000-strong armies daily expected from the duc de Lorraine, the duc d'Espernon, the duc de Bouillon or the duke of

[43] Groenveld, *Verlopend Getij, Secret Writing*, pp. 127–29.
[44] Groenveld, *Verlopend Getij*, p. 238; *Calendar of Clarendon State Papers* (*Cal. Clar. S. P.*), ed. O. Ogle and W. D. Macray (Oxford, 1869), I, nos. 1729, 1733, 1753, 1884, 1912–13, etc.; *Royalist Ordnance Papers*, pp. 42–43; *Digby's Cabinet*, pp. 19–22, 31–33, 40–41, 48.

Courland. In 1646, after Digby had left England, 6,000 French troops, it was still being reported in royalist circles, were instantly expected at Hastings.[45]

The queen's letter to the king of January 1646 offered a sour comment on the cooperation achieved between the two courts over the previous years. It was intercepted by the Parliamentary authorities but it was completely enciphered from the original French, and they could not read it. Had they been able to, they would have been reassured. The letter was an admission of defeat. The queen, sick and gloomy, petulantly scolds Charles for giving her such affliction that, if she could, she would prefer to retire to a convent. She and Jermyn had previously complained that all her schemes were frustrated; the Irish refused to cooperate, the Pope was obdurate, the king had made public her secret negotiations with the French and Scots. Now his ill-timed actions and sudden changes of plan added to her woe: as did, we can be sure although she did not say so, an unrealistic assessment of the prospects for him in England, continuously provided by his former secretary. While she was offering her son to leading personages in Europe he was negotiating an alliance, she had found out, between the young Charles and the new crown of Portugal. In this way Spain, a potential ally, was being alienated. The fact that unreality reigned in Paris also, however, was apparent from the accompanying letter to the king from Jermyn. The 6,000 troops destined for England were delayed, it was said, only by the freezing of the rivers in the Netherlands.[46]

When all was lost, in 1647, Henrietta Maria sought divine guidance. Pope Innocent X had refused to give her material aid when it mattered, and his envoy had sunk their Irish hopes. Now she beseeched him to canonise a long-departed French monk who had once advised kings of England. Might his blessed soul, joined with the heavenly host, intercede with the Almighty to halt the slide of her husband's unfortunate nation to perdition? The queen was rapidly assuming the role, which she played for years before and after Charles I's death, of Cassandra at the French court.[47]

Growing estrangement between the courts of Oxford and Paris, as royalist fortunes declined in 1645, was matched by the divisions in the

---

[45] *Digby's Cabinet*, pp. 51–55; BL, Add. MSS 33, 596, fos. 11–12; PRO, SP 16/510, fos. 223–24, 239–41; HMC, *Portland*, I, pp. 245–46, 287; *Secret Writing*, pp. 121–22, 125–26; Carte, *Letters*, I, pp. 76–83, 90–95; *Cal. Clar. S. P.*, I, no. 1958.

[46] I. Roy, 'Les Puissances Europeennes et la chute de Charles I', *Revue d'Histoire Diplomatique*, 92, 1978, pp. 92–109; *Secret Writing*, pp. 128–31, 136–37. The queen's and Jermyn's letters of 16/26 January 1646, entirely in cipher, are SP 106/10, unnumbered folios, marked '3' and '21' respectively.

[47] *CSPD*, 1645–47, pp. 438, 552; P. Knachel, *England and the Fronde* (Ithaca, 1967), pp. 39, 41–42.

councils at home. A key relationship was that between Digby and Rupert. The initial warmth and admiration, at least on Digby's part, was a thing of the past by 1644. The prickly letter Digby wrote to the soldier most trusted by both men, William Legge, in November 1643 is revealing of the trend.[48] Rupert had been humiliated and his troops damaged by the fiasco of Aylesbury.

The prince's anger, however, was soon to have a different or at least wider focus. In the months leading up to the relief of York, and Marston Moor, and the trapping of Essex at Lostwithiel in Cornwall, a major conspiracy was hatched in royalist counsels. Rupert had heard that Wilmot, his second-in-command, Culpepper and Digby had said that it was a matter of indifference to them whether Rupert or the Scots prevailed in the north that summer. His fury was such that he halted his march to York for ten days and contemplated handing in his commission. He also blamed Percy, now very much not the prince's favourite, for failing to supply his forces. Rupert needed an ally with the king if he was to be rid of Wilmot and Percy. Digby was not a friend to Percy, 'generally unloved, as a proud and supercilious person', and could easily sacrifice Wilmot. Even in the face of the enemy, in August 1644, both generals were dismissed, allegedly for communicating with Essex.[49]

This dramatic event did not remove the distrust Rupert and Digby felt for each other. Rupert's 'Diary', composed long after the event, blamed the secretary for the gap in the prince's new command-in-chief, November 1644, that left the guards independently brigaded. It is obvious too that Rupert resented the latitude granted by the king to the council of the Prince of Wales, as much as he liked the prince himself: he wanted to rescue the young Charles from his council at Bristol, he said. And although he had agreed to the setting up of a separate army under Lord Goring, as he had to Goring's replacement of Wilmot after Lostwithiel, to free himself from a rival at court, he was aware that Goring's command was designed in part as 'a counterpoise' to his own. He was soon suspicious of Goring's pre-eminence in the west and in the prince's council. He respected no general except Sir Richard Grenville, 'the only soldier in the West', and was contemptuous of the civilian advisers, such as Culpepper and Hyde.[50]

The political atmosphere at Oxford was not improved during the winter of 1644–45 by the secretary's last attempt to suborn an enemy stronghold,

---

[48] Digby to Legge, Oxford, 1 November 1643: Staffs. Rec. Office, Dartmouth Papers, S.MS.345, no. 34.

[49] Carte, *Ormond*, vi, pp. 87, 150–52, 167; Clarendon, *History*, iii, pp. 388–93.

[50] BL (formerly at Wilts. Rec. Office), Pythouse Papers, Rupert's 'Diary', p. 62; Warburton, *Prince Rupert*, iii, pp. 27–28, 32, 73, 75; HMC, *Ormond*, n.s. ii, p. 385.

this time Abingdon, which had been for some months a threat to the royal headquarters. But again the Parliamentarian officers involved were playing a double game, hoping thereby to persuade their masters to make the supply of the garrison a higher priority, and Oxford forces were sent out on a futile errand. 'The traffic in treachery', as Digby described this ruse, was one all could play. He appears to have been increasingly isolated; among the Oxford politicians only Lord Treasurer Cottington was mentioned as a supporter.[51]

For the campaign of 1645 Digby and Rupert were yoked together in the council of war. Close proximity heightened the tension rather than closed the gap between them. Both headed independent parties and sources of intelligence. Rupert's promotion had carried into the top military posts many of his followers, such as his brother Maurice at Worcester and Charles Gerard in South Wales. Most important too was the fact that the new governor of Oxford was the prince's associate William Legge. His information therefore came from the combatants in the field, mostly career soldiers. Digby's circle, as revealed by his cipher keys and correspondence, consisted of some local commanders, who had fallen out with the commander-in-chief, such as Blagge at Wallingford, close friends and relatives, such as his brother Dyve, O'Neill and members of the Boyle family, or his agents in provincial garrisons reporting on Rupert's appointees, or Goring's debauches, or the squabbling in the western armies.[52]

Of the forty-eight ciphers taken at Sherburn, twelve related to his international diplomatic network; eight were for major figures in Irish affairs. He had close and secret links with both the royal and the enemy capital. Several were through women, who played a vital role in communications during the war. Four women of the Boyle family, headed by the earl of Cork, had married into the Digby, Goring and other prominent families in England and Ireland. They, and the countess of Cork, merited their own ciphers. Mrs Jane Whorwood at Oxford was a source of intelligence at this time, and was an intimate of the king later. His most private line, however, from which he received the juiciest gossip from Oxford, London and the army, was the young Catholic intellectual in his household, Edward Walsingham. A brilliantly gifted man, he had composed the hagiographical accounts of the most celebrated of the Catholic

[51] F. Varley, *The Siege of Oxford* (London, 1932), pp. 79–80; *The Lord Digbies Designe to betray Abingdon* (London, 1645), Madan, no. 1727; Warburton, *Prince Rupert*, III, p. 156; Carte, *Letters*, I, pp. 76–83.

[52] I. Roy, 'The Royalist Council of War, 1642–6', *Bulletin of the Institute of Historical Research* 35, 1962; *Diary of the Marches of the Royal Army ... by Richard Symonds*, ed. C. Long (Camden Soc. 74, 1859), p. 271; BL, Trumbull MSS Add. 43, ciphers; Bodl., Tanner MSS 60, fos. 327–29; *Secret Writing*, pp. 120–21; *CSPD*, 1645–47, pp. 122, 157–58, 160, 456.

soldiers who had died for the king in the Civil War. Sir Edward Nicholas and others regarded him later, however, as a 'pragmatical knave'.[53]

The two men and their followers disagreed violently over the course to pursue on the summer's campaign which culminated at Naseby. That disaster sparked much recrimination. Had it occurred because the crown had been 'absolutely given away' to Rupert, who, in the eyes of Digby's men, was attempting to replace, with his elder brother and mother in the pay of Parliament, one branch of the Stuarts by another?[54] Or because Digby was the classic evil adviser of the crown, pouring poison in the ear of the king? It was poison, moreover, distilled by the king's own entourage, which included, Rupert wrote to Legge, 'two cuckold lawyers, a herald and a barber'.[55]

Walsingham's London spies claimed that Rupert, disillusioned by defeat at Naseby, for which he accepted no blame, was in touch with the Independents at Westminster. *The King's Cabinet Opened*, published two months after Naseby, had revealed to the world (his nephew included) the king's secret negotiations with Catholic Europe and Ireland. If he did not want a Catholic takeover the prince did not relish either a deal, in the king's declining days, between the monarchy, Presbyterians and Scots. It is probable that some of the published correspondence was new to Digby as well. He believed it was 'heedlessly lost' and congratulated himself that 'I lost none of mine'.[56]

Rupert retired in a huff to his governorship of Bristol, and soon advised the king to make the best peace possible with his enemies. Whether as cavalry general or commander-in-chief the prince had always run a tight ship, and it was a measure of his black mood that the city, plague-ridden and devastated, was rumoured to be a giant 'bawdy house'. He did not attend to his duties, it was said, as his hands were full with 'Paps', his best friend's beautiful young wife. A London newsbook explained to its readers, in a footnote to an intercepted letter from O'Neill to Digby, that 'The Dutches of Richmond is caled Pap. by a nickname'.[57]

---

[53] BL, Trumbull MSS Add. 43, ciphers; Bodl., Tanner MSS 60, fos. 327–29; *DNB*, 'Edward Walsingham'; *CSPD*, 1644–45, pp. 450, 521; *CSPD*, 1645–47, pp. 47–49, 58–60, 116, 134–37, 140–42, 157–58; *Digby's Cabinet*, pp. 62–67; Carte, *Letters*, I, p. 217.

[54] Digby to Jermyn (Raglan, 10 July, and Cardiff, 5 August 1645), BL, Add. MSS 33, 596, fos. 9–10, 11–12; SP 16/510, fos. 87–88, 223–24; *Evelyn's Diary*, ed. Wheatley, IV, pp. 168–69.

[55] Rupert to Legge (Belvoir, 3 November 1645), SP.16.511, fo. 89. I am grateful to Mr John Moore for assistance with the cipher passages. It is not at present clear whom Rupert had in mind.

[56] *The King's Cabinet Opened* (London, August 1645), 72pp., reprinted in various editions of the *Harleian Miscellany*, vol. VII; *Digby's Cabinet*, pp. 60–62.

[57] 'Papers relating to the delinquency of Lord Savile, 1642–1646', ed. J. J. Cartwright,

Digby's chance for revenge came with the surrender of Bristol by Rupert in September 1645. Charles was outraged. His nephew had promised in August, when the king was in South Wales attempting to raise a new army, that he could subsist for four months. Coming upon Rupert's plea for peace and his desire for a pass to continue his career in arms abroad, Digby had an easy task in discrediting him. With betrayal and accusations of treachery rife as the royal cause stumbled to disaster, the king took panic measures. The queen spread the rumour in Paris that he had sold the town. Rupert was cashiered, and with him fell most of the officers and commanders he had promoted as Lord General. The governor of Oxford, William Legge, was arrested. It was not only Walsingham's London spies who suggested that he was about to betray the city: it was the common talk of the capital in the wake of Lord Saville's disclosures, and Charles even came to believe that Nicholas at Oxford had evidence against him. The divisions in the highest counsels of the royalists were out of control. It was extraordinary that the king's most loyal soldier could be suspected by his most honest minister; and that Charles should write in his own private cipher to warn Nicholas to reveal nothing to his council there.[58]

Digby's triumph was complete – he was made Lieutenant General north of the Trent – but he did not enjoy it long. No new armies could be raised, the high command was decimated by the sackings and resignations, and within a month it was known that Montrose's brilliant career had come to an end. At Newark he heard that Rupert and about 200 of his followers were on their way to demand justice of the king. They had already strongly signalled their displeasure by letter. He lost no time in heading north with the experienced Yorkshire commander, Sir Marmaduke Langdale, and a strong party of Horse, to see if they could join any part of Montrose's forces. On 15 October 1645 his little army was routed and his coach, with its vital papers, taken. His remark about the king's discomfiture on that score proved premature. He escaped to Ireland, but his career with Charles I was over. The Newark scene of 26 October followed.[59]

Digby had been accused of High Treason in 1642, but it was not Parliament which first exacted justice upon him. A royalist irreconcilable,

Camden Miscellany, 8; The King's Packet of Letters (London, October 1645); Carte, Ormond, VI, pp. 166, 277.

[58] Warburton, Prince Rupert, III, pp. 162, 185; 'Papers relating to Lord Savile'; Evelyn's Diary, ed. Wheatley, IV, pp. 168–69, 176–77, 178–79. Some words were not deciphered by Nicholas, or were discreetly blotted out. The printed version lacks 'hate', and 'Legge' for '401', on p. 168, 'you' for '316' on p. 177, and 'conceale what I have written' on p. 178.

[59] DNB, 'George Digby'; note of letters received, September 1645, in Bodl., Tanner MSS 60, fos. 327–29; Digby explained to the king that Sherburn had been almost a victory, ibid., fos. 322–23.

he remained in exile during the Interregnum. It was the judgement of his peers he had to face after the publication of the king's and his own cabinets. *Lord George Digby's Cabinet* appeared in March 1646, after some delay while Parliament decided which parts, especially those dealing with the Scots' secret negotiations with the king, were too politically sensitive to be printed. The bitter quarrels of the court and high command of the defeated party were now open to scrutiny, not least by the participants themselves. Digby faced the hostility and burning desire for vengeance of his fellow Cavaliers, who were now penniless exiles, deprived of office and power, with little to do but seek scapegoats for the disaster that had overtaken them. He was the prime candidate.

Two years after his flight from Newark he arrived in France. He had been undismayed by his defeat in England, had gone to Ireland (and had Glamorgan arrested), and found himself involved again in the politics of the court, this time that of the Prince of Wales. Correspondence of the time suggests that the roads of northern France were full of well-armed ex-Cavaliers hastening to exact private vengeance for slights received during their service in the Civil War. *En route* to the queen's court at St Germain Digby took the precaution of hiring a guard.

At one point, on the road to Paris, his men met an aggrieved Cavalier, 'running post with a great duelling sword', but it is not clear whom he intended to fight. Then Wilmot arrived to challenge Digby for disparaging him to the queen, referring to the slurs on his character printed in the *Cabinets*. But both men had their allotted places in the royalist exiles' cascade of disdain. Wilmot warned Digby that a bigger beast of prey lurked close by; Rupert himself intended foul play. The duel with Wilmot, a lesser attraction, was postponed to a more propitious time, but the place was agreed: the court at St Germain.[60]

The denouement could not be delayed much longer. Digby's principal enemy, a veritable prince of darkness in this dark chapter of royalist misfortune, sent a message that he wanted satisfaction from Digby at the cross at Poissy. Lord Jermyn and Daniel O'Neill attempted a reconciliation. The depth of feeling, however, not only prevented it but led to their taking part as seconds. Other leading royalist statesmen and generals were involved (Lords Wentworth, Gerard and Culpepper, as well as prominent courtiers). The quarrel was now so general and notorious that the queen's guards were forced to intervene and arrest several of them, including Digby. At the same time, or possibly a little later, the seventeen-year-old Prince of Wales himself, hunting in the forest, stumbled on his warring courtiers and separated them.

[60] Carte, *Letters*, i, p. 146.

Another attempt to bring the parties together proved unsuccessful; and a free-for-all developed. It is a telling comment on the demoralising effect of failure and the uplifting effect of success, as well as on the character of the two sides at this moment, that another group of soldiers, the victors in the civil wars, was meeting at Putney, in an atmosphere of great seriousness and piety, to decide the nation's fate. 'Out flew bilboes', wrote O'Neill, 'and to work we went *à la mode de France*'. That this was a fight in which the seconds also took part is indicated by his description of the scene. One of the combatants was John Digby, the enormously fat son of Sir Kenelm, George's ingenious cousin. In the mêlée he fell on top of Wentworth, who grasped O'Neill while warding off a thrust from our Digby. His fall, according to O'Neill, 'almost squeezed them to death'.[61]

It could be argued that this ludicrous tableau of brawling overweight Cavaliers is of a piece with the undignified and self-destructive end of a party which had at one time gained the allegiance of half of England. It is a picture that merits, on several grounds, the famous *Punch* line: 'Collapse of stout party'. The royalist cause had gone down in a welter of mutual fear and loathing, and suitably enough, many might feel, George Digby was at the centre of it.

His peer group had made a judgement about his share of the blame. The impeachment, had it taken place, might have provided better evidence. Might there have emerged a Civil War model of ministerial responsibility to add to those thrown up by the case of Strafford earlier or Danby later? Digby claimed, in his own defence against Wilmot's charges, that as secretary of state he was 'forced by the duty of his place' to write and speak as he did. Rupert appeared to accept this argument when he stated that he wanted satisfaction only for what Digby had said in a private capacity.[62]

We have seen that in his work Digby took the initiative in some matters, such as the bribing of enemy commanders, the publicising of military actions, the defence of Oxford, some of the dealings with foreign powers and different groups in Ireland. He dealt directly with the shippers of munitions. He was at the centre of royalist affairs for two years, and possessed his own private network of spies and informers, which played an important role in the downfall of his rivals at court. In many fields, however, he was as much the willing tool of his sovereign and the sovereign's wife as the author of policy. The royal pair kept many of the most important matters very secret, even from their trusted secretary.

[61] Ibid., I, p. 158. Bilboes are swords, the blades originally made at Bilboa, Spain.
[62] Ibid., I, pp. 152, 158.

They encoded their own communications, which they hid from their advisers. The bearers of letters were not allowed to know the contents.

Given the enormous disadvantages – fewer resources, less money – the royalists faced in the Civil War, what the king most required was realistic advice which directly addressed the chief difficulties. The European situation was not favourable; the Parliamentary blockade restricted the amount of aid available; the queen headed her own court, and fell out with her husband. In these circumstances Digby was not right for the king, as Clarendon, in his pen portrait of his erstwhile friend, showed. His nature mixed brilliant gifts and severe weaknesses. He was too fanciful and sanguine, providing an over-optimistic rather than realistic picture. In this he resembled both his master and mistress. His fatal flaw was that 'he too often thinks difficult things very easy; and doth not consider possible consequences'. He never learned from his mistakes. Clarendon's final judgement was one an assessment of his work will confirm. 'He was equal to a very good part in the greatest affair, but the unfittest man alive to conduct it.'[63]

The king had long taken the view that he could best preserve his freedom of action by giving complete trust to no one minister, and even playing off one against the other. This policy was only too effective at Oxford; the king came to preside over a regime at war with itself. The challenges to Digby in 1647, and the duels that ensued, were the result. In the violent aftermath of the royalists' collapse Rupert was willing to make a distinction between the public servant and the private man. Was the prince therefore not conceding the point that a good deal of the blame for their predicament lay with the soon-to-be-martyred royal sovereign himself? His martyr's crown precluded any criticism by his erstwhile followers at the time, but historians have not been so generous.

In answer to the questions posed at the start of this paper – arising from the Newark scene – it would be fair to conclude that Digby was largely responsible for one major decision only: the downfall of Rupert's followers in September 1645. But even in that he could not have succeeded without the approval of the king, and possibly the queen. In general, therefore, Charles at Newark got it right. Digby did not lead him by the nose; the king remained sovereign. The secretary was an honest man and a loyal official, not a traitor. But he was also the wrong man for the job.

[63] Ollard (ed.), *Clarendon's Four Portraits*, pp. 61–62; Clarendon, *History*, I, pp. 461–63.

4

The iconography of revolution: England 1642–1649[*]

IAN GENTLES

A wide variety of evidence apart from the written word can extend and enrich our knowledge of the past. Pictures, tapestries, buildings, sculpture, music, coins, tools and clothing are among the forms of evidence that historians have exploited with increasing frequency in recent decades. The fields of numismatics, musicology, art history, emblematics and other disciplines are contributing more broadly to the study of history than ever before. As this essay will show, emblematics has a particular relevance to the English Revolution.

Emblems and impresas were among the most distinctive of Renaissance art forms. Typically, the emblem consisted of a combination of motto, picture and short poem. The motto was usually a proverb or some well-known heraldic phrase or literary quotation. Its function was didactic: the conveying of some general truth. The impresa was an emblematic device that expressed the intention or convictions of a particular individual in a personal, sometimes enigmatic fashion. In sixteenth- and early seventeenth-century England impresas were to be found everywhere – in tapestries, jewellery, medals, coins, household decorations, masques, pageants, monumental sculpture, costumes and portraits.[1] Several English emblem books were published during the half-century or so before the Civil War: Jan Van der Noot, *A Theatre for Worldlings* (1569), Paolo Giovio's *The Worthy Tract of Paulus Jovius* (translated by Samuel Daniel, 1585), Geffrey Whitney's *A Choice of Emblemes and other Devises* (1586), the anonymous P.S.'s *The Heroicall Devises of M. Claudius Paradin [and] the Purtratures or*

[*] I am grateful to many people for help in preparing this essay: Ian Roy, Victor Morgan, Alan Young, Jeanette Neeson, Tim LeGoff, Steven Pincus, John Morrill, Blair Worden, Michelle White, and the members of the Toronto Seminar on Early-Modern English History.
[1] For useful discussions of emblems and impresas see Mario Praz, *Studies in Seventeenth-Century Imagery* (2nd edn, Rome, 1964), chs. 1, 2; Michael Bath, *Speaking Pictures: English Emblem Books and Renaissance Culture* (London, 1994), pp. 19–27.

Emblemes of Gabriel Simeon, a Florentine (1591), Andrew Willett, *Sacrorum Emblematum Centuria Una* (1591–92), and Thomas Combe, *The Theatre of Fine Devices* (c. 1593). In 1612 Henry Peacham brought out *Minerva Britanna* in two parts, dedicated to the young Prince Henry. It was the first original illustrated emblem book by an English author.[2]

When a generation later Thomas Blount translated the work of the French author Henri Estienne as *The Making of Devises* (1646) he was attempting to establish the antiquity and codify the rules of emblematics and heraldry. 'Devises', as Blount called them, can be traced back to the earliest of epochs, that of the ancient Egyptians. Reference to them is also found in the Old Testament; indeed God can be identified as the author of the first device when he planted the tree of knowledge of good and evil and explained himself with the words 'Ne comedas': 'do not eat'. Blount defined a device as 'that which beareth the picture of some living creature, plant, root, sun, moon, starres, or of any other corporeal subject, with some words, sentence or proverb, which serve as it were for its soule'.[3] Practised originally by the ancient Egyptians, Greeks and Romans, the tradition was still a vital one in the Renaissance. At tiltings, tournaments and masques, knights placed impresas on their shields, first to identify themselves and, second, to express the social worth and precedence of the individual who was being summoned whether for battle or for a festive function.[4] To his first edition of Henri Estienne's treatise Blount appended a catalogue of some of the 'cornet-devises' carried in the royalist and parliamentarian armies during the Civil War. This catalogue was enlarged and updated in the subsequent editions of 1648, 1650 and 1655.

Estienne and Blount had a clear conception of the dos and don'ts for designing devices, which were not, however, all strictly adhered to by the participants in the mid-seventeenth-century conflict. First of all, there should be 'a just proportion or relation of the soule to the body', the soul being the motto and the body the picture. The social snobbery underlying the making of devices was revealed in the prescription that the motto 'be not so obscure as to need a Sybill to interpret it; nor yet so plain, as the common people may comprehend it'. In order to shut out the common people and preserve the esoteric nature of the communication, the motto was to be 'in a strange language'. Estienne thought that Latin was the best, '... since that truely is that language which is most knowne, most pleasant, most energ[et]ique, and most authentick of any other in all Europe'. Greek

---

[2] Alan R. Young, *Henry Peacham* (Boston, 1979), pp. 34–36. The emblem books referred to above have been collected and republished by Peter M. Daly *et al.* as *The English Emblem Tradition*, 2 vols. (Toronto, 1988, 1993).

[3] Thomas Blount, *The Art of Making Devises* (London, 1650), p. 10.

[4] Alan Harding, *England in the Thirteenth Century* (Cambridge, 1993), p. 182.

was acceptable as well, apart from the drawback that it was understood by too few. He went on, '... I think that those mottoes are much more exquisite and better accepted, which are taken out of some famous author, as Virgil, Horace, Catallus, Ovid, Lucan, or others'. Another requirement was that the standard be aesthetically appealing, that it have 'a sweet appearance, which shall succeed by inserting therein either stars, sun, moon, fire, water, green trees, mechanicall instruments, diversified and fantasticall beasts and birds ...'[5]

Luckily we do not have to rely exclusively on Blount's catalogue for information about the military banners of the English Revolution. Watercolour drawings of nearly 500 of these banners, or 'colours', 'cornets' and 'ensigns' as they were known at the time, have been preserved in over half a dozen collections. While they comprise only a fraction of the several thousand colours that were manufactured and used during the civil wars, and while the bulk of them date from the early 1640s, they are broadly enough distributed among the various armies and garrison forces to provide valuable insight into the attitudes and thinking of officers on both sides. The mere fact that such care was taken to keep a record of these perishable bits of cloth itself demonstrates that contemporaries recognised their social and cultural significance. They were designed by commissioned officers of the rank of captain and higher for their companies, troops and regiments. Since each officer appears to have had a free hand in creating his colour and selecting the motto which it bore, it is evident, given the large numbers which have survived, that they provide important clues to the reasons why men on either side – royalist and parliamentarian – in the three kingdoms took up arms, what they thought they were fighting for, or, to use a modern phrase, their combat motivation. They also shed light on what they wanted other people to think were their reasons for taking up arms.

In designing their colours the officers were both perpetuating and transforming the heraldic and emblematic traditions of their day. Among the 447 colours (128 royalist and 319 parliamentarian) which are the basis of the present study, many were plainly copied from medieval heraldry and Renaissance emblem books. But a far greater number were novel in their images and their statements, and embodied a propagandist intent more extreme than had been witnessed on the battlefields of earlier centuries. In the 1640s the aristocratic, gentlemanly hobbies of heraldry and emblematics were enlisted in a deadly struggle for the hearts and minds of the English, Scots and Irish people.[6]

[5] Blount, *Art of Making Devises*, pp. 17–18, 21, 29, 59.
[6] They are found in the following repositories: Dr Williams's Library (London), Modern MS, Folio 7 ('Book of Cornets'); British Library, Add. MS 5247 (also known as Sloane MS

Royalist and parliamentary colours were seen by many, not just the soldiers on both sides. They were public artifacts, which drew comment from writers and politicians. Highly prized as trophies of war, captured colours were put on display – for example by being paraded through the streets of London after the battles of Marston Moor and Naseby, and hung in Westminster Hall.[7] To lose one's 'colour' was regarded as a disgrace worse than death. 'Indeed, a greater act of cowardice cannot be found', declared Captain Thomas Venn, 'than to suffer the colours to be lost'.[8] In a palpable sense the standard was thought to represent the men and the commanding officer who were identified with it. Thus, in the *Lawes and Ordinances of Warr* of Essex's army in 1642 it was baldly stated that 'no man shall abandon his colours, or flye away in battail, upon pain of death'.[9] The importance of military colours is illustrated in a memorable incident at the battle of Edgehill in 1642. Charles I's standard bearer, Edmund Verney, found himself surrounded by parliamentarians, who offered him his life on condition that he surrender his standard. Defiantly he replied that while his life was his own, the standard belonged to their sovereign, and he would never surrender it while he lived. He then fought on, killing several parliamentarians before falling with his left arm cut off. According to the story, which was almost certainly embellished in the retelling, his body was not found, only the severed hand still grasping the broken staff of the colour. When the colour was eventually recovered by a royalist officer of the king's life guards he was rewarded with a knighthood.[10] What this episode illustrates is that mediaeval and classical conceptions of honour continued to animate both sides throughout the civil wars.[11] The colour

5247) ('"Cornetes" or flags and arms ... of the Earl of Essex's army, and of the Scotch and Irish forces, in the time of the Commonwealth'); Add. MS 14308 (Arms and Banners of the Trained Bands of London, 1647); Harley MS 2275; National Army Museum (London), MSS 6208-1 ('Standards taken in the Civil Wars'); Bodleian Library, MSS Rawlinson D942 (Book of civil war colours), B48 ('London in Armes displayed'). They are also referred to and described in numerous pamphlets and newsbooks of the time. These and a few others have been collected and published in Alan R. Young, *The English Emblem Tradition*, III, *Emblematic Flag Devices of the English Civil Wars 1642–1660* (Toronto, 1995). This admirable work lists and illustrates 487 flags, including 40 that I do not consider in this essay: those from the Bishops' Wars, the Scottish Covenanting Army, and one flag each from the Fifth Monarchists and Clubmen. In a handful of cases I have also dissented from Professor Young's assignment of particular flags to the royalist or parliamentary camps.

[7] Young, *Emblematic Flag Devices*, pp. xxvii–xxviii.

[8] Thomas Venn, *Military Observations* (London, 1672), p. 183.

[9] Printed in C. H. Firth, *Cromwell's Army* (London, 4th edn, 1962), p. 407.

[10] *Memoirs of the Verney Family during the Civil War*, ed. Frances Parthenope Verney, 4 vols. (London, 1892; repr. 1970), II, pp. 115–16, 118.

[11] On this point, see Ian Gentles, *The New Model Army in England, Ireland and Scotland, 1645–1653* (Oxford, 1992), pp. 421–22.

also embodied the honour and good name of the regiment or troop it represented. For example, when the Prince of Wales' troop surrendered their standard at Hopton Heath in March 1643, they were forbidden to carry another until they had collectively redeemed their honour by capturing a colour from the enemy. This they did three months later at Chalgrove.[12]

Most of the colours that were copied at the time belonged to cavalry regiments. They were carried by the most junior commissioned officer of each troop, the cornet, and were called cornets. They measured about two feet square, the same dimensions as the guidons carried by the cornets of dragoons – the dragoons of the seventeenth century being mounted infantry. The infantry colours were also known as ensigns, and were carried by the non-commissioned officer of that name. Because they did not have to be carried on horseback, they could be much bigger than the cavalry cornets – usually about six-and-a-half feet square – and were supported on a staff seven-and-a-half to eight feet in height.[13] The functions served by colours were at least as much practical as they were decorative. On the battlefield they showed the rank and file where their units were situated, and where the individual soldier was supposed to be. They would also act as rallying points if the regiment broke under the stress of combat, and as a focus for regrouping.

In keeping with their high symbolic importance, colours were elaborately wrought from expensive materials. Accounts from the First Bishops' War (1639) show Montrose's Scottish army paying £4 15s. for each of its ensigns. The total cost per regiment was £61 15s. for the thirteen ensigns that were deemed necessary. Fabrics were 'the best duocape', taffeta and sarcenet in a variety of hues, with mottoes in gold lettering, the flags being supported on staves 'with gold and silver heads and tassells'. The trade that catered to this specialised demand appears to have been based in London. In 1650 Colonel Charles Fairfax of the northern army wrote to his friend Adam Baynes there, asking him to procure colours for his regiments, and to have them painted 'by my old friend Mr Knight, a herault that dwells in Shoe Lane towards Fleet Street Conduit.' A decade later we read of Sir Richard Temple ordering colours for his regiment from a tradesman 'at the Sunn in Burchin Laine neare the Exchainge'.[14]

---

[12] Charles Carlton, *Going to the Wars: The Experience of the British Civil Wars, 1638–1651* (London, 1992), p. 83.

[13] Peter Young, *Civil War England* (London, 1981), p. 58.

[14] PRO, WO49/68 (supply warrants for the king's army, 1639), fo. 69. I am indebted to Mark Fissel for this reference, but have been unable to find a definition for 'duocape'. For Colonel Fairfax, see *Proceedings of the Society of Antiquaries* 2, 1849–53, p. 250; for Sir Richard Temple, see Huntington Library, CA., Stowe Temple Accounts Box 26 (A) 16 May 1660. I am grateful to Paul Hardacre for these last two references.

Table 1 *The language of royalist and parliamentary battle standards*

	Royalist		Parliamentarian	
	No.	(%)	No.	(%)
Latin	104	(81)	244	(76)
English	16	(12)	48	(15)
French	7	(5)	18	(6)
Italian	0	(0)	1	(0.5)
Spanish	0	(0)	1	(0.5)
No motto	2	(2)	9	(3)
(Totals)*	129	(100)	321	(101)

* These totals include three bilingual standards, one royalist and two parliamentarian.

The New Model Army under Sir Thomas Fairfax was more frugal. The treasurers allowed an infantry colonel a maximum of £22 15s. for ten colours for his regiment – barely a third of what Montrose allotted.[15] There are no warrants for colours for cavalry regiments, which may indicate that cavalry officers procured them at their own expense.

Under the stress of war, colours were sometimes manufactured from humbler materials than taffeta. After the battle of Naseby (1645) a parliamentary propagandist sought to embarrass the royalists by announcing that at least one of their captured colours was made of red flowered damask. 'These have surely been hard put to it for colours; for they look like peeces of old petticoats.'[16] On another occasion a royalist commander made a positive virtue of the improvised nature of his flag. Referring in the motto itself to the piece of satin petticoat supplied to him by a lady, he quoted the *Aeneid* to the effect that it was 'a gift not sought after for such use'.[17]

Both sides respected the precept that it was appropriate for mottoes to be expressed in a foreign language. The preferred tongue was Latin – over eighty per cent on the royalist side, and over seventy-five on the parliamentarian – with English coming a distant second. Only a handful of mottoes were in other languages: French, Italian and Spanish.

This evident preference for a language familiar only to the educated demonstrates that in a formal sense the officers on both sides adhered to

---

[15] The supply warrants for the New Model Army are preserved in PRO, SP28, vols. 29–37 and 352. See SP28/29, fos. 170, 180, 209, 227, 237, 247, 248, 270; vol. 30, fo. 339, etc.

[16] *The Manner how the Prisoners are to be brought into the City of London, This present Saturday being the 21th day of Iune, 1645* ... (London, 1645), p. 4.

[17] 'Non hos quaesitum munus in usus' (*Aeneid*, 4, 647). Young, *Emblematic Flag Devices*, p. 139.

the precept that their mottoes should be '... a little removed from common capacities'.[18] We need not, however, infer that the standards were merely a dialogue between military élites. Both fellow and enemy officers were undoubtedly the primary audience to whom the standards addressed their messages. By conforming to a tradition of emblematics extending several millennia into the past, and by quoting from classical and sacred literature, the individual officer advertised himself as an educated and sophisticated man. But that was not all. More than in any previous period these devices were vehicles of political and religious propaganda. They told anyone who was willing to pay attention, why the officer believed he was fighting. I think it also likely that most officers would have explained carefully to the men of their units the significance of the design of their colours, and the meaning of the classical or biblical quotations which adorned them. If this is so, battle standards were also a vehicle for inculcating rank-and-file soldiers, many of whom were not willing participants but conscripts, 'pressed men',[19] with the officer's interpretation of why they were fighting. As was the practice with most armies since the Middle Ages, the colours of each soldier's unit were paraded before him regularly to ensure that he would have no trouble recognising them in battle.[20] At least one commentator at the time was in no doubt about the possible impact of the religious images featured on one set of parliamentary colours. The newswriter of the royalist *Mercurius Aulicus* singled out for condemnation those from Essex's army that 'were set out gloriously with three faire Bibles, to make poore simple folke believe they fought in defence of the Word of God ...'[21] A further sign of the importance attached to flags as instruments of propaganda was the effort sometimes made to discredit the mottoes and images of one's enemy, thereby generating negative publicity. Thus, after the Irish Catholic Confederacy had thrown itself behind the king's cause in 1644, *The True Informer*, a parliamentary newsbook, reported with evident satisfaction the messages contained on twelve of its flags. At the end of the catalogue of crowns, crosses, the chalice, the rosary, the Blessed Virgin Mary and the burning of Calvin's *Institutes*, each with its supporting motto, the writer concluded, '... if any man, after so many evident demonstrations concerning the concurrence of the designs of the Papists, both here in England, and in Ireland, will not be undeceived, let him so

---

[18] Blount, *Art of Making Devises* (1650), p. 21.

[19] Most pressed men were infantry. For the extent to which each side resorted to conscription see Ian Gentles, 'Why men fought in the British civil wars, 1638–1652', *The History Teacher*, 26, 1993, 407–8; and Gentles, *New Model Army*, pp. 31–40.

[20] Cf. W. A. Smy, 'Standards, guidons and colours of the British army and provincial corps during the American Revolution', *Loyalist Gazette*, 31, 1993, 16.

[21] *Mercurius Aulicus*, 25th week (18 June 1643), p. 323.

Table 2 *Classical and scriptural mottoes*

	Parliamentary	Royalist
Latin classics	8	9
Old Testament	25	9
New Testament	13	5

continue ... till they see an utter extirpation of themselves and their families, by those vipers whose cause they [the royalists] defend.'[22]

Many officers did not make up new mottoes; preferring instead to quote the Latin classics or the Bible. Of the parliamentary standards four quoted Horace, one Vergil, two Cicero and one Ovid. The royalist banners quoted Horace twice, Vergil six times and Cicero once. Parliamentary officers quoted scripture thirty-eight times; royalists fourteen times. Given, however, that our sample of parliamentary standards is almost three times as large as the royalist sample, the proportion of biblical quotations is nearly equivalent. There is, however, visual evidence that the Bible loomed much larger in parliamentary than in royalist minds. Twenty-eight parliamentary flags bore images of the Bible, in comparison with only three royalist flags. What was selected from the Bible was also revealing. Parliamentary officers manifested a clear preference for texts that were confident, militant, fire breathing. 'If God be with us who can be against us?'[23] (Romans 8:31) was the favourite. Other choices included '[Our God is] like a consuming fire'[24] (Deuteronomy 9:3), 'Let God arise and his enemies be scattered' (Psalm 68:1),[25] and 'Thov shall breake them with a rod of iron'[26] (Psalm 2:9). The royalist texts stressed loyalty, obedience and the sanctity of kingship. Thus, 'Render unto Caesar the things which are Caesar's'[27] (Matthew 22:21), and 'Touch not mine anointed'[28] (Psalm 105:15). One flag bore the simple motto 'Romans XIII',[29] confident that the phrase 'The powers that be are ordained of God' would flash through the minds of those who saw it.

A significant number of officers on both sides evidently copied or

[22] *The True Informer*, no. 28 (28 Sept.–5 Oct. 1644), p. 357. See also Alan R. Young, 'Ireland 1641–1642: some emblematic flag devices', *The Flag Bulletin*, 24:5, Sept.–Oct 1995, 178–91.

[23] Sloane MS 5247, fos. 28, 38, 75; 'Book of cornets', fo. 112; Young, *Emblematic Flag Devices*, pp. 83, 137.

[24] Sloane MS 5247, fo. 85.

[25] Sloane MS 5247, fos. 8v, 60v; Young, *Emblematic Flag Devices*, p. 60.

[26] Young, *Emblematic Flag Devices*, p. 239.

[27] Blount, *Art of Making Devises* (3rd edn, London, 1655), sig. A4a, pp. 72–73.

[28] Young, *Emblematic Flag Devices*, p. 138.   [29] Blount, *Art of Making Devises* (1650), p. 75.

1 'For these I will live and die' (Dr Williams's Library, Modern Folio MS 7, fo. 132)

2 'Thus it stands foursquare' (Modern Folio MS 7, fo. 132)

3 'As they are outside, so will they be inside' – Sir Thomas Bosvile's cornet (Modern Folio MS 7, fo. 130)

4 'Cuckold wee come' (Modern Folio MS 7, fo. 149)

adapted their mottoes and images from the emblem books that had been published in England since the late sixteenth century. The classical legend of the pelican feeding its young with blood from its own breast had been transmuted in the Middle Ages into a metaphor of Christ's redemptive sacrifice.[30] By the seventeenth century it had become one of the most frequently repeated religious symbols, finding a prominent place in George Wither's *A Collection of Emblemes* (1635).[31] The four flags bearing this image were divided equally between the royalist and parliamentary armies.[32] The haughty royalist motto flaunted by Sir Marmaduke Rawdon, 'I would rather die than be defiled', had previously been used by Ferrante, son of Alfonso I, king of Naples.[33] Colonel John Urry copied the motto of Francesco Sforza, Duke of Milan, 'No one attacks me with impunity.'[34] When Colonel Sir James Montgomery proclaimed 'there will be another reward', he too was adapting an Italian emblem.[35] The unidentified royalist commander at Naseby who portrayed bullrushes being dashed by waves with the tag 'we are cleansed not crushed' was likewise using a common theme in emblem literature.[36] Captain Benjamin Mason of Essex's life-guard who boasted 'I break that which tries to break' was echoing the Marquis of Pescara's motto recorded by Giovio.[37] 'Ready for both [war or peace]' was copied by one parliamentary and two royalist officers, who would have found it in the emblem book of either Whitney or Paradin.[38] 'Make haste slowly' was also found in Whitney and Paradin.[39] Charles I's favourite motto, 'As long as I breathe I hope', used by Sir William Courtney, was recorded in Andrew Willett's *Sacrorum Emblematum*.[40] Even

---

[30] John Horden, 'The connotation of symbols', in Michael Bath *et al.*, *The Art of the Emblem: Essays in Honour of Karl Josef Höltgen* (New York, 1993), p. 72.

[31] Rosemary Freeman, *English Emblem Books* (London, 1948), p. 145 and plate 24.

[32] Young, *Emblematic Flag Devices*, p. 290.

[33] 'malem mori qvam faedari'. 'Book of Cornets', fo. 149; *The English Emblem Tradition*, I, eds. Peter M. Daly *et al.* (Toronto, 1988), p. 41.

[34] 'nemo me impune lacessit'. 'Book of Cornets', fo. 27; *English Emblem Tradition*, I, p. 42. Blair Worden reminds me that this was also the motto of Marchamont Nedham in his parliamentary newsbooks.

[35] 'erit altera merces'. Sloane MS 5247, fo. 122v; *English Emblem Tradition*, I, p. 47.

[36] 'abluimur non obruimur'. Blount, *Art of Making Devices* (1655), sig. L4a; *English Emblem Tradition*, I, p. 48.

[37] 'conantia frangere frango'. Sloane MS 5247, fo. 46; *English Emblem Tradition*, I, p. 55.

[38] 'in utrumque paratus'. Sloane MS 5247, fos. 89, 123; *English Emblem Tradition*, I, p. 160; II, p. 96.

[39] 'festine [*sic*] lente'. Sloane MS 5247, fo. 93; *English Emblem Tradition*, I, p. 213; II, pp. 210–11.

[40] 'dum spiro spero'. Sloane MS 5247, fo. 3v; *English Emblem Tradition*, II, p. 300; Roger Lockyer, *The Trial of Charles I: A Contemporary Account from the Memoirs of Sir Thomas Herbert and John Rushworth* (London, 1959), p. 36.

two of the most militantly political and religious mottoes, 'If God be with us, who can be against us' and 'Not without cause', had previously been noted by Whitney and Paradin, respectively.[41]

For all this evidence of borrowing from the emblem books, most officers still concocted their own mottoes and the pictures that accompanied them. What is extraordinary is that there were almost as many mottoes as there were colours, none being repeated more than five times. Satire and wit were found in only a minority of banners, but they were twelve times as likely to be featured on a royalist than a parliamentarian banner. Most notorious perhaps was the one directed against the unfortunate Earl of Essex, whose first wife had divorced him for impotence, and whose second had run off to Oxford with a lover at the beginning of the Civil War. With no image accompanying it, the banner read 'cuckold wee come'.[42] Its sardonic force must have been reduced, however, by the fact that Essex was no longer on the battlefield: it was captured at Naseby, several months after he had been forced to surrender his commission under the terms of the Self-Denying Ordinance. No fewer than five royalist colours explicitly mocked the cuckoldry of the Earl of Essex, while at least two more deployed the imagery of horns and crescents to allude to it. Lieutenant-Colonel Caryl Molyneux pictured a reindeer's head supported by five hands, standing for the Five MPs whom Charles had tried to arrest in January 1642, above the motto 'To what do you exalt this horn?'[43] His older brother Richard, Viscount Molyneux created a flag showing a crescent moon obscuring the sun, with the motto 'But if I shine, alas for my horns.'[44] The most obscene royalist standard portrayed a naked soldier with an unsheathed sword and an erect penis. 'Ready to use both', boasted the shameless officer in the familiar words of the Latin emblem.[45] On another banner the royalists advertised their willingness to take risks, and their repudiation of roundheads. Bearing the image of a die, it read 'whichever way it falls, it stands four square'.[46] The die shows only the odd numbers, one, three and five, which were considered lucky. Not surprisingly, the only satirical quotation from the Bible appeared on a royalist flag. Beneath a picture of a loaded cannon and a hand issuing from a cloud holding a lintstick and a lighted match was the inscription from Psalm 51:15, 'Open thou my lips and my mouth shall show forth [thy

---

[41] *English Emblem Tradition*, I, p. 264; II, p. 24.   [42] 'Book of Cornets', fo. 149.
[43] 'Ad quid exaltatis cornu?' Blount, *Art of Making Devises* (1650), p. 72.
[44] 'Quid si refulsero? Vae cornibus meis'. Blount, *Art of Making Devises* (1650), pp. 72, 74; Young, *Emblematic Flag Devices*, pp. 5, 206, 314.
[45] 'In utrumque paratus'. Blount, *Art of Making Devises* (1650), p. 74.
[46] 'Book of Cornets', fo. 115.

Table 3 *The Civil War colours by theme*

	Parliament		King	
	No.	(%)	No.	(%)
Political	30	(9)	21	(17)
Constitution/legal	25	(8)	5	(4)
Political-religious	28	(9)	20	(16)
Religious/providential	87	(27)	17	(13)
Biblical	67	(21)	16	(13)
Protestant zeal	32	(10)	–	
Anti-episcopal	8	(3)	–	
Anti-Catholic	9	(3)	–	
Submission/resignation	–		11	(9)
Martial	29	(9)	11	(9)
Classical/civic virtue	51	(16)	16	(13)
Ethical	13	(4)	–	
Loyalty	–		27	(21)
Wit, humour, personal	4	(1)	15	(12)
Heraldic or family crest/motto	11	(3)	3	(2)
Unclassified	3	(1)	–	
(Totals)*	388		162	

For Parliament, the braced group (Political-religious through Anti-Catholic) totals 231 (72). For King, the braced group (Political-religious through Submission/resignation) totals 64 (50).

* Note: the totals exceed the numbers of colours because some have been assigned to more than one category. The percentages similarly add up to more than 100.

praise].[47] As we shall see, the only humour to appear on puritan banners was anti-clerical.

Analysing the cornets and ensigns thematically, we find that they fall into three main categories: politics and the constitution, religion, and classical or civic virtue.

If we group all the colours that contain some religious reference, whether pictorial or verbal, we find that seventy-two per cent of the parliamentary, but only fifty per cent of the royalist, colours can be classified as partly or wholly religious. More remarkable than the greater frequency of parliamentarian reference to religious themes is the contrasting flavour of roundhead and royalist piety. Both sides thought that God was backing their cause, but for the roundheads this assurance led to aggressive confidence in military victory. All the colours manifesting protestant zeal are on the parliamentary side.

Thus, the younger son of the radical peer, Viscount Saye and Sele, marched under the motto 'Let [God] arise and [his enemies] will be

[47] Neither the name of the (presumably) artillery officer who designed it, nor a drawing of the flag has survived. It is referred to in Blount, *Art of Making Devises* (1655), p. 90. See Young, *Emblematic Flag Devices*, p. 150.

5 'Wealth is not courage' – Sir James Montgomery (Modern Folio MS 7, fo. 64)

6 'For Reformation' – Captain Copley (British Library, Sloane MS 5247, fo. 37v)

7 'Antichrist mvst downe' – Captain William Gwilliams (BL Sloane MS 5247, fo. 64)

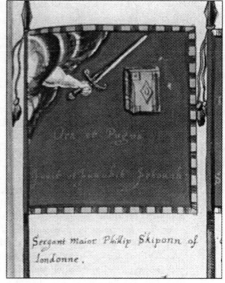

8 'Pray and fight. Jehovah helps, and he will help' – Sergeant-major-general Philip Skippon (Modern Folio MS 7, fo. 53)

scattered',[48] the first verse of Psalm 68, whose words were also uttered by Oliver Cromwell when he led his troops at the battle of Dunbar in 1650. Captain James Berry, later to become a Cromwellian major-general, used the frequently reiterated phrase, 'If God is with us, who can be against us?'[49] Philip Skippon, captain and sergeant-major of the London forces in 1642 and later major-general of the New Model infantry, showed a sword of heaven and a Bible, with the tag, 'Pray and fight: Jehovah helps, and he will continue to help.'[50] Captain, later Lieutenant-General, Thomas Hammond gave voice to a quintessentially puritan view that virtue, far from being a passive quality, is dynamic, constantly on the move: 'Virtue does not know how to stay standing in one place.'[51] Captain John Graves depicted an armed man, sword drawn and galloping on horseback with the tag 'for the protestants we thus make our country tremble'.[52] Captain John Blackwell of Oliver Cromwell's horse regiment pictured a walled city above a clutch of flaming hearts and the motto 'aflame with love for Sion'.[53] A number of other standards proclaimed their adherence to Protestantism and the Reformation, together with a readiness to fight on their behalf.[54]

Among the scores of religious and quasi-religious roundhead flags only a handful were negative. Eight were hostile to bishops, showing them holding the king in thrall,[55] trying to tear down the City of God that the puritans were building,[56] in league with the pope and other enemies of the Bible,[57] or as one of the heads of the many-headed beast in Revelation.[58] Two of the very few puritan standards which displayed any wit were anti-clerical or anti-episcopal. One showed a soldier clipping the corners of a cleric's square cap in order to turn him into a roundhead.[59] Another had a

---

[48] 'Exvrgat et dissipabvntvr'. Sloane MS 5247, fo. 8v.

[49] 'Si devs nobiscvm qvis contra nos'. Ibid., fo. 103. For the related motto 'Iehova nisi' ('Unless the Lord [builds the house they labour in vain that build it]'), see Add. MS 14308 (Arms and banners of the trained bands of London, 1647), fo. 17v (Richard Turner).

[50] 'Ora et pvgna. Ivvat et ivvabit Jehovah'. Ibid., fo. 15v.

[51] 'Nescit virtus stare loco'. Sloane MS 5247, fo. 33.

[52] 'pro protestantibvs sic patria quatimus'. Ibid., fo. 99v.

[53] 'accendia cura sionis'. 'Book of Cornets', fo. 83.

[54] Thus: 'Pro reformatione pugnandum' ('The Reformation must be fought for') – Capt Knights ('Book of Cornets', fo. 99); 'for reformation' – Capt Copley (Sloane MS 5247, fo. 37v); 'Only in heaven' – Sir Arthur Hesilrige (ibid., fo. 28v); 'I live in this hope' (In hec [sic] spe vivo), the sword of heaven – Capt Tho. Pennyfather (ibid., fo. 23).

[55] Bodl. Lib., MS Rawlinson D942, fo. 30v.   [56] Sloane MS 5247, fo. 76v.

[57] MS Rawlinson D942, fo. 9.   [58] Young, Emblematic Flag Devices, p. 257.

[59] 'Mutato quadrata rotundis'. 'Book of Cornets', fo. 42. For the long-standing controversy over 'popish vestments' to which this cornet refers, see Norman Jones, The Birth of the Elizabethan Age: England in the 1560s (Oxford, 1993), pp. 53–65.

9 'Our country asks for a man who is prepared [to sacrifice his life]' – Captain Barnard (Modern Folio MS 7, fo. 50)

10 'If God is with us who can be against us?' – Lieutenant-colonel Sir Edward Peto, governor of Warwick Castle (Modern Folio MS 7, fo. 18)

11 'By removing the wicked from the king's sight the throne is established in justice' – Captain Ward, alias Farmer of Leicestershire (Modern Folio MS 7, fo. 46)

12 'So you want to be a bishop? No, no, no, I don't!' – Captain Sandberd of Devon (Modern Folio MS 7, fo. 60)

soldier pointing his sword at a cleric's chest, demanding, 'So you want to be a bishop?' To which the terrified cleric is replying, 'No, no, no, I don't.'[60]

In view of the stress historians have placed on the theme of anti-popery in the English Revolution, it is surprising that only nine parliamentary colours expressed hostility to Catholicism, sometimes in conjunction with other themes. Captain Llangrish put it most bluntly with his skull and bishop's mitre, illustrating the motto, 'I would rather die than be a papist' or more colloquially, 'Better dead than Catholic'.[61] Another ebullient picture shows a swordsman pushing the pope off his throne while a puritan in a high-crowned hat rips his triple crown from his head. Above it William Gwilliams, captain of a New Model troop of horse, wrote in English, 'Antichrist must down'.[62] Colonel Edmund Ludlowe showed an open Bible over the pope's crown, crosier, staff and rosary lying on their side. 'I yield to the truth, the word of God', was his slogan.[63]

It was the highly exaggerated and inflammatory stories about the atrocities committed by the native Catholic population of Ireland against the Protestant settlers from England and Scotland that provoked the most extreme expressions of anti-popery from the parliamentary officers who prepared to invade that kingdom in order to put down the rebellion. In one striking image Ireland was represented as a house on fire, being consumed by the flames of popish rebellion.[64] The Scottish major John Niarne meant to jolt his enemies with a picture of a supposedly typical Irish Catholic atrocity against an innocent Protestant settler: a swordsman slaying a naked woman. 'Heaven avenges cruelty', he warned.[65] Sir William Selenger showed Ireland as a tree that has been cut down, but with a new sapling sprouting, thanks to the rescue efforts of the Protestant army.[66] William Cecil, younger son of the Earl of Salisbury, who would later serve in the New Model regiment of Henry Ireton, commissioned a gruesome picture of a man hanging on a gibbet, with the menacing inscription, 'he is a rebel and deserves it'.[67] What many of these banners – the ones from the Protestant army for Ireland especially – bear witness to is a puritan self-righteousness, stemming from the utter certainty that their cause is sanctified by God.

The royalists too were certain that they were supported by a providence, one which would not let rebellion prosper indefinitely. But their conviction was less triumphalist, subdued, and focused strongly on the

---

[60] 'vis ne episcopare [?] Nolo, nolo, nolo.' Sloane MS 5247, fo. 5v.
[61] 'Mori potvi qvam papatvs'. Ibid., fo. 102.   [62] Ibid., fo. 64.
[63] 'Verbvm dei, Veritati succvmbo'. Ibid., fo. 79v.   [64] 'Book of Cornets', fo. 64.
[65] 'Crvdella vindicat aether'. Ibid., fo. 34.   [66] Sloane MS 5247, fo. 124.
[67] 'Book of Cornets', fo. 144.

person of the king and the theological obligation of loyalty to him. One of
the few exceptions to this generalisation was Lieutenant-Colonel Henry
Constable's motto 'In this sign [the Cross] you conquer.'[68] More typical
was Colonel Sir John Cansfield: 'May there be peace in your strength.'[69]
For some royalists religion was a source of consolation before the prospect
of defeat. 'God comforts my heart and consoles my soul' were the words in
French found on one colour at Exeter.[70] A few officers bore flags that were
almost shockingly explicit in their prefiguring of defeat. Thus, Major
Christopher Wormsley's cornet showed religion as a woman in blue
standing on a skeleton with a broken cross close by. The motto was 'I hope
for better things.'[71] Another officer whose colour was captured at the first
battle of Newbury (1643) expressed a similar sentiment in the words 'I live
and will die for these things' surrounding images of a crown, sword, Bible,
olive branch and landscape (country).[72] Stoic constancy with defeatist
overtones is again the theme of a cornet that quotes Psalm 57, 'Until this
tyranny be over past', above a picture of a parliamentary committee (the
Committee of Safety?) seated around a table.[73] Constancy in the face of
defeat is the clear message of another quotation from the Psalms: 'In the
darkness a light has arisen for the upright in heart.' The image is of a cloud
with the sun's rays streaming from it, with an armed hand and a sword.[74] A
colour captured at the battle of Marston Moor (1644) almost forecast the
king's martyrdom five years later. Displaying the three crowns of England,
Ireland and Scotland, it proclaimed 'the fourth will be eternal'.[75]

Next to religion in frequency were politics, law and the constitution.
Given that the king had yielded to almost all the political and constitu-
tional demands of parliament by the beginning of 1642, this is a surprising
finding. On parliamentary banners frequent allusion was made to Magna
Carta, as a bulwark of the rights of the subject against royal tyranny.[76]
Captain Hooker's motto, 'Preserve the law, oh Lord', was illustrated by a
parchment scroll stamped with a red seal, standing for Magna Carta.
Francis Dowett also featured Magna Carta and the Bible. The theme of

---

[68] 'In hoc signo + vinces'. Ibid., fo. 72.
[69] 'Fiat pax in virtute tua'. (Psalm 121:7 [*Vulgate*]). Ibid., fo. 73. This is rendered as 'peace be
within thy walls' in the Authorised Version (Palm 122:7).
[70] 'Dieu comforte [sic] mon coeur et console mon ame.' Young, *Emblematic Flag Devices*, p.
45.
[71] 'Meliora spero'. 'Book of Cornets', fo. 131.
[72] 'Spiro his. His expirabo'. Ibid., fo. 132.
[73] Ibid., fo. 75.
[74] 'Extortum est in tenebris lumen rectis corde'. (Psalm 111:4 [*Vulgate*]). Ibid., fo. 73. The
bearer, Colonel Thomas Dalton, was a Lancashire Catholic.
[75] 'Quarta perennis erit'. Young, *Emblematic Flag Devices*, p. 203.
[76] 'Book of Cornets', fo. 31; Sloane MS 5247, fos. 47 (Hooker), 9 (Dowett); National Army
Museum, MS 6208-1, fo. 156.

13 'Thus I change square heads into roundheads' –
Colonel Cooke of Gloucestershire (Modern Folio
MS 7, fo. 42)

14 'If God is for us, who can be against us?' –
Captain James Berry (Modern Folio MS 7, fo. 112)

15 'Let God arise and his enemies be scattered' –
Captain John Fiennes (Modern Folio MS 7, fo. 22)

16 'The people's safety is the highest law' –
Major William Rainborowe (Modern Folio MS 7,
fo. 115)

constitutional legality was promoted in a more general way in the standard of Master Wansey, 'For lawfull lawes and liberties', and Captain John Carmichael and others who proclaimed that they were fighting 'for the law and for the people'.[77] An attempt to strike a pose of moderation is clear in several early parliamentary colours, most notably that of the future major-general, John Lambart. Above a picture of a hand from heaven placing a regal crown atop a Corinthian column representing the state or polity, he wrote, 'may he [the king] preserve us unharmed'.[78] Other colours avoided attacking the king directly by suggesting that he had been led astray by evil counsellors. Ferdinando Lord Fairfax's motto, the only one in Spanish on either side, declared, 'Long live the king, and death to bad government.'[79] Sergeant-Major Ralph Weldon's colour bore the image of a damaged column representing the commonwealth weakened by the king's wicked advisers, but with the reassuring motto, 'still it stands'.[80] Captain Ward of Leicestershire was blunter. Quoting from the Book of Proverbs, this swordsman exhorted his foes to 'take away the wicked from before the king, and his throne shall be established in righteousness'.[81] Who were the wicked? According to the image they were bishops, monks and papists. Far more radical was the standard devised by Major William Rainborowe in July 1649, on the eve of the New Model Army's departure for Ireland. 'The safety of the people is the supreme law', he announced, quoting Horace, beneath an image of a severed head and an axe dripping with blood.[82]

The royalists used their colours too to make serious and often angry constitutional arguments. The episode they alluded to most often was Charles's hapless attempt to arrest the Five revolutionary MPs in January 1642. On the earl of Carnarvon's device, which affected the weary *hauteur* of Cicero's rhetoric in the First Cataline Oration – 'For how long will you abuse our patience?' – six dogs baited the royal lion. The largest of the six was labelled Kimbolton, the future earl of Manchester, while the other five each wore the tag 'Pym' streaming from their mouths.[83] Many royalists regarded the parliamentarians as nothing less than traitors to the king, and took grim pleasure in portraying the punishment for treason. One standard

---

[77] 'Pro lege et grege'. Young, *Emblematic Flag Devices*, p. 71 (Wansey); Sloane MS 5247, fos. 67 (Carmichael), 62.

[78] 'vt servat in columem'. Ibid., fo. 59v.

[79] 'Viva el rey y muerra el mal govierno'. Ibid., fo. 20v.

[80] 'stat adhuc'. 'Book of Cornets', fo. 40.

[81] 'Eripiendo malos a conspectu regis stabilitur iustitiae solium' (Proverbs 25:5). Sloane MS 5247, fo. 58v.

[82] 'Salus populi suprema lex'. 'Book of Cornets', fo. 115.

[83] 'Quousque tandem abuteris patientia nostra?'. 'Book of Cornets', fo. 71. See also ibid., fo. 72 (three examples), and Blount, *Art of Making Devises* (1655), pp. 71, 72.

depicted three human heads with short hair, beneath the motto, 'They will be turned around [converted] or confounded for ever.'[84] In a transparent reference to William Prynne, scourge of the bishops, an unknown officer's banner depicted a human head slashed and mangled with its ears cut off. The mocking tag was 'not square'.[85] Another showed the Parliament House in Westminster with the heads of two traitors stuck on spikes at either end of the roof, with the motto, 'as they are outside, so they will be inside'.[86] This captured colour particularly scandalised MPs when it was delivered to the House of Commons after the first battle of Newbury.[87]

A significant number of political royalist devices edge into the category of social panic, masquerading as scorn for the low status of the roundheads. One obscure cornet carried the message 'It is fitting that the king should rule the commons.'[88] Colonel Sir John Berkeley showed an opulent, peaceful landscape of houses and cornfields being invaded by a crowd of beggars, and posed the question, 'Will a barbarian reap these crops?'[89] Sir William Compton was more insulting: from an ode of Horace he culled the line, 'I detest and keep away from the common crowd.'[90] Even more disdainful was the motto of Sir Marmaduke Rawdon, 'I would rather die than be defiled.'[91]

Occasionally the royalists boasted the excellence of monarchy as a form of government and the best guarantee of harmony in the commonwealth.[92] More often they merely declared their loyalty to the person of Charles I. 'I will strive to serve my sovereign king' was the forthright statement of Sir Ralph Hopton at the battle of Torrington in 1646.[93] 'Love loyalty', exhorted the Catholic Marquess of Winchester at the siege of Basing House in 1645.[94] Loyalty was acknowledged on both sides as one of the virtues; however, the roundheads' feeble pretence that their rebellion was directed not against the king but against his evil counsellors convinced

---

[84] 'Convertentur vel confundentur in aeternum'. Ibid., p. 90.

[85] 'Non quadratus'. Young, *Emblematic Flag Devices*, p. 141.

[86] 'Ut extra sic intra'. 'Book of Cornets', fo. 130.

[87] BL, Add. MS 31116 (Lawrence Whitacre's diary), p. 160 (28 Sept. 1643).

[88] 'Decet regem regere plebem'. Blount, *Art of Making Devises*, p. 76.

[89] 'Barbarus has segetes?' Ibid., p. 72.   [90] 'Odi profanum vulgus et arceo.' Ibid., p. 73.

[91] 'Mallem mori quam foedari'. 'Book of Cornets', fo. 148v. Another version carries the image of an ermine, symbol of royalty, which would not survive the pollution of its fur according to common belief. Young, *Emblematic Flag Devices*, p. 111.

[92] For example, 'perfectissima gubernatio', the cornet of Arthur Lord Capel. Blount, *Art of Making Devises* (1655), p. 72. Another officer, unknown, linked the crown with the harmonious music of the harp: 'mvsica, monarchica, lyra'. 'Book of Cornets', fo. 131.

[93] Ioshua Sprigge, *Anglia Rediviva* (London, 1647), p. 195.

[94] 'Aimez loyaulté'. This was also his heraldic motto. Blount, *Art of Making Devises* (1650), p. 71.

few. Having monopolised this political virtue, the cavaliers not surprisingly bragged about it often.

What is perhaps surprising is the frequency with which both sides invoked the classical or civic virtues, without any reference to Christianity. Stoicism, moderation, honour, the sacredness of one's word, carelessness towards death – these are the themes found on several dozen standards. Much emphasis was placed, especially by parliamentarian commanders, on the ethical character of their cause, but their colours were devoid of any reference to republicanism. Even Algernon Sidney, who would later die for his republican convictions, made only a veiled reference to his liking for that form of government when he stated, 'sacred love of country gives courage'.[95] Another future prominent republican, Colonel Edmund Ludlowe, chose, as we have seen, to stress his anti-Catholicism. Other officers eschewed politics and religion altogether. 'Virtue rejoices in trial' was the stoical reflection of the parliamentary colonel Valentine Wauton.[96] 'If I perish I perish', said Captain Markham with affected unconcern.[97] A captain in Colonel Alexander Popham's regiment vaunted his 'total magnanimity in difficult circumstances'.[98] 'Neither timid nor puffed up' was the modest boast of Colonel Thomas Sheffield.[99] Royalists tended to draw attention to the deplorable effects of discord on the body politic,[100] and to scoff at death. 'Either death or a fitting life' was the way one unknown officer phrased it beneath the image of a skull and nothing else.[101]

Another theme unrelated to politics or religion was martial valour and, related to it, the sheer glorification of war. A small percentage of the colours on each side poured contempt on cowardice, praised the joys of victory in battle, and flaunted their fearlessness before the prospect of death. Already by the seventeenth century this species of *machismo* could boast a long pedigree, and for a few it was their most significant motive. 'Win it and wear it', meaning the sword, announced the ensign of a captain in Colonel Barkstead's regiment.[102] 'I shall find [them] or make [them] quiet', threatened a royalist officer in the earl of Spencer's regiment.[103]

---

[95] 'Sanctus amor patriae dat animus'. 'Book of Cornets', fo. 95.
[96] 'Gaudet tertamine [sic] virtus'. Sloane MS 5247, fo. 82.
[97] 'Si pereo pereo'. Ibid., fo. 101.
[98] 'In arduis et tote magnanimi'. Blount, *Art of Making Devises* (1655), p. 91.
[99] 'Nec timid ned tumid [sic]'. Sloane MS 5247, fo. 22. For other expressions of balance and moderation see ibid., fo. 90; Young, *Emblematic Flag Devices*, pp. 123, 160.
[100] 'En quo discordia cives'. Blount, *Art of Making Devises* (1655), p. 73.
[101] 'Aut mors aut vita decora'. John Rushworth, *Historical Collections The Third Part* (London, 1692), II, 635.
[102] Blount, *Art of Making Devises* (1655), p. 91.
[103] 'Avt inveniam avt faciam'. 'Book of Cornets', fo. 130.

'Let the bolder man advance against the enemy' was the challenge of Sir Charles Compton, younger brother to the earl of Northampton.[104]

Finally, a small but significant number of officers, both roundhead and cavalier, sidestepped political and religious issues by adopting their ancestral coats of arms. The earl of Essex used his family motto, 'Envy is the companion of virtue';[105] Colonel William Waller proclaimed 'The fruit of virtue',[106] showing three gold fleurs de lys hanging from a walnut tree; Colonel William Constable exhorted, 'Be firm',[107] with the image of a gold anchor suspended by its flukes from a cloud symbolising heavenly aid; while Captain Edward Hungerford announced that 'God is my support.'[108] Royalist officers, however, resorted less to heraldic mottoes and crests, perhaps because they were less apprehensive about their social status and origins. The exception to this generalisation is the king's own cornet carried by his lifeguard, which bore the royal coat of arms and motto: 'Dieu et mon droit'.[109]

To sum up, the standards created by the royalist and parliamentarian army officers during the English Revolution were part of a still-vital tradition of emblematics dating back to ancient and medieval times. These devices served the practical functions of identifying which side the officer and his unit were on, furnishing a rallying point during the terror and confusion of battle, and at the same time representing in a public way the social worth of the individuals on whose behalf they were borne. To these were added a fourth and new function, that of propaganda. Since there was no centralised control or censorship over the making of devices, they are an unusually illuminating source of evidence for the combat motivation of the several thousand military leaders who put their lives on the line to advance the cause in which they believed.

For the royalists the cause was more personal than theoretical. They were moved by considerations of honour, fidelity and devotion to the person of the king. That the king in question was a political incompetent and an unprepossessing military commander did not matter. The treachery of those who fought against him was so abhorrent that it inspired the most savage mockery and hatred. A number of royalist standards also reveal a persistent suspicion and fear of the vulgar mob. Religious references are found in many of the royalist devices, but less as a galvanising force than a source of consolation. Religion also seemed to validate the charismatic nature of kingship.

---

[104] 'Contra audentior ito' (Vergil, *Aeneid*, VI, 95). Blount, *Art of Making Devises* (1650), p. 74; Young, *Emblematic Flag Devices*, p. 24.

[105] 'Virtvtis comes invidia'. 'Book of Cornets', fo. 1.

[106] 'Fructus virtutis'. Ibid., fo. 10.   [107] 'Soies ferme'. Ibid., fo. 12.

[108] 'Et dieu mon appuy'. Ibid., fo. 13.   [109] Blount, *Art of Making Devises* (1650), p. 71.

For the parliamentarian officers, by contrast, religion – the Bible, detestation of prelates and Catholics, the conviction that they were instruments in the hands of the Almighty – sanctified their struggle. 'If God is for us, who can be against us?' was the message, either explicit or implicit, conveyed by scores of cornets and ensigns. Their occasional attempts at humour were neither as suave nor as scatological as those of the cavaliers. While the royalist colours sometimes took aim at *bêtes noires* such as Essex, Kimbolton and Pym, the roundheads paid little attention to personalities. Instead they focused on the political grievances of unconstitutional taxation and tyrannical rule. But what animated them most strongly was puritanism, less in the negative sense of fear of popery than as a positive expression of confidence that their triumph would come, not through the 'arm of flesh', but as a reward for unquestioning faith in divine power. The study of these 447 banners lends force to John Morrill's observation that the events of 1642–49 should be construed, not so much as Europe's first revolution, as the last of its wars of religion.[110]

[110] 'The religious context of the English Civil War', *Transactions of the Royal Historical Society*, 5th ser., 34, 1984, 178.

5

The casualties of war: treatment of the dead and wounded in the English Civil War

BARBARA DONAGAN

Amidst these times of killing and destroying, it is a work of Charity to Save such as may be Saved.

[B]esides the just charity of such Care, who can expect the Soldiery shall frankly hazard themselves, if due provision be not made for the wounded and sick.[1]

Respect for the dead and care for the sick and wounded were part of the international codes of war of early modern Europe. They were moral obligations, but they also had a utilitarian dimension for, as the earl of Orrery observed, provision of care was 'as much the Interest, as the Duty' of a commander who wished to have willing troops.[2] The English practices we shall examine here were not unique. England shared problems and solutions with continental Europe, with whose wars many soldiers, medical practitioners and civilian observers were familiar. Unlike their continental counterparts, however, and despite their recent northern excursions, the English were not accustomed to the presence of war and armies. In 1642 they had to create systems of care virtually from scratch.

Obligation to the dead and wounded was taken seriously by both sides. It extended to enemies as well as friends, for the former could not decently be left to die. Bipartisan observance was – like adherence to laws of war that governed conduct to the defeated, to prisoners, to women and children – an ameliorating factor in relations between enemies, one that facilitated post-war co-existence and social and political reconciliation. Unfortunately, as in all wars, reality fell short of the ideal. The traditional charitable duty to the unfortunate, and professional duty to inferiors, were offset by inadequate administrative and physical means, by human failings,

---

[1] John Rushworth, *Historical Collections*, 8 vols. (London, 1680–1701), VII, p. 1205; Roger Boyle, earl of Orrery, *A Treatise of the Art of War* ([London], 1677), p. 53.
[2] Ibid.

and by a reluctance to foot the bills. And the best efforts could be overwhelmed by disasters such as epidemics or by sheer numbers.

Care for the war's victims has been little studied, in part because much of it was small-scale, localised and *ad hoc*, and records are consequently dispersed and fragmentary.[3] A further difficulty lies in the nature of surviving 'statistics', for most estimates are uncertain at best. Numbers of dead in particular actions, although freely bandied about by both sides, prove soft, and figures for the wounded were admittedly only probable calculations. Yet if it is impossible to give quantitative form to the fate of the victims of war, there is much to be learned about its quality. A study of their sufferings and of the attempt to care for them enables us to recover something of the experience of those who survived or died in the war, to observe the playing out of obligation to friend and foe, and to appreciate the massive challenge represented by the need to construct systems of care in a state lacking any infrastructure for centrally directed, effectively managed welfare.

I. THE SICK AND WOUNDED

(a) Wounds, sickness and survival

Much public discourse about military actions revelled in the horrors of blood and disaster, but the practical efforts of both sides to moderate their effects on wounded bodies were sensible, humane and extensive. There was little difficulty in defining what was needed, but much in delivering it. Army establishments provided for medical staffs of physicians, surgeons, surgeon's mates and apothecaries at all levels from the general's staff down to each regiment of foot or troop of horse, and these military practitioners ranged from the great William Harvey to obscure regimental surgeons and provincial apothecaries. As the war went on, however, it became increasingly difficult to sustain the generous levels of manning originally adumbrated. By 1647 the provisions for Fairfax's army were less generous than those for the king's army sent against Scotland in 1640.[4] The earl of Orrery, a veteran of thirty-four years' service, distilled the basic needs of both preventive and curative medicine, which included good food, warm clothing, adequate lodging, hygienic conditions, and the services of attendants and laundresses as well as medical practitioners. Providing them was another matter, as harried administrators like Thomas Clarges

---

[3] C. H. Firth, *Cromwell's Army* (4th edn, London, 1962), pp. 251–75 remains the best general survey but is heavily weighted towards the 1650s.

[4] San Marino, Henry E. Huntington Library (H.E.H.), Bridgewater MSS 7682; *Lords' Journals (LJ)* x, 67.

found in Oxford in 1643, where he scrambled with mixed success to provide the laundered shirts, clean straw, beds raised above vermin level, wholesome food and nursing that he knew in theory his charges should have.[5]

Little can be said here about preventive care, but its basic principles did not differ from those applicable to the sick and wounded. Attention to cleanliness, clothing, lodging, food and quarantine all helped to keep troops healthy and their morale intact. Hygiene, it should be noted, was a constant preoccupation. The contemporary sense of cleanliness and freshness was nice if not clinical, and soldiers, like civilians, knew that exposure to foul smells, overcrowding and ordure, and deprivation of fresh air and fresh clothes, endangered health. So it was recognised that soldiers' linen should be washed and their camps kept clean; army regulations, for example, had long prohibited fouling camps with human or animal wastes. Although cleanliness in garrison, camp and hospital was an uphill battle in the face of overcrowding, carelessness and competing demands for resources (such as horses for scavengers' carts), money and man- and woman-power were regularly assigned to the task.[6]

Curative medicine included care not only for wounds, the prototypical harms of war, but also for sickness, from devastating epidemics to common colds. Battle wounds were treated either initially on the field, where surgeons, their mates and apprentices shared soldiers' dangers, or after the wounded had straggled off or been borne away in cartloads. Only later did they move to hospitals or into the care of locals or relatives. The medical reasons for front-line presence were strong. Practitioners recognised the value of speedy treatment. Wounds left 'some days undrest', noted the great royalist surgeon Richard Wiseman, were 'full of Maggots', and bullet wounds quickly grew infected. Similarly, amputation, when it must be performed – although Wiseman cautioned that it was 'more for your Credit to save one Member, then to cut off many' – was best done promptly. So baggage trains carried 'Medicaments' as well as ammunition, and the ambulatory wounded who 'retreated to be drest' were attended to within sight of action. Both sides recognised the humanity and utility of field treatment, and allowed captured surgeons to continue their work with the wounded.[7]

[5] Orrery, *Art of War*, pp. 49, 53; London, British Library (BL), Harleian (Harl.) MSS 6804, fos. 202–4; 6851, fo. 163; 6852, fos. 41, 74, 86–90, 181–81v.

[6] London, Public Record Office (PRO), State Papers (SP) 28/141A, fos. 5, 35, 37; Oxford, Bodleian Library (Bodl.), MS Additional (Add.) D. 114, fos. 45, 103; *Lawes and ordinances of warre ... by ... the Earle of Essex* (London, 1642), p. 19.

[7] Richard Symonds, *Diary of the Marches of the Royal Army*, ed. C. E. Long (Camden Society, 74, 1859), pp. 63–64; John Washbourn, *Bibliotheca Gloucestrensis* (Gloucester, 1825), p. 172;

The harms of battle were laconically, almost casually, present in innumerable accounts of field actions. Wounds came from many sources besides bullets. Burns, slashing cuts from sword and pike, fragmentation agents like chain or case shot, and blows from butt ends of muskets and pistols all claimed their victims. Accidents were frequent, through either carelessness or inherent instability of materials. Nathaniel Nye saw explosions and burns as a normal part of the artilleryman's life, and knowledge of remedies as an aspect of professional preparation. Wiseman's *Chirurgicall Treatises* offer a humane, observant, clinical survey of war wounds and treatments. Although he was a particularly distinguished representative of his profession, his practice was clearly in many ways representative, and his accounts reveal an approach to wounds that is a mixture of the homely and the horrifying. He provides in passing some of the best evidence for the experience of civil-war battles, from hacking close encounters and gunshot wounds at such close range that powder stuck to the skin, to the desperation and confusion of flight.[8]

Wiseman's exemplary cases ranged from instances of relatively clean wounds by pike and sword, to which general surgical principles applied, to the gunshot wounds that, although not confined to war, were essentially military and demanded special techniques. Wounds of the first kind were often the result of multiple blows, and his account of how they were inflicted reveals the messy, painful and intimate character of civil war combat:

> These kind of Wounds are not so often seen in times of Peace, but in the Wars they are frequent, especially when the Horse-men fall in amongst the Infantry, and cruelly hack them; the poor Souldiers the while sheltring their Heads with their Arms, sometime with the one, then the other, untill they be both most cruelly mangled: and yet the Head fareth little the better the while for their Defence, many of them not escaping with lesse then two or three Wounds through the Scull to the Membranes, and often into the Brain. And if the man fly, and the Enemy pursue, his Hinder parts meet with great Wounds, as over the Thighs, Back, and Shoulders and Neck.[9]

Gunshot wounds presented even more problems than compound battery wounds. They had distinctive, confusing and unpleasant characteristics: their openings were ragged and contused; they had a 'deadly Colour' and a tendency to inflame if undressed; they produced 'Matter ... of a foetid

---

Richard Wiseman, *Severall Chirurgicall Treatises* (London, 1676), pp. 349, 400, 410, 420–21, 456; *A Relation of the Battaile Lately Fought Between Keynton and Edgehill* (Oxford, 1642), p. 5.

[8] Nathaniel Nye, *The Art of Gunnery* (London, 1648), II, pp. 100–1; Wiseman, *Chirurgicall Treatises*, pp. 348–49, 408–9, 427.

[9] Ibid., pp. 348–49.

smell'; and if not properly cared for they gangrened, 'and so the Patient commonly dies'. Although Wiseman maintained that they healed if 'rationally drest', he admitted that even many of his experienced colleagues were mistaken in treatment, while their 'ugly aspect' dismayed the inexperienced. Case histories suggest that local civilian surgeons called on for emergency aid but unfamiliar with military wounds may have killed before they learned the knack of curing.[10]

Wiseman discussed the relationship between practitioner and wounded, the victim's role in his own cure or death, and his attitude to suffering. Victims tend to appear as passive subjects in medical accounts of heroic measures designed for their welfare, but Wiseman also saw the person in the patient. The amount of suffering and stoicism was surely enormous, and pain must have been universal, yet it is rare to catch a glimpse such as that he gives us of the common soldier shot through the breast who 'lay roaring very grievously, complaining of a pain in his Back', and who, once the bullet was removed, 'ceased his crying'. Wiseman recognised the clinical uses of pain as a guide to diagnosis, but he also knew the need for alleviation. The means available were limited, but 'in case of extremity' the patient might have 'a grain or two of *ladanum*'.[11]

Endurance had limits, and arguments for rapid field amputation, if it was deemed necessary, were based not only on patients' increasing weakness but also on their increased awareness and unwillingness. Wiseman's motto was 'cut it off quickly, while the Souldier is heated and in mettle', but some refused to undergo the ordeal. One such case sums up the horrors of military medical treatment even when it was skilful and well intentioned. Confronted by a Scottish soldier whose elbow joint had been shattered by a musket bullet, Wiseman prepared to cut off his arm and at the same time encouraged the soldier to endure it:

> In answer thereto he onely cried, Give me drink, and I will die. They did give him drink, and he made good his promise, and died soon after; yet had no other Wound then that. By which may be perceived the danger in delaying this work to the next day, when the foresaid Accidents have kept them watching all night, and totally debilitated their Spirits. Which happens not, if it be done in heat of Fight; for then, while they are surprized and, as it were amazed with the Accident, the Lim is taken off much easier ... In the heat of Fight ... [some] have urged me to dismember their shattered Lims at such a time, when the next day they profest rather to die.[12]

The anaesthetising daze of shock saw some through surgical horrors, but it is not surprising that the patience and submission of some sufferers were

---

[10] Ibid., pp. 407–9.   [11] Ibid., pp. 352–53, 409, 411–12, 425–28.   [12] Ibid., pp. 420, 451.

offset by the debilitated spirits, physical decline, apprehension and defiance of others.

Much treatment was less draconian. Some was still appalling. The surgeon's duties included extraction of bullets, suturing, splinting, bandaging, bleeding and cauterising as well as application of ointments and medicines. Even with the best initial care, the victim was vulnerable to 'many Accidents' that 'not onely impede the Cure, but often ... destroy the Patient'. Mistaken diagnoses and faulty treatment, then as now, might cause 'persons [to] die miserably afflicted'. Risks were multiple, and the progression from 'vehement Pain' to gangrene and ultimately 'Mortification' was familiar.[13] Yet some treatment was for routine ailments: warts and corns, king's evil (scrofula) and gonorrhea, were also part of the surgeon's practice. Moreover, if further crises did not develop, much post-trauma care was un-invasive and common-sense. Wiseman trusted to nature's curative powers. He also paid attention to warmth, rest, tranquillity, drink and diet. Great wounds, he observed, required a spare diet 'as Barly-grewells, Panadoes, thin Broth, or a Potched egge' – he preferred them new-laid – and 'Jellies'. At the same time he recognised that sudden interruption to past habits of eating and drinking could be harmful. '*A Hair of the same Dog*, ... Brandy-wine is a common relief' – could strengthen wounded drinkers whom a week on 'Ptisan ..., nay two days' would cause to 'faint and languish'.[14] And he advised moderation in such conventional but drastic treatments as purging and bleeding in the regimen of already weakened men. Recommendations for devastating surgery appeared side by side with those for soothing drinks compounded from traditional English 'Simples' such as 'Comfry, Bugle, Ladies-mantle ... boiled in Water, or White wine'.[15]

One striking feature of Wiseman's account is its working assumption that in most cases a cure was there for the seeking. Despite inevitable failures, and despite the heroism required of the patient, there was no fatalism and no passivity before the will of God. Even hopeless cases demanded effort and kindness. The frightful wounds of the soldier 'shot in the Face by Case-shot ... and ... without Eye, Face, Nose, or Mouth' were dressed and bound up, and a fellow-soldier brought milk in a little wooden dish 'to pour some of it down his Throat' while others brought a blanket and fresh straw for 'that deplorable creature' to lie on. Many injuries to brain and lungs were equally hopeless, and gangrene was usually fatal.

[13] Ibid., pp. 342–43, 353, 409–11, 415–17, 421–25, 443–44.

[14] 'You may laugh at my pleading for them', wrote Wiseman defensively, 'but I hope you will consider I am a Water-drinker the while'. Ibid., pp. 346–48, 414. A 'ptisan' was a nourishing drink, often barley-water.

[15] Ibid., p. 347.

Ultimately, after his best efforts, there came a point at which the surgeon must 'leave it to Nature, lest the Patient die under your hands, and you be thought to hasten his death'.[16] Yet the results of dangerous cases and draconian surgery were not always fatal. Sir Arthur Aston's head injury left him deeply unconscious for days, but 'his skull being opened he ... expressed more sense, & some hope [was] conceived that he [was] not past recovery'. He was in action again within three months.[17] Professional and humane obligation required effort to alleviate what could not be cured.[18] Nevertheless, despite the efforts of physicians and surgeons, the lot of the sick and wounded remained dangerous, uncomfortable at best, excruciating at worst, and subject to the vagaries of combat, supply and chance.

Sickness too accompanied war. 'Sickly times', 'diseases and fluxes', 'grievous plague-time', were its expected concomitants, and the sufferings of soldiers in this respect could not be separated from civilians' especially when, in sieges and garrison towns, they lived at close quarters.[19] In addition, concentrations of troops and their prisoners were especially vulnerable once infection took hold. Although the principles of quarantine were well understood, they could not always be applied, and epidemics could decimate military and civilian populations. When Colonel Bampfield surrendered Arundel castle in 1644 he claimed that fewer than two hundred of his original nine hundred men were alive to march out with him; most had died of bloody flux or spotted fever. After Dunbar in 1650 Hesilrige received 3,900 Scottish prisoners, but he wrote from Durham in October that 1,600 had already died of the flux, and 'they still dye[d] daily'. Oxford, the crowded royalist capital, was wracked by epidemics. Armies were sometimes paralysed by sickness, and disease was no respecter of rank. The war was punctuated by occasions when commanders were too ill to march with their men and lead planned operations. In 1643, for example, Prince Maurice succumbed to 'the ordinary raging disease of the army', which also infected his general of artillery and his major-general. In December 1645 Fairfax's officers and men were stricken by 'the *New disease*'.[20] Nor should we forget the disabling and disruptive

---

[16] Ibid., pp. 383, 402–3.   [17] Stafford, William Salt Library, Salt MS 564.

[18] Wiseman, *Chirurgicall Treatises*, pp. 402–3.

[19] *The Swedish Discipline, Religious, Civile, and Military* (London, 1632), pp. 26–27; *The Swedish Intelligencer*, part III (London, 1633), p. 23; *Monro His Expedition with the Worthy Scots Regiment* (London, 1637), part II, pp. 10, 12.

[20] *Colonel Joseph Bamfeild's Apologie* ([The Hague?], 1685), pp. 7, 10; Eliot Warburton, *Memoirs of Prince Rupert and the Cavaliers*, 3 vols. (London, 1849), II, pp. 307–8; 'A Letter from Sir Arthur Hesilrige ... concerning the Scots prisoners' (London, 1650), in *Original Memoirs, Written During the Great Civil War: Being the Life of Sir Henry Slingsby* (Edinburgh, 1806), pp. 339–46; Ioshua Sprigge, *Anglia Rediviva: Englands Recovery* (London, 1647), p. 155.

effects of everyday afflictions. Medicine could do little for Fairfax's chronic gout, and who cannot sympathise with Sir Richard Grenville, who wrote one cold January that he had lain 'all this night, coughing and sneezing, with a violent cold, which ... makes me both head sick, and stomach sick'.[21]

If the military effects of sickness were clear, its nature often was not. Plague and typhus were great hazards, but while plague was normally identifiable its incidence was, relatively, restricted and sporadic. It took its toll, for example, on civilians and soldiers in besieged Bristol, Pontefract and Oxford, and attacked both besiegers and marching armies.[22] Nonetheless other less certainly identifiable diseases wrought more havoc; of these, typhus was probably the greatest killer, but while we may be reasonably sure that references to spotted fever mean typhus it is less certain, although probable, that it was the 'New disease' of Fairfax's army of 1645 and the 'ordinary raging disease' of Maurice's. A whole range of dysenteric diseases remain unspecific and extremely common. Other diagnoses can be accepted with fair confidence, as in cases of soldiers sick of smallpox or consumption, but much was lumped together under the general head of great and contagious disease.[23]

In practice, at the regimental level, surgeons and apothecaries confronted a mixed bag of ailments. A surgeon's bill for Colonel Pickering's regiment in 1644 listed twenty-four men 'sick both of fevers and fluxes' against fifteen with 'wounds', a category that included ulcers, scurvy, and 'impostumes' on the feet. Only ten of the fifteen were unequivocal battle casualties, with flesh wounds and shattered bones.[24] Epidemics or major engagements tipped the balance of cases heavily towards sickness or wounds, but generally civil-war medical men conducted a very mixed practice.

The word 'cure' recurs with notable and perhaps surprising frequency in writings such as Wiseman's and in accounts rendered by and paid to practitioners, further evidence of the activist and optimistic character of their approach to treatment. Death rates in action were of course high, but the chances of those who survived initial trauma in combat and escaped the more virulent and probably more dangerous epidemic diseases were

---

[21] Bodl., MS Clarendon, 27, fo. 3.

[22] Bodl., MS Add. D.114, fo. 101; William Salt Library, Salt MS 550/23; *A Brief Relation of the Taking of Bridgewater ... Together with ... the Delivering up of Pontefract Castle* (London, 1645), p. 6; for identification of plague, see Paul Slack, *The Impact of Plague in Tudor and Stuart England* (London, 1985), pp. 25–26, 64–65, 275–76.

[23] PRO, SP 28/25, fo. 335; 28/26, fo. 29; Exeter, Devon Record Office (DRO), Seymour MS 1392 M/L 1643/61; Slack, *Impact of Plague*, pp. 72–73, 98, 120–21.

[24] PRO, SP 28/18, fos. 140–40v; 28/21, fo. 54; 28/23, fos. 457, 458, [480].

better than we might have expected. Records from a royalist hospital set up in 1643 for the Dartmouth garrison suggest that although cures were slow the death rate was slight. Over a six-week period from October to early December thirty-five men were brought in; in that time only two or three 'went out' cured, but only two men and a boy died. The Bristol hospital similarly sent men back to service cured, while the records of farmed-out care of soldiers of the Eastern Association in 1644 give a similar impression, with their references to those 'that was sick and now sent home' and bills for men well enough to rejoin their regiments. Even an apothecary's request to attach the wages of ungrateful soldiers who left without paying for his medicines reflected successful cures.[25]

(b) Ministering to victims

If professional expertise was to achieve good long-term recovery rates it needed the comfort, cleanliness and solicitude that enlightened practition-ers and administrators hoped to achieve. Their provision, in the day-to-day life of the sick, was largely in the hands of non-professionals, many hired from local populations to meet current needs.

Such long-term care sometimes took place in hospitals but was often a kind of putting-out system, a form of domestic industry. The military hospital as a permanent organisation set up to house the sick did not exist, although the Savoy hospital in London was adapted for care of wounded soldiers in 1642 and in 1648 Ely House was converted for this purpose.[26] In 1642 parliament had optimistically hoped that all its wounded soldiers could be handled at the Savoy, but its two hundred beds were soon swamped, and numbers and need for local care forced makeshift arrange-ments whereby existing buildings were pressed into service. Sometimes, as at St Bartholomew's and St Thomas's in London, military victims could be sent to civilian institutions, but the war demanded many on-the-spot, short-term solutions. The results were erratic. In Oxford an impressive system providing for acute care, convalescence and quarantine was established but was often overwhelmed by demand. Even at the Savoy, under parliament's immediate eye, care often fell short. In November 1647 its 'poor wounded Soldiers' were 'ready to starve', and a month later, in hard weather, money was so far in arrears that there was no wood to warm them. On that occasion parliament itself ultimately took remedial action, but in most cases provision of care was the responsibility of army

---

[25] DRO, Seymour MSS 1392 M/L 1643/8, 41; PRO, SP 28/18, fo. 140v; 28/19, fo. 313; 28/21, fos. 44, 56; 28/23, fo. 134.

[26] *Commons' Journals (CJ)*, II, 847; David Stewart, 'Some early military hospitals', *Journal of the Society for Army Historical Research*, 28, 1950, 174–75.

commanders and local committees.[27] They provided a remarkably comprehensive safety net for the sick and wounded, but temporary hospitals such as that established at Bristol in 1645 could not meet all needs, nor were they always the best solution, notably when casualties were low or scattered. Hence the dependence on the ministrations of freelance attendants, of whom 'Parliament Joan', nurse and spy, was one of the more picturesque.[28]

The royalist hospital in Dartmouth offers an example of the institutional approach. There a surgeon, Richard Irish, supervised care of soldiers and received payment for his labour and for medical supplies for his chest, all under the watchful eye of John Thomasin, the garrison's methodical paymaster and accountant. The pay of the women attendants who looked after the men was low, but expenditure on food and supplies was generous. Soldiers were supplied with candles, shot pots, spoons, platters and chamber pots. Their diet consisted not only of beer, bread, butter, mutton and soup, but also sugar, prunes, pepper, fruit, salt pork and pies.[29] The effort to adapt diet to need was not an isolated case; Hesilrige, for example, supplied his sick Scottish prisoners with 'very good' mutton and veal broth, and milk especially brought in and boiled with water or bean flower, 'the physitians holding it exceeding good for recovery of their health'.[30] Dartmouth offered a more interesting menu than the north of England in late October and there, more happily than for the Scots, the result of surgeon's and attendant's care, equipment and diet was a gratifying recovery rate.

The alternative putting-out system recruited involuntary hosts through forced quartering or made more voluntary, contractual arrangements with landlords and attendants. The first method was unpopular, and placed even heavier burdens on the poor than did ordinary quartering of the healthy. In 1643 the poor of Chester were ready to desert their homes to

[27] Rushworth, *Historical Collections*, VII, pp. 870, 928; Stewart, 'Some early military hospitals', p. 175; for Oxford see BL, Harl. MSS 6804, 6851, 6852 passim.

[28] G. E. Manwaring, *The Flower of England's Garland* (London, [1936]), pp. 76–79; *Calendar of... the Committee for Advance of Money, 1642–1656* (London, 1888), I, pp. 517–18; *CJ*, v, 334; Historical Manuscripts Commission (HMC), *Thirteenth report*, Appendix, Part I, *The Manuscripts of the Duke of Portland*, I (London, 1891), p. 309; Firth, *Cromwell's Army*, pp. 258–61.

[29] DRO, Seymour MSS 1392 M/L 1643/8, 27, 38, 41, 67; the women's daily rate was under 3*d.*; cf. 2*s.* a day for each of the regimental surgeon's mates, ibid., 1643/67. For Thomasin (or Thomasius) see I. Palfrey, 'The Royalist war effort revisited: Edward Seymour and the royalist garrison at Dartmouth, 1643–44', *Report & Transactions. Devonshire Assoc. for the Advancement of Science*, 123, 1991, 41–55.

[30] 'Letter from Sir Arthur Hesilrige', pp. 343–44. Hesilrige also provided coals, straw, and 'old women ... to look to' the sick. Ibid., pp. 342–44. See also Nellie J. M. Kerling, 'A seventeenth century hospital matron: Margaret Blague (Matron of St. Bartholomew's Hospital, 1643–1675)', *Transactions of the London & Middlesex Archaeological Society*, 22, part 3, 1970, 30–36. I am grateful to Paul Hardacre for leading me to Matron Blague and 'Parliament Joan'.

avoid the burden.[31] Parliament's quartering of wounded cavalrymen in the country around Bristol in 1645 elicited similar reluctance, for good reasons: 'disquiet of theyr houses, distruction of theyr beddinge, linnen, and consumption of theyr fiering', all made more unendurable by the severity of the men's wounds. Parliament's commissioners congratulated themselves that at least they had 'paied in money for the most part', but the remainder had still to be settled, as did replacement of household goods, food and fuel. A soldier's pay was supposed to cover his maintenance while sick, while attendants received pay for labour, but arrears were as common for the sick as for the sound, and the poor burdened with their care were ill equipped to sustain non-payment.[32]

Contractual care also brought difficulties to the poor who cared for the poor, although their grievances appear to have been sympathetically treated if they could get a hearing. Cicely Plaskett, a poor widow with three children, was to receive 6d. a day for nursing a soldier and his wife, both very sick. After two weeks without payment she petitioned the Cambridge committee, explaining that she was in want and could forbear no longer. They promptly paid the 6s. 6d. due to her. The records of parliament's army in East Anglia contain many similar cases in which sums were small and recipients humble; the kind of bulk consignment for which Judith Massey was paid £10 for 150 soldiers wounded at the siege of York is exceptional.[33]

The economic effects of care for the sick were diffuse but considerable. Victims' sufferings brought cash to poor village women in yet another variation on the swings and roundabouts of civil war. Their care clearly injected significant amounts into some local economies through accretions of small payments. On a larger scale, surviving accounts for the Savoy and Ely House in the 1650s indicate the diversity of labour and goods that had to be paid for. Patients were supplied with clothing, from shirts to dimity caps. Coals, brooms and mops had to be bought, besides drugs, cows to provide milk, earthen vessels for surgeons, faggots to boil fomentations, lime for laundry, and lavender and sweet herbs to 'sweeten' the washed linen. Some labour payments were for relatively skilled and expensive operations, such as monthly cleaning and repair of stoves. Others went to cleaners, porters, water-bearers and 'watchers' over the sick, and for necessary but unattractive tasks, low in pay and status, such as cleansing the surgery room and the house of office and emptying close stools.

[31] BL, Harl. MS 2135, fo. 9, and see fos. 55, 57.

[32] HMC, *Portland MSS*, I, 309; PRO, SP 28/21, fo. 46; 28/23, fos. 134, 166, 361; and see e.g. 28/26, fos. 5, 317v.

[33] PRO, SP 28/19, fo. 333; 28/25, fo. 137; for similar examples of small-scale payments see e.g. SP 28/21, fos. 44, 65; 28/26, fo. 317v.

Laundry, done on a large scale, appears to have provided an opening for female entrepreneurship, for although some was done in small, individual batches, a few women acted as regular, large-scale middlemen between hospital and laundresses.[34]

Such payments were specifically due to war: recipients performed services that would not otherwise have been called for. Others represent 'displacement' income. Some of the women who nursed soldiers may already have been accustomed to nursing civilians, but demand – although irregular and unpredictable – increased, and even established hospitals needed extra hands.[35] Other payments directly substituted war-related for peacetime sources of income, as when existing inns were used to house the wounded. In April 1644, for example, the Cambridge committee paid 14s. towards six weeks' quarter of a sick soldier at the Katherine Wheel, and five men from the same company were distributed between the Eagle, the Black Boy, the White Horse and the Three Blackbirds.[36] Such payments represented income from war, as did payment to reluctant private hosts, even if the overall economic gain was sometimes problematic. The choice of public or private spaces, of institutionalised care or private nursing by strangers or relatives (such as wives who came to care for their husbands), was largely an *ad hoc* matter dependent on the availability of accommodation and personnel rather than one of policy and administrative principle. The result, however, was that care was not a segregated activity that took place behind hospital walls, but one that was visible and integrated into the fabric of civilian society through labour, lodging and payment.

It was also an activity that reflected the contemporary sense of communal and personal obligation. To be ill and suffering through service to the cause constituted a moral claim for special consideration although it brought no formal entitlement to aid. Public obligation mingled with professional solidarity, with simple compassion, with noblesse oblige and the ties binding patron and client, which often extended beyond those between officer and man to civilian relationships interrupted but not cancelled by war. Public and military obligation was evident, for example, in concern for the sick who could not be moved with the army; they were not abandoned but left with guards and provision for their welfare, while surrender treaties after sieges normally contained provisions for the continued care of the sick and wounded of the defeated side.[37] It was, as

---

[34] PRO, SP 28/141A, fos. 1, 3, 5, 35, 37–38, 85–86, 126–27.
[35] Kerling, 'Seventeenth century hospital matron', p. 33.
[36] PRO, SP 28/23, fo. 158; 28/25, fo. 335.
[37] Edward Walker, 'His Majesty's happy progress ... 1644', in Edward Walker, *Historical Discourses, Upon Several Occasions* (London, 1705), pp. 106, 115; *Articles of Agreement betweene*

armies before and since have realised, prudent for it to be known that they did not abandon their own.

Promises about the wounded were as imperfectly kept as other terms of surrender-treaties, but the important point was the combination of intent, continued efforts by both sides to enforce, and refusal officially to abandon victims, one's own or the enemy's, to neglect or cruelty. It was sensible to provide medical care for enemy prisoners if one wished to assure similar attention to men of one's own side. To leave a prisoner unattended to die of wounds was grounds for obloquy, while active cruelty was an unqualified atrocity. Professional and moral obligation, which was not limited to officers but extended to ordinary soldiers, was joined to considerations of utilitarian reciprocity. It was important to convince the other side that their wounded had been well cared for. So a parliamentarian officer anxiously assured his royalist counterpart, after the death of a prisoner, that it was 'not by want of care or conveniency ... he being accommodated at Mr. Murry the surgeon's house, who neglected not any thing for his recovery'. And a royalist surgeon wrote to a parliamentarian, 'It is very well known how careful I have ever been in dressing your wounded men whensoever they have fallen into our hands.'[38]

The greatest, most conscientious care was of course owed to victims of one's own side. In their case the obligations of public debt, professional responsibility and compassion joined forces. So parliament's commissioners in Bristol urged the House of Commons in 1645 'to reach forth [their] arme of comfort' on behalf of 'these poore men', wounded in the capture of the city and now 'in extremities', who were 'noe lesse patient in theyr sufferings and constant in theyr resolutions, then they were couragious in theyr undertakings'.[39] In the same vein, Prince Rupert urged 'all charitable and well-disposed persons' of Chester to contribute to the relief of their wounded soldiers. Individual cases also elicited compassion and special treatment, as in the case of John Barton, in debt and 'in distress for moneys', and sick of smallpox. A petitioner wrote on his behalf, 'I conceive his necessity great, though I know not what is his due, yet you may be pleased to compassionate him.' The 'poor fellow's' quarter was paid and he was given '6 shillings beside'.[40] Particular connection helped to warm charity and speed payment, as in Essex's special concern for members of

His Excellency Prince Maurice, and the Earle of Stamford upon the Delivery of the City of Excester (London, 1643), p. 1; Rushworth, *Historical Collections*, v, p. 266; S. Sheppard, *The Yeare of Jubile* (London, 1646), pp. 31, 64; PRO, SP28/26, fo. 5.

[38] BL, Additional (Add.) MS 11, 332, fo. 105; BL, Egerton MS 787, fo. 65v.

[39] HMC, *Portland MSS*, I, 309.

[40] Warburton, *Rupert*, II, p. 432; PRO, SP 28/25, fo. 335.

his army after Lostwithiel. And simple pity sometimes moved even official hearts.[41]

The sick and wounded merited the protections and kindnesses due to other weak and powerless persons like women, children and the old, and these traditional Christian and moral obligations were reinforced by considerations of professional reciprocity. There were limits to obligation, however. We are not talking here of a system of entitlements, by which soldiers had a legislated right to care or to compensation for injury beyond regular pay. Rather, there was an attempt to respond to needs that were recognised both practically, in the hope of sustaining troop morale and loyalty and of returning men to active service, and morally, as part of a general duty to aid the afflicted and a special duty to those who suffered for one's own cause. Efforts on behalf of individual soldiers normally resulted in payment, in whole or part, of what was already legally due to them, while charitable collections addressed themselves to relief for urgent necessities. The extra payments required – for medicine, nursing, surgery, laundry, special diet – were channelled through army services that, stumbling but conscientious, both sides set up. Charity and obligation to those disabled on a long-term basis, for whom today special provision would be made, remained sporadic and uninstitutionalised, operating through the mixture of public and private charity, of *ad hoc* and systematised effort, characteristic of other forms of seventeenth-century social welfare. In the shorter term care for sick and wounded soldiers demonstrated again the mixed and transitional state of military organisation, in which soldiers were in theory paid to support themselves in normal circumstances, but in which an infrastructure, still rudimentary and not yet effectively centralised, was developed to deliver emergency and exceptional care. It also revealed the mixed concept of responsibility. The state (whether royal or parliamentary), the patron, the officer and the charitable Christian all bore a share of the obligation to care for sick and wounded victims of war.

II. THE DEAD

The dead called up many of the same moral obligations as the living, but they also touched a primeval nerve. The basic need to care for their bodies joined a Christian obligation to despatch them to their maker with appropriate religious rites and professional tribute to honour and courage. The Bible commanded pious and respectful burial of the dead after battle. The fate of the defeated should arouse compassion, not rejoicing, declared

[41] PRO, SP 28/18, fos. 112, 130, 131; 28/19, fos. 20, 22; 28/26, fos. 29, 32.

a clerical theorist of war, who quoted with revulsion the remark of Charles IX of France after the massacre of Saint Bartholomew in 1572: '[O]h how good is the smell of the dead enemies.'[42] In practice the degree of respect with which the dead were treated reflected the size of the problem on any given occasion.

Although some precise figures have recently been advanced, the total number of war dead must remain uncertain. Published figures for particular engagements were usually partisan and incomplete. A parliamentarian set 800 royalist deaths (excluding Irish) at Naseby against 300 parliamentary common soldiers killed; an equally partisan royalist declared that the 'whole number on both sides slaine was conceived not to exceed 400'.[43] Creative accounting was not the only reason for such differences. Whenever possible the defeated carried off their own dead, as at Cheriton in 1644, where the royalists 'fetch'd off cart-loads of dead men, and some they buried, and some they carried with them'. Battlefield estimates rarely took account of the wounded who died later, like the drummer found by Nehemiah Wharton 'two miles of, with his arme shot of, and lay a dieinge'. Scale too, added to difficulties, when the dead were buried *en masse*. After a bloody victory at Bolton, Prince Rupert caused '[t]he dead bodies ... to be buried in the trenches throwing the mud walls on them', and after Hopton Heath it was claimed that the parliamentarians 'threw hundreds ... into pooles and pitts'.[44] Individually, some estimates were more reliable than others, and those compiled for the use of one's own side were more trustworthy than those disseminated for partisan motives. The country people who came out to bury the dead, for obvious reasons of public health and profit, provided some of the most accurate totals for battle deaths, as in their body counts after Marston Moor.[45] In general, however, reports of battle deaths are consistent only in their discrepancies, while the problem of total war mortality is even more vexing, for combat deaths accounted for only a part of military deaths, and they in turn constituted only a part of all war deaths, just as the wounded were only a part of the larger body who grew sick through war. Nevertheless it is clear that England did not

[42] Richard Bernard, *The Bible-battells: Or, The Sacred Art Military* ([London], 1629), p. 249.
[43] Compare figures given by Josiah Ricraft, *A Survey of England's Champions* (London, 1647), pp. 116–25, and *Mercurius Belgicus* (n.p., 1646), sig. Bv–B2, C3v, E2v, and 17–20 Sept. 1643, n.p.; and see Austin Woolrych, *Battles of the English Civil War* (London, 1966), p. 135. Cf. Charles Carlton, *Going to the Wars. The Experience of the British Civil Wars 1638–1651* (London, 1992), pp. 204–6.
[44] [E.A.], *A Fuller Relation of the Great Victory ... at Alsford* (London, 1644), pp. [2, 5]; BL, Harl. MS 2125, fo. 140v; [Nehemiah Wharton], 'Letters from a subaltern officer of the earl of Essex's army', *Archaeologia*, 35, 1853, 316; 'The battle of Hopton Heath 1643', *Collections for a History of Staffordshire* (1936), p. 184.
[45] Rushworth, *Historical Collections*, v, p. 635.

approach the Continental carnage of the Thirty Years War, either in the tallies for individual engagements or in cumulative effect.[46]

The dead did not present a purely statistical problem. The duty to give them proper burial was older than Christianity. In the Civil War, religious, professional and atavistic obligation joined with hygiene to require prompt and when possible respectful disposal of bodies. The carts that carried them off did so to allow honourable burial by their fellows as well as to deprive the enemy of information. Civilian victims of military action were given ordinary Christian burial, but for soldiers military observance joined religious whenever practicable. One of a victorious general's first duties, after he had given thanks to God, was 'to have ... his Dead honourably buried'. Ritual asserted solidarity of the living with the dead; it also, like a good wake, heartened survivors.[47] It was a public recognition that the soldier had value beyond cannon fodder, by which superiors and fellows paid tribute not only to his Christian soul but also to his human and soldierly worth, while friends offered a last office of love. After Sir William Campion was killed at Colchester in 1648 a friend wrote to his widow:

> He was buried with as much decency & honour as the place & suddenness could afford to a gentleman & soldier of his quality & merit and with as much general sorrow of all as if everyone had been his particular friend.[48]

After an unsuccessful assault on Donnington castle parliamentarians negotiated a truce to retrieve the dead, and spent the next day in solemnising their burial with drums, trumpets, volleys of shot, 'and now and then a Psalme'.[49]

The respect that could be preserved towards individuals and small groups of victims was overwhelmed by large disasters. For obvious reasons, burials were as quick as possible, often on the battlefield itself; the morning after the first battle of Newbury John Gwynn could already count scores of graves in the field. After Naseby they were so hastily dug and so shallow 'that the bodies, in a short time, became very offensive'.[50] Some at

---

[46] Cf. 4,500 total dead at Marston Moor, 1644 (the most deadly battle of the English Civil War), and 7,500 Spanish alone at Rocroi, 1643; ironically and uncharacteristically, the total number of troops engaged at Marston Moor (c. 46,000) exceed that at Rocroi (c. 41,000). Woolrych, *Battles of the English Civil War*, p. 78; David G. Chandler, *Atlas of Military Strategy* (New York, 1980), p. 28; Simon Adams, 'Tactics or politics? "The military revolution" and the Hapsburg hegemony, 1525–1648', in John A. Lynn, ed., *Tools of War. Instruments, Ideas, and Institutions of Warfare, 1445–1871* (Urbana, 1990), p. 32.

[47] Orrery, *Art of War*, p. 205; PRO, SP 28/141A, fos. 5, 38 (for issues of beer to accompany soldiers' burials).

[48] Oxford, Worcester College, Clarke MSS, cxiv, fo. 47.

[49] *Mercurius Aulicus*, 27 Sept. 1644, p. 1173 [sic, properly 1181].

[50] BL, Add. MS 11,810, fo. 24v.; John Mastin, *The History and Antiquities of Naseby* (Cambridge, 1792), p. 117.

least of the victims were buried in a communal grave. Yet even when circumstances forced unceremonious and mass disposal, meliorating courtesies survived bipartisanly. Class and status still had claims in death, and after Marston Moor Sir Charles Lucas – like the Constable of France after Agincourt – was allowed to 'book the dead' so that the better sort could be reserved for more dignified burial.[51]

The ceremony of sending off was a last mark of the respect due in life, and officers were buried accordingly. The day after Colonel Lister was killed at Tadcaster in 1642, 'My Lord Fairfax with the rest of the Commanders laide him in his Grave' before marching on. When Captain Horsey was killed by a sharpshooter at Sherborne, he was given a military funeral in the abbey where his ancestors were buried.[52] Money for such last honours was found out of war funds; the 'disbursements for Major Jackson's funeral' appeared alongside the disposition of proceeds from cattle seized in the Cheshire countryside. The expense of burial varied according to the degree of honour required, which in turn was related to rank, but basic costs did not vary greatly. A grave could be dug for a shilling, and different prices for shrouds – commonly from 2 to 5 shillings – do not seem to reflect the status of their wearers.[53] Insistence on the obligation to provide, if possible, 'decent' Christian burial for all, and acceptance of the right of 'considerable' men to special privilege, were yet other means by which social continuities were asserted in war.

Every effort was made to bury one's own, not to leave them to the enemy, and courtesies to this end were mutual. So Hopton wrote to Waller after the engagement at Alton, 'I desire you, if Colonel Boles be living to propound a fit exchange; if dead, that you will send me his corps.'[54] When a parliamentary prisoner died at Chester, a royalist lieutenant-colonel wrote to the parliamentary commander:

> If you desire his corpse it shall be brought to a convenient distance from my fort, to be delivered to where you shall send for it, upon notice from you this night in what manner or condition, either coffined or otherwise you will have him sent, it shall be performed.[55]

[51] Woolrych, *Battles of the English Civil War*, p. 78; *Henry V*, IV, vii. 76–79.

[52] Henry Foulis, *An Exact and True Relation of a Bloody Fight … before Tadcaster* (London, 1642), p. 6; A. R. Bayley, *The Great Civil War in Dorset 1642–1660* (Taunton, 1910), p. 283.

[53] *The Letter Books of Sir William Brereton*, ed. R. N. Dore, vol. 1 (Record Society of Lancaster and Cheshire, 123, 1984), p. 256; PRO, SP 28/126, fos. 35, 36; DRO, Seymour MSS 1392 M/L 1643/8, 41.

[54] John Vicars, *Gods Arke overtopping the Worlds Waves* (London, 1646), p. 99, in John Vicars, *Magnalia Dei Anglicana* (London, 1646).

[55] BL, Add. MS 11,332, fo. 105.

Most soldiers were buried in church or field where they died, but the eminent dead might hope to lie with their ancestors. Efforts to achieve this end proclaimed, by their very visibility, that civility and religion had not been abandoned. In 1645, after the royalist defeat at Rowton Heath, a parliamentary colonel informed Lord Byron in Chester that he held the body of the earl of Lichfield, and both sides then gave young Lord Bernard Stuart his full measure of honour:

> with great civility [the colonel] brought the Corpse with a guard of foot and forty horse to a place agreed upon ... without the walls of the City, where [Byron] met it: with such Noblemen and Gentlemen as were in the garrison and an equal number of horse and so conveyed it into the City where [he] caused it to be embalmed and kept, till the Duke of Richmond should otherwise dispose of it, which, afterwards (upon rendition of the Town) he sent for to Oxford, and there interred it with two other noble gentlemen his Brothers, slain in his Majestie's service.[56]

The transportation of the body to Oxford was itself a bipartisan recognition of courtesies due to the eminent dead, for it depended upon parliamentary permission.

The story is not one of unalloyed mutual respect. Sir John Gell refused access to the surgeon sent to embalm the earl of Northampton's body to preserve it for future rites unless the royalists, in exchange, surrendered all the prisoners and spoil of Hopton Heath. When this blackmail failed, the body was 'carried ... in triumph through several counties, till it corrupted, and bur[ied] ... without ceremony'.[57] Rough humour and vindictive satisfaction also survived, as in the newsletter that rejoiced that the victors of Leicester had so quickly become the defeated of Naseby; their friends might now 'think it an honour, if they hear a Turfe was cast upon their Noses, that the worms might feed upon their carkasses.' At Colchester parliamentary troops, in a mob frenzy, desecrated the recently buried bodies of women of the family of Sir Charles Lucas, their royalist opponent.[58] The satisfaction of such popular reversals of respect and decency lay in part in their denial of observance of honour; the levelling effect of death was potentially subversive. The profit to be wrested from the dead also worked against the maintenance of honour and of human

---

[56] 'John Byron's account of the siege of Chester 1645–1646', *The Cheshire Sheaf*, 4th ser., 6, 1971, 11.

[57] Warburton, *Rupert*, II, pp. 137–8; G. E. C[okayne], *The Complete Peerage*, 13 vols. (1910–59), IX, p. 680; Edward Hyde, earl of Clarendon, *The History of the Rebellion and Civil Wars in England*, 3 vols. (Oxford, 1702–4), II, p. 116.

[58] *The Weekly Account* (XXIV Week, 1645, 11–18 June), sig. Aa; HMC, *Twelfth Report*, Appendix, part XI (London, 1891), 'Beaufort MSS', p. 28.

dignity, for they were routinely stripped by civilians and soldiers. Army regulations prohibited predation from the dead of one's own side, with limited effect, but takings from enemy bodies were a customary battlefield perquisite.[59] Nevertheless, attempts such as Gell's to exploit death for gain by holding bodies to ransom aroused revulsion: his was an 'unparraleld and unchristian' act betraying ignorance of 'the honner of a souldier'.[60]

Wilful cruelty and neglect of the suffering living were ethically abhorrent, but when cruelty, neglect and mockery were extended to the dead they aroused an ancient horror as well as Christian distress. Furthermore, failure to respect the dead denied the bond between soldiers as well as that between Christians. It seemed to foreshadow withdrawal of a proper respect to the living and a return to barbarism, and to betoken the overthrow of religion and civility which, to many Englishmen, was always frighteningly possible and which was brought closer by war.

Such concerns have not vanished. Mass burials still arouse dismay, and mockery and mutilation of the dead still call up fears of a return to a barbaric past. Medical care too remains a chancy and uneven business, but its variations were far greater in seventeenth-century England. I have argued that care was better, more extensive, more conscientious, more efficient than has previously been recognised. Nevertheless practice too often failed to live up to aspiration, and even at its best still fills us with pity and horror for those subjected to its ministrations. Yet for all these failings, commitment to care for the military victims of war was, like respect for the souls and bodies of the dead, an affirmation of humane and social obligation. Reciprocal recognition of that obligation contributed to the maintenance of a sense of residual community among warring Englishmen.

---

[59] *Lawes and Ordinances ... Essex*, p. [12]; Mastin, *Naseby*, p. 117; John Vicars, *The Burning-Bush not Consumed* (London, 1646), p. 34, in *Magnalia Dei Anglicana; Mercurius Aulicus*, 27 Sept. 1644, p. 1173 [sic, properly 1181].

[60] 'Battle of Hopton Heath', p. 183; Clarendon, *History*, II, p. 116.

6

'A bastard kind of militia', localism, and tactics in the second civil war

SARAH BARBER

In the spring of 1648, the English parliament prepared for a new war. It had spent the previous year trying to secure a peace settlement and disband its armies. The Scots were about to march south again, now in alliance with King Charles I and, in England and Wales, people anxious to see an end to their hardships rose up in armed frustration. Parliament strengthened strategic garrisons, such as Berwick, and 'resolving to reinforce the militia of each county', it 'sent down some of their members to give life to the preparations'.[1] On 25 May, the Commons proposed that the Derby House Committee issue commissions for the raising of county forces by persons of known fidelity to the parliament. The measure did not pass, though an exception was made in the case of Edmund Ludlow's county of Wiltshire.[2] Ludlow agreed to raise two artillery regiments and one of cavalry.

Gentry frustration at the difficulties which persisted in obtaining a lasting settlement covered the whole range of political opinions. At one end of the spectrum was royalist revivalism: there were armed demonstrations against taxation levels, calls for the New Model Army to be disbanded and for a personal treaty with Charles. These were particularly a feature of Wales and the south-eastern counties of England.[3] At the other end of the spectrum was direct action taken by county gentlemen who were among the most hawkish of the parliamentarians. Their role is intriguing, under-researched, patchily-documented. They volunteered

---

[1] Edmund Ludlow, *Memoirs of Edmund Ludlow*, ed. C. H. Firth, 2 vols. (Oxford, 1894), I, p. 187; Jonathan Scott, *Algernon Sidney and the English Republic* (Cambridge, 1988), p. 90.

[2] *Commons' Journals* (*CJ*), v, 573, 579, confirmed by the House in September. Wiltshire may have been excepted, possibly because it was strategically positioned between the royalist risings in the counties to the west of London and those in south Wales. The royalists' joining forces would have made the risings harder to quell.

[3] Robert Ashton, *Counter-revolution: The Second Civil War and its Origins, 1646–8* (New Haven and London, 1994), pp. 197ff.

auxiliary forces, with the claim that they were support troops for the more 'official' struggle conducted by Fairfax's New Model and the militia raised by parliamentary commissioners. This essay looks at three such men; the MPs Thomas, Lord Grey of Groby, John Pyne and Henry Marten. These are the examples for which we have the most evidence.

During June 1648, Thomas, Lord Grey of Groby raised troops in Leicestershire: according to Ludlow, 'about three thousand horse and foot to preserve the country from plunder, and to take all possible advantages against the enemy'.[4] The troop was imbued with the principles of its commander. Grey had occupied the shire seat in the Commons since 1640, when he had been a mere seventeen, and at nineteen he was created commander of the Midland Association, as the only peer in the area to declare for parliament. Until the mid-1640s he had been a loyal supporter of his patron, Essex, but at an indeterminable point, somewhere around 1646, he was converted to sectarian religion and his politics veered sharply towards those who were hawkish towards the king, the Scots and the Presbyterian faction. Therefore, at the end of June 1648, 'loyal citizens' of the east midlands addressed three dispatches to parliament, making great play of Grey's efforts to raise a militia force. The first tract claimed that Leicestershire was so forward in the promotion of common safety and in

> such a formidable posture, that I think they may be the patterne to the rest of the Counties of England, for they have chosen their Officers, and formed their Regiments, *viz.* six Regiments of Horse and Dragoones, three hundred in each; the Foot are not as yet completed, my Lord *Grey* is chosen Commander in chiefe, so that now there wants nothing but power from the House, to inable my Lord *Grey* to give Commissions to the officers thus chosen by the Countrey.[5]

Rutland and Northamptonshire vowed to join Leicestershire in a new Association, in which the petitioners believed, with unwarranted optimism, both Presbyterians and Independents would join. A second petition was more specific.[6] Grey had come down from the House in order to settle the

---

[4] Ludlow, *Memoirs*, I, p. 202.

[5] *Two Letters sent out of Scotland ... with another Letter written from a Friend concerning the affaires in Leicester, Rutland and Northamptonshire*, 24 June, BL Thomason Tracts E449(24), p. 5. Another at E449(29), dated 22 June, repeats the same material except for the inclusion of Market Harborough. When dates to printed pamphlets are given, these are the dates on which they were acquired by Thomason.

[6] *A Petition presented at a Common-Hall in London on satturday last concerning the Kings Majesty*, 26 June 1648, E449(35). This is sometimes included in the lists of pro-personal treaty petitions, because it appends a statement made at a common hall in London to that effect, but it is, in the main, a news letter of the activities of Grey and opposition to royalist and Scottish activities.

militia, in accordance with the decision of the 'well affected party of that County' to be the 'ways and meanes, as might put the said county into such a posture, as should be for the defence of themselves, and render them most serviceable to the peace and safety of the Kingdome'.[7] The third petition was masterminded by the same people. Rutland and Northamptonshire – 'other Counties ... which have formerly felt the miserie of a Civill War' – were continuing to establish their forces on the same model. These were localised bands, mustered by a highly politicised, committed, 'well-affected' section of the population. Initially claiming to act in self-defence, they encouraged recruitment through radical political principles and elected a commander from amongst their number. Only then did they seek approval from the authorities in London and request permission to commission junior officers.[8]

During the first war, Grey had been accused of being too tied to his county.[9] The charge was repeated during the second war. In July 1648, royalist forces around Newark in Nottinghamshire were tackled by the troops of Colonel Rossiter.[10] Only when they fled into Leicestershire did Grey 'fall upon them ... and so finished their scattering'.[11] A month later, Cromwell informed the Committee for Both Kingdoms of the dire situation at the siege of Pontefract, and tried to encourage Grey to take his Leicestershire forces north:

> You cannot but know how necessary it is that our forces in the North should receive all the increase we can give them, so that the work there may be carried on with effect, speed, and reputation, for if that be so done the distempers in other places will be more easily calmed. We enclose a copy of ours to the Committee of Leicestershire and desire you to promote the sending of as many horse as may be spared with safety to your county.[12]

---

[7] Ibid., p. 3.

[8] Ludlow cites a force of 3,000; the letter of June talked of 1,800 cavalry. The only evidence we have of junior officers is a Colonel Wayte, to whom, Ludlow says, Hamilton surrendered on 22 August. Hamilton says he surrendered to Lambert. Wayte was described as 'an officer of the Leicestershire party'. There is no evidence that the Leicestershire troops were paid by the state and Cromwell's forces also complained of lack of provision whilst they were in the county; Ludlow, *Memoirs*, I, p. 202; S. R. Gardiner, *History of the Great Civil War*, 4 vols. (Windrush Press reprint, 1987), IV, p. 178; *The Moderate*, E457(21); Lucy Hutchinson, *Memoirs of the Life of Colonel Hutchinson* (London, 1965 edn) p. 255.

[9] Clive Holmes, *The Eastern Association in the English Civil War* (Cambridge, 1974), pp. 73–74.

[10] C. H. Firth and G. Davies, *The Regimental History of Cromwell's Army*, 2 vols. (Oxford, 1940), I, pp. 165–66.

[11] *Calendar of State Papers Domestic* (*CSPD*), 1648–49, p. 168.

[12] *CSPD* p. 236, 8 August 1648, Inter. 24E, pp. 301–2.

Grey returned word to the committee that his forces were at 'great readiness to serve the public' but required £500 for arms, a request which the Committee referred to the Commons.

However, about three weeks later, Grey downplayed the urgency for pay and provision in a letter to Philip Skippon, printed up for wider circulation by the sectarian publisher, Giles Calvert. Although he was ready to serve in 'all our neighbouring Counties', his emotive rhetoric was a potent mixture of localist sentiment and millenarian religion. He attracted the attention of his audience with shire parochialism. These were soldiers who, he said, had demonstrated that 'old English blood [was] boyling afresh in Leicestershire men'. They were fired by zeal for the cause, a sense of community and patriotism for their native soil. A threat to England's liberties was a threat to Leicestershire:

> When we understood that our *proclaimed enemies* (the Scots) were drawing towards us, even to fall upon this Nation when it was weak ... wee tryed what volunteers would appear, which were not a few, that tendred themselves and their own horses, and those that wanted wee horsed upon those that were dissenters, insomuch that ... we have mounted a considerable number for so inconsiderable a County ... not waiting upon the customary way of pay and quarter, which would retard us, and such a work as this.
>
> We had our men so willing to goe forth as if they should finde their *wages in their worke*, yea though in the highest of this harvest, and this unseasonable weather; At our meeting a March being propounded, they cryed, ONE AND ALL.[13]

It was not until early September, however, that the Leicestershire forces reached Pontefract, and only then that the Committee for Both Kingdoms recommended that Grey's plea for maintenance be granted. Two weeks later the Committee was still receiving requests from local commanders, including Grey, that provisions be sent to the parliamentary forces.[14]

Grey did not differ from the New Model Army or the Parliament in believing that the defensive needs of the country were uppermost. There was disagreement about the means to secure this. Two other local militias – in Somerset and Berkshire – proclaimed their solidarity with the New Model Army and (more faintly) with the House of Commons, but they also maintained a real autonomy and used the rhetoric of autonomy. Whilst the New Model and the Parliament struggled to win the war on

---

[13] *Old English Blood boyling afresh in Leicestershire Men*, 28 August 1648, E461(7), p. 2.

[14] *CSPD* 1648–49 p. 269, Inter. 25E pp. 6, 7 and p. 283, 4 and 19 September. The complaints of Cromwell's barefoot soldiers were met. There is no evidence to determine whether Grey's forces received provisions; Gardiner, *History*, IV, p. 178.

the one hand and find a settlement on the other, the autonomous militia was a constant reminder of the revolutionary tendencies within the ranks of their supposed supporters.

The parliamentary cause in Somerset was riven with internicine strife, and the county committee was effectively run by a faction led by John Pyne of Curry Mallet. These divisions made it impossible to appoint one acceptable commissioner to raise militia troops and the county committee levied divisional forces instead. In the summer of 1648 Pyne raised 600 horse and 2,500 foot soldiers to defend his home county.[15] This was a red rag to moderates who had long seen Pyne as an extremist of the demagogic kind. He was said to have used undue influence to ensure that only supporters of his faction held posts on the county committee and had persecuted all who stood in his way, whatever their political persuasion, using and abusing the powers granted to him by parliament.[16] He allegedly enforced *ex officio* oaths, led an unrepresentative cabal on the committee, and 'mutinously and seditiously by power carried and indeavoured to carry *Elections of parliament men* for his favourites, and wilfully disobayed many *Orders, and Ordinances of Parliament*'.

By the spring of 1649 Pyne's closest allies were at the centre of government, and it would therefore seem the most fruitless time for his local opponents to complain of Pyne's actions during the war.[17] Nevertheless, the Presbyterian faction in Somerset chose this moment to reveal the means whereby he had preserved the parliamentary cause from almost certain ruin: 'thousands of the said County, faithfull Servants, and Sufferers, for the King and Parliament' accused Pyne of high treason. The articles published by the Somerset men accused their most extreme opponents of military incompetence and cowardice. The regiment which Pyne had raised in July 1642 – consisting of 500 foot and horse – had been forced to flee by a mere sixty of the enemy's cavalry. In the spring of 1643, another force of 6,000 had been mustered, 'most Horse, well-affected and stout men, and raised great summs of mony', but Pyne had 'run away with the Countries mony before the Enemy (not halfe so many) came within twenty miles of him'.[18] Between 1646 and 1648 he had campaigned for the

---

[15] David Underdown, *Somerset in the Civil War and Interregnum* (Newton Abbot, 1973), p. 148. Pyne was MP for Poole in neighbouring Dorset.

[16] Ashton, *Counter-revolution* pp. 90–92; Underdown, *Somerset*, pp. 125–26, 132 and *passim*.

[17] Ian F. W. Beckett, *The Amateur Military Tradition, 1558–1945* (Manchester, 1991), p. 45; David Underdown, '"Honest" radicals in the counties, 1642–1649', in Donald Pennington and Keith Thomas (eds.), *Puritans and Revolutionaries* (Oxford, 1986), pp. 186–205, 201–5.

[18] *Articles of Treason and high Misimeanours (sic), committed by John Pine of Curry-Mallet, in the county of Somerset*, 2 April 1649, 669.f.14(15), broadsheet, articles 1, 2. Another copy is dated by Thomason, 2 March 1649 at 669.f.13(94).

Anglo-Scottish link to be severed and for a settlement which excluded the king,

> and when we hoped for peace by the late Treaty, whilst it lasted, he declared in the Country, *that the Parliament should make no peace with the King, but that the Kings life should be taken from him.* And for that purpose, he and his confederates have listed and raised divers new forces without the authority of *Pa[r]liament, to alter the fundamentall Lawes and government of the Kingdome, disinherit the King and his issue of the Crowne,* and inslave the free people of *England* to Martiall Law and Government, and the County to his tyranny and violence.[19]

Despite this campaign, Pyne's career continued to flourish under the Commonwealth, although there seems to be no evidence that action was taken against the perpetrators of this particular pamphlet.

A similar activity was being undertaken by Henry Marten around his estates in Berkshire. Marten had had an undistinguished career in charge of a regiment of trained bands. He was first governor of Reading and, after 1644, of Aylesbury,[20] though his contribution to campaigns prior to 1648 had been financial, not military. Nevertheless, in June 1648, he went down to Abingdon to place his county in a state of defence. The committee of the county raised a company of foot soldiers in Reading. These were disbanded and dispersed to serve at Colchester and at the garrison posts of Wallingford and Windsor. Parliament regarrisoned Reading and levied fresh troops, but all this time Marten was told to 'forbear'. He carried on regardless, refusing to return to the Commons. He justified the independence of his actions in a letter to Lenthall: the House would 'rather bee served than waited on', so he would not attend in person.[21] *Mercurius Pragmaticus*, which had a good knowledge of the region to the west of London, reported that Marten was rallying 'the holy tribe of levellers'.[22] He continued his efforts to raise cavalry: 'by the help of some friends & my own care & cost I have gotten up a troop of honest men ... resonably well appointed, notwithstanding the strange obstructions I mett with from those that owed their contrey as much assistance as my self'.[23]

He recruited with the slogan 'freedom and common justice against tyranny and oppression'. *Mercurius Pragmaticus* described the company banner as a motto '[f]or the People's Freedom against all tyrants what-

---

[19] Ibid., article 6.   [20] *CJ*, III, 503.
[21] Bodleian Library (Bod.Lib.), Tanner MS 57, fo. 197, dated August 1648.
[22] *Mercurius Pragmaticus* 6–13 June 1648, E447(5); *Lords' Journals* (*LJ*), x, 302, 3 June 1648; Chris Durston, 'Henry Marten and the High Shoon of Berkshire: the Levellers in Berkshire in 1648' in *Berks Archaeological Journal* 70, 1979–80, 87–95.
[23] Bod.Lib., Tanner MS 57, fo. 197.

soever'.[24] His justification for commissioning a junior officer called Simon Rice was 'by virtue of that right which I was born to as an Englishman and in pursuance of that duty which I owe my said country'.[25] Another officer was the Leveller, William Eyres. Eyres' name had appeared on the key to the cipher with which the activists of 1647 had communicated between army, levellers and MPs. The key was held by Henry Marten.[26] Eyres was probably a yeoman farmer from the village of Pusey, Oxfordshire, which lay immediately to the south of Marten's land. The combination of radical politics and national and local sentiment which fuelled Marten's recruitment found willing adherents amongst the yeomanry on his estates. Some soldiers were already serving with other commanders, but were encouraged to desert and to join his unofficial band by the egalitarian principles which Marten espoused. The author of *Mercurius Elenticus* believed that 'Henry Marten is resolved to level all of Berkshire ... the greatest part of the Agitators of the Army and such others as stand for the doctrine of levelling are come unto him so that within 8 days he is wonderfully encreased, being nigh 1500 strong already'.[27]

In August, agents of the New Model reported to Fairfax that '[t]he House this day (16 August 1648) voted That Mr Martin should be required to attend the service of the House, That Col. Ayres [and] Mr Walrond that were with him bee sumoned in safe Custody, That the Horse raised by them be disbanded [and] restor'd to the parties from whome they were taken'.[28] He seems to have 'borrowed' mounts from malignant sections of the Berkshire gentry because of the dilatoriness of his masters at Westminster. The shortfall in the number of horses required for a cavalry regiment was filled by taking them from travellers. Marten would claim that he was commandeering them as a necessary means to defend the cause, but since his regiment was unauthorised and had no official status, he was guilty of stealing horses.

Arms and ammunition were taken from the houses of local royalist gentry. Several reports related the attacks made on the property of royalist

[24] *Mercurius Pragmaticus* 22–29 August 1648, E461(17), n.p.

[25] Worcester College, Oxford, Clarke MSS cxiv fo. 104b.

[26] BL Add. MS 71532 fo. 23; There may have been two William Eyres. The Leveller, republican activity of captain (later colonel) Eyres throughout the later 1640s and the 1650s, his close friendship with Marten and his political activity with Thomas Scot and John Wildman, point to the same person; Firth and Davies, *Cromwell's Army*, I, pp. 9, 179, 378, II, pp. 528–29, 689; Ian Gentles, *The New Model Army in England, Ireland and Scotland, 1645–1653* (Oxford, 1992), pp. 222 and *passim*.

[27] *Mercurius Elenticus* 23–30 August 1648, E461(20). Underdown adds that Marten welcomed recruits from Wiltshire, Kent and elsewhere, but I have been unable to verify this; Underdown, 'Honest radicals', p. 201.

[28] Worc.Coll., Clarke MSS cxiv fo. 67.

gentlemen and aristocrats such as Lord Craven,[29] Sir Richard Langsmill, Sir Humphrey Forster and Charles Garrard, as well as the more random attacks on travellers. The attack on Forster was described in some detail in a complaint to parliament. The soldiers made two visits to Forster's home in Aldermaston. On the first they 'p[r]tended to be under the comand of one Colonell Ayer and demanded quarter but produced no order'. It is unclear whether they were asked to produce their order and failed to do so, or whether they deliberately did not show it and hoped to brazen it out in the hope that Forster would not demand to see evidence of their authority. Forster was ready to comply, obviously believing these to be soldiers of the New Model, and he showed them Fairfax's order granting him protection for the house. He agreed to provide for the soldiers in other premises. Later that evening whilst Forster's party were at dinner, the troop returned, shot the butler in the hand, ransacked the house and took eight horses 'using uncivill Speeches towards the Parliam[t] [and] disrespecting the generalls proteccon'. So long as Forster thought they were an authorised regiment, he was prepared to yield to army authority, protecting his property as much as he was able. The soldiers, on the other hand, demonstrated that they had no authority from parliament or Fairfax and were 'barbarous and uncivill'.[30] Three 'officers', Captain Waldron,[31] Lieutenant Seymor and Corporal Knowles, were due to appear before Wiltshire assizes for robbery. The soldiers brandished the sword as their source of power, but claimed that the centuries of oppression which the people had suffered by the levying of tithes conveyed their authority.[32]

Marten was aware that his 'levellers' had been reported to have demonstrated a zeal which went beyond the letter of his order, for he attempted to obliterate part of his report to Lenthall. He had initially meant to say that 'if they have exceeded [orders] as I have been informed they have' he would answer them 'very strictly'. He decided better of such

---

[29] To whom Marten was in debt and of whose sequestered estates he had control; University of Leeds, Marten Loder MSS 66/116; 85/32; 90/1.

[30] Bod.Lib., Tanner MS 57/1 fo. 199, 16 August 1648. The Commons ordered the forces to be disbanded on 21 August, CJ, v, 676.

[31] This is likely to be the same man named as Walrond in the report of the New Model agents to Fairfax. The Martens were involved with the royalist, Humphrey Walrond, in Barbados, but a link is highly improbable.

[32] Bod.Lib., Tanner MS 57, fo. 199; Mercurius Pragmaticus, 22–29 August 1648, E461(20). Bulstrode Whitelocke was a guest of Sir Humphrey Forster on the night of this alleged event and made no mention of an incident which one might have expected him to find sufficiently scandalous to include in his diary; Ruth Spalding (ed.), The Diary of Bulstrode Whitelocke 1605–1675 (Oxford, 1990), p. 221. The case does not appear to have come before the Committee for Indemnity, despite the change in the chair from the Presbyterian stalwart, Sir Robert Pye, to the Independent, John Weaver; PRO SP 24/3, pp. 88–89.

a confession and instead offered ignorance – 'I hope they will appear not to have exceeded. Besides', he continued, 'I presume the House will consider that the extraordinariness of the occasion in this iuncture of affairs may excuse a little over-acting in a service of this nature, for which I do not doubt … but I shall receive the happines of being favourably understood, if not well accepted by the House'. This was, of course, far from the case in August 1648; after the Commons had been purged of those who supported accommodation with Charles, Marten returned to the chamber and the Rump subsequently welcomed his regiment into the New Model.[33]

Royalists gleefully exploited Marten's reputation, for they could make much of the apparent connection between libertinism, licentiousness, anarchy and violence. Those alarmed at Marten's potential to take power were quick to discredit his forces. The stalwart Presbyterian MP, Sir John Maynard, commented on Marten's ambitions. He was 'all for parity and Anarchy' and aimed to be chosen 'one of the Tribunes of the People, or a John of Leiden'.[34] A citizen of Leicester, one W. Turvil, published a report on the activities of Marten's regiment during September 1648 in the vicinity of Market Harborough.[35] The woodcut on the frontispiece of this pamphlet portrayed Marten in the foreground, wearing an ostentatious feathered hat, strutting in front of his troop while his soldiers raped and murdered the population and burnt down the town. These were 'the basest and vilest' men. They had been persuaded to join by their commander's 'strange politick and subtle delusions'. The text of the pamphlet told a different tale. Although the townsfolk had been terrified at the prospect of losing their property to the 'levellers', Marten identified the focal points of the town and read a proclamation, declaring that the regiment was peaceable and had no intention of levelling property. They stayed overnight and moved on.

The troop had come to Leicestershire in order to evade attempts to disband it. On 21 August, the Derby House committee requested quarter-master Fincher to liaise with the county committees of Surrey, Wiltshire, Oxfordshire, Berkshire and Buckinghamshire forcibly to suppress Marten's

---

[33] *CJ*, vi, 129, 2 February 1649; the regiment continued to have a poor disciplinary record.

[34] 'A Speech in answer to Mr Martyn who railest against the king Lords & Commons. Said to be Sr John Maynards for the wch he was turned out of the house.' In manuscript in Thomason's hand, n.d. (January) E422(32).

[35] W[illiam] Turvil, *Terrible and bloudy newes from the disloyall army in the North*, 7 September 1648, E462(28). The implications this fascinating pamphlet bear for Marten's reputation are discussed in the author's study of Marten, currently in preparation. The woodcut is used again in 1650 to discredit the Ranters, and subsequently appears in school textbooks as evidence of the atrocities of royalists. An article tracing the history of the woodcut is also in preparation.

forces and those under his command led by William Eyres and John Walrond.[36] The soldiers fled Berkshire and first placed themselves under the 'protection' of the governor of Oxford.[37] They then went to Leicestershire and joined Grey's garrison at Ashby de la Zouche.[38] That Fincher had failed to disband Marten's forces was confirmed on 4 September, when the Committee for Both Kingdoms received orders from the Commons to suppress the forces of Colonel William Eyres. The notoriety of Marten's auxiliary regiment was probably a reflection of the colourfulness of its commander. The prospect of England's most infamous incendiary and lecher in charge of similarly-minded, undisciplined, uncontrollable, armed ruffians masquerading as an autonomous militia force caused widespread alarm. By the end of that month, the Commons was attempting to regain a semblance of control over both the New Model and the various types of auxiliary forces. Approximately 200 MPs were excused attendance at the House on the grounds that they were engaged in officially sanctioned military duties. The Commons named twenty-six who were not excused. These included Henry Marten, who had indicated that he would not be attending. This group was described as those 'who they thinke are doing ill services in their Counties'.[39]

One Presbyterian, outraged at the behaviour of radicals in the counties, was Clement Walker, who railed against the county committees as factions of agitators dedicated to overriding the representativeness of the parliamentary system in order to seize power for themselves. Many of Walker's examples seem to have had John Pyne as an archetype. The phrases used about anonymous demagogues in the *History of Independency* were repeated in the 'charges' against Pyne sent to London in April 1649, so Walker may well have been the chief organiser of the campaign against him. These were men who would 'tramp *Magna Charta* under their feet ... transgresse all Orders and Ordinances of Parliament, and break the Solemn League and Covenant'.[40] But although Walker was particularly concerned to

---

[36] *CSPD* 1648 p. 268, Interregnum 10E pp. 117–21.

[37] *Mercurius Pragmaticus* 22–29 August 1648, E461(17), n.p.

[38] This link between the Berkshire and Leicestershire forces cannot be extended to Somerset, except to say that one of Pyne's closest allies on the county committee was Marten's friend Alexander Popham.

[39] Worc.Coll., Clarke MSS cxiv fo. 80.

[40] Clement Walker, *The compleat history of Independency upon the Parliament begun 1640* (London, 1661), pp. 5–6. There were charges of arbitrary behaviour in Wells and Bridgwater, Somerset; 'how ignorantly and unjustly they exercise a power to *hear and determine*, or rather to determine without hearing, or hear without understanding, *private controversies of Meum & Tuum for debt* ...' and 'how frequently they leavy one Tax three or four times over, and continue their leavies after the Ordinance expires; How cruelly they raise the twentieth and fifth part upon the well-affected, exercising an illegal, arbitrary, tyrannicall power over their fellow Subjects' (p. 6).

counter the power of the New Model, which he saw as the breeding ground for Independents and the root of the undemocratic moves in the county committees, he worried that the local forces posed the greater danger. He believed the aim of the exercise was to subvert legitimate authority by establishing tentacles outside the main body. Hence, when the radical MPs had forged an alliance with the New Model which boosted the confidence of the army,

> their brutish General sent forth Warrants *to raise the Trained Bands* of some Counties to march with him against the City and both Houses; although Trained Bands are not under any pay of Parliament; and therefore not under command of the General, by any Order or Ordinance.[41]

One example he gave was Sir Hardress Waller – 'that one eyed *Polyphemus* of Pastebord'. In May 1648 Waller had issued a warrant to enlist volunteers in Devon. This was sent up to the Commons a month later, along with 'an Engagement of divers well-affected Volunteers in the Town of *Ilfordcombe*, of 12 *Junii*, desiring Sir *Hardres Waller* to appoint a fit Person to command them'.[42] As far as Walker was concerned, he was arming a faction, though Waller's forces were vital to protect the west country and he was actively involved in both the south-west of England and the Scilly Isles.[43] Waller maintained, in language Walker obviously thought dissembling, that his forces would be

> no burden to the Country, but be in pay with the rest of the army. In these Commissions he stileth himself (untruly) *Commander in chief of all the Forces of the five Western Associat Counties* and gave authority and encouragement to the well-affected (that is, to Independents, Sectaries, Antimonarchists, and the more desperate, forlorn sort of people) to enter into, and subscribe Engagements, *to live and die with the Army* (an imitation of the Members Engagement) *in defence of the Parliament*, (that is, of the ingaged faction of Independents, Schismaticks, and corrupt persons).

Grey of Groby had addressed his letters on the state of Leicestershire to Philip Skippon, who was, according to Walker, also raising a cavalry troop officered by 'schismaticall Apprentices' who in turn would raise men 'underhand'.[44]

---

[41] Ibid., p. 43.   [42] *CJ*, v, 606, 19 June 1648.

[43] Walker, *History*, p. 106; Worc.Coll., Clarke MSS 114, fo. 54; *The Moderate*, 22–29 August 1648, E461(16), n.p.; Ashton, *Counter-revolution* pp. 445–46.

[44] Ibid., p. 117. A number of the auxiliary forces in London seem to have been a breeding ground for the most radical politics; see Ian Gentles, 'The struggle for London in the second civil war' *Historical Journal*, 26, 1983; Keith Roberts, *London and Liberty: Ensigns of the London Trained Bands* (Partizan Press, 1987); L. C. Nagel, 'The militia of London 1641–1649', Ph.D., University of London (1982).

The correspondent responsible for *Mercurius Pragmaticus*[45] had a particular concern with the subversive actions of the garrison of Oxford. Marten's unauthorised regiment sought refuge with this garrison and its troops were alleged to have levied taxes on the local people in order to pay for what was here referred to as 'a *Bastard* kind of *Militia*, called the *County Troop*'.[46] The people were charged a monthly assessment, thinly justified by an ordinance of 1644, which it was claimed had not applied to the Oxford region until the crisis of 1648.[47] 'It is conceived by many intelligent men', continued the report, 'that this is done without the privity and consent of the *Houses* of Parliament', although Oxfordshire was the county in which Commons' Speaker William Lenthall had the greatest interest.[48]

The efforts of the local forces were reinforced by civilian lobbying. Pyne had sent 'scandalous and seditious Petitions in the Country ... in the Counties name' in order to oppose the links between the English and Scottish Commissioners, and was subsequently accused of promoting regicide and republicanism.[49] The concerns expressed in 1648 continued to address the links between the Scottish Commissioners, those in England who sued for peace and the king himself. During 1648, petitions submitted in favour of a personal treaty with Charles outnumbered those against by three to one.[50] Those which aimed to counter a personal treaty came disproportionately from Somerset, Berkshire and Leicestershire, and were collected during two waves of activity. The first followed the vote of no addresses to Charles, passed on 3 January, at a time when both parliament and army were in hawkish mood. The town of Taunton –

---

[45] Marchamont Nedham edited *Mercurius Pragmaticus*. He was resident in London in 1648, but was born, and maintained a base, in Burford, Oxfordshire, where he could procure a ready supply of first-hand information; Joseph Frank, *Cromwell's Press Agent: A Critical Biography of Marchamont Nedham, 1620–1678* (Lanham MD, 1980); Joad Raymond (ed.), *Making the News: an Anthology of Newsbooks of Revolutionary England, 1641–1660* (Gloucester, 1993).

[46] *Mercurius Pragmaticus* 27, 26 September–3 October 1648, E465(19).

[47] It was claimed to be legitimate as a result of a militia ordinance of 27 June 1644. There is no such record for 27 June, but on 21 June the House of Lords committed an ordinance from the Commons for raising money to send to Oxfordshire to lords Rutland, Sarum and Howard. On 25 June an ordinance from both Houses created three committees, for Berkshire, Buckinghamshire and Oxfordshire, with the task of implementing previous ordinances, including those for voluntary loans, the weekly assessment, fifths and twentieths and the sequestration; *LJ*, VI, 600, 605–6.

[48] The centres of his estates were at Burford, and he was named to the committees of Oxfordshire and Berkshire.

[49] *Articles of Treason*, article 3.

[50] During January to June 1648 there were six petitions which included Essex, eight from Kent, and four from London, plus several from Surrey, Sussex, Wales and occasional northern counties. These are the extant copies registered in the Thomason collection.

in which Pyne would subsequently raise 800 men in addition to his divisional county forces – petitioned in favour of the vote in February. The petitioners wanted parliament to believe that the area had been at the forefront of support for the true cause during the first war. Now they would continue to defend it: 'no Danger in the world may cause us to desert'.[51]

Henry Marten, whose previous contributions to pamphlet literature had been anonymous,[52] put his name to two calls for the total defeat of the king and a revolutionary settlement. In January 1648 he reopened the attack which he and Thomas Chaloner had launched against the Scottish Commissioners in 1646.[53] The Scots were one of his favourite targets because they were keen to uphold the terms of the Solemn League and Covenant which bound them to protect the person of the king. Marten poured scorn on the Scottish Commissioners and their army, rallying his readers with patriotic English talk. He called on his supporters to continue to fight for their liberties, for 'there is another and more naturall way to peace and to the ending of a warre then by agreement, namely by conquest'.[54] The following month he addressed his 'fellow citizens'.[55] The military force of the nation must either be in the hands of a representative and accountable parliament or in local hands to defend local communities. In the hands of a monarch, the sword was the tool necessary to maintain absolute power: 'in the hands of a Parliament (or the representatives of a free Nation) is not so much the power of the Sword as of the Buckler, and will not be exercised at all, but in cases of Rebellion or Invasion'.[56]

A second wave of radical pamphleteering came at the end of the year. Twenty 'gentlemen, ministers and other inhabitants of the county of Leicester' became the first to make an unambiguous demand that the king

---

[51] *The Humble Petition and grateful Acknowledgement of the town of Taunton*, 9 February 1647(8), printed by order, 17 February E427(21); Underdown, 'Honest radicals', p. 201.

[52] Marten had been ordered from the House and briefly imprisoned in 1643 for statements against the king. He thereafter anonymously produced a series of sarcastic and vitriolic pamphlets against the king and his Scottish supporters, such as *A Corrector of the Answerer of the Speech out of Doores*, and *An Vnhappie Game at Scotch and English*, which are recognisably his in both style and content.

[53] Sarah Barber, 'Scotland and Ireland under the Commonwealth: a question of loyalty', in S. G. Ellis and Sarah Barber (eds.), *Conquest and Union: Fashioning a British State, 1485–1625* (London, 1995), pp. 195–221.

[54] Henry Marten, *The Independency of England endeavoured to be maintained*, 11 January 1648, E422(16), p. 15.

[55] This was a message which his nephew-in-law, John Wildman, and Thomas Saunders were to make about Cromwell in the petition of the three colonels, *To his Highness the Lord Protector*, 18 October 1654, 669.f.19(21).

[56] Henry Marten, *The Parliaments proceedings justified, in declining a Personall Treaty with the King*, 7 February 1648, E426(2), p. 15.

be brought to trial.[57] In November 1648, Marten's county addressed a petition to the Council of War sitting at Windsor, complaining that committeemen, gentlemen, ministers and the well-affected of Berkshire had had to wait at the Commons for a month to present a petition which it continually refused to receive. The Berkshire gentlemen reminded the nation of 'our Countreymen of Leicestershire, [who] in behalfe of themselves and the whole Nation, did fully impresse our Sense of the present Condition of Affaires'.[58] Was it pure coincidence that when the New Model drove Marten's troop out of the south, Marten ran to Leicestershire? Now Berkshire folk expressed their willingness to expend the last of their lives and estates for the public good, called for judicial action against the chief author of the nation's troubles, and '(either by this present Parliament purg'd, or another and more equall Representative chosen) to have a true Accompt requir'd of all the Bloud spilt, and Treasure spent'. The warning against centralised military power continued, for the army was:

> Waging a successfull Warre; carried on throughout with such a Frame of Spirit, that all the World shall see it was in Your Hearts only to serve the Necessity of the Nation, not to set your selves above it, not to become a new Oppression to us, but (under God) our Redemption from all Our Oppressions. For the present, and (*sic*) our Bullwarke, and Preservation against them or the like for time to come.[59]

Just one week later Grey was a central figure at Pride's Purge, pointing out those members to be ejected from the House for continuing to press for an accommodation with the king.[60] Cromwell and Marten subsequently re-entered the House together. The following month was the only occasion on which they co-operated. Marten thanked the Lieutenant General for preserving the nation, carefully ignoring the ambivalent attitude which the grandees had expressed towards his own efforts. At the turn of the year, John Pyne supported a Somerset petition presented by the Particular Baptist, Thomas Collier, which drew attention to the miraculous redemption of the parliamentary cause in the face of a 'dispersed Army, weakened by neglect of friends'. The gentlemen, ministers and well-affected of Somerset reminded the Commons in January 1649 that they would soon

---

[57] The House replied that it was engaged in a treaty with the king, 'wherein they will take care for the preservation of Religion, Laws, Liberties, and Protection of those that have engaged with them'.

[58] *A True Copie of the Berkshire Petition*, 30 November 1648, E475(2), p. 1.

[59] Ibid., p. 6, echoing Marten's phrase about the army, 'the greatest Bulwark, under God, of our Liberties', *The Independency of England*, p. 8.

[60] Ludlow, *Memoirs* I, p. 204; David Underdown, *Pride's Purge: Politics in the Puritan Revolution* (London, 1971), pp. 132–33.

enjoy peace and stability provided the vote of no addresses was not forgotten. This petition was enthusiastically received by the now purged and sympathetic Commons.[61]

These three militias were raised by radicals of far from mean background. Henry Marten was in control of extensive estates in Berkshire, although his father (a prominent civil lawyer) was the first in his family to have such wealth. Clarendon described Pyne as 'well known, and of fair estate'[62] and Grey of Groby was the son of the earl of Stamford and descendant of the ill-starred Lady Jane. The Grey estate at Bradgate, just north of Leicester, was considerable, and the family had a long and recent history of violent feuding with the neighbouring Cavendish dukes of Newcastle.[63] The three commanders had a tendency to stress the material sacrifice which both the first and second war entailed. An investment of their estate had been made by both themselves, holders of a major stake in the land, but also by their soldiers.

Pyne was reluctant to leave his county for fear he would lose his power base.[64] Grey's reluctance to move away from Leicestershire was a result of the isolation which a man of his politics felt in a county dominated by the powers of the dukes of Rutland and Loughborough. Keeping control of the Bradgate estate, and the support of his tenantry, were intimately tied to his physical presence in the shire. Grey had been keen to stress the way in which his adherents were prepared to desert their harvesting, and constantly badgered parliament for recognition for his forces by way of pay and provision. The lucrative Thames-side lands which Marten's father had bought in the 1620s lay at the point at which, during most of the war, royalist forces met those of their opposition. Thus, a combination of the taxes which he was forced to pay for soldiers of both armies, and the money which he invested in the parliamentary war effort, left Marten's estates, which had been encumbered by debt even before the war, in a sorry state by 1648.[65] Hence the negotiations with the king, the Scottish

---

[61] *To the Honourable the Commons assembled in Parliament*, the petition of the gentlemen, ministers and well-affected of Somerset, ordered to be printed and published 5 January 1648(9), 669.f.13(68); Underdown, *Somerset*, pp. 149–50; *True Copie of the Berkshire Petition*, p. 2; *CJ*, VI, 102.

[62] Edward Hyde, earl of Clarendon, *The History of the Rebellion and Civil Wars in England*, ed. W. D. Macray, 6 vols. (Oxford, 1888), III, p. 491.

[63] To Underdown, Grey and Marten are greater gentry and Pyne county gentry, all three in the top income bracket of over £1,000 p.a.: *Pride's Purge*, pp. 375, 479, 383; J. Richards, 'The Greys of Bradgate in the English Civil War: a study of Henry Grey, first earl of Stamford, and his son and heir Thomas, lord Grey of Groby', *Transactions of the Leicestershire Archaeological and Historical Society* 62, 1988, 32–52.

[64] Bod.Lib., Tanner MS 59, fo. 353.

[65] Marten Loder MS 89/29; 85/32; 4/137; 92/35–38.

Commissioners and the English Parliament during 1646 would set 'the ruine of so many honest families at so cheap a rate'.[66] Marten also had concern for the ordinary citizen ruined by the war:

> Sir *Thomas Fairfax* knows he hath indeed no open force at all, and yet the objection hath force enough, for the Parliament knowes that there is need of keeping Sir *Thomas Fairfax* and the army under his command, or else they would not put the Kingdome to the charge of sixtie thousand pounds *per* moneth; they are not ignorant, that ... there is a daily swarme of discontented persons in all parts ... some for want of employment, some for want of what they earned when they were employed, others for pure want ...[67]

The Berkshire petition called for an account of 'all the Bloud spilt, and Treasure spent' for good reason.

The language of materialism was tied with that of principle through the promotion of the slippery phrase 'England's liberties'. The New Model Army soldiers were claiming to be more than 'mere mercenary soldiers', and in order to make claim to a similar notion of virtue, the auxiliary regiments had also to demonstrate a dedication to the cause such that no danger in the world would cause them to desert. Even at the height of the fighting, it seemed possible that parliament would conclude an agreement with Charles which would wipe out the soldiers' efforts. An attempt to quantify and rationalise the soldiers' commitment, in both monetary and political terms, had been part of radical politics since the Putney debates.[68] The case was even more urgent in 1648: Charles had been twice defeated. The auxiliary regiments were recruited with slogans which promised a fight against any person or centralising institution which sought to deprive local people of their rights to property. They would fight any tyranny and continue to fight to any length.

The county sentiment which recruited such regiments was of the utmost importance. The auxiliary regiments were drawn from within their local areas to defend their homes and livelihoods. The potential presence of a Scottish army in England injected an urgent note of English patriotism

---

[66] [Henry Marten], *A Corrector of the Answerer to the Speech out of Doores. Iustifying the worthy Speech of Master Thomas Chaloner*, 26 October 1646, E364(9), p. 8.

[67] Marten, *Parliaments Proceedings Justified*, pp. 13–14.

[68] Edward Sexby expressed it at Putney, '[w]e have engaged in this Kingdome and ventur'd our lives, and itt was all for this: to recover our birthrights and priviledges as Englishmen ... There are many thousand of us souldiers that have ventur'd our lives; yet wee have had a birthright ... If wee had nott a right in this Kingdome, wee were mere mercenarie souldiers. There are many in my condition, that have as good a condition ... itt may be little estate they have att present ... I am resolved to give my birthright to none'; C. H. Firth (ed.), *Clarke Papers*, 4 vols. (Camden Society, New Series xlix, liv, lxi, lxii, 1891–1901), i, pp. 322–23.

into the call to defend England's liberties, and the county element was a localised act of defiance at those institutions such as the House of Commons and the New Model Army which did not seem to be doing enough to secure the liberties of ordinary citizens.

A combination of the localism of the forces, their dependence on a local gentleman or county committee sponsor, and the radicalism of the forces' commanders, provided ample ammunition for royalist and Presbyterian critics to be scathingly dismissive of these regiments. This was the case in Somerset, where power had passed to men of lower social status and the balance between gentry families had shifted.[69] There was an established tradition in which local militia forces and trained bands were seen as rather laughable and incompetent, and those who were panicked by the regiments of 1648 could tap into this language which neutralised danger by poking fun.[70] Hence, it was necessary to decry the military acumen of Pyne and Grey. Marten's reputation as a libertine was used to castigate his military competence: he was unable to control troops whose disorder was a consequence of their commander's politics. Alarmed critics of these radicals could weave together a number of factors which were not necessarily linked, in order to discredit their opponents. Localist retrenchment and a failure to serve the wider cause, extreme political and/or religious views, mayhem, disorder, bungling and a shortage of military acumen, were wrapped up together. The criticisms extended to those who were ostensibly on the same side, with failure to fight outside county boundaries being portrayed as cowardice, rather than as an attempt to defend beleaguered areas.[71]

However, the New Model needed these local forces because a standing army could not command sufficient resources.[72] The localised royalist rebellions of the second civil war could best be met by pinpointed

---

[69] Beckett, *Amateur Military Tradition*, p. 45. Beckett cites Sussex, Cornwall and Suffolk as counties where the traditional elites maintained control.

[70] Lois Schwoerer, *'No standing armies!': the Antimilitary Ideology in Seventeenth-century England* (Baltimore/London, 1974), pp. 8–14; Nagel, 'The militia of London'; Beckett, *Amateur Military Tradition*, p. 41; modern equivalents of this attitude can be found in people's responses to the Home Guard or the Territorial Army.

[71] A Derbyshire minority attempted to oust Colonel John Gell whose first defence was to accuse his major, Thomas Saunders, of incompetence and cowardice, and Saunders' troops of mutiny, political radicalism and sectarianism. Lucy Hutchinson was glowing in her praises of fellow Nottinghamshire man, Colonel Thornhaugh, but less generous about Saunders. He was 'a Derbyshire man, who was a very godly, honest, country gentleman, but had not many things requisite for a great soldier'; Derbyshire Record Office, Sanders MSS, D1232M; Lucy Hutchinson, *Memoirs of Colonel Hutchinson* (London, 1965), p. 256.

[72] J. R. Western, *The English Militia in the Eighteenth Century: the Story of a Political Issue, 1660–1802* (London, 1965).

suppression, in which local counter-forces proved ideal assistance. Only in the case of Henry Marten, whose reputation was notorious, did Fairfax consider forcible disbandment. The local auxiliary militia provided some assistance to the official forces of parliament during the second civil war, but were also a means to ensure that neither parliament nor the New Model Army forgot the radical decisions which had been made earlier in the year. They reminded people of the vote of no addresses in January. Ironically, however, the purging of parliament could only be accomplished in cooperation with the New Model soldiers. The use of arms to bring about the revolution injected new fervour into the debate about whether the New Model really was the bulwark of England's liberties.

7

Cromwell's commissioners for preserving the peace of the Commonwealth: a Staffordshire case study*

JOHN SUTTON

I

Cromwell's commissioners for preserving the peace of the Commonwealth are the invisible men of Interregnum politics. They were the special agents appointed by the Lord Protector to assist the Major-Generals during their brief rule between 1655 and 1656. Yet while much has been written about their military superiors, an almost complete veil of anonymity surrounds these officials. Virtually the only modern historian to be impressed by the commissioners and their work is Stephen Roberts in his fine study of Devon during the period 1646–70; for him they possessed 'the ultimate bureaucratic virtue': 'thoroughness'.[1]

Manifestly it is high time Cromwell's commissioners were rescued from oblivion and in this essay an in-depth case study will be made of his appointees in Staffordshire, focusing on certain key issues. Were they a set of colourless nonentities? Is it fair to characterise them, as Ronald Hutton has done, as 'usurpers within the social as well as the political (and often the religious) order'? And what of Ivan Roots' assertion that the Major-Generals and their helpmates 'were a heterogenous lot' especially in terms of their 'age, education, experience and so on'? Hopefully our investigation

---

* I would like to thank Ian Gentles, John Morrill and Blair Worden for their invaluable comments and criticisms on an earlier draft of this essay.

[1] At least three modern historians investigating the rule of the Major-Generals make only a cryptic reference to the commissioners or ignore them completely: Toby Barnard, *The English Republic, 1649–1660* (London, 1982), p. 52; Michael Lynch, *The Interregnum 1649–1660* (London, 1994), pp. 44–47; Andrew Colby, *Central Government and the Localities: Hampshire 1649–1689* (Cambridge, 1987), p. 34. Even when the Major-Generals' deputies are acknowledged, they tend to be treated in dismissive terms. Cf. Ivan Roots, 'Swordsmen and decimators – Cromwell's Major-Generals' in R. H. Parry (ed.), *The English Civil War and After 1642–1658* (London, 1970), pp. 83–84; David Underdown, 'Settlement in the counties 1653–1658' in G. E. Aylmer (ed.), *The Interregnum* (London, 1972), p. 175. For the notable exception see Stephen K. Roberts, *Recovery and Restoration in an English County: Devon Local Administration 1646–1670* (Exeter, 1985), p. 52.

will answer these questions and in the process throw new light on the character of local government personnel during what David Underdown has described as the revolutionary phase of the Protectorate when direct military rule temporarily superseded traditional methods of 'settlement'.[2]

II

In the 'cantonisation' of the nation in October 1655, Staffordshire was associated with Cheshire and Lancashire and placed under the authority of Major-General Charles Worsley, an uncompromising zealot determined in his own words 'to strike while the iron is hott' and to be 'a terror to the bad'. During his frenetic and hard-line administration Worsley proved an exacting taskmaster, expecting his subordinates in regard to their collective mission 'not to be wanting in that, but to make it our study night and day'. Small wonder that the Staffordshire commissioners were soon 'presinge' the dour Major-General that they be individually sent full particulars about 'every one' of their expected duties.[3]

And the list of tasks assigned by Worsley to his Staffordshire agents was truly daunting. Some indication of the sheer range of their responsibilities is furnished by the detailed orders and instructions which Worsley issued at Chester to the commissioners in all three counties on 4 January 1656. Their prime function was to police royalist delinquents whose 'restless and irreconcileable malice' had recently manifested itself in Penruddock's revolt. All 'such dangerous and suspicious persons' were not only to be disarmed but were to be kept under the strictest surveillance. Apart from being gendarmes, the commissioners also had another crucial role to play, namely that of moral crusaders in the battle against 'Merrie England'. They were to spearhead a reformation of manners through a concerted attack on 'Drunkenness, Sabbath-breaking, swearing, and unwarrantable ... Plays ... Mirths and Jollities'. To achieve these ambitious goals Worsley authorised 'a full, exact and impartial return' to be compiled of 'all persons that have been in arms for the late King, or Charles Stuart his son ... or are disaffected to the present Government'; 'all Delinquent, Scandalous or

---

[2] Ronald Hutton, *The British Republic 1649–1660* (Basingstoke, 1990), p. 85; Roots, 'Swordsmen and decimators', p. 83; Underdown, 'Settlement', p. 172.

[3] The standard account of this period of direct military rule is still the article by D. W. Rannie, 'Cromwell's Major-Generals', *English Historical Review*, 10, 1895, 471–506. For Worsley see BL, Harl. Ms 21000, fos. 63–65; and the entry on him in the *Dictionary of National Biography* (*DNB*); and J. S. Morrill, *Cheshire 1630–1660: County Government and Society during the English Revolution* (Oxford, 1974), p. 277. On Worsley's tough stance towards his subordinates and the corresponding response of the Staffordshire commissioners see *Thurloe State Papers*, ed. T. Birch [henceforth *TSP*], 7 vols. (1782), IV, pp. 189, 224, 247–48, 495.

Ignorant Preachers [and] Schoolmasters'; 'all idle and vagabond fellows'; 'all frequenters of Tipling houses'; and finally all those that attended 'horse-races, cock-fights, bear-baiting, stage-plays, Interludes and all other unlawful assemblies' throughout his area of jurisdiction – by any reckoning a formidable undertaking![4]

Who were the Staffordshire commissioners chosen to assist Worsley in this grand design? The source-material makes it possible to identify twenty-two men earmarked for service as guardians of the Common-wealth's 'welfare' and 'security' in the shire (see Appendix 1 for their names and essential biographical details). This tally is very much in line with the numbers of commissioners serving in other counties: twenty in Oxfordshire, twenty-one in Norfolk, twenty-two in Suffolk, and twenty-six in Sussex to cite but four parallel examples.[5]

Nomination was one thing; activity another. By and large the majority of the Staffordshire commissioners seem to have taken their assignment seriously: thus when Major-General Worsley first arrived at the county town, in late November 1655, eighteen of them turned out to greet him – over eighty per cent of the entire complement. According to *Mercurius Politicus*, the government newspaper, the Staffordshire commissioners subsequently fulfilled their duties with 'much cheerfulness' and showed every sign of being 'as forward in their work, as any of the counties'. Such praise might be dismissed as mere propaganda, but we also possess the testimony of Major-General Worsley himself. He held his Staffordshire assistants in the highest esteem, describing them to Secretary Thurloe as 'men in whom I am persuaded his highnese may very much confide'.[6]

As the accompanying map shows, the Staffordshire commissioners were drawn from all parts of the shire. Four hailed from in or near Stafford, a sensible deployment since it was the hub of the county's administrative life and the nerve-centre of the commissioners' own work during the brief nine months of their active existence. The seats of the commissioners were to be found in all of the seven geographical subdivisions of Staffordshire, each of them having three or four commissioners except for the south-west lowland which had only one representative (Thomas Pudsey). Half the

---

[4] The printed version of Worsley's instructions to the commissioners in his district is given in: BL, Thomason Tracts, E.491(14), *Mercurius Politicus*, 23–31 January 1656, pp. 1598–1600.

[5] The names of the twenty-two Staffordshire commissioners can be gleaned from BL, Stowe Ms 155, fo. 89; and *TSP*, IV, pp. 432, 648. My calculations of the numbers of commissioners serving in Oxfordshire, Norfolk, Suffolk and Sussex make no pretense to be definitive, but are based on *TSP*, IV, pp. 161–62, 171, 185, 225, 394, 595.

[6] For the alacrity of the Staffordshire commissioners in carrying out their responsibilities see BL, Thomason Tracts, E.489(18), *Mercurius Politicus*, 22–27 November 1655, p. 57; *TSP*, IV, p. 224.

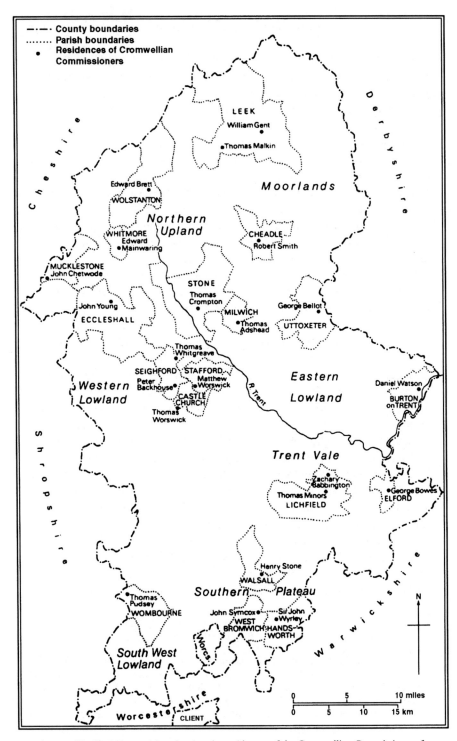

Cheshire

Derbyshire

LEEK
• William Gent
• Thomas Malkin

Moorlands

Edward Brett
WOLSTANTON

Northern Upland

WHITMORE
Edward
• Mainwaring

CHEADLE
• Robert Smith

MUCKLESTONE
• John Chetwode

STONE
Thomas
Crompton
MILWICH
• Thomas
Adshead

George Bellot
UTTOXETER

John Young
ECCLESHALL

Thomas
Whitgreave

SEIGHFORD   STAFFORD
Peter   Matthew
Backhouse•   • Worswick
CASTLE
CHURCH
Thomas
Worswick

Western Lowland

Eastern Lowland

Daniel Watson
BURTON
onTRENT

R. Trent

Trent Vale

Shropshire

Zachary
Babbington
Thomas Minors
LICHFIELD

• George Bowes
ELFORD

Henry Stone
WALSALL

Southern Plateau

Thomas
Pudsey
WOMBOURNE

John Symcox•   Sir John
WEST   • Wyrley
BROMWICH   HANDS-
WORTH

Worcestershire

Warwickshire

South West Lowland

N

Worcestershire   CLIENT

0   5   10 miles
0   5   10   15 km

A map of Staffordshire parishes showing the residences of the Cromwellian Commissioners for Preserving the Peace of the Commonwealth, 1655–56

commissioners lived north of the Trent, the other half south of it, thus ensuring a pretty even spread across the county.[7]

Turning from their geographical distribution to the men themselves, we find that no easy generalisation can be made of their personalities, which were varied and contrasting. An anonymous royalist commentator, writing shortly after the Restoration, furnishes us with pen-portraits of eight of the commissioners. Overall he was impressed by their capacity, intelligence and worth. Thus he characterised Zachary Babbington as 'an understanding person'; Robert Smith as 'able'; and Henry Stone as 'a prudent, wise ... [and] suttle man'. Only one commissioner seems to have possessed a serious vice, namely Sir John Wyrley who was apparently 'a great drinker', a weakness which, coupled with his known dandyism, must have given him a certain Cavalier flamboyance that stood in sharp contrast to the earnestness of more 'sober' colleagues like John Chetwode and Edward Mainwaring. Far and away the most attractive commissioner was Thomas Crompton, described as 'a witty man and a good fellow'; his presence doubtless enlivened the proceedings of the Major-General's deputies in Staffordshire.[8]

III

The sterling qualities of the commissioners were matched by their ripe years. From a variety of sources such as baptismal entries in parish registers, demographic details in heraldic visitations, memorial inscriptions and depositions we can glean the ages of all but three of the twenty-two Staffordshire commissioners at the time of their nomination in October 1655. They were a predominantly middle-aged group. No fewer than twelve of the nineteen commissioners whose dates of birth can be ascertained were more than forty years old. Both the average and median age of the cohort as a whole was approximately forty-three. This is not to say there were no youthful commissioners: five were 'thirty-something' and another two – Thomas Worswick and Thomas Whitgreave – in their late twenties. But even these were hardly striplings. At the other extreme 'the ancients' among the commissioners – those over fifty, an old age by mid-seventeenth-century standards – numbered merely three. At sixty-five Thomas Malkin was the most venerable commissioner; John Chetwode (fifty-six) and Edward Mainwaring (fifty-two) were less advanced in years

---

[7] I would like to express my deep appreciation to Mrs Sandy Haynes for drawing the map.

[8] See Staffordshire Record Office [henceforth SRO], 100/1 for the original manuscript containing these observations on the Staffordshire commissioners. For a transcription see *Staffordshire Historical Collections* [henceforth *SHC*], 4th series (1958), II, pp. 11–12, 28, 30, 32, 36–37. On Sir John Wyrley's sartorial elegance, see his will: PRO, Prob. 11/399/80.

but still a decade above the mean. The solid core of the Staffordshire commissioners thus consisted of the nine men in their forties. This must have endowed them with considerable experience and maturity.[9]

We must next determine whether the commissioners were single or married men, heirs to estates or younger sons. This is an important issue in view of David Underdown's claim that the revolutionary MPs of 1648–49 had a greater tendency to be bachelors and younger sons than their conservative opponents who, by contrast, were more prone to be yoked in matrimony and heads of families. Could the same be said of the Staffordshire appointees of 1655? The answer is no.[10]

For a start an investigation of their familial status reveals that they were nearly all married. Twenty are definitely known to have tied the matrimonial knot by October 1655. The records do not reveal the marital status of the remaining two, but since they were each under thirty they may still have been bachelors: in any event they had both become married men by the Restoration. At least five of the commissioners were married more than once. Thomas Crompton's memorial inscription states that 'he lived in the holy state of wedlock' four times, his last marriage to Eleanor, daughter of Sir George Morton of Millburn in Dorset, lasting for thirty-one years.

---

[9] The baptismal dates of four commissioners have been ascertained from printed parish registers: for Peter Backhouse see *Staffordshire Parish Register Society* [henceforth *SPRS*], 1977–78: Seighford 1561–1712, p. 32; Edward Brett: *SPRS*, 1949–50: Keele 1540–1812, p. 75; and Matthew and Thomas Worswick: *SPRS*, 1935–36: St Mary's Stafford, 1559–1671, pp. 147, 210. The ages of four further commissioners have been gleaned from three original registers and the copy of a fourth: see SRO, D.3332/1/1: Whitmore (Mainwaring); D4219/1/1: Burton-upon-Trent (Watson); D3891/1/2: Uttoxeter (Minors); and William Salt Library, Stafford (WSL), Staffordshire parish register transcripts: Cheadle, 1574–1682 (Smith). Demographic details contained in Dugdale's heraldic visitation have enabled me to calculate the ages of seven more commissioners: Babbington, Bowes, Chetwode, Crompton, Pudsey, Whitgreave and Wyrley. See H. S. Grazebrook, *The Heraldic Visitations of Staffordshire ... 1614, 1663–4* [henceforth *Staffs. Pedigrees*] (1885), pp. 24, 47, 75, 102, 246, 308, 335. Miscellaneous sources furnish the ages of four additional commissioners: George Bellot's is traceable from the information he gave when he matriculated at Hart Hall, Oxford in May 1640; he was then aged 16. Cf. Joseph Forster (ed.), *Alumni Oxonienses: The Members of the University of Oxford 1500–1714* (London, 1891), I, p. 104. That of Thomas Malkin can be derived from an affidavit he supplied to the Committee for Compounding on 3 October 1653 when he stated that he was 63 years old, making him 65 two years later. Cf. SP23/168/535. For Henry Stone's age I have relied on the figure given in the post-Restoration survey: *SHC*, 4th Series (1958), II, p. 30. This latter source is also useful for verifying the ages of several other commissioners: Forster, *Alumni Oxoniensis*, I, pp. 11–12, 28, 32, 36, 37. The date of John Young's christening is recorded in his family's papers: SRO, D1082/8/17/35.

[10] D. Underdown, *Pride's Purge: Politics in the Puritan Revolution* (Oxford, 1971), pp. 225–26. A fuller exploration of the plight of younger sons in the seventeenth century is to be found in Joan Thirsk, *The Rural Economy of England: Collected Essays* (London, 1984), Chapter XIX.

'Much-married' is thus a good description of the Staffordshire commissioners.[11]

What then of Underdown's point about younger sons? In an age of primogeniture the lot of non-inheriting sons was an unenviable one and this bitter experience, it has been argued, often drove them into political extremism. We can ascertain the family positions of nineteen of the Staffordshire commissioners. All but four of them were first-born sons and as inheritors of estates, whether large or small, may have had a natural bias towards a more conservative brand of politics.[12]

Though the Underdown thesis only applies to a handful of the Staffordshire commissioners, it does illuminate those cases. Of the four commissioners known to have been younger sons, three were radical in church or state. George Bellot, who served in the Nominated Assembly in 1653, was opposed to a publicly maintained ministry. Perhaps that sentiment was born of his experience as a poorly endowed younger son eking out an existence on an annuity of £8. Daniel Watson, another younger son, was radical in politics rather than religion. A self-made man, who had acquired an estate by the Restoration worth £200 a year thanks to his thriving legal practice, Watson was a republican sympathiser. For example when the Rump Parliament was threatened by Sir George Booth's rebellion in August 1659 he made a solemn pledge 'to be true, faithfull and constant to this commonwealth without a single person, kingship or House of Peers'. The third commissioner who fell into this category of militant younger son, Peter Backhouse, was likewise 'a Commonwealth's man', demonstrating a real enthusiasm for the restored Rump in 1659. He would later be prominent in 'the radical underground' of the 1660s. The likes of Bellot, Watson and Backhouse, however, were the exception rather than the rule in terms of the overall stamp of the Staffordshire commissioners, most of whom were first-born, not younger sons.[13]

[11] Information about the marital status of the commissioners has been mainly derived from *Staffs. Pedigrees: 1614 and 1663–4*, pp. 24, 47, 55, 75, 102, 208, 246, 299, 308, 335. Otherwise I have relied on parish register material; see note 9 above. The two possible bachelors among the commissioners were Thomas Worswick and Sir Thomas Whitgreave. Whitgreave was probably wed to his first wife Mary, the daughter of Sir William Bowyer, sometime in the mid-1650s, though conclusive evidence of their union is only furnished by the family pedigree of 1663. *Staffs. Pedigrees: 1614 and 1663–4*, p. 308. Worswick had certainly married the latter's sister by 1657: *SPRS*, 1935–36: St Mary's, Stafford 1559–1671, p. 290.

[12] To determine whether the commissioners were first-born or younger sons, I have again used the source material referred to in notes 9 and 11.

[13] For Bellot's religious radicalism see BL, Thomason Tracts, 669.f.19, *A Catalogue of the Names of the Members of the Last Parliament* (London, 1654), fo. 3; Austin Woolrych, *Commonwealth to Protectorate* (Oxford, 1982), pp. 410–11. For his small annuity, see below note 25. For Watson's subscription to the pro-republican declaration of August 14 1659

IV

We can learn something, though not much, of the commissioners' education. The only record we have of their schooling reveals that Sir John Wyrley was a pupil of Wolverhampton grammar school. However we should not conclude from this that these men lacked education, for at a higher level eight of them are known to have attended the universities and/or the Inns of Court. At least five commissioners were university alumni, with a distinct bias towards Oxford: there was only one Cambridge man to Oxford's four.[14]

Of the five commissioners who went to university, four also had a legal education at the Inns of Court, among them Daniel Watson who was the only one to become a practising barrister; his was clearly a vocational education. Of the other three, Zachary Babbington is a curious case. He was admitted to the Inner Temple in 1646, then in his thirty-fifth year and having already, in his own words, enjoyed the 'happiness' of sitting at the feet of 'learned Judges' for 'many years'. The legal studies of the other two commissioners – Edward Mainwaring and John Young – were much more straightforward: as the heirs of well-to-do gentry families both men followed convention in acquiring a basic knowledge of the law to stand them in good stead in a litigious age. Alongside the four commissioners who attended both university and an inn of court, there were three who attended an inn of court alone. Of those seven, four went to the Inner Temple, two to Gray's Inn and one to the Middle Temple. The fact that a core of the commissioners possessed this university and legal background demonstrates that it would be wrong to characterise them as uneducated men.[15]

---

see Hereford and Worcestershire Record Office, Hereford, E12/F/P3. NB. his continuing radicalism after the Restoration: he became a Whig and supported the Duke of Monmouth during the Exclusion crisis. Cf. B. D. Henning (ed.), *The House of Commons 1660–1690* (The History of Parliament Trust, London, 1983), p. 678: *Calendar of State Papers Domestic (CSPD)*, 1677–78, p. 33. Like Watson, Backhouse signed the republican declaration cited above and played a leading role in the suppression of the Staffordshire Royalists during Sir George Booth's rebellion in August 1659: Bodl. Lib., Clarendon Ms, vol. 62, fos. 222–23; *CSPD*, 1659, p. 23. On his subversive activities in the 1660s see PRO, SP29/75/115; and SP29/76/46.

[14] For Wyrley's schooling, see H. R. Thomas and John Ryan (eds.), *Wolverhampton Grammar School Register 1515–1920* (Kendal, 1926), p. 8. On the five university-educated commissioners see Forster, *Alumni Oxoniensis*, I, pp. 104, 268 (Bellot, Chetwode); IV, pp. 1582, 1696 (Watson, Wyrley); and J. and J. A. Venn (ed.), *Alumni Cantabrigiensis: A Biographical List of All Students, Graduates and Holders of Office at the University of Cambridge from the earliest times to 1900* (Cambridge, 1922), I, p. 190 (Bowes).

[15] For the seven commissioners who were Inns of Court men see Joseph Forster (ed.), *The Register of Admissions to Gray's Inn, 1521–1889* (London, 1889), pp. 177, 212 (Wyrley and

It is also worth observing that four of the commissioners who had not themselves received a higher education sent their sons to Oxford after the Restoration. Thomas Pudsey's two sons, William and Thomas, and John Symcox's boy Josiah were students there in the 1660s; while the following decade the halls of learning included the male offspring of William Gent and Henry Stone. The latter's son Aaron proved a particularly wayward pupil, his studies at St Edmund Hall being cut short despite a considerable financial investment. Even when his indulgent father permitted him to continue his education abroad – at Leiden University – Aaron continued to be a disappointment. The great pains Henry Stone took over his errant son's education surely provide convincing proof that the 'nongraduate' commissioners were no enemies to academe.[16]

V

Of no less interest is the economic and social status of Worsley's Staffordshire representatives. Were they 'usurpers' in terms of the pre-civil War hierarchical structure as Ronald Hutton has asserted of the Cromwellian commissioners in general? At first sight the Staffordshire commissioners appear to have been solid members of the gentry class. When nominated collectors for the monthly assessment and army tax in the late 1640s/early 1650s, one was described as a knight and another thirteen as esquires. This clearly suggests that the majority were drawn from the upper echelons of Staffordshire society. And of the remaining eight commissioners, four were intermittently designated as esquires, leaving just four plain gentlemen. However, here we need to be wary. There was a considerable 'inflation of honours' during the Interregnum when men of a lower social standing often exaggerated their status on attaining office, raising it above the gradations assigned to them – or their families – before 1640.[17]

Watson); H. A. C. Sturgess (ed.), *Register of Admissions to the Honourable Society of the Middle Temple: From the fifteenth century to the year 1944* (London, 1877), I, p. 110 (Mainwaring); Anon., *Students admitted to the Inner Temple 1547–1660* (London, 1877), pp. 220, 302, 322 (Chetwode, Young and Babbington). For Babbington's comment about his legal studies cf. Bodl. Lib., Zachary Babbington, *Advice to Grand Jurors in Cases of Blood* (London, 1677), Introduction.

[16] For the four non-university-educated commissioners who sent their sons to Oxford: Forster, *Alumni Oxonienses*, I, p. 557 (William Gent's son, Thomas); Ibid., III, p. 1218 (Thomas Pudsey's sons Thomas and William); Ibid., IV, pp. 1357, 1428 (John Symcox's son Josiah and Henry Stone's son Aaron). On Aaron Stone's wayward education: BL, Add. Mss 29910, fo. 52.

[17] For the 'usurpation' of lower social types during the Interregnum in general see A. H. Dodd, *Studies in Stuart Wales* (Cardiff, 1952), pp. 110–12; Christopher Hill, *Puritanism and Revolution: Studies in Interpretation of the English Revolution of the 17th Century* (London, 1958),

When a more searching investigation is made into the pre-Civil War ranking of the Staffordshire commissioners, a subtler picture emerges. Only six men can truly be said to have been socially pre-eminent prior to 1642. Sir John Wyrley had been knighted by the king at Whitehall on 4 June 1641; the seigneurial status of George Bowes and John Chetwode was that of well-established county gentry, while Thomas Crompton, Edward Mainwaring and John Young were the sons of esquires, all having succeeded to their fathers' titles by the time of their nomination in 1655. Yet those six men accounted for less than a third of the Staffordshire commissioners, a figure which raises serious doubts about the social classification of the remainder.[18]

Detailed examination reveals that six of these were gentlemen of a distinctly parochial kind. Perhaps they are best epitomised by Thomas Adshead, whose father had purchased a fourth part of the manor in Milwich in 1620. Another two commissioners (Peter Backhouse and Thomas Malkin) were of yeoman stock with pretensions to gentility. A further five reeked of the counting house. Admittedly, Thomas Minors belonged to a medieval gentry family from Uttoxeter that had fallen on financially evil days, and had been driven into commerce to restore its fortunes. He set up as a mercer with a shop in Sadler Street, Lichfield. Minors apart, the other four commissioners were pure merchant types. Robert Smith of Cheadle was another mercer who vended 'cloth stuffs, linen and drapery ware'; as for the other three, John Symcox from West Bromwich was an enterprising ironmonger, catering for both the local and national markets; William Gent a prosperous grocer in Leek; and Henry Stone of Walsall both a tobacco merchant and a retailer of West Midland ironware, making him a man with 'a great interest in the cuntre'.[19]

---

pp. 21–23; Alan Everitt, *The Community of Kent and the Great Rebellion 1640–1660* (Leicester, 1966), p. 143. To gain an initial impression of the social status of Major-General Worsley's Staffordshire deputies, I have used the rankings assigned them in the six assessment commissions of 23 June 1647, 16 February 1648, 7 April and 7 December 1649, 26 November 1650 and 10 December 1652. See C. H. Firth and R. S. Rait, *Acts and Ordinances of the Interregnum* [henceforth *A&O*], 3 vols. (1911), I, pp. 973–74, 1091; II, pp. 42, 307, 376, 673.

[18] For Wyrley's knighthood see W. A. Shaw (ed.), *The Knights of England: A Complete Record from the Earliest Time to the Present Day* (London, 1906), II, p. 209. The pre-Civil War seigneurial status of the families of the other five commissioners is confirmed by the Parliamentary subsidy rolls, Protestation returns and poll-tax certificates for Staffordshire in 1641–42: PRO, E179/179/310–312; House of Lords Record Office (HLRO), Protestation Returns, Offlow Hundred, Staffs, February–March 1642; HLRO, Main Papers, 28 February 1642: Staffordshire Poll Tax Certificates: Offlow and Pirehill Hundreds.

[19] For the Adshead estate at Milwich see T. Harwood, *Sampson Erdeswicks' Survey of Staffordshire* (Westminster, 1820), pp. 45–46; *SHC*, New Series, XII (1909), p. 159. Though designated a gentleman himself, Peter Backhouse's father, Robert, was described as a

Finally there were four commissioners with professional occupations. All but one of them pursued careers in the law. Daniel Watson combined his activities as a barrister, however, with running a brewery or 'Brorehouse', in his native Burton-upon-Trent. The attorney Thomas Worswick ended his days as a gentleman-farmer with a solid estate near his home town of Stafford. Zachary Babbington's wide-ranging legal pursuits – from associate clerk on the Oxford Circuit to a variety of judicial posts (judge, JP and deputy clerk of the peace) in his own county – converted an estimated income of £10 per annum in 1641 into £200 a year by the Restoration. The odd man out in this small knot of professional gentry was Matthew Worswick of Stafford who found his vocation in medicine. His skills as an apothecary were called upon not just in his birthplace but as far afield as Shrewsbury.[20]

So far our investigation into the social standing of the Staffordshire commissioners before 1642 has revealed a perceptible division between a small inner circle (six in all) of genuine rank and distinction; and a much larger outer fringe, comprising minor/borderline gentry and mercantile and professional arrivistes. This dichotomy becomes even more evident when one examines the armorial status of the twenty-two men under review: no fewer than eleven, possibly twelve, Staffordshire commissioners were non-armigerous. During Sir William Dugdale's heraldic visitation of Staffordshire in 1663 five of these men did not apply for this much-

yeoman when interred at Seighford on 2 January 1632: *SPRS* 1977–78: Seighford 1561–1812, p. 45. Thomas Malkin had the classification of a yeoman in the pre-Civil War poll tax: HLRO, Main Papers, 28 February 1642: Staffordshire Poll Tax Certificates: Totmonslow Hundred. On Thomas Minors' gentry descent see note 24. For details of his trade as mercer in Lichfield see PRO, Prob. 4/5879; Prob. 11/355/100; E. A. Watkin, 'Staffordshire tokens and their place in the coinage of England', *North Staffordshire Journal of Field Studies*, I, 1961, p. 12. On Robert Smith's commercial background: *SHC* 4th Series, II, p. 28; Lichfield Joint Record Office (LJRO), WP, 4 April 1674. For John Symcox, the ironmonger, see HLRO, Parchment Collection: 2 May 1645: Depositions of witnesses in the dispute between the Earl of Denbigh and Staffordshire Parliamentary Committee; Marie B. Rowlands, *Masters and Men in the West Midland Metalware Trades before the Industrial Revolution* (Manchester, 1975), pp. 11, 72. William Gent's will confirms his status as a grocer and refers to 'my shop and warehouse in Leek': PRO, Prob. 11/381/108. For Henry Stone's career as a tobacco merchant and a retailer of West Midland ironware see PRO, SP29/101/29 part II; SP24/42/Crompton vs Fitzwilliam; *SHC*, 4th Series, II, p. 30; E. J. Homeshaw, *The Corporation of the Borough and Foreign of Walsall* (Walsall, 1960), pp. 32–33; Rowlands, *Masters and Men*, p. 118.

20 For Watson, the barrister-cum-brewer: Colin Owen, *Burton upon Trent: The Illustrated History* (Derby, 1994), pp. 51–52: *SHC*, 1923, p. 199; on attorney Thomas Worswick's conversion into a farmer see his will: LJRO, WP, 10 March 1664; for Babbington's legal career, see J. S. Cockburn, *A History of English Assizes 1558–1714* (Cambridge, 1972), pp. 81–82, 317, 324–25; and on Matthew Worswick's practice as an apothecary: D. H. Pennington and I. Roots, *The Committee at Stafford 1643–1645* (Manchester, 1957), p. 59.

coveted prestige symbol. Nor had any of their forbears laid claim to arms in the heraldic visitations of 1614 and 1583. A lack of social ambition may have lain behind this reluctance; but more probably it was prompted by a hard-nosed realisation that, given their lowly origins, any efforts to secure armigerous status would doubtless end in the humiliation of being pronounced 'ignobilis' by over-officious heralds.[21]

The heraldic aspirations of three other non-armigerous commissioners – Matthew and Thomas Worswick and Thomas Adshead – cannot be ascertained, since these men were dead by the time of Dugdale's visitation in 1663. However another three were alive and did try to have their alleged coats of arms recorded. One, Thomas Pudsey, proved successful; another, Daniel Watson, was granted leave 'to exhibit' proof of his armorial pretensions, though he never furnished any. The third candidate, Henry Stone, who panted after an escutcheon like a miser after gold, not only had his claims rejected but also suffered the acute humiliation of being publicly disclaimed at the Stafford assizes in August 1664. Finally there was a commissioner in a special category of his own, namely John Young of Charnes, whose family blazon had never received official sanction: it was spurned in both 1583 and 1614, while in 1663 Young's widow Catherine prudently avoided a third rejection by the snobbish Dugdale. Acceptance, however, did finally come in the 1680s at the hands of the more amenable herald Gregory King.[22]

If we look at the ten armigerous commissioners, few could boast of an unbroken line of gentry descent legitimised by 'an ancient use of arms'. Three belonged to families which had only acquired armorial bearings in the Jacobean period, those of George Bowes and Thomas Crompton dating back to just 1614 and Zachary Babbington's merely to 1619. Poor Thomas Crompton's merchant ancestors in the City of London were dismissed by the late Elizabethan Staffordshire antiquary, Sampson Erdeswick, as 'ex humili loco natus'. To these three relative newcomers to the ranks of the armigerous gentry in the county one could add Edward

---

[21] The eleven non-armigerous commissioners are listed in Appendix 1. The five who made no effort to procure a coat of arms in 1663 were Peter Backhouse, William Gent, Thomas Malkin, Robert Smith and John Symcox. The numbers of Staffordshire men pronounced 'ignoblis' for making bogus claims to gentility, both in 1583 and 1664, were quite considerable: cf. *Staffs. Pedigrees: 1584*, pp. 14–15; and *Staffs. Pedigrees: 1614 and 1663–64*, pp. 342–46.

[22] For the success or failure of Pudsey, Watson and Stone in their heraldic pretensions see *Staffs. Pedigrees: 1614 and 1663–64*, pp. 245–46, 299, 344. On the chequered history of the armigerous pretensions of the Young family: *Staffs. Pedigrees: 1583*, p. 10; *Staffs. Pedigrees: 1614 and 1663–64*, p. 337; eds. Sir George Armytage and W. H. Rylands, *Staffordshire Pedigrees ... 1680 & 1700*, edited for the Harleian Society, LXII (1912), p. 260.

Brett, whose grandfather and namesake had been granted a coat of arms in October 1599. This was subsequently carved on an oak beam in the family seat at Dimsdale Hall in an ostentatious flourish. Thus half of the so-called armigerous commissioners were in fact 'greenhorn' gentry with escutcheons of only recent vintage.[23]

Thus we are left with a hard core of half a dozen commissioners who truly possessed ancient lineage. All six men could take pride in their pedigrees, none more so than Thomas Whitgreave, whose family took its name from the small village of Whitgreave, a few miles north-west of Stafford, where they had reportedly been in residence since pre-Conquest days. The knighthood which Cromwell bestowed on Whitgreave in July 1658 was thus a simple acknowledgement of his time-hallowed ancestry. Other commissioners boasting antiquity of blood were Sir John Wyrley, with forbears going back to Henry II's reign, if not before; John Chetwode, whose progenitors had been established at Oakley in north-west Staffordshire since the late fourteenth century; Thomas Minors, the proud owner of a family shield which dated back to at least 1433 and which he had engraved in miniature on his gold signet ring; Edward Mainwaring, the scion of a family that, though only settled in Staffordshire since 1546, could trace its roots in neighbouring Cheshire deep into the Middle Ages; and George Bellot, descendant of Thomas Bellot of Great Moreton Hall, who occurs in a Cheshire heraldic listing of c. 1490 known as Ballad's Roll.[24]

[23] The arms of George Bowes' great-grandfather, Sir John, had been declared 'doubtful' in 1583; while those of Thomas Crompton's ancestor, William, were rejected outright, though both were accepted in 1614. Cf. *Staffs. Pedigrees: 1583*, pp. 5, 15, 29; *Staffs. Pedigrees: 1614 and 1663*, pp. 46–47, 101–2. On the Jacobean escutcheon acquired by Zachary Babbington's father, William, see John Fetherston (ed.), *The Visitation of the County of Leicester in the Year 1619*, Harleian Society Publications (London, 1870), II, pp. 205–6. For the Crompton's mercantile origins and the spiteful comments this provoked: WSL, Salt Ms 201, 1, p. 44; Harwood, *Erdeswick*, p. 34. On the armorial pride of the Bretts see *Staffs. Pedigrees: 1614 and 1663*, p. 55; John Ward, *The Borough of Stoke-upon-Trent* (London, 1843), p. 117.

[24] Regarding the medieval ancestry of these six commissioners; for Bellot see Ralph Griffen (ed.), *Cheshire Arms c1490*, Miscellanea Genealogica et Heraldica, September 1933, p. 4; Sir George Armytage and J. P. Rylands (eds.), *Pedigrees made at the Visitation of Cheshire, 1613*, Lancashire and Cheshire Record Society, LI (1909), pp. 20, 22; Chetwode: WSL, Salt Mss 154, p. 58; and ibid., 201, vol. 1, p. 43; *Staffs. Pedigrees: 1680–1700*, p. 48; Mainwaring: Harwood, *Erdeswick*, pp. 7–8; *SHC*; 1934, pp. 47, 52; Minors: Harwood, *Erdeswick*, pp. 386–87; Whitgreave: BL, Stowe Mss 878, fo. 22; Shaw (ed.), *The Knights of England*, II, p. 224; *Staffs. Pedigrees: 1680–1700*, pp. 241–42; Wyrley: Harwood, *Erdeswick*, pp. 288, 306; William Wyrley, *A True Use of Armorie* (London, 1592), pp. 17, 18; S. Shaw, *The History and Antiquities of Staffordshire (Staffs.)*, 2 vols. (1798–1801) II, pp. 110, 115, 116.

VI

We still need to explore the economic fortunes of the commissioners in Staffordshire. This is important in view of the discrepancy that could exist between a landowner's armorial standing and his financial position. Simple possession of a coat of arms did not automatically indicate wealth, as the case of George Bellot, a very poor gentleman of ancient pedigree, shows.[25]

Three key indicators exist for determining the economic status of the twenty-two men under review. The first of these is income per annum. A considerable amount of information is available about the incomes of all but six of the commissioners, including the valuations given in the 1641 Staffordshire poll-tax returns; an anonymous catalogue of prominent Parliamentarian supporters in the county dated c. 1644; and a more wide-ranging list of the Staffordshire gentry – including Royalist and neutral landowners as well as Parliamentarian adherents – drawn up in the immediate wake of the Restoration. The sums given are suspiciously rounded but provide a broad indication of the distribution of income among the Staffordshire commissioners.[26]

By far the wealthiest of them was Edward Mainwaring whose annual income was assessed at £1,000 in c. 1662/3, a figure hardly surprising when we remember his extensive property-holdings not only in Stafford-shire but also in neighbouring Cheshire and distant Kent. 'Moneyed' indeed! Immediately beneath Mainwaring came three commissioners with respectable incomes in the £500–£700 per annum bracket: George Bowes, John Chetwode, John Young. In financial terms these men can best be classified as middling gentry. The same might be said of Thomas Crompton, who was reported by a post-Restoration observer to have an income of £400 a year. This intermediate category should probably also include Sir John Wyrley. The valuation of his estate at a mere £100 per annum in the early 1660s seems unrealistic. Later in the century his demesne lands at Hampstead alone were reputed to be worth £300–£400 annually, a figure which did not include the other Wyrley holdings in the county like the manor of Tipton.[27]

[25] On Bellot's minuscule annuity see PRO, SP23/180/754.
[26] For the three main sources for the commissioners' annual incomes see HLRO, Main Papers, 28 February 1642; *Staffordshire Poll Tax Certificates.* Offlow, Pirehill and Totmon-slow Hundreds (Adshead, Symcox, Matthew Worswick); BL Harl. 378/4 (Bowes and Young); and *SHC*, 4th Series (1958), vol. II, pp. 11–12, 30, 32, 36, 37 (Babbington, Crompton, Chetwode, Mainwaring, Stone, Wyrley). Cf. note 28 for additional information on this subject.
[27] A mark of Edward Mainwaring's affluence in the 1650s was his extensive involvement in the property market: J. G. Cavenagh-Mainwaring, 'The Mainwarings of Whitmore and Biddulph in the County of Stafford', *SHC* (1934), pp. 66–67. For the solid incomes of

At the lower end of the income scale was a much larger group of commissioners – ten in all – whose economic circumstances differed markedly from those of their well-to-do colleagues. Four of these lesser types had incomes below £100 a year, among them Peter Backhouse, whose son Thomas was said by Gregory King in c. 1680 to own lands in Doxey worth a modest £80 per annum. Three of the remaining six commissioners, Adshead, Brett and Pudsey, were only marginally better off, hovering just above the £100 per annum borderline. The trio whose annual income lay around the more respectable £200 mark – Babbington, Stone, Watson – were either tradesmen or professional gentry and thus not entirely dependent on agriculture for a livelihood. Judged overall, then, the majority of the Staffordshire commissioners were among the financial lees of the gentry with only a few who could be characterised as affluent.[28]

A second guide to the wealth of the Staffordshire commissioners is provided by their hearth-tax assessments. According to Margaret Spufford, the number of hearths in an occupant's house gives a rough indication of his relative position in the economic hierarchy. By far the best hearth-tax return for Staffordshire, in terms of both its scope and comprehensiveness, is that surviving for 1665–66, only a decade after the commissioners held power. From this we can glean the hearth-tax valuations of nineteen commissioners.[29]

Most modern commentators would agree that those householders assessed for fewer than five hearths can usually be deemed members of 'the middling sort' rather than gentlefolk. By this yardstick, three commissioners fell into that lower category. Thomas Malkin's son Charles was residing in a three-hearth house in the mid-1660s which, while commensurate with the family's yeoman status, hardly matched their pretensions to gentility! The hearth-tax assessments of the other two commissioners were equally modest: the widow of apothecary Matthew Worswick was

---

Bowes, Chetwode and Young see note 26 above. Though described as 'a man of good estate', Thomas Crompton's financial fortunes were, in fact, declining: cf. PRO SP29/101/29 part II; PRO E134/24 Charles II/Mich 10. Over the baffling variations in the estimates of Sir John Wyrley's annual income, see SHC, 4th Series (1958), p. 32; PRO, E134/8 William III/Easter no. 13.

28 For the yearly income of Peter Backhouse's son, Thomas, in 1680 see SHC (1919), p. 227. In a pre-Civil War chancery dispute Edward Brett's father was said to have a 'good estate of inheritance' worth around £100 per annum. Cf. PRO, C3/Ser II/435/24. A similar estimate was made of Thomas Pudsey's income in 1645: HLRO, Parchment Collection: 2 May 1645: Staffordshire depositions re. the Earl of Denbigh. On the annual wealth of Babbington, Stone and Watson see notes 19 and 20.

29 The way in which the hearth-tax returns can be used as 'general guides to wealth' is discussed in Margaret Spufford, 'The Significance of the Cambridgeshire Hearth Tax', Proceedings of the Cambridgeshire Antiquarian Society, 55, 1962, pp. 53–64. Fortunately, the 1665–66 Staffordshire hearth-tax return has been printed in extenso in SHC (1921, 1923, 1925, 1936).

occupying a tenement in the county town with four fireplaces, while Robert Smith's grocery 'store' at Cheadle contained three hearths.[30]

Turning to the remaining sixteen commissioners, we find that ten possessed intermediate dwellings with between five and nine flues. Some of these edifices were clearly solid farmhouses like those of the yeoman Peter Backhouse at Doxey and the minor country gentleman Thomas Pudsey at Seisdon, each containing six hearths. Others belonged to the miniature manor-house category such as the eight-hearthed Bridgeford Hall, home of Thomas Whitgreave, and the similarly rated Charnes Hall where John Young's widow Catherine was living in 1665–66. Young's status as an esquire and £500-a-year income marched hand in hand with the hearth-tax assessment of his property. But one must be wary of simplification, since there was by no means an automatic association between wealth and hearth-tax rating. The mismatch which could exist between these two variables is shown in the cases of Edward Brett (£100 p.a. and nine chimneys), Henry Stone (£200 p.a. and two properties with nine and four hearths respectively), John Symcox (£50 p.a. and five grates) and Daniel Watson (£200 p.a. and eight fireplaces).[31]

Only with the six commissioners who resided in large halls – those assessed for ten hearths and above – can the chimney tax be said to furnish a fairly accurate measure of their means. There was a clear-cut correlation between the financial livelihood of men like George Bowes and John Chetwode, who respectively commanded £700 and £600 a year, and their hearth-tax assessments, namely for fifteen grates at Elford Hall, the former's country mansion, and for eleven at Oakley Hall, the latter's. An even closer fit is to be found in the case of Edward Mainwaring, whose post-Restoration income of £1,000 per annum exactly dovetailed with the number of hearths – nineteen – in his ancestral pile. Only Zachary Babbington, whose thirteen-hearthed hall at Curborough stood in contrast to his modest income of £200 a year in the early 1660s, proved the exception to the rule. Despite the fluctuations in the data, it should once again be apparent that, while the majority of the Staffordshire commissioners were men of solid property, they tended to be drawn from the bottom rung of the landowning élite.[32]

The third and final means of ascertaining the economic position of the

---

[30] For the hearth-tax assessments of these three commissioners – or their kith and kin – see *SHC*, 1925, pp. 160, 164; *SHC*, 1921, p. 44.

[31] The hearth-tax ratings of the ten commissioners mentioned in this paragraph are given in: *SHC* (1921) pp. 89, 107, 126, 141: *SHC* (1923), pp. 102, 126, 199, 202, 247; *SHC* (1925), p. 164; and *SHC* (1936), p. 152.

[32] On the hearth-tax valuations of these six well-to-do commissioners see *SHC* (1921), pp. 96, 133, 136; *SHC* (1923), pp. 122, 228, 243.

Staffordshire commissioners is through a study of their probate inventories. Ten of these invaluable documents have been traced, a reasonably representative sample covering just under half of the men in question. Needless to say, the aggregated sums in the probate inventories under examination are valuations of personal, not real, estate. Thus they provide only a partial guide to the financial health of the individuals concerned. It is nonetheless instructive to compare the variations in the gross values given in the probate accounts, since they afford a measure, however crude, of the deceased's living standards.[33]

Such an analysis reveals that only one commissioner was in straitened economic circumstances at the time of his death. This was Thomas Adshead who, to escape his creditors, had migrated to Ireland, leaving behind a few sticks of furniture in a house at Uttoxeter worth a mere £33. At the opposite end of the spectrum a solitary commissioner, Thomas Minors, enjoyed a truly plutocratic fortune: his moveable property amounted to a staggering £2,331. All of the remaining eight commissioners had solid personal wealth, with five falling in the lower range of £100–£499 and three in the upper category, between £500 and £999. Altogether the cumulative value of the moveable goods appraised in these ten inventories was a little short of £6,000. The arithmetical mean, for what it is worth in such a small number of cases, works out at £579 17s. 2d.; while the median, perhaps a more valuable calculation since it avoids the extreme variations in the distribution of the data, produces a figure of £420 7s. 2d. By the yardstick of their probate inventories, then, the Staffordshire commissioners had a spread of personal wealth that broadly ran in tandem with their income per annum and hearth assessments and which clearly locates them among the lesser gentry or the more prosperous 'middling sort of people'.[34]

VII

Let us turn to the commissioners' administrative experience. They had impressive records both of national and local expertise. Five had served as

---

[33] An excellent review of the problems which beset modern historians using this material is Philip Riden (ed.), *Probate Records and the Local Community* (Gloucester, 1985), Introduction.

[34] For the whereabouts of the ten probate inventories sampled here, two – those of Thomas Minors and Thomas Pudsey – are located at PRO, Prob. 4/5879 and 7024. Another seven can be consulted at LJRO: Thomas Adshead, WP. 17 February 1662; Peter Backhouse, WP. 20 April 1675; Robert Smith, WP. 4 April 1674; John Chetwode, WP. 15 October 1667; Edward Mainwaring, WP. 24 July 1675; Zachary Babbington, WP. 9 December 1687; Thomas Worswick, WP. 9 March 1664. The tenth, that of George Bowes, in Birmingham Reference Library (BRL), Elford Hall Ms, 294.

MPs before 1655. The most outstanding was Thomas Crompton: elected to the Long Parliament in 1647, this 'recruiter' MP survived Pride's Purge to become Staffordshire's principal representative in the Rump. He also sat in the first Protectorate Parliament. Two other commissioners, Bellot and Chetwode, had been members of the Nominated Assembly; while two more – Whitgreave and Minors – were returned to the Parliament of 1654.[35]

It also says something about the calibre of these men that a number of them secured election to subsequent parliaments. Crompton, Minors and Whitgreave were again selected in June 1656 and January 1659. Daniel Watson was MP for Lichfield in Richard Cromwell's Parliament and again – until he was unseated by Minors for electoral malpractice – in the Convention Parliament; while Edward Mainwaring even managed to get himself elected to the Cavalier Parliament in the unpropitious climate of 1661. Less successful was Henry Stone, who, according to Sir Simon Degge, sought to become one of the knights of the shire during the elections to the second Protectorate Parliament in June 1656, 'but was put back in disgrace'.[36]

That the Staffordshire commissioners possessed solid administrative experience is further shown by a review of their work in local government. No fewer than fourteen were acting JPs in 1655. Admittedly none of them had been members of the bench in the pre-Civil War days. Yet the paternal grandfathers of Babbington and Bowes and the fathers of Crompton, Mainwaring and Wyrley had served as magistrates in the reigns of James I and Charles I. Nearly two thirds of the commissioners were justices of more than five years' standing. Five had been appointed between November 1645 and April 1647; four more in June 1649; and the remaining five in the early 1650s. Between them the fourteen men could notch up just over a century of magisterial work. It should also be noted that, one year after his nomination, Matthew Worswick was appointed a JP in his native Stafford, though by then his work as a commissioner was effectively over.[37]

These men had experience of other forms of local government too.

[35] On the Parliamentary careers of Crompton, Bellot, Chetwode and Whitgreave see J. C. Wedgwood, *Staffordshire Parliamentary History from the Earliest Times to the Present Day*, vol. II: *SHC* (1920–22), pp. 74–76, 93–94, 97–98, 101.

[36] For the Parliamentary careers of Minors, Watson and Mainwaring: *SHC* (1920–22), pp. 99–100, 103, 107–8, 126; and B. D. Henning (ed.), *The House of Commons 1660–1690* (1979) III, pp. 2, 70, 678. For Henry Stone's abortive electoral bid in 1656 see Shaw, *Staffs.* II, p. 74.

[37] The identity of the fourteen commissioners with magisterial experience down to 1655–56 has been ascertained by using three principal sources: (1). PRO, C193/13/3, fos. 58–59; C193/13/4, fos. 89–91; C193/13/5; (2). SRO, SQSR: 1645 (Michaelmas), fo. 36;

Fourteen had acted as assessors for the army tax prior to 1655; and while none of the group was a sheriff before this date, two did hold sheriffdoms after the Restoration (Wyrley in 1664–65 and Stone from November 1676 to January 1677). Five had an impressive record in urban administration, occupying positions such as mayor (Matthew Worswick at Stafford 1655–56), sheriff (Thomas Minors at Lichfield in 1642), bailiff (Minors again, 1648–49 and 1657–58), recorder and steward (Daniel Watson at Stafford 1652, Newcastle-under-Lyme 1659 and Lichfield after the Restoration), capital burgess and feoffee of town lands and revenues (Henry Stone at Walsall from May 1647) and churchwarden and vestryman (Robert Smith at Cheadle between April 1658 and May 1673).[38]

More pertinently to the task required of them in 1655, the commissioners had a wealth of experience as militia officers, in both a civilian and military capacity. Six had served as commissioners for the Staffordshire militia back in 1648; while eleven, including four of the former, were members of the militia commission which Cromwell had issued in March 1655 shortly after Penruddock's revolt. This had instructed them to monitor closely the 'conspiracies and secret meetings of the disaffected' in Staffordshire and their work in this sphere must have proved an invaluable preparation for their more wide-ranging surveillance activities the following autumn. A bonus was the fact that nine of the appointees in October 1655 had been, or currently were, field officers in the local militia. These included two colonels, a lieutenant-colonel, a major, four captains and a lieutenant. Most prominent among them was Colonel Thomas Crompton, aptly described by a modern historian as 'the Sword of the Government' in the shire throughout the Interregnum. The security operation in Staffordshire could only have been enhanced by the presence of such 'swordsmen'.[39]

1648 (Easter), fo. 76; 1650 (Michaelmas), fo. 40; 1656 (Easter), fo. 77; (3). *SHC*, 1912, pp. 333–37.

[38] For the fourteen commissioners identified as assessors for the army tax, see *A&O*, I, pp. 973–74, 1091; II, pp. 42, 307, 476, 673. On the sheriffdoms of Wyrley and Stone: *SHC* (1912), pp. 287–88. Concerning the five commissioners with experience of urban administration: for Matthew Worswick see J. W. Bradley (ed.), *The Royal Charters and Letters Patent Granted to the Burgesses of Stafford AD 1206–1828* (Stafford, 1897), p. 206; for Thomas Minors see Thomas Harwood, *The History and Antiquities of the Church and City of Lichfield* (Gloucester, 1806), pp. 426–27; for Daniel Watson, see ibid., p. 438 and T. Pape, *Newcastle-under-Lyme in Tudor and Early Stuart times* (Manchester, 1938), pp. 74, 334 and *CSPD*, 1677–78, p. 33; for Henry Stone see Homeshaw, *The Corporation of the Borough and Foreign of Walsall*, pp. 54–56; and Robert Smith: SRO, D233/A/PC Cheadle Account Book: entries for 1658, 1660, 1673.

[39] For the thirteen deputies who had been appointed commissioners for the Staffordshire militia in December 1648 and/or March 1655 see *A&O*, I, p. 1242 and PRO, SP25/76/30. NB that Thomas Whitgreave was first appointed to the militia commission in July 1650:

VIII

We have examined the administrative expertise of the commissioners. What then of their political reliability? Wherever possible, Cromwell and his advisers seem to have chosen for commissioners men with a record of firm attachment to the parliamentary cause in the 1640s. We can particularise about the earlier political behaviour of all but one of the Staffordshire personnel, the exception being William Gent whose civil war loyalties are shrouded in obscurity. Only four had less than impeccable Parliamentarian backgrounds. George Bellot hailed from a fervently royalist family, though his own parliamentarian sympathies were not in doubt. Thomas Whitgreave had been conspicuous by his absence in the first and second civil wars, yet not in the third when he spent twenty-eight days as a cavalry captain in the local militia hunting down royalist fugitives from the battle of Worcester. Zachary Babbington had been an arch-trimmer, incurring the wrath of Royalists and Parliamentarians alike for his mercurial behaviour. Equally suspect was Sir John Wyrley, an elusive figure who resided in London and Surrey during the war years and who is perhaps best classified as a parliamentary-inclined neutral.[40]

The remaining seventeen men had demonstrated their fidelity to the Long Parliament during the fratricidal conflicts of the 1640s. Of course, one must recognise that there were degrees of loyalty. Even so, only two commissioners can be characterised as passive parliamentary adherents, Thomas Malkin and Thomas Minors. Activists, by contrast, numbered fifteen. Of these, six had served the Parliamentary cause in a purely

---

CSPD, 1650, p. 25. The military ranks of the nine deputies with experience as field officers in the Staffordshire militia were gleaned from the following sources; PRO, SP25/76/34–5; PRO, SP28/242/part 3, fos. 379–80: Bodl. Lib., Clarendon Ms, vol. 62, fos. 222–23; *TSP*, III, pp. 94–95; Ibid., IV, pp. 647–48; *CSPD*, 1650, p. 506.

[40] Though he himself 'remained in the Parliament's service', George Bellot's father, John, was sequestered in the Civil War 'for residing in the King's quarters'; while four of his brothers espoused the royal cause, three being taken prisoner at the surrender of Biddulph Hall on 21 February 1644. See PRO, SP23/1844, 755, 758; BL, Harl. Mss 2144, fos. 75, 160; BL, Thomason Tracts, E37(4), *The Military Scribe 5–12 March 1644*, p. 19; E35(25), *The Kingdom's Weekly Intelligence, 29 February–6 March 1644*, pp. 170, 172; *Memoirs of the Civil War in Cheshire by Thomas Malbon and Edward Burghall*, Lancashire and Cheshire Record Society (1889), pp. 122–23. In 1650 George Bellot served as a captain of horse in the Staffordshire militia with whom he saw action in Scotland: PRO, SP28/242/part 3, fo. 379. For Whitgreave's military service during the Worcester campaign: Ibid., fo. 380. On Babbington's tortuous neutrality during the Civil War see WSL, D1553/81; D. A. Johnson and D. G. Vaisey (ed.), *Staffordshire and the Great Rebellion* (Staffordshire County Council, 1964), pp. 35–36; Huntingdon Library: Henry Hastings Ms, HA 5571. Evidence of Wyrley's low profile in the Civil War: PRO, SP23/143/307, 321–322; PRO, SP19/63/109; and 75/174.

civilian capacity: John Chetwode was a receiver of the money and plate raised in London for the relief of Staffordshire at the commencement of hostilities; John Symcox the first treasurer of the Staffordshire Parliamentary Committee in 1643; Matthew Worswick a conductor for the Roundhead troops mustered in Stafford in 1645; Edward Mainwaring a sequestrator of Royalist estates from 1643–46; while Edward Brett and Thomas Adshead both served as commissioners for taking the accounts of the kingdom in their native shire at the war's end.[41]

The remaining nine commissioners had seen military action in the parliamentary service. Among their ranks were to be found two former colonels and six captains. Four of these officers had also served as governors of parliamentarian garrisons in the county during 'the brother-killing days'. The governorships of Caverswall Castle, Lapley House and Wrottesley Hall had been held by John Young, Robert Smith and Peter Backhouse, respectively; while Henry Stone was the governor of both Eccleshall Castle and Stafford. Three ex-servicemen among the commissioners – including two of the above – could even be described as war heroes. There was Colonel Thomas Crompton who boasted in September 1645 that 'it is verie well knowne by men of eminancie yt my zeale and affection hath to ye utmost been demonstrated with ye often hazard of my life'. There was Captain, later Colonel, Henry Stone, of whom Sir William Brereton had said in March 1645: 'I dare affirm that his single troop of horse … hath done as much service as any in England.' And there was Captain Peter Backhouse, whose actions in the first Civil War were said to be 'valient, faithful and successful', and who showed equally sterling prowess during the Scottish invasion of Staffordshire in August 1648.[42]

---

[41] Thomas Malkin signed two pro-Parliamentary petitions during the 1640s, but appears to have done little else. See HLRO, Main Papers, Staffordshire petitions of 16 May 1642 and 1 October 1644. Thomas Minors declared in a petition to the Committee of Indemnity in February 1653 that he 'did all these late warres adhere to ye Parliamt', though what form that allegiance took is not known: PRO, SP24/74 Saxon, Mott, Minors and Wilmot vs Finney. For the work of John Chetwode as receiver and John Symcox as treasurer of the funds raised for the Parliamentary war-effort in Staffordshire early in 1643 see PRO, SP28/176/part 1: John Symcox's accounts. On Matthew Worswicke's role as a conductor of Parliamentary troops in Stafford during the Civil War: BL, Add. Ms 28716, fo. 19. On Edward Mainwaring's service as a sequestrator: *Commons' Journals* (*CJ*), III, p. 119. On Edward Brett's and Thomas Adshead's work as Staffordshire commissioners for taking the accounts of the Kingdom: PRO, SP28/144/part 6, fo. 28.

[42] For the two commissioners who were former Parliamentary colonels – Thomas Crompton and Henry Stone – see below. The six commissioners who had held captaincies in the Parliamentary army included: Peter Backhouse: PRO, E121/2/10; *TSP*, IV, pp. 647–48: George Bowes: PRO, SP28/131, part 12/21; BRL, Elford Hall Ms 280: Thomas Pudsey: PRO, SP23/168/455; PRO, SP28/200/Pudsey's accounts; Robert Smith: see below: Daniel Watson: PRO, SP28/226/Watson's accounts; R. N. Dore, *The Letter Books of Sir William Brereton*, 2 vols. (1984, 1990), I, pp. 73, 96, 205, 216, 233. For John

Seven commissioners had been members of the Staffordshire Parliamentary Committee during the previous decade. In their study of this body, Donald Pennington and Ivan Roots drew attention to an ideological division between 'the adherents of Sir William Brereton who in general favoured the most energetic and uncompromising prosecution of the (civil) war' and 'those of the Earl of Denbigh who were attracted by peacemaking'. Four of the ex-committeemen had been pro-Brereton supporters, as against two who were pro-Denbigh (the seventh, John Chetwode, seems to have been non-aligned during the controversy between the two sides). This might seem to suggest that former Parliamentarian hardliners were chosen by the Protector to serve as commissioners in the county in 1655: but such a gloss would be erroneous. Of the fifteen commissioners who had not themselves been members of the Staffordshire Committee, none (with the possible exception of Backhouse) are known to have been henchmen of Brereton but five did express their support for Denbigh in a petition in September 1644. On the basis of this evidence, the political moderates on the commission thus outnumbered their more radical colleagues by a ratio of nearly two to one.[43]

IX

There remains the vexed question of the commissioners' religious affiliations. That they were a godly group of men is beyond doubt. Six of them can be shown to have been particularly pious. Peter Backhouse was said by fourteen of his colleagues in March 1656 to have 'procured esteem from the religious'. George Bowes had signed a petition in March 1642 calling for a thorough reformation in the Anglican church. Henry Stone main-

Young, see below. Concerning the four commissioners who were erstwhile governors of Parliamentary garrisons in the county during the first Civil War: for Young see *Committee at Stafford*, pp. 5–6; for Smith, see ibid., pp. 10, 18; for Backhouse see *Historical Manuscripts Commission* (*HMC*), 13th Report (1891) Portland Mss, I, p. 306; and for Stone see PRO, E112/566 (Deposition of Henry Stone). For the three 'war heroes' among the commissioners: for Backhouse: *TSP*, IV, pp. 647–49; PRO, SP23/66/463, 475–77; for Crompton see Warwickshire Record Office (WRO), CR2017, vol. 2, fo. 92; for Stone: Dore, *Brereton*, I, pp. 150–51.

[43] Brief biographies of the seven commissioners who were former members of the Staffordshire Parliamentary Committee are to be found in *Committee at Stafford*, pp. 351–56. The four pro-Brereton supporters were Pudsey, Stone, Symcox and Watson, and the two pro-Denbigh adherents Crompton and Mainwaring. For the stance adopted by these men during the Brereton–Denbigh dispute: Dore, *Brereton*, I, pp. xxiv–lxxxi, 148, 152, 346; HLRO, Parchment Collection: 2 May 1645: *Staffordshire Depositions, Lords' Journals* (*LJ*), VI, pp. 651–52, 654, 682 and VII, pp. 173, 416–18. Bowes, Young, Brett, Malkin and Matthew Worswick signed the pro-Denbigh address of 30 September 1644: HLRO, Main Papers, 1 October 1644: Staffordshire Petition.

tained a fervent religious correspondence with Sir William Brereton during the first Civil War. Edward Brett was appointed a feoffee of the impropriate rectory of Wolstanton in January 1647, administering the profits for the maintenance of 'honest, godly, learned and religious preaching ministers' there. Matthew Worswick promoted an address to the Protector in December 1657 'for advanceing ye gospel and encouraging and promoting of godlynes' in the shire town; and John Young won renown in the early 1650s for his determined efforts that 'godly people' in his locality should be able 'to hear Christ taught' by 'godly men'.[44]

Such zeal should not be confused with fanaticism. Most of the commissioners seem to have been on the conservative ends of the Puritan spectrum. Four can be unambiguously labelled 'Presbyterians': Babbington, Smith, Minors and Stone. Henry Stone was particularly keen to promote Presbyterian clergymen during the Interregnum, as shown by his presentation of 'my welbeloved in Christ, Joseph Eccleshall' to the rectory of Sedgley in February 1657. His friend, Thomas Minors, proved an even greater patron to clerics of this persuasion, especially after the Restoration when he provided financial relief for a number of those who had been ejected. One other commissioner can probably also be rated a Presbyterian: Thomas Crompton. He was reported to be 'of any religion' in the early 1660s; but his membership of the select committee set up in the first Protectorate Parliament to examine the effectiveness of the ordinance for ejecting scandalous ministers hardly suggests a religiously indifferent man.[45]

More surprising, perhaps, is the presence of two men with Anglican

---

[44] The godly zeal of these six commissioners is attested in the following sources: for Backhouse: *TSP*, IV, p. 647; for Bowes, HLRO, Main Papers, 16 May 1642, Staffordshire Petition (actually dated 25 March 1642, though not submitted to the Lords until the following May); for Brett see PRO, SP28/331/31; for Stone see BL, Add. Ms 11333, fos. 18, 82v, 125; for (Matthew) Worswicke: PRO, SP18/179/62; for Young see BL, Thomason Tracts, E219(26) *Severall Proceedings of State Affaires in England, Ireland and Scotland*, 13–20 October 1653, p. 3354.

[45] Three of these four commissioners – Babbington, Smith and Stone – were classified as Presbyterians in the post-Restoration survey of the Staffordshire gentry. See *SHC*, 4th ser. (1958), II, pp. 28, 30, 37. For Henry Stone's patronage of the Presbyterian minister, Joseph Ecclesall: Lambeth Palace Library Ms, Comm. II, no. 594. Thomas Minors left bequests in his will to the following Presbyterian ministers: Dr Obadiah Grew; William Grace; Thomas Miles; Thomas Bakewell; Thomas Ford. See PRO, Prob. 11/355/100; A. G. Matthews (ed.), *Calamy Revised* (2nd edn, Oxford, 1988), pp. 94, 207, 231, 236, 350; *The Victoria History of the Counties of England: Staffordshire*, vols. XIV, XVII (Oxford, 1976, 1990) (*VCH, Staffs*), vol. XIV, pp. 93, 158. Minors had a running battle with bishop John Hacket for his 'violent' nonconformity throughout the 1660s; and licensed his house as a Presbyterian meeting place in 1672: cf. A. G. Matthews, *The Congregational Churches of Staffordshire* (London, 1924), pp. 72–75, 78. On Thomas Crompton's religious affiliations: *SHC* 1920 and 1922, pp. 74–76; *SHC*, 4th Series (1958), p. 11; *CJ*, V, p. 370.

sympathies among the commissioners. Sir John Wyrley belonged to a staunchly Church of England family, though firm evidence of his own Anglicanism only dates from the Restoration period. He contributed £20 to the rebuilding of Lichfield cathedral in July 1663, and as a JP took part with relish in the suppression of 'seditious' conventicles. Edward Mainwaring, despite a strict Puritan upbringing, retained an attachment to the traditional church. While acting as a commissioner, he defied a Protectoral ordinance that prohibited sequestered Royalist divines from acting as teachers, and permitted Dr William Higgens, former precentor of Lichfield cathedral and a rabid Cavalier, to set up a school in a poor cottage in his own 'lordship' of Whitmore. Even more maverick was Thomas Whitgreave. In the 1650s he was an epitome of Puritan correctness, and as a member of the first Protectorate Parliament helped draft a declaration for a day of solemn fasting and humiliation. For most of Charles II's reign he was, in his own words, 'a member of the Church of England'. Under James II he became an avowed Roman Catholic.[46]

Only three commissioners possessed radical religious reputations and on examination these turn out to be largely false. George Bellot certainly displayed sectarian tendencies. But it was a different story with the 'Fanatique' John Chetwode. Admittedly, he was reputed to be no friend to a publicly maintained ministry during his membership of Barebone's Parliament in 1653. There is also a hint that he harboured Fifth Monarchist sympathies, being hailed by the millenarian prophetess, Hannah Trapnel, as one of the Lord's 'glorious instruments', destined to complete 'the Temple work'. For all his much-vaunted religious radicalism, however, he was fully prepared to cooperate in schemes to regulate and reorganise the Cromwellian state church – hardly the hallmark of a sectary. Daniel Watson furnishes a similar case. He was branded a 'separatist' whilst serving in the Derbyshire regiment of Colonel Thomas Saunders in 1645, though his commanding officer vehemently denied this

---

[46] Both Mainwaring and Wyrley were classified as 'orthodox' Anglicans in c. 1662–63. See *SHC*, 4th Series (1948), II, pp. 32, 36. For Wyrley's contribution to the restoration of Lichfield cathedral and his role in suppressing the conventicle at Oldbury chapel, Salop: BL, Add. Ms 43857, fo. 2; SP29/217/15, 60, 60:1. For Edward Mainwaring's Puritan upbringing and his protection of the Anglican divine, William Higgens, during his commissionership: Samuel Clarke, *A General Martyrologie Together with the Lives of Thirty Two English Divines* (London, 1677), p. 148; John Walker, *An Attempt towards Recovering an Account of the Numbers and Sufferings of the Clergy of the Churches of England in the late Times of the Grand Rebellion* (London, 1714), Part II, p. 40; William Hamper (ed.), *The Life, Diary and Correspondence of Sir William Dugdale* (London, 1827), p. 319. On Thomas Whitgreave's religious tergiversations see *CJ*, V, pp. 368, 397, 541, 581 and 9, p. 673; William Cobbett (ed.), *Complete Collection of State Trials* (London, 1811), X for 1680–85, pp. 1271–72; Bodl. Lib, Rawlinson Mss A136, fo. 484; PRO, SP31/4/15, 16: Sir George Duckett (ed.), *Penal Laws and Test Act* (London, 1883), p. 206.

imputation. After the Restoration, Watson was said to be 'orthodox' in his religious outlook, a view confirmed by his known opposition to 'unlawful conventicles' whilst acting as magistrate for Charles II. In this he typified the religious preferences of the Staffordshire commissioners who were, for the most part, Church-type rather than Sect-type Puritans.[47]

The basic religious conservatism of these officials can be demonstrated by two further examples. In August 1654 nine members of the group had been appointed commissioners for ejecting scandalous ministers in the county, and subsequently three more were made 'Ejectors'. Their nomination is a clear sign that Cromwell believed that they supported his national church. Among them was John Chetwode. In January 1656 all twelve men, plus one other commissioner, were given a further 'godly' assignment. This was the task of subdividing the larger, and amalgamating the smaller, parishes in Staffordshire, as part of a major overhaul of the country's ecclesiastical structure. Four men were particularly active in this work, among them John Chetwode. His participation should confirm that Major-General Worsley's Staffordshire agents were far from being a set of religious fanatics.[48]

X

Finally, were the Staffordshire commissioners men of integrity? Doubts exist about the probity of two of them. Peter Backhouse had an unenviable reputation as a 'discoverer' of concealed royalist estates. He was nearly dismissed by Cromwell himself during his stint as a commissioner in 1655/56. The Protector's 'displeasure' apparently arose from his secret, underhand dealings, the precise details of which are unfortunately not specified. A cloud of suspicion also hangs over Henry Stone who allegedly 'gained a great estate' through being 'a busy man in sequestrations [and] decimations'. During the first Civil War the confiscated goods of defeated

---

[47] On Watson's religious outlook see Derbyshire Rec. Off., Saunders Ms D1232 M/09b, 025, 070; Dore, *Brereton*, I, pp. 524–25 and II, p. 219. For all his alleged religious radicalism, George Bellot was a Trier and a member of the commission of enquiry into the union and division of Staffordshire parishes. See note 48 below. On the complexities of John Chetwode's so-called 'radical sectarian tendencies' cf. Anna Trapnel, *The Cry of a Stone or a Relation of Something Spoken in Whitehall by Anna Trapnel, being in the Visions of God* (London, 1654), pp. 2, 11; Woolrych, *Commonwealth To Protectorate*, pp. 140, 388, 414; *SHC* (1920 and 1922), II, p. 9; *SHC* (1958), II, p. 12.

[48] Eight commissioners were appointed triers for ejecting scandalous ministers in the county by the first ordinance of 28 August 1654; and five more by an additional ordinance of 7 August 1656. See *A&O*, II, p. 974; PRO, SP25/77/part 1, fo. 321. For the eleven commissioners who were chosen members of the official enquiry into the union and division of Staffordshire parishes in January 1656, and their subsequent activities, see Lambeth Palace Library Ms, Comm. XIIb/12; and XIIc, fos. 12–13, 60–60v.

royalist gentry do seem to have stuck to his fingers like glue, though whether he was guilty of corruption in the collection of the decimation tax a decade later is not known.[49]

These individuals apart, the rest of the commissioners seem to have been honourable men. Throughout his life, Sir John Wyrley was ever deemed 'a worthy, honest gentleman and a man of very great credit and repute in his country'. The commissioners were public-spirited too. Even after the Restoration Thomas Pudsey was valued as an 'arbitrator' in a property dispute among the warring Turtons of West Bromwich. That 'noble Justice', Edward Mainwaring, was a 'vir generosus' in the mould of Sir Philip Sidney. He dispensed his largesse not just to distressed Anglican clergymen like Dr William Higgens whose household of 'hungry bellies' he liberally supplied with food when it was smitten with smallpox, but also to psychologically disturbed Puritans such as James Bell who, but for Mainwaring's diligent and watchful care over him at Whitmore Hall, would have committed suicide. But the commissioner who commanded most respect for his service to the community was Zachary Babbington. He led the Staffordshire opposition to plans to disafforest Needwood Chace in the autumn of 1654, intensively lobbying the first Protectorate Parliament and the Council, and even securing an interview with Cromwell himself which may have played a part in his selection as a commissioner a year later.[50]

A strain of altruism can be discerned in the commissioners. This is best demonstrated by their charitable activities, both public and private. At a communal level the work of the fourteen commissioners appointed to investigate the administration of charitable legacies in the county, in June 1656, deserves mention. Particularly active and diligent were Edward Brett and John Chetwode in north-west Staffordshire. They compelled two recalcitrant squires, William Sneyd and John Offley, to meet their charitable obligations towards the poor in the parishes of Wolstanton and

[49] For the allegation that Smith was 'willing to doe mischefe' see *SHC*, 4th Series (1958), II, p. 28. On Backhouse's misdemeanours: PRO, SP19/138/70, 71, 74–76, 79–80, 169–175; SP23/81/235; *TSP*, IV, pp. 647–49. Stone is said to have purloined goods belonging to Bishop Wright – from Eccleshall Castle in 1643 and Lichfield Close in 1646 – worth an estimated £70,000, not to mention his misappropriation of the sequestered goods of Ralph Sneyd esq. of Keele and the sequestered rents of Lord Gerrard of Gerrards Bromley. See PRO, E178/6589: E134/1650/Easter No. 12: HLRO, Parchment Collection: 2 May 1645: Staffordshire Depositions; Shaw, *Staffs*, II, p. 74.

[50] For Wyrley's honourable reputation, see PRO, E134/8 William III/Easter No. 13. For Pudsey's role as an arbitrator: PRO, E134/20 Charles II/Mich. No. 20. On Mainwaring's noblesse oblige and Christian charity see John Walker, *An Attempt*, Part II, p. 40; Richard Parkinson (ed.), *The Autobiography of Henry Newcome*, The Chetham Society (1852), I, pp. 78–79. For Babbington's leadership of the Needwood Chace anti-enclosure movement and his interview with Cromwell: BL, Stowe Ms 878, fos. 74, 76.

Madely, respectively, as well as seeing that the executors of the late Earl of Essex did likewise in Newcastle-under-Lyme. They also took steps to guarantee the payment of a series of yearly stipends for the maintenance of godly preaching ministers at Talke Chapel and at the churches of Maer and Biddulph. Elsewhere in the county, Zachary Babbington, Thomas Minors and Henry Stone helped to ensure that two yearly rent charges for the upkeep of the free schools of Rugeley and Leigh were honestly applied.[51]

In terms of individual philanthropy, six commissioners stand out. Zachary Babbington bequeathed £5 to the destitute of Whittington. Sir John Wyrley donated £12 for the relief of the indigent inhabitants of Handsworth; and £2 to those of Great Barr. Thomas Pudsey's charitable donations, amounting to £7 in all, extended to three Staffordshire parishes, Trysull, Harborne and Womborne. Even the money-grubbing Henry Stone proved a generous benefactor, leaving £20 to 'be disposed of as a dole to the poor of the parish of Walsall at my decease' as well as a £15 annuity for the provision of five coats and five gowns to ten other poverty-stricken men and women there. John Young gave succour to the paupers of Charnes; while Thomas Minors was charity itself. He not only paid 2s. 6d. to every needy householder in Uttoxeter Woodland, but also established a free school for thirty poor boys, not to mention leaving a lump sum of £5 for the beggars of his adopted city of Lichfield.[52]

XI

Current theories about the calibre of the men who served under the Major-Generals in 1655–56 need to be qualified in the light of this investigation. Our case study furnishes little evidence to support David Underdown's assertion that the Cromwellian commissioners represented a different kind of local government personnel from that which had so far been prevalent under the Protectorate. Indeed, those from Staffordshire seem to have been that usual 'blend of older gentry, Commonwealth upstarts and military men' identified by Underdown himself as typical members of the county oligarchies during the first phase of the Protector-

---

[51] For the names of the deputies who served on the commission for charitable uses and their work, see PRO, C93/24/1. Cf. also SRO, SQSR, 1656 (Michaelmas), fo. 19.

[52] On the private charitable bequests of these six commissioners see their wills: LJRO, Zachary Babbington WP. 9 December 1687; PRO, Prob. 11/259/409 (Young); PRO, Prob. 11/351/69 (Pudsey); PRO, Prob. 11/355/100 (Minors); PRO, Prob. 11/399/80 (Wyrley); PRO, Prob. 11/399/80 (Stone). Further information about the charitable activities of Minors and Stone can be found in VCH, Staffs, xiv, pp. 141, 173, 189; and xvii, p. 273.

ate (December 1653 to March 1655). Admittedly the traditional elements were in the minority, with merely five commissioners belonging to the élite landowning families who had ruled the shire before 1642. That said, it would be wrong to characterise the remaining seventeen commissioners as complete newcomers to county government in 1655. All of them had held office – of one sort or another – in local administration in the decade before the institution of the Major-Generals.[53]

Nor does our survey substantiate Ronald Hutton's claim that the Cromwellian commissioners were social and religious as well as political 'usurpers'. Socially speaking, the Staffordshire deputies were largely drawn from the gentry class. While only one representative of the greater gentry (Mainwaring) was to be found among them, another four – and possibly two more – hailed from the ranks of the middling gentry. Of the remainder, it is possible to classify four as members of the lesser gentry, six as merchant gentry and three as professional gentry. This leaves just two (Backhouse and Malkin) who could be described as 'commoners' and, as we have seen, even they fall into the category of borderline gentry.[54]

As for the Staffordshire commissioners being religious 'usurpers', this, too, is wide of the mark. The majority of them supported the Cromwellian state church. Two at most were sectaries. All this suggests – if the Staffordshire experience was typical – that the men spearheading the Major-Generals' campaign in the localities were not such an 'aberration' from the officeholders who had immediately preceded them. Indeed, they were often the same people.[55]

Appendix 1 *The Staffordshire Commissioners for Preserving the Peace of the Commonwealth, 1655–56*

This appendix lists all the known men who served as Cromwell's commissioners in Staffordshire during the rule of the Major-Generals. The system of classification follows that of David Underdown in the appendix on the members of the Long

---

[53] Underdown, 'Settlement in the counties', pp. 175, 179. Admittedly, some of the commissioners had occupied relatively minor positions in county government before 1655 like Thomas Malkin, the High Constable of the north part of Totmonslow Hundred in April 1645. See *Committee at Stafford*, p. 300.

[54] Ronald Hutton contends that the Major-Generals, especially Worsley, 'tended to promote commoners into local power': Hutton, *The British Republic 1649–1660*, p. 83. This is simply not borne out by the Staffordshire experience, at least so far as Worsley's commissioners were concerned. Cf. the broad social classification of the Staffordshire commissioners in Appendix 1, column 6 (a).

[55] The term 'aberration' is used by David Underdown to describe the entire rule of the Major-Generals. This is clearly an overstatement of the case. See Underdown, 'Settlement in the counties', p. 172.

Parliament in his *Pride's Purge* (Oxford, 1971); and that adopted by Austin Woolrych in his study of the members of Barebone's Parliament (*Commonwealth to Protectorate* [Oxford, 1982]). The names of the Staffordshire commissioners are arranged alphabetically and their biographical details summarised in twelve columns. The key to these columns is as follows:

1. Place of residence: parish where commissioner lived, with individual locations given in brackets if different from the parent settlement.

2. Age as known or estimated in October 1655.

3. Position in family:
    E = Eldest, or eldest surviving son who inherited.
    YS = Younger son.
    H = Heir, with father still living.

4. Marital status:
    M = Married.
    S = Single.

5. Education:
    University: C = Cambridge.
                     O = Oxford.
    Inns of Court: G = Grays's Inn.
                     IT = Inner Temple.
                     MT = Middle Temple.

6. Social status:
    Sub-column (a) General ranking.
    GG = Greater gentry.
     IG = Intermediate gentry.
     LG = Lesser gentry.
    MG = Merchant gentry.
    PG = Professional gentry.
    BG = Borderline gentry.

    Sub-column (b) Pre- and post-Civil War classification.
        E = Esquire.   G = Gentleman.
        K = Knight.   Y = Yeoman.
        U = Undifferentiated.

    Sub-column (c) Armorial designation.
        A = Armigerous.   NA = Nonarmigerous.

7. Wealth:
    Sub-columns (a) Income per annum.
                 (b) Hearth-tax assessment (H).
                 (c) Personal wealth in probate inventory.

8. Parliamentary career:
    LP = MP in Long Parliament (recruiter).
    R = MP in Rump Parliament.
    N = MP in Nominated Assembly.
    P1 = MP in first Protectorate Parliament.
    P2 = MP in second Protectorate Parliament.
    RC = MP in Richard Cromwell's Parliament.
    RR = MP in the restored Rump Parliament.
    C = MP in Convention Parliament.
    Cav = MP in Cavalier Parliament.

9. Local government experience:
    JP = Justice of the Peace
        (with date of first appointment in brackets).
    A = Assessment Commissioner 1647–52
        (with number of times selected in brackets).
    C = Commissioner for charitable uses 1656
        (asterisk indicates active involvement).

10. Civil War background:
    Sub-column (a) Civilian occupations.
        S = Member of the Staffordshire Parliamentary Committee 1643–49.
        T = Treasurer to the above.
        CA = Commissioner for taking the Accounts of the Kingdom, 1646–49.
        CDR = Conductor of Parliamentary troops.

    Sub-column (b) Military occupations.
        G = Governor of Parliamentary garrison.   M = Major.
        C = Colonel.   CP = Captain.
        LC = Lieutenant-Colonel.   L = Lieutenant.

11. Militia service in the 1650s:
    MC = Militia Commissioner
        (with dates of appointment in brackets).
    FO = Field Officer.
        Abbreviations for military rank the same as those given above in (10)
        sub-column (b).

12. Religious stance:
    E = Ejector.
    UD = Member of the commission of enquiry into the union and division of
        Staffordshire parishes from January 1656.
    A = Anglican.   S = Sectarian.
    P = Presbyterian.   T = Religious trimmer.

Name	Place of residence	Age	Position in family	Marital status	Education Univ.	Inn	Social status (a)	(b)	(c)
Thomas Adshead	Milwich	–	E	M			LG	G/E	NA
Zachary Babbington	Lichfield (Curborough)	44	E	M		IT	PG	G/E	A
Peter Backhouse	Seighford (Doxey)	40	YS	M			BG	Y/G	NA
George Bellot	Uttoxeter	31	YS	M			LG	G/E	A
George Bowes	Elford	35	E	M	O	IT	IG	E/E	A
Edward Brett	Wolstanton (Dimsdale)	31	E	M	C		LG	E/E	A
John Cherwode	Mucclestone (Oakley)	56	E	M	O	IT	IG	E/E	A
Thomas Crompton	Stone (Park)	48	E	M			IG	G/E	A
William Gent	Leek	–	–	M			MG	U/G	NA
Edward Mainwaring	Whitmore	52	E	M		MT	GG	G/E	A
Thomas Malkin	Leek	c.65	–	M			BG	Y/G	NA
Thomas Minors	Lichfield	46	E	M			MG	G/E	A
Thomas Pudsey	Trysull (Seisdon)	46	E	M			LG	G/E	NA
Robert Smith	Cheadle	42	–	M			MG	U/G	NA
Henry Stone	Walsall	c.43?	E	M			MG	G/E	NA
John Symcox	West Bromwich	–	–	M			MG	G/E	NA
Daniel Watson	Burton-on-Trent	38	YS	M			PG	G/E	NA
(Sir) Thomas Whitgreave	Seighford (Gt Bridgford)	c. 29/30	E	S?	O	GI	IG?	G/E	A
Matthew Worswick	Stafford	49	YS	M			MG	G/E	NA
Thomas Worswick	Castle Church (Lees Farm)	28	–	S?			PG	G/E	NA
Sir John Wyrley	Handsworth (Hampstead)	48	E	M	O	GI	IG?	K/K	A
John Young	Eccleshall (Charnes)	35	E	M		IT	IG	G/E	NA?

Name	Wealth (a)	Wealth (b)	Wealth (c)	Parliamentary career	Local government experience	Civil War background (a)	Civil War background (b)	Militia service in the 1650s	Religious stance
Thomas Adshead	£100 (1641)		£33		JP(1649), A(4), C	CA		MC (1655) FO(LC)	E, UD
Zachary Babbington	£200 (1662)	13H	£249		JP(1653), C*			MC (1655) FO (CP)	E, UD, P
Peter Backhouse	£80 (1680)	6H	£154.15s.2d.				G, CP	MC (1655) FO (CP)	?P
George Bellot	£8 (1646)			MP (N)	JP (1650), A(4), C			MC (1655) FO (CP)	E, UD, S
George Bowes	£700 (1644)	15H	£570.7s.4d.		JP (1645), A(1), C		CP	MC (1648, 1655)	
Edward Brett	£100 (1641)	9H			JP (1649), C*	CA			
John Chetwode	£600 (1662)	11H	£346.3s.4d.	MP(N)	JP (1647), A(5), C*	S, T		MC (1648, 1655)	E, UD, S
Thomas Crompton	£400 (1662)	12H		MP (LP, R, P1, P2, P3, RR)	JP (1645), A(6), C	S	C	MC (1648, 1655) FO(C)	?P
William Gent		8H						MC (1655)	E, UD
Edward Mainwaring	£1,000 (1662)	19H	£900.5s.6d.	MP (Cav)	JP (1645), A(5), C	S		MC (1648)	E, UD, A
Thomas Malkin		3H							
Thomas Minors		9H	£2,331	MP (P1, P2, RC, C)	JP (1653), AA(4), C*				E, UD, P
Thomas Pudsey	£100 (1645)	6H	£494.11s.0d.		A(2)	S	CP		P
Robert Smith		3H	£139.3s.1d.				G, CP	FO(M)	P
Henry Stone	£200 (1662)	9H		MP (RC, C)	JP (1645), A(5), C*	S	G, C	MC (1648, 1655) FO (C)	E, UD, P
John Symcox	£50 (1641)	5H			A(2)	S, T			
Daniel Watson	£200 (1662)	8H		MP (P1, P2, RC)	JP (1649), A(1), C	S	CP	MC (1655) FO(CP)	E, UD, ?S
(Sir) Thomas Whitgreave		8H			JP (1651), A(1), C			MC (1655) FO (CP)	T
Matthew Worswick	£5 (1641)	4H			JP (1656)	CDR			
Thomas Worswick		19H					L	FO(L)	
Sir John Wyrley	£100 (1662)		£580.8s.4d.		JP (1649), A(1), C			MC (1655)	E, UD, A
John Young	£300/£400 (1696) £500 (1644)	8H			JP (1653), A(1), C		G, CP	MC (1648)	E, UD, ?S

8

Colonel Gervase Benson, Captain John Archer, and
the corporation of Kendal, c. 1644–c. 1655*

C. B. PHILLIPS

Gervase Benson and John Archer entered the government of the Cumbrian market town of Kendal in 1640. Once the royalists in south Westmorland had been neutralised by the Scots in 1644, the two men became increasingly important in Kendal corporation. Unlike a number of their corporation seniors, they did not support the king in the second civil war in 1648. Later they pushed to dismiss those royalists from the government of Kendal. Benson and Archer removed a third of the corporation, royalists and others, in a purge mounted through the imposition of the Engagement in 1650. At some point, Benson's religious opinions led him to sectarianism, eventually as a Quaker. Thus his old but more conservative ally John Archer assisted in his removal from the corporation in 1653. Their public disagreement in that year helped to ensure that a vitriolic quarrel in print and pulpit, street and jail, was carried on in Kendal. The corporation finally removed its last Quaker member in 1655, though Quakers remained in the town.

Two points emerged from this contribution to the history of Kendal. The first, which has been given little emphasis, is the relationship between local and central government. It was a concern recurrently prominent during the revolutionary decades: for example, the second civil war can be explained by the dissatisfaction of the localities with the policies of the London parliament; later, Cromwell's major-generals proved a centralising imposition on the localities, resented and thus unworkable. In the confines of Kendal corporation, the Engagement, a device of the central government intended to promote unity, became a partisan stick with which to beat not only opponents, but also allies of

* My thanks to the librarians and archivists whose collections figure here; especially to all the staff of the Kendal Record Office over the past thirty years, and to the staff of the John Rylands University Library of Manchester. I am grateful to the editors of this volume for their interest, and especially to Professor Blair Worden who saved me from many errors.

the centre.[1] The readiness of central government to interfere in local town affairs, while asserting that it intended no threat to the independence of a town,[2] was a precursor of interference by the later Stuarts.[3] The second point to emerge is a glimpse of small-town politics,[4] and especially of the part played by religion. This essay will emphasise the place of religion in the politics of Kendal, although the town of course was too large for religion to be the only concern. To understand the politics, we need first to know something of Kendal and of its government.

I

Kendal was the 'county' town for south Westmorland.[5] The population of the borough was in the order of 2,500 in the seventeenth century. Its large hinterland extended to the west into Furness and Cumberland, and to the east into the Dent and Sedbergh area of Yorkshire. John Archer's occupation as a mercer selling cloths and foodstuffs, and Gervase Benson's

---

[1] For the Engagement see A. B. Worden, *The Rump Parliament 1648–1653* (London, 1974), pp. 19–32. The Rump offended towns by the Engagement: A. Woolrych, *Commonwealth to Protectorate* (Oxford, 1982), p. 8. Cf. R. Hutton, *The British Republic 1649–1660* (Basingstoke, 1990), p. 38.

[2] Exactly the claim made by the House of Commons when intervening in Kendal in 1650 – *Commons' Journals* (*CJ*), VI, 481; below, p. 189.

[3] E.g. J. Miller, 'The crown and the borough charters in the reign of Charles II', *English Historical Review*, 100 (1985), 53–84.

[4] Elsewhere I shall set the findings of this essay against the recent urban historiography of the 1640s and 1650s which has concentrated largely on parliamentary boroughs and big towns, categories to which Kendal does not belong. See the essays on Bristol (David Sacks), Coventry (Ann Hughes), Oxford (Ian Roy), and York (David Wilson) in *Town and Country in the English Revolution*, ed. R. C. Richardson (Manchester, 1992). Other specifically urban studies are R. Howell, Jr, *Newcastle upon Tyne and the Puritan Revolution* (Oxford, 1967); *The Chamber Order Book of Worcester*, ed. S. Bond (Worcestershire Historical Society, new series (WHS), VIII, 1974); P. Styles, *Studies in Seventeenth-century West Midlands History* (Kineton, 1978); R. Howell, Jr, 'The structure of urban politics in the English Civil War', *Albion*, 11 (1979); R. Howell, 'Neutralism, conservatism and political alignment in the English revolution: the case of the towns, 1642–1649', in *Reactions to the English Civil War 1642–1649*, ed. J. S. Morrill (London, 1982); I. Roy, 'The English republic, 1649–1660: the view from the town hall', in *Republiken und Republikanismus im Europa der Frühen Neuzeit* (Schriften des Historischen Kollegs, Kolloquien 11, Munich, 1988); R. Howell, Jr, 'Resistance to change: the political élites of provincial towns during the English revolution', in *The First Modern Society*, ed. A. L. Beier, D. Cannadine and J. M. Rosenheim (Cambridge, 1989). My debt to these works will be obvious in the following pages. See also *Grantham during the Interregnum: The Hallbook of Grantham, 1641–1649*, ed. B. Couth (The Lincoln Record Society, CLXXXIII, 1995).

[5] See C. B. Phillips, 'Town and country: economic change in Kendal c. 1550–1700', in *The Transformation of English Provincial Towns 1600–1800*, ed. P. Clark (London, 1984), pp. 99–132.

role as a probate official in the Archdeaconry of Richmond,[6] were typical of the functions and services on which Kendal thrived. As a manufacturing town Kendal specialised in textiles and leather. The structure of Kendal's government, set out in its charter of incorporation in 1575, was significantly modified by the grant of a new charter, completed in 1637.[7] The new corporation hierarchy can be summarised as a chief officer, the mayor, presiding over a two-tier structure in which an upper tier of twelve aldermen were superior to a lower tier of twenty (capital) burgesses.[8] Much of the burden of government was shouldered by the mayor, and by the top tier, whose two senior members were, with the mayor and the recorder, justices of the peace. A *cursus honorum* for these office holders had become established under the 1575 charter and this continued in the 1640s and 1650s. The mayor and aldermen elected new members of the lower tier, and chose new members of the top tier from that lower tier. Lower- and top-tier men normally served for life. Charles I's charter restricted the nomination and election of a new mayor to the current mayor, aldermen, and capital burgesses, thereby ending voting by the 'inhabitants'. The chief officer was usually chosen in order of seniority.[9] In July each year the top tier nominated two aldermen to stand for election as mayor. If there was agreement on the name of the next mayor, one of the senior aldermen would stand as a make-weight candidate. The election took place the following September.[10] The ex-mayor reverted to the top tier after his year of office which ran from Michaelmas. The corporation was thus a self-perpetuating body, in which some individuals served for decades. In 1642 the longest-serving top-tier man had been in the corporation (both tiers) for thirty years, the most recent recruit but a year; the mayor and

[6] Archer: see e.g. Kendal, Cumbria County Record Office (CROK), Kendal Corporation MSS (WD/MBK), Kendal chamberlains' accounts (KCA), dated by year beginning at Michaelmas, 1635 for clothes bought by the corporation, or London, Public Record Office (PRO), Chancery, equity proceedings, bills and answers, Bridge's Division, C5/619/7. Benson: Preston, Lancashire County Record Office (LRO), Archdeaconry of Richmond wills, WRW, passim; B. Nightingale, *The Ejected of 1662 in Cumberland and Westmorland* (Manchester, 1911), p. 898; Carlisle, Cumbria County Record Office (CRO), miscellaneous deposits, DX/46/BRA/6/7, 24 June 1651 (probate for commissioners of the keepers of the liberties of England).

[7] Transcripts and translations in *A boke off recorde of ... Kirkbie Kendall ... (BOR)*, ed. R. S. Ferguson (Cumberland and Westmorland Antiquarian and Archaeological Society, Extra Series, VII, Kendal, 1892), 274–356.

[8] For the membership of the corporation see *BOR*, pp. 18–21 (1645–59), 22–39 (from 1575); CROK, WD/MBK, enrolment of apprentices (1645–1784), for 1640–42 at the rear; WD/ MBK, file of mayors' elections, 1647–82 (FME), plus a stray in WD/MBK, documents sorted by the Historical Manuscripts Commission (WD/MBK HMC), A12.

[9] However, the mayors elected for the years 1637–43 were the longer-serving aldermen taking their turn in the newly named mayoralty.

[10] *BOR*, p. 319; FME, passim.

aldermen averaged seventeen years' service on both tiers. In the 1640s, self-perpetuation seems to have produced a body of men exhibiting only limited evidence of a tradition of family service, or of kingship connections. They were, however, drawn from amongst the most wealthy townsmen.

One family had members present in the corporation from 1575 until 1641, and again from 1646. In 1642 three burgesses were sons of previous or serving top-tier men. Two aldermen were related by marriage to two burgesses. It is difficult to decide how much influence, if any, such alliances might have had on corporation politics.[11] Apprenticeship links among members of the top tier seem to have been of little importance in Kendal corporation. Generally, the corporation men followed the requirement to live within the town's boundaries. A fulsome description of the personal qualities required dates from 1576: corporation men were to be the 'mooste honeste Discrete Sober wise and Substanciall' of townsmen.[12] If probate valuations are a reasonably accurate guide to a man's wealth, the corporation men between 1575 and 1635 were, on average, the most wealthy townsmen;[13] nothing suggests that the 1640s were any different. Trade as mercers or merchants provided this wealth for 50 per cent of the members in the 1640s, though a third followed manufacturing occupations. Most of the manufacturers were, however, members of the lower tier, while men whose occupations can be grouped as professions or as distributors made up 78 per cent of the top tier.

II

The role of Gervase Benson and John Archer in Kendal corporation became noticeable after 'the first reducing of Westmorland' by occupying Scottish forces in the early autumn of 1644.[14] Fragmentary evidence suggests that some individuals on Kendal corporation may have favoured parliament in the early years of the civil war. They no doubt found the recorder of the town, Sir John Lowther of Lowther, Bt, sympathetic. His neutralist position in gentry struggles before the Scots came inclined him to help the corporation to preserve its military independence from the royalist gentry.[15] But it was Gervase Benson who made the first known

---

[11] J. T. Evans, 'The decline of oligarchy in seventeenth-century Norwich', *Journal of British Studies*, 14 (1974), 57–8.

[12] *BOR*, p. 82.

[13] C. B. Phillips, 'Probate records and the Kendal shoemakers in the seventeenth century', in *Probate Records and the Local Community*, ed. P. Riden (Gloucester, 1985), p. 47.

[14] PRO, State papers domestic, committee for compounding, SP23/G197/457.

[15] C. B. Phillips, 'County committees and local government in Cumberland and West-

attempt by a member of the corporation to commit the town to parliament when on 9 May 1644 he tried but failed to get Lancashire parliamentarian forces to come to Kendal.[16] He was elected mayor of Kendal at Michaelmas 1644. Benson was soon an ally[17] of the Presbyterian vicar of Kendal, Henry Masy.[18] Although the Scots had made possible Masy's return to his living, from which he had been driven by royalist gentry in 1642,[19] they had not installed their creatures on the corporation. The great majority of Benson's fellow aldermen had been elected by Michaelmas 1642, and included long-serving members. Benson had been an alderman since 1641, but an indicator of his importance is that he had leapfrogged the *cursus honorum* to become mayor. When the mayor of Kendal for the time being was added to the Westmorland commission of the peace, Benson was the first to serve in this capacity.[20] He was known as Colonel Benson by 15 August 1645, and in command of the small garrison in the town.[21] It was difficult for Benson to get into the Westmorland commission of the peace in his own name, for he had held barely sufficient land to be accepted as a JP, and most of that was in Sedbergh, Yorkshire. He eventually became a justice in his own name on 27 April 1646.[22] John Archer was a newcomer as an alderman. He was elected in September 1644, and ranked as Captain Archer by 14 May 1645; he was another ally of the vicar by early 1646.[23]

The consequences of the second civil war enhanced the status of Benson and Archer in the county, more than in Kendal. Many of the Westmorland county committee had sided with the royalists in 1648. Thereafter both men became more prominent in militia and assessment commissions.[24] By 1649 they were known in London through their

morland 1642–1660', *Northern History*, 5 (1970), 40–6; and C. B. Phillips, 'The royalist north: the Cumberland and Westmorland gentry, 1642–1660', *Northern History*, 14 (1978), 170–4.

[16] CRO, Musgrave Manuscripts, civil war letters, Miles Atkinson to Sir P. Musgrave, 9 May 1644.

[17] Nightingale, *Ejected*, p. 884.

[18] Nightingale, *Ejected*, pp. 109, 891, 905, 906, 909, 912. For the dangers inherent in labelling individuals as Presbyterian or independent see A. Woolrych, *Soldiers and Statesmen* (Oxford, 1987), pp. 5–6, and A. L. Hughes, 'The frustrations of the godly', in *Revolution and Restoration*, ed. J. S. Morrill (London, 1992), pp. 70–1.

[19] Nightingale, *Ejected*, p. 916.

[20] BOR, p. 24; HMC, *13th Report, appendix*, 1, 186; *CJ*, III, 678.

[21] PRO, State papers, domestic, commonwealth exchequer papers, SP28/249 (Westmorland).

[22] Nightingale, *Ejected*, p. 900; PRO, Chancery, crown office docquet books, IND4213, p. 45.

[23] BOR, p. 18; PRO, SP28/216 (Westmorland), accounts of Richard Pindreth; Nightingale, *Ejected*, pp. 896, 908.

[24] *Acts and Ordinances of the Interregnum*, ed. C. H. Firth and R. S. Rait (3 vols., London, 1911), I, 1246; II, 46, 53, 312.

involvement in Westmorland's sequestration business;[25] Benson was also active on the Northern Committee for Compounding at Newcastle.[26] They were both made commissioners for propagating the Gospel in the north on 1 March 1650.[27] Archer joined Benson in the commission of the peace in July 1650.[28]

Although it is true that John Archer's stock in the town rose when he became mayor at Michaelmas 1648, his election owed much to the *cursus honorum*. No changes in the membership of the corporation followed the second civil war, yet two, perhaps four, aldermen, and two or three burgesses, had supported the king.[29] In the two years between Michaelmas 1648 and Michaelmas 1650 the corporation was divided between a group of junior aldermen (Benson, Archer, and Thomas Sandes), and a group of senior men led by Roland Dawson and including Edward Turner.[30] It would oversimplify a complex situation to label these groups parliamentarian and royalist, respectively. Thus some of the royalists had voted for Archer in the 1648 election, in the aftermath of the second war, votes which seem to have followed the *cursus honorum*.[31] With the benefit of hindsight, it appears that the two groups can be traced as far back as Benson's election as mayor in 1644, when he overtook the *cursus honorum* candidate, Edward Turner.[32] Turner was not elected mayor in the 1640s, although he is known to have been a candidate in 1647 and in 1649. His failure to become mayor by process of seniority demonstrated a lack of confidence in him on the part of a majority of corporation men. Nevertheless he obtained a third of the votes in the 1647 election. In subsequent years in which voting behaviour suggests a *cursus honorum* election, and that there was only one serious candidate, the make-weight candidate polled between one and six votes.[33] In 1647 the breakdown of the vote suggests that neither Edward Turner nor his opponent, Thomas Sandes,

[25] Benson: *Calendar of the Proceedings of the Committee for Compounding*, ed. M. A. E. Green (London, 1889–29. Hereafter *CCC*), p. 247. Archer: PRO, SP28/240 (Northumberland), Westmorland receipt, 14 June 1649; *CCC*, p. 257.

[26] PRO, SP28/240 (Northumberland), order dated 14 June 1649.

[27] F. Nicholson and E. Axon, *The Older Nonconformity in Kendal* (Kendal, 1915), pp. 19–22.

[28] PRO, IND4213, p. 193.

[29] *CCC*, pp. 203, 510, 521; plus PRO, Chancery proceedings, bills and answers, series II, C3/397/58 (also for Roland Dawson); and PRO, State papers, domestic, Charles II, SP29/68/19 (for Richard Prissoe).

[30] FME, 24 September 1649; PRO, Prerogative Court of Canterbury, registered wills, PROB11/243, fo. 2 (Roland Dawson); 11/251, fo. 434 (William Bank).

[31] FME, 25 September 1648.

[32] Alderman Crossfield 'retired' in July 1645, and Alderman Barrowe was 'dislocat pro contempt' in August 1646 (*BOR*, p. 18). Three of the lower tier drop out of sight at this time. I cannot relate these changes to the division suggested here.

[33] For the nomination of candidates see p. 185 above.

were make-weights. Turner had been backed by three very long-serving aldermen, all, like him, mercers. Established members and newcomers amongst the burgesses, including both traders and manufacturers, raised Turner's vote to eleven,[34] yet, so far as is known, none of his supporters were beholden to him as kinsmen or ex-apprentices. In 1649 he was supported by just two aldermen, including Roland Dawson.[35]

If it is too simplistic to label these groups royalist and parliamentarian, it is nevertheless the case that Dawson, and others, had been royalists in 1648, and that allegations of royalism in 1648 against Turner were made. But they did not lead to his sequestration, and were, indeed, denied.[36] The fact that the royalist minority was not removed after the end of the second civil war implies that, if any such intention existed, there was insufficient support within the divided top tier of the corporation to expel them.

III

The committed royalists were removed for failing to take the Engagement. There is no contemporary narrative of the purge in 1650, but we can reconstruct the essentials of what happened. The annual ceremony in which the new mayor had to be sworn in presented an obvious occasion to put the Engagement to the corporation. In 1650 the election should have taken place on 23 September. Gervase Benson and John Archer wrote to the House of Commons on 28 September to complain that many of the corporation had not taken the Engagement.[37] Given their involvement in county affairs in Westmorland, the two men would have been known in London, and their anxiety given some attention. On 9 October the Rump discussed their letter and resolved 'that all such Aldermen and Burgesses ... who have not subscribed the Engagement ... are discharged and disabled ... and that such of the Aldermen and Burgesses of the said Borough as have subscribed the Engagement do proceed to the Election of new Burgesses ...'[38] The clues to what then happened in Kendal lie in the extensively altered lists of names of members of both tiers of the corporation: some description of these manuscript pages in the 'Boke off Recorde' is called for, not least because the century-old printed edition requires re-interpretation.[39] Lists of members had been drawn up in 1645, in order of seniority as aldermen or burgesses. Thereafter, as men left

---

[34] FME, 27 September 1647.   [35] FME, 24 September 1649.

[36] See note 29. Turner was called a cavalier in 1655, below p. 199.

[37] The mayor had, presumably, been sworn in on 23 September, though in some years the swearing-in ceremony followed a week later.

[38] *CJ*, vi, 481 left the names of the corporation blank.

[39] WD/MBK, 'Boke off recorde', fos. 20, 21, printed in *BOR*, pp. 18–21. Changes of ink and

office their names were annotated, usually with the date in the left margin, and a brief explanation to the right. The names of replacements were added at the bottom, followed to the right by the date sworn. Thus the top-tier list always totalled thirteen.[40]

The date of the Rump's resolution, '9 October 1650', to the left of a name in the 'Boke off Recorde' seems to indicate that dismissals occurred on that date. It appears from the notes of the House of Commons discussion that the mayor, Benson and Archer were the only three members of the top tier who had taken the Engagement.[41] Thus Benson and Archer became the senior aldermen, and, with the mayor, JPs. The three men were empowered to rebuild the top tier by taking subscriptions to the Engagement. The senior, Roland Dawson, apparently resigned.[42] Five other aldermen survived. Five replacement aldermen were elected, and a sixth after the mayor's death near the end of his term in September 1651. The top-tier list in the 'Boke off Recorde' was then partially re-cast, no doubt in preparation for the mayor's election at Michaelmas: the names of Benson and Archer were not moved but the other eleven names were re-written lower down the page.[43] The upheaval amongst the members of the lower tier was greater than amongst the top tier: the next surviving list, dated September 1653,[44] contains only six names from September 1650. In 1650 six were displaced and four promoted.[45]

The impact of these changes was to remove committed royalists and, apparently, some 'Presbyterians'. Of those aldermen who had been displaced, two, perhaps three, had been royalists.[46] One of the burgesses who went was a sequestered royalist (while another sequestered royalist was allowed to stay).[47] But the dismissal of two aldermen, Thomas Sandes and Alan Gilpin, was different. Gilpin (possibly) and Sandes (certainly)

---

of hand are important in dating events. Cf. *BOR*, p. 18, I read the date by Dawson's name as 1651 (see note 30), and 1651 for Anthony Preston's death (cf. *BOR*, p. 24).

[40] The current mayor reverted to the position of alderman at the end of his mayoralty, see p. 185 above.

[41] *CJ*, VI, 481.

[42] Cf. the lack of annotation of Dawson's name and those of three burgesses who, nevertheless, remained on the corporation.

[43] WD/MBK, 'Boke off recorde', fo. 20; *BOR*, middle of p. 18, and top two names on p. 19.

[44] WD/MBK, HMC, A12.

[45] I have been unable to find any reference to these, or any other, dismissals discussed in this essay, in PRO, State papers domestic, committee for indemnity, SP24.

[46] I read the 'Boke off recorde' to bracket one of these men, Richard Prissoe in the same 'dislocat per ordin Parlti' as Sandes and Gilpin, in contrast to *BOR*'s exclusion of Prissoe from the bracket (p. 18). For the royalists see note 29 above.

[47] John Beck went, Joseph Edmundson stayed, but had disappeared by 1653 (*CCC*, p. 203; WD/MBK, HMC, A12). Three burgesses were apparently not present to take the oath but remained on the lower tier.

were still serving parliament:[48] they appear to be 'Presbyterians' who would not take the Engagement.

IV

Now we know what happened to Kendal corporation, some attempt can be made to account for the expulsions, though in the absence of statements as to motive, one can only offer suggestions as to why Benson and Archer acted to purge the corporation, why they did it at Michaelmas 1650, and why the House of Commons was involved. Two possibilities stand out, of which the more likely is that Benson and Archer were determined to propel the corporation into the realities of Commonwealth England but were prevented from doing so by conservatives on the corporation. (Later in the year John Archer signalled his republican mood by purchasing from the town, and thus removing from the corporation's inventory, the old king's arms and sergeants' maces.[49]) Benson and Archer had to seek help from outside the corporation. They invoked the authority of the House of Commons to enforce the controversial Engagement at a time when it had regained support after the seemingly God-given victory at Dunbar early in September.[50] Thus internal divisions within the corporation may explain why the Engagement was applied in Kendal nearly a year after town officials first became liable to it, and eight months after the legislation had been finalised in January 1650.[51] The second possibility follows on, namely that of pressure from the county administration. Even though two victims of the Engagement in the town, aldermen Gilpin and Sandes, were active in county affairs, Benson and Archer were also prominent, as we have seen. The county assessment commissions had shed all the county committee men who had turned royalist in 1648, and most royalists had disappeared from the county bench.[52] The county was being purged, but not yet the town. Despite the position of Benson and Archer in the county, there are no grounds for suggesting that either alderman represented a Westmorland military element in the purge of Kendal corporation.

---

[48] Gilpin: PRO, SP23/G207/195 (Nov. 1648). Sandes: A&O, II, 46, 53, 312, 460 (Nov. 1650), 678, 1248; accounts October 1648 to January 1650 as treasurer for sequestrations: PRO, SP28/216 (Westmorland); placed on county commission of the peace, 18 March 1652: PRO, IND4213, p. 234.

[49] KCA, 1650 extraordinary receipts. However, some monarchist plate was still in corporation possession in 1658 (WD/MBK, unlisted receipt of George Archer, 4 October 1658).

[50] Worden, *The Rump*, p. 232.   [51] Worden, *The Rump*, pp. 220, 227.

[52] PRO, chancery, crown office entry books, C193/13/3. It includes '[blank] Prissoe Mayor of Kendal', a confusion persisting to 1653 in Cambridge University Library MS Dd 8/1. PRO, IND4213, pp. 162, 193.

Neither Colonel Benson nor Captain Archer had established a reputation as a fighting soldier.[53]

V

The Engagement was intended not only to ensure that those who governed supported the achievements of the revolution, but also to unite officials behind the new republican state. It should have removed royalists and, probably, Presbyterians whose political and/or religious position was too conservative to support the republic. We can apply these tests to Kendal corporation, and examine how far the general character of the personnel changed; how far the corporation was united; and how far the corporation was radicalised.

The election of John Towers, who in 1651 became the first mayor after the purge, showed the effect of the Engagement. He had neither royalist nor Presbyterian connections. The senior of the newly appointed top-tier men, he overtook two before him in seniority, effectively bypassing any hostility latent in the older members. Towers was followed in 1652 as mayor by Edward Turner, a man previously passed over for the office, and one who had denied allegations that he had supported the royalists in 1648. The prosopography of the incoming aldermen and burgesses does not suggest any obvious motivation governing their choice. Royalist shades in the past of one newly promoted alderman were tolerated, just as the alderman concerned tolerated the Engagement.[54] Amongst those promoted aldermen, two came from established corporation families, but one of the two had not previously been a burgess. His immediate promotion through the lower tier indicates that he was especially valued, and his subsequent membership of the Committee for Scandalous Ministers suggests a religious motive.[55] The top-tier men averaged thirteen years of service on the corporation, rather less than the pre-war average of seventeen,[56] which implies that the new top tier was less immersed in the traditions of the town, and more open to innovation. John Towers also embodied a noticeable, if small, alteration in the social make-up of the

---

[53] Nightingale, *Ejected*, pp. 884, 888. Cf. *The Letter Books of Sir William Brereton*, ed. R. N. Dore (Record Society of Lancashire and Cheshire, 2 vols., cxxiii, cxxviii, 1984, 1990), ii, 137. Cf. the conclusion of M. E. Hirst, *The Quakers in Peace and War* (London, 1923), p. 527 that Benson served in the New Model, which is not supported by C. H. Firth and G. Davies, *The Regimental History of Cromwell's army* (London, 1940).

[54] William Potter, see note 29.

[55] James Cock: PRO, SP28/216 (Westmorland); PRO, Exchequer, special commissions, E178/6116.

[56] Cf. p. 186 above.

corporation.[57] He was the first shearman, the principal cloth-making occupation in Kendal, to be chief officer since 1631. For both tiers, the proportion of members from manufacturing occupations exceeded that from the distributive occupations. The change was apparent in the top tier alone which had four manufacturing members after the Engagement, compared with one before. The trend continued throughout the 1650s, with members from the distributive occupations totalling less than 50 percent of the whole. This may reflect the departure of royalists who were tradesmen. But it was also a consequence of the fact that active parliamentarians from manufacturing occupations handled state monies, and leased or purchased sequestered estates. Thus, from means outside their regular business, such men emulated the wealth of the distributive tradesmen who had hitherto dominated membership of the corporation.[58] The elections of Towers and of Turner,[59] and the changes in the social composition of the corporation, were perhaps indicators of the unity and reconciliation which the Engagement had been intended to foster. The new corporation was one in which conservative ideas continued to appeal. However, alongside the suggestions of unity and reconciliation, there is evidence of persisting division. Two episodes reveal the strength of conservative thinking and the extent of division: the appointments of the clerics, William Cole and Thomas Walker, in Kendal in 1651 and 1652; and the removal of the sectarian Gervase Benson in 1653.

VI

The background to the corporation's involvement with Cole and Walker is the pulsating evolution of religious opinion. Unfortunately, our knowledge of religious developments in south Westmorland and Kendal about 1650 has many gaps. There is, however, evidence of religious radicalism within Kendal's hinterland, which reached the town from perhaps as early as 1647.[60] One recorded event in Kendal church is the debate sometime in 1650 between the Anabaptist-Separatist Thomas Taylor and three

---

[57] I.e. the top tier of 1650–51 (*BOR*, pp. 18–19) and the list of lower-tier names dated September 1653 (WD/MBK, HMC, A12). Poor evidence for the 1650s obviates reaching any conclusions about dynasties or kinship.

[58] Examples are Alderman George Archer, cordwainer (*CCC*, pp. 187, 348, 386; e.g. PRO, SP28/249 treasurer of the Westmorland Committee; CROK, Fleming of Rydal MSS, WD/Ry, MS. R, p. 119 (1658), sequestered land), and the burgesses John French, glover, (receiver for the Bottom of Westmorland) and George Taylor, hardwareman (farmed sequestered estates, PRO, E178/6116).

[59] Was the conservative Turner elected to hammer the Quakers, see p. 197?

[60] D. Boulton, *Early Friends in Dent* (Dent, 1986), p. 23.

anonymous but more orthodox 'priests'.[61] People from Kendal went to hear Taylor at his own chapel at Preston Patrick, some six miles south of the town.[62] To the west of Kendal, at Underbarrow, and at about the same time, the future Quaker Edward Burrough was finding Presbyterianism too restrictive.[63] It may be that the religious beliefs of the vicar of Kendal, Henry Masy, developed over time. He took the Engagement in January 1650. A few years earlier he had expressed staunchly Presbyterian sentiments. Although a number of Presbyterians did take the Engagement, Masy's subscription may imply some flexibility of thought on his part.[64] He became ill early in 1651, and let it be known that William Cole should act as his *locum.* Masy and Cole were old friends, and when Masy died some weeks later, Cole preached his funeral sermon.[65] When Cole moved to Newcastle, early in 1653, he had contact with Congregationalists, before returning to a Presbyterian living in Lancashire around 1658. Like those of his friend Masy, his beliefs were evolving, but not radical.[66]

A vacant vicarage was evidently a matter of concern to corporation and parish alike, and they had solicited Trinity College Cambridge, the patron of the benefice, on Cole's behalf before Masy had died. The signatories to a second letter to the College dated 12 April 1651 included but half of the corporation, which suggests that the Engagement had failed to unite the members.[67] The April signatories included four of the five displaced top-tier men. If Cole was not a religious radical, those corporation men, and ex-corporation men, who supported him, were conservatives. The Master and Fellows of Trinity College appointed one of their number, Thomas

---

[61] Nicholson and Axon, *Older Nonconformity,* p. 32.

[62] For Taylor see Robert Barrow's testimony in T. Taylor, *Truth's Innocency and Simplicity Shining* (London, 1697).

[63] Edward Burrough, *A Warning from the Lord to the Inhabitants of Underbarrow* (London, 1654), p. 31.

[64] Nightingale, *Ejected,* p. 928. Cf. ibid., p. 920, Worden, *The Rump,* p. 231, and Nicholson and Axon, *Older Nonconformity,* p. 46, for financial pressures on Masy to subscribe.

[65] Nightingale, *Ejected,* pp. 895, 899, 928; Cambridge, Trinity College Library Mss (TCC), box 40, no. 31; see also KCA 1650, disbursements December 1650, February 1651 and June 1651. On Masy's death cf. Nightingale, *Ejected,* p. 928, and Nicholson and Axon, *Older Nonconformity,* pp. 46–7.

[66] Nightingale, *Ejected,* pp. 928, 931. Nicholson and Axon, *Older Nonconformity,* p. 55; R. P. Bohn, 'The controversy between puritans and Quakers, to 1660' (unpublished Ph.D. dissertation, Edinburgh University, 1956), p. 82, n. 4; G. F. Nuttall, *Visible Saints* (Oxford, 1957), p. 125, n. 6. Cole was, or had been, minister of Kirkby Lonsdale, replacing a sequestered royalist who had been appointed by Trinity College, Cambridge in 1640 (Nightingale, *Ejected,* pp. 1014–28).

[67] No text is known of the earlier letter, which is summarised in the April letter, TCC Mss, box 40, no. 31.

Walker, as vicar on 18 April.[68] The corporation endorsed his appointment by making him town lecturer.[69] The appointment looks like a religiously conservative one, though little is known of Thomas Walker. We do know that he was reported in 1652[70] to enjoy an augmentation of tithes, that he successfully applied in 1655 to continue it,[71] and that he became a Trier.[72] So we can take it that he favoured a maintained, parochial clergy.[73] There seems to have been little difference in belief between Walker and Cole.[74] As with their support for Cole, the selection of Walker as lecturer suggests that the Engaged corporation was conservative.

Kendal corporation's intention to renew Walker's annual appointment as lecturer provoked opposition and a split within the corporation. Once more, the evidence does not present the corporation in a radical guise, for it again suggests the existence of a more conservative faction linked with some of those displaced from the top tier at the Engagement. Sixteen 'well affected' townsmen, including two aldermen and three burgesses, and also the displaced Thomas Sandes,[75] petitioned the corporation on 1 July 1652 to appoint Cole to be the lecturer.[76] Cole's continuation in Kendal was '... of soe greate Concernment to many poor soules (the paucity and small number of godly and painfull ministers settled in this county Considered) ...' This hostility to Walker may have been left over from 1651, but his allies were a majority of the corporation, and he remained as lecturer.[77]

---

[68] TCC Mss, Conclusion book 1607–1673, p. 219. The College Mss generally give no explanation of such appointments.

[69] References in note 65.

[70] WD/MBK, Box 2, unlisted petition, 1 July 1652; cf. Nicholson and Axon, *Older Nonconformity*, p. 47.

[71] Nightingale, *Ejected*, pp. 930–31.   [72] Nightingale, *Ejected*, pp. 930–31, 1206.

[73] Woolrych, *Commonwealth to Protectorate*, pp. 236–37, summarises the argument over tithes.

[74] Woolrych, *Commonwealth to Protectorate*, p. 58, has noted a drawing together of the orthodox denominations in 1651–52.

[75] An indication of the importance of Sandes is his lease of Kendal Castle mills, the corporation's major single source of revenue, from 1649 to 1656 (KCA, 1649–57).

[76] WD/MBK, Box 2, unlisted petition, 1 July 1652.

[77] It is worth offering a conjecture here. In 1648 Thomas Sandes was well regarded by the Presbyterian Masy (Nightingale, *Ejected*, pp. 922–23). The group of petitioners whom Sandes led in 1652 included men who had been close to Henry Masy (PRO, PROB11/ 246, fo. 246 – will of Walter Cowper), who saw William Cole as a Presbyterian minister and wanted him to lecture in Kendal. Finally, the committed Presbyterian William Syll (Nicholson and Axon, *Older Nonconformity*, p. 99) was associated with Sandes and the re-issue of *The Quakers Shaken* in 1655 (below, p. 199). The conjecture is that Sandes led a group of committed religious Presbyterians including some corporation men, and that Thomas Walker was too independent for them.

VII

The second episode which allows us to make some estimate of the character of the corporation in the Commonwealth period is the dismissal of Alderman Gervase Benson. Those who in July 1652 wanted to keep William Cole in Kendal as an additional 'godly and painfull' minister wanted him to help combat the growth of sectarian churches in the region. The challenge of the sects was to pierce the corporation to the core in the next twelve months, for Gervase Benson was prominent in the Separated church he had formed at Sedbergh. Although it is unclear whether Benson's church was in existence before or after he had helped to remodel Kendal corporation in October 1650,[78] in 1652 the church was well enough known for the Quaker George Fox to visit it on 6 June, and Fox made contact with other Separatists in the Kendal region in the following weeks. It is a measure of the vitality of these churches that Fox's contact with them in the summer of 1652 is now construed as a meeting of like minds, rather than as conversion by the evangelising Quaker leader.[79] The petition to retain William Cole in Kendal as town lecturer, dated 1 July 1652, must have been influenced by Fox's arrival. In the autumn, James Nayler was reported to have received a hostile reception at Kendal, while Benson's position as a Quaker no doubt became common knowledge when he tried to shield Nayler in the latter's trial at the Westmorland sessions in Appleby on 11 January 1653.[80] Later that year the discord involved the corporation directly when Alderman Gervase Benson debated in Kendal in public with William Cole and others.[81]

The corporation combated Quakerism on two fronts: first, in print with a book entitled *The Quakers Shaken*, ostensibly written by John Gilpin of

---

[78] Cf. Boulton, *Early Friends in Dent*, p. 23. The tone of Benson's letter to Sir John Lowther of Lowther, on composition business, written 19 May 1651 does not suggest that Benson had yet moved to such a radical position (CRO, Earl of Lonsdale's Mss, D/Lons/L13/1/9). Then Benson was still a probate official (note 6 above).

[79] *The First Publishers of the Truth*, ed. N. Penney (London, 1907), pp. 242–63 is an edition of contemporary Quaker memories of this time written some two decades later. Burrough, *A Warning*, pp. 34–35. W. C. Braithwaite, *The Beginnings of Quakerism* (2nd edn, revised; Cambridge, 1955), pp. 80–81; R. T. Vann, *The Social Development of English Quakerism* (Cambridge, Mass., 1969), ch. 1; B. Reay, *The Quakers and the English Revolution* (Hounslow, 1985), pp. 8–9; and *New Light on George Fox 1624–1691*, ed. M. A. Mullet (York, [1991]), provide modern comment. Most recently, H. L. Ingle, *First Among Friends* (New York, 1994), pp. 82–84 appears to restate the importance of Fox.

[80] J. Nayler and G. Fox, *Several Petitions ... by the Priests of Westmorland ...* (London, 1653), sig. H2; Braithwaite, *Beginnings of Quakerism*, pp. 83, 98, 111.

[81] Wm Cole et al., *The Perfect Pharise* (London, 1654. [Nightingale, *Ejected*, p. 932 gives a date of 14 January 1654]), pp. 6, 10, 11; J. Nayler, *An Answer to the ... Perfect Pharisee* [1654], p. 6; T. Weld et al., *A Further Discovery ...* (Gateside, 1654), p. 9.

Kendal and published by July 1653.[82] (Gervase Benson later placed the responsibility for this book on Thomas Walker and the grammar school master the Revd John Myriell.[83]) Amongst those who endorsed the book, if they did not help to write it, were the mayor (Edward Turner), John Awher (i.e. Archer), and three men who had been displaced in 1650. The perceived threat of the Quakers brought the supporters of Walker and of Cole on the corporation to joint action. The second response of the corporation was for its (unnamed) JPs to imprison some people who had challenged the authority of town or clerics: on 10 September 1653 there were between sixteen and twenty Quaker prisoners in Kendal jail.[84] This response presented a dilemma for the Quaker Benson, who as a senior alderman was a JP. It seems likely that it was the mayor, Edward Turner, and the other senior alderman, John Archer, who had filled the jail.[85] The Quaker JP for Westmorland, Anthony Pearson, reported that seven people had spoken out in church and been imprisoned, but that eleven persons were committed merely for speaking to a justice of the peace against '... this persecution and Tyranny ...' On 11 September five more individuals were jailed for speaking to a clergyman or the mayor.[86]

On 26 September 1653 when the corporation met to elect the mayor, Benson was dismissed.[87] There is no indication as to who initiated the attack. He was vulnerable to the first charge against him: he '... lives out of the towne ... so that the towne hath had little use and service of him'. But the Quaker flatly denied non-attendance at town meetings and courts, and pointed out that he was not the only non-resident corporation man, to which the other aldermen could only respond feebly. Nevertheless, in mid-1653 a non-resident JP who had further weakened the magistracy by publicly arguing with learned clergymen was an embarrassment. The second charge was sharp-witted and opportunistic. It arose from Benson's non-participation in the mayoral election that day. He explained his abstention by promising to vote when either candidate was '... a man of courage fearing the lord and hateing covetiousnes ...' This response was

[82] J. Gilpin, *The Quakers Shaken* (London, 1653). Nightingale, *Ejected*, p. 127, dates it to 4 July 1653.

[83] G. Benson, *An Answer to John Gilpin's Book* (London, 1655), sig. A1.

[84] C. Atkinson, *The Standard of the Lord ... Or an Answer to John Gilpin's Book ...* (London, 1653), p. 31 (I owe this reference to Ms Kate Peters). Atkinson was in Kendal jail. A. Pearson, *To the Parliament of the Commonwealth of England* (London, dated 3 October 1653), pp. 4–5.

[85] The fourth JP, the recorder, did not necessarily sit.

[86] Pearson, *To the Parliament*, p. 5. 'Speaking' may mean interrupting.

[87] WD/MBK A12, from which the following quotations are taken. The note dated 27 July 1653 in FME implies that Benson had been present at the nomination meeting, but the date must be an error, for the listed candidates are for the 1654 election.

too equivocal to be accepted. When it was pointed out to him that he normally exercised his vote, Benson's retort went to the heart of the matter, '... at that time they [the aldermen] had not declared them selves to be enemies of the trueth of God'. Benson was presumably referring to the attack on Quaker thought contained in *The Quakers Shaken* published in July 1653, and to those jailed in August and September. Nine of the ten aldermen present (including John Archer) voted for Benson's removal; one voted to refer it to the recorder, which was done anyway; but Benson was struck off.

The alliance of Benson and Archer was fractured, and the more conservative of the two had won. To the extent that John Archer had found himself working with Edward Turner (mayor in 1652–53), the pressure of sectarianism had helped to bring a degree of unity to the corporation. Equally, old divisions remained, and with them the influence of those dismissed from the corporation in 1650. The events of Benson's dismissal parallel the debate at national level in the Nominated Parliament, and the town government, like the centre, turned away from a sectarian agenda.

VIII

The struggle between Benson and Archer was not yet finished, although Gervase Benson's preoccupation with London affairs in the autumn, and then with a family tragedy, make it uncertain how soon he again became involved in conflict with the Kendal authorities.[88] Benson's removal helped to ensure that Archer, and other members of the corporation, had to face fierce criticism of their anti-Quaker stand, and Benson's absence did nothing to mute that criticism. The complaints came, however, from a small minority, for the number of Quakers resident in Kendal was about three dozen.[89] Only one, George Taylor, was a member of the corporation (a burgess).

Those Quakers in jail at the time of Benson's dismissal replied to *The Quakers Shaken*, and also highlighted their own harsh treatment by the Kendal justices.[90] The corporation men who had endorsed that tract and had imprisoned friends were told that 'The Lord will beat the mountains to dust! How will you stand against the Almighty?' they were asked.[91] The Quaker prisoners' complaints were directed

---

[88] Boulton, *Early Friends in Dent*, pp. 32–35.

[89] See CROK, records of the Society of Friends, Westmorland, book no. 93, fo. 7, dated 1656.

[90] Atkinson, *The Standard of the Lord*.

[91] Francis Howgill, in Atkinson, *The Standard of the Lord*, p. 25.

To the Maior and justices of Kendal ... we for witnessing truth are kept in prison by the corrupt magistrates who live in the world and turn the grace of God into wantonness, and refuse to do justice for they have perverted the way of the Lord.

... the corrupt wills of the Magistrates have restrained us of our liberty, who are free born of England.[92]

Reports that preachers were confronted, and that men and women had walked naked through the streets, were published in January 1654, and a story of John Archer's discomfort at the hands of the Quakers[93] appeared in print in William Cole's theological disputes with James Nayler.[94] The fact that in January 1654 Archer had taken a lease of the tithes of Kendal rectory is a measure of the gulf between him and the Quakers.[95] George Taylor did not attend the election meeting at Michaelmas 1654,[96] and we know that by October 1654 Taylor had written against John Archer,[97] and had been imprisoned for twenty days by him.

The corporation continued to be identified with some of those dismissed in 1650 when, early in 1655, Thomas Sandes headed the endorsers of a re-issue, with additional material, of *The Quakers Shaken*.[98] Two aldermen were amongst those who signed. In April 1655 Gervase Benson returned to the Kendal conflict, this time as a writer, with his answer to both editions of *The Quakers Shaken*. Amongst other signatories of Benson's book, it was George Taylor, rather than Benson, who attacked personalities. John Archer was '... a detestable Blasphemer, a notorious liar and a persecutor of the Saints ... whose name and nature stinkes in the nostrills of the Lord God'. Edward Turner was called a 'cavalier' and, Taylor claimed, had been fined for swearing. Taylor also attacked as a slander John Archer's accusation that Quakers condoned buggery, which had caused great offence.[99] This was enough to bring about Taylor's dismissal from the corporation in September 1655,

---

[92] Atkinson, *The Standard of the Lord*, pp. 25, 27, 31.

[93] CROK, records of the Society of Friends, book of sufferings, no. 51D, makes no mention of such events. However, the volume was written up in 1716.

[94] Cole *et al.*, *Perfect Pharise*, pp. 23, 24, 45; Weld *et al.*, *A Further Discoverie* ..., pp. 83, 84.

[95] PRO, Exchequer, equity proceedings, bills and answers, E112/532/15. Gervase Benson's pamphlet against tithes, *A True Tryall of the Ministers and Ministry of England*, was published at London in 1655.

[96] FME, 'The names of the aldermen September 1654'; I do not know why this document is annotated: 'Simplenes of heart/ diligence in the office', and, separately, '2 Sam: 13' [sic].

[97] London, Friends Library, Swarthmore Transcripts (microfilm), III, 501 (14 October 1654). Ms Kate Peters drew my attention to this reference.

[98] J. Gilpin, *The Quakers Shaken* (London, 1655), p. 17.

[99] Benson, *An Answer to John Gilpin's book*, pp. 4–8.

for that he neglects comeing to church and reviles some of the Magistrates of the towne and that he said there was none of the Companie containing the Aldermen of this Burgh fit to be Maior. And is an incourager of those that disturbes the publique assemblie <meat together for the worship of God> and an abettor of them he is ejected for beinge a Burgesse.[100]

By early October he was reported to be in jail because of what he had written to John Archer.[101] The reasons given for Taylor's removal were a frank attack on Quaker practices, for there was no need to hide behind the fiction of a member failing in his obligations to the corporation that had been used to remove Benson. His departure marked the end of confrontation with Quakers within the corporation. John Archer continued in his power bases outside the town, in clerical appointments across the north of England, and in the county, where he was easily the most zealous attender of the magistrates at Westmorland quarter sessions in Kendal between midsummer 1655 and midsummer 1659.[102] He remained as a senior alderman of Kendal, a position which he had acquired through the Engagement purge.

IX

In Kendal, the corporation men appeared to ignore the implications of their civil-war allegiance, and preserved their chartered independence until 1650. Continuity of membership prevailed over internal division in the corporation brought about by the war. In order to defeat the royalists on the Corporation, Benson and Archer imperilled the independence of the town. In 1650 they had to turn to the House of Commons and the Engagement. Even after the Engagement, there was some continuity, epitomised by the career of Edward Turner, alderman between 1637 and 1672. But fifteen out of the thirty-three members of the Engaged corporation were newcomers to one or both tiers, a greater upset than either the restoration or natural disasters effected.[103] Men whose role in the economy centred on manufacturing rather than distribution became proportionately more important. Yet these changes left the corporation inclined to conservatism. Some of those dismissed in 1650 retained influence even though excluded. Thus the corporation could swiftly agree to use its charter to remove two Quakers from their number. Benson must

---

[100] FME, 17 Sept. 1655 (the words within < > are interlined after an erasure).
[101] Swarthmore TS (microfilm), III, 662 (7 October 1655).
[102] C. B. Phillips, 'The corporation of Kendal under Charles II', *Northern History*, 31 (1995), 161. Archer resigned as commissioner for sequestrations in 1654 (*CCC*, pp. 696, 2588).
[103] Phillips, 'Kendal under Charles II', p. 172.

have been one of the first English Quakers to be put out of office.[104] He probably lobbied for the anti-tithe cause in London that autumn,[105] and so may have contributed to the pyrrhic victory of the radicals in a parliamentary division on 10 December 1653 (chronicled so masterfully by Austin Woolrych), which precipitated the demise of the Nominated Parliament.[106]

[104] E.g. *Victoria County History, Hull*, p. 109; *VCH Oxfordshire*, IV (Oxford), 415, and X (Banbury), 74–75; C. Holmes, *Seventeenth-century Lincolnshire* (Lincoln, 1980), pp. 205–6; and D. Sacks, in Richardson, *Town and country*, pp. 120–21, on Bristol, do not report the ejection of Quakers from corporations. One was put off Evesham corporation in 1655, see *Evesham Borough Records of the Seventeenth Century, 1605–1687*, ed. S. K. Roberts (WHS, XIV, 1994), xxii.

[105] Ms Kate Peters suggested this to me. For some estimate of Benson's wider importance see Boulton, *Early Friends in Dent*, pp. 33–34, 47, 55–56, 64.

[106] Woolrych, *Commonwealth to Protectorate*, pp. 333–39.

9

Repacifying the polity: the responses of Hobbes and Harrington to the 'crisis of the common law'

GLENN BURGESS

(I) THE 'CRISIS OF THE COMMON LAW' AND CONSEQUENT PROBLEMS

Political thinkers, especially the most creative of them, tend to develop their ideas within a great variety of intellectual contexts. Few of them can satisfactorily be studied in relation to only one or two of those contexts. It is often true, as well, that the ways in which thinkers respond to their contexts can interact with one another to produce unexpected results. The following essay is an examination of some of the less-explored dimensions of the political writings produced after 1650 by Thomas Hobbes and James Harrington; and it suggests that it is possible to consider them as having responded to a 'crisis of the common law' that engulfed English political life in the years 1640 to 1642, and beyond. I do not suppose that this context can lead us to an exhaustive analysis of either of these thinkers; and I therefore wish to deny neither that there are other, better-known and perhaps contradictory, aspects of their thinking that can only be explained in other contexts, nor that these other aspects may predominate over the dimensions explored below.

Before 1640 many in English public life believed that they lived in a 'pacified polity', a view underpinned by the assumptions and attitudes that made up what we know as the idea of the 'ancient constitution'. Hobbes and Harrington were often severe critics of the 'ancient constitution'; but they shared its ideal of the 'pacified polity'.[1] By 1640 that ideal was in crisis, as faith in the political role of the common law faded.[2] The 'crisis of

---

[1] For this concept of the 'pacified polity' see Glenn Burgess, *Absolute Monarchy and the Stuart Constitution* (New Haven, 1996), pp. 159–64; and Deborah Baumgold, 'Pacifying politics: resistance, violence, and accountability in seventeenth-century contract theory', *Political Theory*, 21 (1993), 6–27.

[2] The following discussion is based on Glenn Burgess, *The Politics of the Ancient Constitution: an Introduction to English Political Thought 1603–1642* (Basingstoke, 1992), chs. VII and VIII. Full references to evidence can be found there.

the common law' amounted to a profound sense that the law of England had failed in its capacity to control royal misgovernment and protect the rights and property of the subject, and that the misuse of the law had undermined its authority and undermined faith in its capacity to prevent tyranny and preserve liberty. The common law had failed, above all, because the king had been able to have his emergency absolute prerogatives accepted as routine legal rights. Writing in the late 1640s, Edward Hyde commented that history should have taught Charles I's ministers that in those times 'when the prerogative went highest ... never any court of law ... was called upon to assist in an act of power'. Trust in the law was necessary for political stability, for without it men were insecure in the possession of their liberties; and nothing should be done to undermine that trust. When the law was trusted, then 'though it [the Crown] might sometimes make sallies upon them by the prerogative, yet the law would keep the people from any invasion of it'. For that reason, paradoxically, it was politically more healthy for the crown to receive 'sharp animadversions and reprehensions' from the courts.[3] But exactly the reverse had happened in England. By 1640 there were doubts about whether the law could control Charles I's misgovernment; by 1642, many were prepared to accept that, in response to Charles I's violence against his subjects, the subject was now able to use violence against him (or, at least, against his ministers and agents). Much of the political thought of the 1640s and 1650s can be read as a response to this crisis. Some asked how this injection of necessary violence into political life could be justified; others, how, in the face of violence and its defenders, a 'pacified polity' could now be built (or rebuilt). Hobbes and Harrington belonged in the latter category. Like the ancient constitutionalists and some of their successors amongst the royalists of the 1640s, these two men grappled with the difficulty of imagining a political community that would contain an irresistible authority, but one that would rule through the law and not against it. From the 1640s the idea of sovereignty became an essential feature of such imaginings, moving thinkers away from the assumptions of the early Stuart world, but also making the task of defending the rule of law even trickier.

One way of defending the resort to violence was to build on the example set by the king, and rely upon *necessity* or *emergency*, rather than law, to justify one's actions. Royalists like John Maxwell, whose explication

---

[3] Edward Hyde, earl of Clarendon, *The History of the Rebellion and Civil Wars in England*, ed. W. Dunn Macray (6 vols., Oxford, 1888), I, 86–9. It is worth nothing that the passage cited here originated in the Ms 'History', written 1646–48, unlike much of the surrounding material which is from the Ms 'Life', written much later in 1668–71 (see Clarendon, *History*, ed. Macray, I, 97, n. 1; C. H. Firth, 'Clarendon's "History of the rebellion"', *English Historical Review*, 19 (1904), 26–54, 246–62, 464–83).

of the maxim *salus populi suprema lex* in 1644 recognised 'that all Lawes should be proportioned to the publike good of the Soveraigne and People', nonetheless continued to stress 'that the Kingdome or State, not onely possibly and probably, but really and existently may be such, that the Soveraigne must exerce and exercise an Arbitrary power ... [and] for the preservation of it selfe and the publick may break thorow all Lawes'. He mentioned specifically cases of foreign invasion and sedition or rebellion.[4] Many royalists, though, quickly abandoned arguments about emergency cases, which, already by 1642, had become the preserve as much of parliamentarians as of royalists. Parliamentarians co-opted them to explain how the two Houses could assume powers and responsibilities that they had hitherto exercised, if at all, only with the king's consent.[5] Henry Parker claimed a similar power for the two Houses to act beyond the law in emergencies, or 'cases of publique extremity'. Parliamentary government, he said, was 'used as Physicke, not dyet'; it has a special function of 'umpirage' between king and kingdom in rare cases of conflict.[6] For those who used this line of argument, royalist and parliamentarian alike, the ancient constitution defined normal politics; but there existed an arbitrary authority that could in cases of necessity override the provisions of that constitution. Another parliamentarian, John Marsh, defended the 'legality' of the militia ordinance in 1642 by arguing 'by reason of the necessity, it is warranted by the Law for them to do it at this time'.[7]

A second reaction to the crisis of confidence in the ancient constitution lay in the development of arguments which appealed to *reason*, in the sense of a rationality against which existing political structures might be judged and (if deemed unsatisfactory) in the name of which they might be replaced. We see this first in parliamentarian propaganda, later in the Levellers. By 1642 we find parliamentarian appeals to 'equity', 'the publike good' and 'the Law taken abstract from its originall reason and end'.[8] The

---

[4] John Maxwell, *Sacro-Sancta Regum Majestas* (Oxford, 1644), p. 176.
[5] This theme has been very thoroughly explored by Michael Mendle, see especially Mendle, 'The ship money case, *The Case of Shipmony*, and the development of Henry Parker's parliamentary absolutism', *Historical Journal*, 32 (1989), 616–20; Mendle, 'Parliamentary sovereignty: a very English absolutism', in Nicholas Phillipson and Quentin Skinner (eds.), *Political Discourse in Early Modern Britain* (Cambridge, 1993), ch. v; and Mendle, *Henry Parker and the English Civil War: the Political Thought of the Public's Privado* (Cambridge, 1995).
[6] Henry Parker, *Observations Upon Some of his Majesties Late Answers and Expresses* (2nd edn, London, 1642), pp. 33, 24, 42; also pp. 16, 27–28; but cf. pp. 30, 34.
[7] John Marsh, *An Argument or, Debate in Law: Of the Great Question Concerning the Militia* (London, 1642), p. 7.
[8] *A Question Answered: How Laws are to be Understood, and Obedience Yeelded?* (London, 1642), which may be by Parker (see Michael Mendle, *Dangerous Positions: Mixed Government, the*

Levellers took over much of this language.[9] In 1645 William Walwyn told John Lilburne to give up his reliance upon the ancient constitution, which, he maintained, had actually been constructed by the oppressive power of kings, imposed at the Norman Conquest. Kings had been aided in their oppressions by their parliaments, rather than resisted by them. It was the law of nature not the law of England that gave men liberty, 'as due unto you as the ayre you breath in'. Lilburne should appeal instead to 'reason, sense, and the common Law of equitie and justice'.[10] The following year, Richard Overton gave emphatic expression to the Levellers' refusal to rest their case on custom, law and tradition (the ancient constitution): 'for whatever our Fore-fathers were; or whatever they did or suffered, or were enforced to yeeld unto; we are men of the present age, and ought to be absolutely free from all kindes of exorbitancies, molestations or Arbitrary Power'.[11] The Levellers never totally abandoned the use of ancient constitutionalist argument.[12] Nonetheless their political platform (succinctly expressed in the *Agreement of the People*) was an attempt to refashion in the light of reason and nature an understanding of what liberties men ought to possess securely, and what sort of political society would ensure that they did so.[13] Judged by the light of reason, the ancient constitution was inadequate and needed to be destroyed and replaced afresh with something better.

Estates of the Realm, and the Making of the Answer to the xix Propositions (University AB, 1985), pp. 187–88). This work was much cited by the Levellers.

[9] For the continuity of ideas between parliamentarians and Levellers see David Wootton, 'From rebellion to revolution: the crisis of the winter of 1642/3 and the origins of civil war radicalism', *English Historical Review*, 105 (1990), 654–69; and Andrew Sharp, 'John Lilburne and the Long Parliament's *Book of Declarations*: a radical's exploitation of the words of authorities', *History of Political Thought*, 9 (1988), 19–44.

[10] William Walwyn, *Englands Lamentable Slaverie* (1645), in *The Writings of William Walwyn*, ed. Jack R. McMichael and Barbara Taft, (Athens OH, 1989), pp. 147–49. The theory of the Norman Yoke is explored most fully in Christopher Hill, 'The Norman yoke', in Hill, *Puritanism and Revolution: Studies in Interpretation of the English Revolution of the 17th Century* (Harmondsworth, 1986; orig. edn 1958), ch. III.

[11] Richard Overton, *A Remonstrance of Many-Thousand Citizens* (1646), in Don M. Wolfe (ed.), *Leveller Manifestoes of the Puritan Revolution* (New York, 1967), p. 114. This whole line of argument was taken furthest in John Warr's *The Corruption and Deficiency of the Laws of England Soberly Discovered* (London, 1649), which saw in the very historical continuity of the ancient constitution a mark of tyranny and oppression.

[12] See J. G. A. Pocock, *The Ancient Constitution and the Feudal Law: a Study of English Historical Thought in the Seventeenth Century – a Reissue with Retrospect* (Cambridge, 1987), pp. 125–27; R. B. Seaberg, 'The Norman Conquest and the common law: the Levellers and the argument from continuity', *Historical Journal*, 24 (1981), 791–806; Burgess, *Politics of the Ancient Constitution*, pp. 90–93, 226–29; and Glenn Burgess, 'Protestant polemic: the Leveller pamphlets', *Parergon*, n.s., 11 (1993), 45–67 for discussion of the roles of common-law and rationalistic argument in the writings of the Levellers.

[13] The various versions of the *Agreement* are all reprinted in Wolfe (ed.), *Leveller Manifestoes*.

Those two lines of argument, necessity and reason, were frequently combined.[14] Together they served to underwrite theories that allowed a role in politics to violent resistance contrary to civil law. There were others, however, who stressed above all else the value of peace and order. They were deeply dissatisfied with arguments from either reason or necessity, and suggested instead that it was possible to distil from the ancient constitution a set of political principles that remained viable, even if the ancient constitution itself, in all its particulars, did not. I will suggest that important elements in the political thinking of both Hobbes and Harrington may have developed in appreciative dialogue with this style of response to the crisis of the common law.

The essential features of this third response are evident in a royalist critic of Parker, probably Sir John Spelman,[15] who in 1643 commented on the idea that parliament could in emergency exercise a natural popular authority which had never been completely alienated.

> Then can they not be assemblies of resumption [sic] of the peoples supposed power, for in such imaginary assemblies, there must be a dissolution of all constitute orders, degrees and qualities of the parts, and all the members must be reduced to a naturall coequality undistinguished by any difference, of quality, degree or priviledges whatsoever: so as there must be neither King, nor peers, nor any office or power of the former State remaining, but all resolved into a meere Chaos, till all be new framed by the deity of the people.[16]

People should rest content with what they were guaranteed by the existing laws and constitution. It was true that England's 'Lawes and auncient setled frame of Government' did allow the people some political authority. They

> were in some sort admitted to a participation of it, but so admitted, as that still the Soveraignty should cleerly remaine to Him that ought to be the Soveraigne. And to this end our law ... did for preventing innovations that might subvert that setled regularity: in such a sort establish the frame of State and government, as that the Prince should have his hands bound up from using the legislative power without the concurrence of the Peers and Commons.[17]

---

[14] Charles Herle, for example, talked of both an emergency right to act when the king himself refused to do so, and in more rationalistic mode of a power of corporate self-defence invested in parliament (Andrew Sharp, *Political Ideas of the English Civil Wars 1641–1648* (London, 1983), pp. 61–62).

[15] The tract has usually been attributed to Dudley Digges. I follow Mendle, *Henry Parker and the English Civil War*, pp. 104–7.

[16] [Sir John Spelman], *A Review of the Observations Upon Some of his Majesties Late Answers and Expresses* (Oxford, 1643), p. 9.

[17] Ibid., pp. 9–10.

Nonetheless, there could be over the king no 'Superintending power', of the sort that Parker allowed the two houses, for that would 'unsoveraigne' him, and the superintending power would itself become sovereign. Thus the law of England had decided 'that a positive knowne law, without any coercive superintendant, was a sufficient and the best boundary of regall power, against any irregularity whatsoever'. If the law were clearly known then the king would not dare to break it. The only alternative lay in an infinite regress of superintendent authorities.[18]

What I want to draw attention to in Spelman's argument is the way in which an understanding of the interdependence of *closure* and *sovereignty* served as a basis for conceptualising the *rule of law*.[19] What compelled many men to accept the need for a clearly defined locus of sovereign authority was their fear that without it there could be no *closure*. By this I mean that the system of laws, customs and traditional practices that made up the English constitution could be complete and self-contained only if it possessed a source of authority beyond which there could be no appeal (a sovereign); and that a system could only guarantee peace and order when it was so closed. It has been frequently contended that Henry Parker was a theorist of sovereignty; but the sort of casuistical absolutism (argued from cases of necessity or emergency) that he represented was well distanced from any concept of sovereignty. He stressed the existence of both a normal and an extraordinary politics. The ancient constitution was not a complete system of law, and appeal – to necessity, or to reason and nature – could be made beyond it. Such appeals might well be euphemisms for an appeal to the sword. Though not all parliamentarians were happy with Parker's form of absolutism,[20] it was largely left to the constitutional royalist writers (especially those of the Great Tew circle[21]) to elaborate

---

[18] Ibid., pp. 14–15.

[19] For some suggestive remarks on this theme see Ivor Wilks, 'A note on sovereignty', in W. J. Stankiewicz, *In Defense of Sovereignty* (New York, 1969), pp. 197–205 passim, but esp. 202–3. Note in particular the importance given in this analysis of sovereignty language to that argument from the impossibility of an infinite regress.

[20] For an excellent discussion of these other parliamentarian voices see Mendle, *Henry Parker and the English Civil War*, pp. 93–97. The most interesting parliamentarians who shared much with the royalist writers discussed below are Charles Herle and Philip Hunton.

[21] The Great Tew circle, which takes its name from Falkland's country house, seems to include, albeit in extremely marginal roles, Digges and Spelman, as well as more famous names including Hyde. The character of their political thought, and their relationship with Hobbes, was discussed in Tuck, *Natural Rights Theories: Their Origin and Development* (Cambridge, 1979), chs v and vi; but that account needs some correction, not least because Hobbes can scarcely be said to be a member of the Tew circle at all, see Perez Zagorin, 'Clarendon and Hobbes', *Journal of Modern History*, 57 (1975), 593–616; and the salutary remarks in Noel Malcolm, 'A summary biography of Hobbes', in Tom Sorell (ed.), *The Cambridge Companion to Hobbes* (Cambridge, 1996), ch. 1, pp. 21–23. For general

the sort of argument that tied together closure, sovereignty and the rule of law.[22]

In thus closely associating closure with sovereignty, the thinkers of the 1640s had moved beyond early Stuart ancient constitutionalism, which had recognised the crucial importance only of the former. They had also taken a step towards the worlds – different worlds though they were in many ways – of Hobbes and Harrington. The significance of constitutional royalism in mediating between ideas of the ancient constitution and the great thinkers of the 1650s can be appreciated if we explore more fully the nuances of royalist thinking. Many royalist authors explored and elaborated the theory of limited but irresistible monarchy. Again and again, they emphasised that the king was both sovereign and bound to rule by law, so that England enjoyed the benefits of being both an absolute and a limited monarchy. By sovereignty they meant that no appeal, peaceful or violent, was possible against the king's *judgements*, rather more than they meant that he was a sovereign *law-maker*, though many did stress his law-making authority as well.[23] The most striking expression of commitment to the idea of sovereignty was in another of Spelman's works from 1643. England, he declared, 'is a Kingdom, an empire, a well regulated monarchie; the Head thereof a Supreme Head, a soveraigne, a King whose Crown is an Imperiall Crown, the Kingdom *His* Kingdom, *His* Realme, *His* Dominion, the People *His* People the Subject *His* Subject ... the very Parliament it self ... *His* Parliament'.[24] But while powers of judgement and law-making were 'inseparably annexed to His Person', nonetheless the king did not possess an arbitrary power of judgement. On matters of 'private interest' (i.e. property rights) his judgements were to be administered by the judges, while in 'matters of publique affaire' his judgements

sketches see Hugh Trevor-Roper, 'The Great Tew circle', in Trevor-Roper, *Catholics, Anglicans and Puritans: Seventeenth Century Essays* (London, 1987), ch. IV; and Michael Mendle, 'The *convivium philosophicum* and the Civil War: a country house and its politics' in Gervase Jackson-Stops et al. (eds.), *The fashioning and functioning of the British Country House* (Washington DC, 1989), pp. 289–97. One should be careful to resist the idea that there is any such thing as a 'Great Tew' political theory. They differed sharply amongst themselves on such subjects as the origin of authority and the idea of mixed monarchy, as well as on much else.

[22] The fullest and best account of the political ideas of constitutional royalism is David L. Smith, *Constitutional Royalism and the Search for Settlement, c. 1640–1649* (Cambridge, 1995), ch. VII; also John Sanderson, *'But the People's Creatures': The Philosophical Basis of the English Civil War* (Manchester, 1989), chs. II and III; and the seminal work of B. H. G. Wormald, *Clarendon: Politics, History, and Religion 1640–1660* (Chicago, 1976; orig. edn 1951).

[23] One needs to read this material against a context in which law-making was frequently seen as a form of giving judgement: see Burgess, *Absolute Monarchy and the Stuart Constitution*, pp. 176–81.

[24] [Sir John Spelman], *The Case of our Affaires in Law, Religion, and Other Circumstances* (Oxford, 1643), p. 1.

and laws required 'the concurrence of the Nobles, and Commons in Parliament'.[25] Thus the king was 'restrained' without any impairment of his sovereignty.[26]

Examples of his position could be multiplied. Henry Ferne, Dudley Digges and Edward Hyde all produced broadly similar portraits of a monarchy sovereign but limited in the years from 1642 to 1645;[27] and Hyde survived to use the same ideas against Hobbes in the Restoration.[28] But the work that explored this line of argument in most detail was Dudley Digges' *The Unlawfulnesse of Subjects taking up Armes*, published in 1643.

In that reflective contribution to the debates of the 1640s, Digges put his chief point in unmistakably Hobbesian language. He was particularly keen to avoid the dangers of the language of mixed-monarchy theory, which had been introduced into royalist thinking in June 1642 by the king's *Answer to the Nineteen Propositions*, written for him by Falkland and Culpepper. They had suggested that sovereign authority in England was shared by the three 'estates', king, lords and commons.[29] The allegiance of royalists to the three-estates model of the *Answer* was from the beginning uncertain. Hyde was appalled by it, and advised that the *Answer* itself should not be published.[30] One problem was that if the king was one of the three estates, part of a collective sovereign power, then it was not clear that the king alone could be an irresistible sovereign. Digges dealt with that problem by abandoning mixed-monarchy theory, and retaining – as did Hyde – a theory of a self-limited sovereign king.[31] The only cure for

---

[25] Ibid., p. 2.   [26] Ibid., p. 3.

[27] See, for example, key statements in Henry Ferne, *A Reply Unto Severall Treatises* (Oxford, 1643), pp. 28–32, 37, 39, 93; Henry Ferne, *The Resolving of Conscience* (Cambridge, 1642), pp. 15–16, 18; [Dudley Digges], *An Answer to a Printed Book Intituled Observations Upon Some of his Majesties Late Answers and Expresses* (Oxford, 1642), pp. 1, 13, 34–35, 36, 37, 43–44, 50–51; [Edward Hyde], *Transcendent and Multiplied Rebellion and Treason, Discovered by the Lawes of the Land* ([Oxford], 1645), pp. 1, 3–4, 15–16.

[28] Edward Hyde, earl of Clarendon, *A Brief View and Survey of the Dangerous and Pernicious Errors to Church and State, in Mr Hobbes's Book, entitled Leviathan* (1676), in G. A. J. Rogers (ed.), *Leviathan: Contemporary Responses to the Political Theory of Hobbes* (Bristol, 1995), esp. pp. 218, 235–56.

[29] J. P. Kenyon, *The Stuart Constitution 1603–1688: Documents and Commentary* (Cambridge, 2nd edn, 1986), pp. 18–20.

[30] Clarendon, *Life*, in Clarendon, *The History of the Rebellion ... Also his Life Written by Himself* (1 vol. edn, Oxford, 1843), p. 953; Wormald, *Clarendon*, p. 12.

[31] It is misleading to say that 'Hyde and his associates ... argued for mixed monarchy in the state', for not only was Hyde never a theorist of mixed monarchy, but at least one of his associates (Digges) quickly distanced himself from it (J. P. Sommerville, 'Lofty science and local politics', in Sorrell (ed.), *Cambridge Companion to Hobbes*, ch. x, p. 266; also Mark Goldie, 'The reception of Hobbes', in J. H. Burns, with Mark Goldie (eds.), *The Cambridge History of Political Thought 1450–1700* (Cambridge, 1991), ch. xx, pp. 595–96). In 1645

the anarchy and chaos of nature, Digges declared, was for men to 'reduce into a civille unitie, by placing over them one head, and by making his will the will of them all'. '[T]here cannot be two powers and yet the Kingdome remaine one.'[32] To appeal to the equality of nature (i.e. to reason) was politically fatal, for it would 'dissolve the bonds of all government, since there can [naturally] be no Magistrate, no Superiour and Inferiour'.[33] Digges' statement implied sovereignty, and the illegitimacy of all appeal against positive laws and existing institutions to nature, reason, equity or conscience; but it did not lessen Digges' commitment to the rule of law. He explained the matter historically. The early monarchies were 'absolute' ones, in which the will of the prince was taken for law. But quickly a remedy was discovered for the inconveniences of such a situation: 'to bound his power within the limits of positive Lawes'. This meant that many monarchies (including the English) were, 'though restrained by Lawes ... yet truly Monarchs ... being not responsible for any breaches, as supreme, though not absolute'. What Digges argued for was not absolute authority, but 'onely *jus regni*, the right of Monarchy, not to be accomptable to any inferiour jurisdiction'.[34] Digges made much clearer in this work than constitutional royalists commonly did that the king alone was the supreme power; that mixed monarchy was in one sense absurd (there could only be one sovereign); but that there was in another reduced sense a sort of mixed monarchy in England constituted by royal grants and concessions. By that process had been created a situation in which kings alone did not make law or tax.[35] Digges scorned that body of opinion which suggested that 'there is not any difference betweene arbitrary government, and government restrained by lawes, if Subjects may not compell their soveraigne to the observation of them'.[36] But Digges did accept that 'obedience to the Kings command against law, is unwarrantable', distinguishing that from 'hostile resistance'. The principle of closure also ensured that one other loophole was closed: there could be no resistance *allowed* by law, for that would dissolve the state whenever the right was exercised.[37]

Hyde glossed the King's *Answer to the* xix *Propositions* in a way that directly reversed what is said about mixed monarchy: see [Hyde], *Transcendent and Multiplied Rebellion*, p. 14; cf. p. 17. For later comment on the subject see his *Brief View and Survey*, in Rogers (ed.), *Leviathan: Contemporary Responses*, p. 213.

[32] [Dudley Digges], *The Unlawfulnesse of Subjects Taking Up Armes against their Soveraigne* (Oxford, 1643), pp. 4, 7–8.

[33] Ibid., p. 26; also p. 59 for another clear statement.   [34] Ibid., pp. 29, 30.

[35] Ibid., pp. 59, 66–69; also pp. 138 ff. for his now rather niggardly use of the language of the three estates.

[36] Ibid., p. 71.   [37] Ibid., p. 128.

(2) HOBBES AS A THEORIST OF THE RULE OF LAW

The framework now established provides us with a context in which to interpret the political thought of Hobbes. How can one combine sovereign closure and the rule of law? Hobbes addressed precisely that question, and in doing so fashioned a rather different answer from those we have come across so far. In a review of David Smith's *Constitutional Royalism*, Mark Goldie revealed himself puzzled by the fact that in Smith's account 'Digges (who was surely close to Hobbes[38]) is said to hold a doctrine of the irrevocable transfer of right to the sovereign, yet is here camped with the constitutionalists.'[39] The puzzle has a solution. The doctrine of irrevocable surrender was one way of ensuring the closure of a legal system, and it was accompanied by a doctrine of sovereignty. Both men emphasised sovereignty, closure (and irresistibility) and the rule of law,[40] though Hobbes developed a way of presenting them that severed the link between the rule of law and the idea that kings were legally limited. Historians have neglected this emphasis on the rule of law, which united Hobbes and the constitutional royalists, because of a common assumption that absolutism and the rule of law are incompatible ideas.[41] It is an odd view, given that the first elaboration of the idea of the rule of law occurred in a work that was also a defence of the absolute sovereignty of parliament.[42] These

---

[38] Goldie presumably alludes to the fact that both Digges and Hobbes argued that sovereigns could not be resisted because subjects had surrendered to them their natural rights. It should be noted, however, that only Hobbes took this principle of irresistibility to *absolutist* conclusions. Cf. Tuck, *Natural Rights Theories*, ch. v.

[39] Mark Goldie, review in *History of Political Thought*, 16 (1995), 447–50, at p. 448. Smith argues that at the core of constitutional royalism were two propositions 'that mixed monarchy did not imply shared sovereignty', and that 'the concept of legally limited monarchy involved a regulation rather than a restriction of the monarch's powers' (Smith, *Constitutional Royalism and the Search for Settlement*, p. 228). That seems right, though I detect much more ambivalence about mixed monarchy than Smith. The essential point to emphasise here was their belief that the king was 'sovereign yet legally limited' (p. 243). Modern historians often side with Hobbes in seeing this as self-contradictory, but it is not: cf. the comments in Maurice Goldsmith, 'Hobbes on law', in Sorell (ed.), *Cambridge Companion to Hobbes*, ch. xi, pp. 277–83.

[40] Goldie is right, in several ways, when he comments that the rule of law will not 'without further specification, serve as a criterion to distinguish constitutionalists from absolutists' ('Review', p. 449).

[41] See the puzzled comments in Francis D. Wormuth, *The Origins of Modern Constitutionalism* (New York, 1949), pp. 211–12 (one of the few writers before very recent times to recognise Hobbes' claims to be a theorist of the rule of law).

[42] A. V. Dicey, *An Introduction to the Law of the Constitution* (Indianapolis IA, 1982; orig. edn. 1885; 8th edn 1915). Cf. Oakeshott's verdict: 'the first condition of the rule of law is a "sovereign" legislative office': Michael Oakeshott, 'The rule of law', in Oakeshott, *On History and Other Essays* (Oxford, 1983), pp. 119–64, at p. 138.

connections between Hobbes and constitutional royalism need to be explored further.[43]

It is, of course, possible and proper to read Hobbes as a critic of constitutional royalism,[44] but he was a critic as much in sorrow as in anger. Too many royalists, even those who had learnt from Hobbes, failed to appreciate the lessons he taught. They were 'in love with *mixarchy*', believing England 'not an absolute, but a mixed monarchy', he wrote in the 1660s.[45] But already in 1640, Hobbes had made it clear that a mixed monarchy was not a pacified one, for 'division ... of the sovereignty ... introduceth war; wherein the private sword hath place again'.[46] However, it is not clear that Hobbes' views on mixed monarchy differed much from those of many constitutional royalists. As he elaborated his criticisms of mixed monarchy in the *Elements of Law* it became clear that he was expressing the *same* points as Digges' *Unlawfulnesse*. Mixture did not qualify the essence of sovereignty, but it had a 'subordinate' place 'in the administration thereof', as sovereigns delegated authority to and worked through various institutions, councils and assemblies.[47] However muddled the situation might look in practice, in theory there was in every commonwealth an absolute sovereign.[48] Constitutional royalists, so far as

---

[43] Especially relevant here is an interesting if small literature on Hobbes and the common law. See especially George L. Mosse, 'Thomas Hobbes: jurisprudence at the crossroads', *University of Toronto Quarterly*, 15 (1946), 346–55; Enid Campbell, 'Thomas Hobbes and the common law', *Tasmanian University Law Review*, 1 (1958), 20–45; Martin Kriele, 'Notes on the controversy between Hobbes and English jurists', in Reinhart Koselleck and Roman Schnur (eds), *Hobbes – Forschungen* (Berlin, 1969), pp. 211–22; D. E. C. Yale, 'Hobbes and Hales on law, legislation and the sovereign', *Cambridge Law Journal*, 31 (1972), 121–56; J. H. Hexter, 'Thomas Hobbes and the law', *Cornell Law Review*, 65 (1980), 491–90; Paulette Carrive, 'Hobbes et les juristes de la common law', in Martin Bertman and M. Malherbe (eds), *Thomas Hobbes: de la métaphysique à la politique* (Paris, 1989), pp. 149–73; and Martin A. Bertman, 'Hobbes on the character and use of civil law', in B. Wilms *et al.* (eds), *Hobbes oggi* (Milan, 1990), pp. 159–76. Most emphasise the conflict between Hobbes and common lawyers and Hobbes' misunderstanding of his adversaries. There are interesting suggestions about the relationship between Hobbes and St German in Robinson A. Grover, 'The legal origins of Thomas Hobbes's doctrine of contract', *Journal of the History of Philosophy*, 18 (1980), 177–94; and Sharon K. Dobbins, 'Equity: the court of conscience or the king's command, the Dialogues of St German and Hobbes compared', *Journal of Law and Religion*, 9 (1991), 113–49. There is an excellent survey of the entire subject in Goldsmith, 'Hobbes on law'.

[44] Smith, *Constitutional Royalism and the Search for Settlement*, pp. 248–53; Sommerville, 'Lofty science and local politics'.

[45] The quotations are from the most explicit of Hobbes' criticisms of the constitutional royalists in Thomas Hobbes, *Behemoth*, ed. Ferdinand Tönnies (Chicago, 1990), pp. 114–17. Hobbes himself does seem to have believed that many royalists were strong believers in mixed monarchy.

[46] Thomas Hobbes, *The Elements of Law, Natural and Politic*, ed. Ferdinand Tönnies (London, 1969), ii.i.16, p. 115.

[47] Ibid., ii,i.17, pp. 115–16.   [48] Ibid., ii.i.18–19, pp. 116–18.

we can tell, would not have disagreed with that way of putting things, and Hobbes' comments read like a blueprint for Digges'.

Hobbes did differ from constitutional royalists on the subject of limited monarchy, if not on that of mixed monarchy; and he had done so from the beginning. There were men, he said in 1640, who 'have imagined that a commonwealth may be constituted in such manner, as the sovereign power may be so limited, and moderated, as they shall think fit themselves'. These men believed that they had 'made a commonwealth, in which it is unlawful for any private man to make use of his own sword for his security; wherein they deceive themselves'.[49] Limited monarchy could not serve as the basis for a pacified polity. The constitutional royalists were wrong because they adopted doctrines of limited monarchy that were as likely to reduce politics to violent chaos as was mixed-monarchy theory. Their response to the crisis of the common law had focused on sovereign closure and a form of the rule of law that limited the sovereign. Hobbes was much more extreme. The collapse of the ancient constitution had occurred, in part, because of this very attempt to combine sovereignty and limitation. Both Hobbes and the other royalists recognised the mutually supportive relationship of sovereignty and legal closure; but in Hobbes' view other royalists had so misunderstood the nature of the rule of law that they breached that very principle of closure itself. Laws were the command of the sovereign power, and therefore how could it be that sovereigns were 'subject to the laws which they may abrogate at their pleasure, or break without fear of punishment'?[50]

In his early writings Hobbes dealt with these subjects concisely and relatively abstractly, but from *Leviathan* (1651) onwards he began to make more pointed and overt attacks on English common-law political traditions. The upshot was a thoroughly absolutist reading of the rule of law. George Lawson, criticising Hobbes' view that the sovereign was above all law, argued that 'Soveraigns are to govern by Laws, not to be subject unto them, or as Subjects obey them, or be punished by them.'[51] Would Hobbes

---

[49] Ibid., II.i.13–14, pp. 113–14.   [50] Ibid., II.viii.6, p. 172.

[51] George Lawson, *An Examination of the Political Part of Mr Hobbes his Leviathan* (1657), in Rogers (ed.), *Leviathan: Contemporary Responses*, p. 97. Lawson was commenting on Hobbes, *Leviathan*, ed. Edwin Curley (Indianapolis IA, 1994), ch. xxix, § 9, p. 213. Lawson's remark might be taken to match part of the definition of the rule of law given by Dicey: 'that no man is punishable or can be lawfully made to suffer in body or goods except for a distinct breach of law established in the ordinary legal manner before the ordinary Courts of the land. In this sense the rule of law is contrasted with every system of government based on the exercise by persons in authority of wide, arbitrary, or discretionary powers of constraint' (*Introduction to … the Law of the Constitution*, p. 110). Most absolutist royalists, including Filmer, were not theorists of the rule of law in this sense; Hobbes was.

have disagreed? Certainly a case could be made for saying that he would. One could point to his curt rejection of the Aristotelian-republican maxim that 'not men should govern, but the laws'.[52] In the world of Leviathan, the sovereign's will rules, not the law.[53] But – as Zuckert has argued – there are other ways of reading Hobbes. For Michael Oakeshott, as well, Hobbes was a pre-eminent philosopher of 'association in terms of the rule of law'.[54]

That Hobbes was a theorist of absolute and irresistible sovereignty, and believed that no sovereign could be considered legally limited, few will doubt. Space will not be wasted here on proving the obvious. But in what ways was he also a theorist of the rule of law, and how did he combine his legalism with his theory of sovereignty? These questions will be answered under three heads.

The sovereign and the law

What, in Hobbes' view, was the sovereign authority in England? The answer is not as obvious as most of us might expect. Responding in Leviathan (1651) to Sir Edward Coke's claim 'that the common law hath no controller but the parliament', Hobbes claimed that the controller of the common law was not parliament but 'rex in parliamento', because the king controlled parliament.[55] In his later Dialogue on the common law (written c. 1666), Hobbes expanded on that comment, blithely recording that 'all the Laws of England have been made by the Kings of England, consulting with the Nobility and Commons in Parliament'.[56] Elsewhere in the Dialogue the implications of this view were developed:

---

[52] Hobbes, Leviathan, ch. XLVI, § 36, p. 465 (cf. p. 476: significantly or not, these remarks were not repeated in the Latin version of 1668).

[53] Considerations of this sort underlie the interesting debate between Jean Hampton and Michael Zuckert: Hampton, 'Democracy and the rule of law'; Zuckert, 'Hobbes, Locke, and the problem of the rule of law'; both in Ian Shapiro (ed.), The Rule of Law [Nomos, XXXVI] (New York, 1994), chs. I and III.

[54] Oakeshott, 'Rule of law', pp. 149–50; also pp. 157–60.

[55] Hobbes, Leviathan, ch. XXVI, §§ 6–7, pp. 175–77. Coke's statement is from Sir Edward Coke, The First Part of the Institutes of the Lawes of England (London, 1628), fo. 115b (parliament).

[56] Thomas Hobbes, A Dialogue between a Philosopher and a Student of the Common Laws of England, ed. Joseph Cropsey (Chicago, 1971), p. 55 (all further references to this work are given parenthetically in the text). Three interesting accounts of the Dialogue are Cropsey's introduction to his edn (pp. 1–49); Susan Moller Okin, '"The soveraign and his counsellours": Hobbes's reevaluation of parliament', Political Theory, 10 (1982), 49–75; and James R. Stoner, Jr, Common Law and Liberal Theory: Coke, Hobbes, and the Origins of American Constitutionalism (Lawrence KS, 1992), ch. VII. I have assumed throughout the legitimacy of using Hobbes's Dialogue (written c. 1666) to interpret and expand on his earlier writing.

> I Grant you that the King is sole Legislator, but with this Restriction, that if he will not Consult with the Lords of Parliament and hear the Complaints, and Informations of the Commons, that are best acquainted with their own wants, he sinneth against God, though he cannot be Compell'd to any thing by his Subject by Arms, and Force (68).

He insisted upon the propriety of the phrase king-*in*-parliament as against king-*and*-parliament, thus emphasising that in attributing sovereign authority to the former one was not denying it to the king (76). The comment occurred in a discussion of the Act of Oblivion (1660), and the philosopher went so far as to concur in the view that such an act could not have been made without the consent of parliament. He did so on the ground that only a person injured could forgive the author of the injury, and the Act of Oblivion effectively forgave injuries to both king *and* commonwealth (76–77).[57] On the same principle it was asserted that 'the punishing of offences can be determined by none but by the King, and that, *if it extend to life or member*, with the assent of Parliament' (131, stress added).[58] Certainly it was stated that statute law was unable to divest the king of his essential authority. '[N]o part of his Legislative Power, or any other essential part of Royalty can be taken from him by a Statute'; but many common lawyers thought similarly (94).[59]

What does this amount to? Kings, it seems, were expected to make law as kings-in-parliament; but that this was essentially a requirement of prudence. Nothing bound the king to such a procedure.

> for there is no King in the World, being of ripe years and sound mind, that made any Law otherwise; for it concerns them in their own interest to make such Laws as the people can endure, and may keep them without impatience ... (165–66)

If a king did not voluntarily respect the principle that he should make law through a consultative process, then he could, in the nature of things, expect to rule over 'impatient' subjects. It takes little imagination to work out what that might be a euphemism for.

---

[57] It is an odd view for Hobbes to espouse, for his doctrine of authorisation meant that the sovereign represented all members of the commonwealth, and ought therefore to be able alone to act for them. The view expressed here in the *Dialogue* would be consistent with this only if Hobbes believed firmly that sovereignty rested with king-in-parliament. Cf. the interesting discussion in Stoner, *Common Law and Liberal Theory*, pp. 125–6.

[58] Cf. *Leviathan*, ch. xxx, § 15, p. 226.

[59] The statement can be read as Hobbes' version of the lawyers' doctrine of inseparable prerogatives (Burgess, *Absolute Monarchy and the Stuart Constitution*, pp. 151–52, 198–200).

A system of laws

Hobbes' account of how sovereigns ought to make law was a surprisingly moderate one. So was his account of what sort of laws they ought to make. One of his central objectives was to delineate the structural features of a closed system of law. The most important thing to recognise in this was that although all law was the sovereign's command, it was not true that all of the sovereign's commands were law. For a king's command to qualify as a command emanating from his body politic (and thus to constitute a law) it had to be issued 'by consent of the People of his Kingdom', or to 'have past the [Great] Seal of England' (162). All civil laws had to be publicly known and promulgated.[60] In *Leviathan* Hobbes had briefly alluded to a distinction between the sovereign's natural and politic persons.[61] What could be done with the distinction was dramatically revealed in *Behemoth*. A question was posed in the course of the dialogue. What should a subject do if the sovereign 'command me with my own hands to execute my father'? The answer was perhaps surprising.

> We never have read nor heard of any King or tyrant so inhuman as to command it. If any did, we are to consider whether the command were one of his laws. For by disobeying Kings, we mean the disobeying of his laws, those laws that were made before they were applied to any particular person; for the king, though as a father of children, and a master of domestic servants command many things which bind those children and servants yet he commands the people in general but by a precedent law, and as a politic, not a natural person. And if such a command as you speak of were contrived into a general law … you were bound to obey it, unless you depart the kingdom after the publication of the law, and before the condemnation of your father.[62]

The implication was that the king's power to command his subject was a power that could be exercised only in so far as commands could be made to satisfy the minimum criteria necessary for them to be considered laws. Other commands need not be obeyed. He also appeared at one point to distinguish between a king's capacity to punish summarily and in other ways, when he said of a man who commits a sinful act 'the King has the power to Punish him (*on this side of Life or Member*) as he please; and with the Assent of Parliament (*if not without*) to make the Crime for the future Capital' (121–22, stress added). In a discussion of the crime of treason Hobbes asked whether the king could execute summary justice against traitors. He implied that he could, on the ground that traitors, as enemies,

---

[60] Hobbes, *Leviathan*, ch. xxvi, §§ 12–20, pp. 177–80.
[61] Ibid., ch. xxiii, § 2, pp. 155–56.   [62] Hobbes, *Behemoth*, p. 51.

had denied the king's jurisdiction and could not therefore avail themselves of the safeguard allowed to those within it (103; also 105). This argument worked on the assumption that for all other crimes the king could lawfully do justice only by the proper process of legal indictment (104–6). Once again, there seems to be present here the thought that the system of laws and justice, while resting on the king's will, was also characterised by a regularity and form that the king himself should not, even if he could, disrupt.

Finally, Hobbes gave some indication of the sorts of criteria that defined good laws. It is crucial to recognise that in his view, though all laws had to be considered just, some were nonetheless iniquitous. Hobbes in the *Dialogue* objected to one definition of law because 'it supposes that a Statute made by the Soveraign Power of a Nation may be unjust. There may indeed in a Statute Law, made by Men be found Iniquity, but not Injustice' (69–70).[63] Of course, even iniquitous laws ought to be obeyed, though Hobbes said enough to make it plain that he did not think that they always would be. In *Leviathan* he asserted that rebellion was the 'natural publishment' for the sovereign's misgovernment,[64] by which he meant that though rebellion was always unjust there were nonetheless things the sovereign could do that in the nature of things would provoke resistance and rebellion. A wise sovereign would not do them. Also in *Leviathan*, Hobbes gave a fairly clear indication of what constituted iniquitous laws. Justice had to be administered 'equally', without respect of persons.[65] The laws thus administered ought to be 'good'. A good law was '*needful* for the *good of the people*, and withal *perspicuous*'. That meant, above all, the laws should only be made when harm to the commonwealth was to be prevented. Otherwise, they were merely 'traps for money'.[66] The sovereign was also, in a sense, subject to the requirements of natural law, which demanded, amongst other things, equity and mercy, and forbade retrospective punishments.[67] A king who failed to ensure that his laws respected these constraints remained in principle beyond correction or coercion; but Hobbes said enough to make it clear that he was aware that such monarchs were likely to undermine their own authority.

---

[63] For a fuller discussion of these terms see Glenn Burgess, 'On Hobbesian resistance theory', *Political Studies*, 42 (1994), 62–83.

[64] Hobbes, *Leviathan*, ch. xxxi, § 40, p. 243.

[65] Ibid., ch. xxx, §§ 15–17, pp. 226–28.   [66] Ibid., ch. xxx, §§ 20–22, pp. 229–30.

[67] See discussion and references in Burgess, 'On Hobbesian resistance theory', pp. 66–69.

The judiciary

One essential characteristic of the rule of law is the existence of a judiciary performing functions distinct from those of the sovereign law-maker.[68] Hobbes' remarks on this subject are important but neglected. The sovereign, he believed, delegated much executive authority to public ministers, which category included judges sitting in courts of law.[69] The role of the judge was to administer laws made by the sovereign's reason. Hobbes agreed with Coke that law was reason; but it was not made by the 'private reason' of judges, as Coke seemed to suppose. It was the public reason of the sovereign, and the judge had to ensure that 'his sentence may be according thereunto; which then is his sovereign's sentence; otherwise it is his own, and an unjust one'. As well as making law, the sovereign's public reason also interpreted laws and settled conflicts between them. A judge's interpretation of the law of nature, for example, was 'authentic, not because it is his private sentence, but because he giveth it by authority of the sovereign'. Judges administered on the sovereign's authority a flexible equity jurisdiction, based on natural law, and were not bound by precedent.[70] The 'right of judicature' was inseparably annexed to sovereignty and could not be alienated,[71] and all sentences given by a judge were the sentences of the sovereign.[72] But the judges seem to have been left to decide cases independently, with the sovereign power serving only as a final appellate jurisdiction (which jurisdiction could itself be delegated). Hobbes did in the *Elements* say that, while 'the due execution of justice' was essential to political stability, judges could not be altogether trusted. So to avoid public discontent there needed to be a 'power extraordinary' to deal with judges who 'shall abuse their authority'.[73] The very term 'extraordinary' makes it sound as if Hobbes was trying to avoid any suggestion of defending the sovereign's capacity to interfere in the ordinary processes of justice. Instead, Hobbes turned to praise the existing English legal system on the ground that it enabled subjects to choose their own judges and thus to give their consent to the verdict reached.[74] All of his comments betray a wariness about talking in ways that would breach

---

[68] Cf. Oakeshott, 'Rule of law', pp. 144–48.   [69] Hobbes, *Leviathan*, ch. xxii, § 7, p. 157.

[70] Ibid., ch. xxvi, § 23, p. 181; see generally §§ 20–25, pp. 180–83.

[71] Ibid., ch. xviii, §§ 11, 17, pp. 114, 116.   [72] Ibid., ch. xxiii, § 7, p. 157.

[73] Hobbes, *Elements*, ii.xix.6, p. 182; also *De cive* xiii.17, p. 270; cf. *Leviathan*, ch. xxx, § 12, p. 224.

[74] Hobbes, *Leviathan*, ch. xxiii, §§ 8–9, pp. 157–58. These rather odd paragraphs were omitted in the Latin version. The view expressed was based on the opinion, which Hobbes expressed a little later, that common-law judges were not really judges at all but *juris consulti*. The actual judge of a case was the jury (ibid., ch. xxvi, § 35, p. 185).

the principle of closure central to the rule of law. That is to say, there seems to be an awareness in Hobbes that if the sovereign's authority is conceived of simply in terms of this untrammelled exercise of private will, then this in itself is fatal to the closure of a legal system, and thus also to the maintenance of peace. The sovereign was free of law because he could lawfully change it rather than because he might openly flout it.

Hobbes' views on the judiciary and its relationship with the sovereign were much more fully expressed in the *Dialogue*. His account there of the jurisdiction of the king's courts was designed to perform two tasks simultaneously. First, to increase the flexibility and ease with which the king could do justice; while, second, maintaining the outlines of the traditional system for the administration of justice. So, for example, he argued that King's Bench, seen in the *Dialogue* as one of the two courts, along with Chancery, to which the king had primarily delegated judicial authority, had a very extensive jurisdiction over all matters criminal and civil, including over all cases generally thought to be within the jurisdiction only of the Court of Common Pleas (81–83). The point, it seems, was to emphasise that King's Bench could not be confined to particular cases because the king's authority to administer justice was committed to it in very general terms. Hobbes at one point insisted on that word *committed*, in contradistinction to *transferred*, implying that the king retained the powers he had committed. Here he did seem to suggest that the king could still sit in the King's Bench and hear all cases in person, though, of course, even when doing so the king would be working within and not outside the institutions established for the administration of justice (88–89; 90).[75] Furthermore, Hobbes argued that the Court of Chancery, the 'Highest ordinary Court in *England*' (91), had a jurisdiction in error over all other courts (86–87; 91–101). Indeed, all courts of law were courts of equity, bound to administer a justice that conformed to the rational intentions of a legislator (it was equitable to require conformity to law in this sense) and not to the strict letter of the law (97–98). The drift of the whole chapter 'Of courts' in the *Dialogue*, especially with its attack on the strict grammatical construction of the law, was to emphasise that if law were to be administered justly then the legal system must be operated in such a way as not to frustrate the sovereign's protean authority to render justice. Hobbes, in the end, stressed not the subordination of the judiciary to sovereign will so much as the role of the judiciary as an agency for

[75] The passage is not perfectly clear. There is a suggestion (85–86) that when Hobbes talked of the king administering justice in person he was referring to the judicial powers of king-in-council. On the question of whether or not the king could sit in person in King's Bench, Hobbes' position may not be as far from Coke's as we generally assume: 'in the King's Bench he may sit, but the Court gives the judgment' (12 Co. Rep., 64).

enforcing the public will of the sovereign expressed in his laws. No justice could exist if it was merely arbitrary.

Hobbes replaced the *potestas irritans*[76] of common law with the extra-legal capacity of nature to frustrate misrule. He did so in order to avoid a breach of the principle of closure that would render unstable and violent the polity that was mid-seventeenth-century England, while recognising in his own way as vividly as the constitutional royalists that sovereigns themselves had a capacity, *against which there could be no formal safeguard*, to de-pacify the societies over which they ruled. He preserved, in his own way, the view that sovereigns (by natural law) had to respect the rule of law; but sharply separated that doctrine from the equally strong conviction that the sovereign was absolute and all his laws had to be obeyed by all subjects. His reaction to the crisis of the common law and to constitutional royalism was, then, to suggest that peace and stability were only possible when the natural restrictions on rulers were not thought of in terms of positive human law and were supported by no sanctions within systems of human law. Always he remained painfully aware that, in the end, sovereigns – not just subjects – were capable of producing disorder.

(3) HARRINGTON ON SOVEREIGNTY AND THE RULE OF LAW

Harrington's key objectives in publishing *Oceana* in 1656 were to explain why the Stuart monarchy collapsed and – above all – to lay down principles that would enable a better polity to be built in its place. In performing those tasks he was led to build on the same foundations as Hobbes and the constitutional royalists: sovereign closure and the rule of law. Of course, it should not be forgotten that though all may have built on similar foundations, the resulting edifices were quite different from one another. They shared certain values, not particular doctrines.

Sovereignty

Harrington, as much as Hobbes, was a theorist of sovereignty.[77] He clearly appreciated the Hobbesian principle of sovereignty, though he made less

---

[76] For the concept see Burgess, *Absolute Monarchy and the Stuart Constitution*, pp. 139–40, 153–54.

[77] There has been much recent work emphasising the affinities between Hobbes and Harrington. See especially Jonathan Scott, 'The rapture of motion: James Harrington's republicanism', in Phillipson and Skinner (eds.), *Political Discourse in Early Modern Britain*, ch. VII; and Scott, 'The peace of silence: Thucydides and the English Civil War', in Miles Fairburn and Bill Oliver (eds.), *The Certainty of Doubt: Tributes to Peter Munz* (Wellington, 1996), pp. 90–116. Similar perspectives can be found in Paul A. Rahe, *Republics Ancient and Modern*, vol. II, *New Modes and Orders in Early Modern Political Thought* (Chapel Hill NC,

effort than Hobbes to translate his definition of the equal commonwealth into the jurisprudential terms required to show where he thought sovereignty lay. '[W]here the ultimate result is, there also must be the sovereignty.'[78] There was in any commonwealth an arbitrary power 'in making, abrogating or interpreting of laws', which rested in 'the sovereign power' (849). An equal commonwealth was defined as 'a government established on an equal agrarian, arising into the superstructures or three orders, the senate debating and proposing, the people resolving, and the magistracy executing by an equal rotation through the suffrage of the people given by the ballot' (181; cf. 424). Presumably, therefore, sovereignty inhered in the operation of the whole and thus in the people as a whole. But Harrington in his debate with Wren came close to suggesting that it was in the many (the people or representative) and not in the few (the senate) (425).[79] The importance of Harrington's attachment to the principle of sovereignty, though, lies less in his muddle over its application than in the fact that it laid the foundation for his appreciation of the principle of closure.

Closure

Harrington, as John Pocock has rightly told us, 'did not believe in the Ancient Constitution'.[80] And yet in places Harrington could himself show tendencies later to be developed by those 'neo-Harringtonians' who attempted to accommodate Harrington's republicanism and the traditionalism inherent in respect for the ancient constitution. He displayed a degree of respect, not for the politics of the ancient constitution, but for the good that it attempted and failed to deliver: 'The monarchy of England was not a government by arms, but a government by laws, though

1994), ch. v; Vickie Sullivan, 'The civic humanist portrait of Machiavelli's English successors', *History of Political Thought*, 14 (1994), 73–96; and Gary Remer, 'James Harrington's new deliberative rhetoric: reflections of an anticlassical republicanism', *History of Political Thought*, 16 (1995), 532–57.

[78] James Harrington, *The Political Works of James Harrington*, ed. J. G. A. Pocock (Cambridge, 1977), p. 695 (all further references to Harrington's writings are to this edition and are given in parentheses in the text).

[79] Cf. also 674–5 (sovereignty in 'parliament' = representative + senate), 676, 695 (which shows a clear appreciation of the principle of sovereignty but locates it in the representative). This combination of firmness on the principle of sovereignty and looseness in defining its exact location indicates Harrington's considerable confidence in the perfection of his equal commonwealth, which will make redundant disputes over the location of sovereignty.

[80] J. G. A. Pocock, 'Machiavelli, Harrington and English political ideologies in the eighteenth century', in Pocock, *Politics, Language and Time: Essays on Political Thought and History* (London, 1972), ch. IV, p. 120.

imperfect or ineffectual laws.' Subsequent governments, especially the Protectorate, had been governments of arms; but '[t]he people, having felt the difference between a government by laws and a government by arms, will always desire the government by laws and abhor that of arms' (762). The ancient constitution was an unstable government of laws, yet there were things about it for which men yearned, things essential to the maintenance of peace. The task men faced was to found or refound a peaceful polity in which there could exist a stable government of laws; and Harrington's political thought was directed to that end. The principle of closure was emphatically asserted in Harrington's commentary on the Levellers' *Agreement of the People*.[81] He noted that the *Agreement* reserved certain matters from the legislative competence of the supreme representative (or parliament): 'That these representatives have sovereign power, save that in some things the people may resist them by arms' (657). Harrington commented:

> Which first is a flat contradiction, and next is downright anarchy. Where the sovereign power is not as entire and absolute as in monarchy itself, there can be no government at all. It is not the limitation of sovereign power that is the cause of a commonwealth, but such a *libration or pose of orders, that there can be in the same no number of men, having the interest, that can have the power, nor any number of men, having the power, that can have the interest, to invade or disturb the government.* As the orders of commonwealth are more approaching to or remote from this maxim (of which this of the Levellers hath nothing), so are they more quiet or turbulent (657–58).

Nonetheless, Harrington agreed with the Levellers in one respect. Both were in favour of 'popular power'. He denied that such a position would 'sow the seed of civil war'; and asserted instead that

> [t]he ways of nature require peace. The ways of peace require obedience unto laws. Laws in England cannot be made but by parliaments. Parliaments in England are come to be mere popular assemblies. The laws made by popular assemblies, though for a time they may be awed or deceived, in the end must be popular laws; and the sum of popular laws must amount to a commonwealth (660).

Thus Harrington, unusually for an English republican, had no commitment to resistance theory. He was entirely concerned with producing a constitutional structure of orders (*ordini*) that would be characterised by

---

[81] Actually, Harrington's commentary is on the so-called Officer's *Agreement*, presented to the Rump following modification of the Levellers' (second) *Agreement* in the Whitehall debates. Its text is in Wolfe (ed.), *Leveller Manifestoes*, pp. 331–54.

sovereign closure, the rule of law, and thus the maintenance of peace.[82] Resistance and violence were the things to be avoided. Harrington thus shared a basic pattern of ideas with many constitutional royalists and with Hobbes. He could even sound a little like the former, as he marvelled that the English 'throne [was] the most indulgent to, and least invasive for so many ages upon, the liberty of a people that the world hath known', while still lamenting that 'through the mere want of fixing her foot by a proportionable agrarian upon a proper foundation ... [it had] fallen with such horror as hath been a spectacle of astonishment unto the whole earth' (235). At its best the ancient constitution had served liberty well enough; but had been undone by the vicissitudes of time and social decay.

The judiciary

In a work probably written immediately after the Restoration, *A System of Politics*, Harrington provided his most succinct and pointed account of the general principles associated with the administration of law. As we might expect from a theorist of sovereignty, Harrington believed, like Hobbes, that all laws were essentially statutes issued by a lawgiver. As he had put it in *The Art of Lawgiving* (1659), 'what is thus proposed by the senate, and resolved by the people, be the law of the land, and no other' (with the exception of the special circumstances in which a dictatorian council could make law) (675). In the *System* this basic principle was followed up with a number of precepts. Wherever 'the power of making law is, there only is the power of interpreting the law'. That led Harrington to confront directly, as had Hobbes, the fact that all governments, because they had no superior, had in the end to be judges in their own cause (848).

A democracy such as Harrington's was ruled by 'such laws as the people, with the advice of their council, or of the senate, shall choose or have chosen' (849). Harrington, like Hobbes, provided some detailed advice on what sort of legal system should be thus created. And like Hobbes', the advice given was implicitly critical of common-law principles, but critical in good part because the common law had failed to achieve the purposes for which it was acknowledged to exist, the preservation of peace and order and the prevention of arbitrary rule. A legal system could have too many laws, in which case they were 'snares of the people' and caused corruption. A superfluity of laws also gave 'arbitrary power' to the judges because it increased their scope for reconciling

[82] For a recent account that shows something of Harrington's place in the construction of a nexus of ideas labelled 'constitutionalism' see Dario Castiglione, 'The political theory of the constitution', *Political Studies*, 44 (1996), 417–35. Much older, but still invaluable, is Wormuth, *Origins of Modern Constitutionalism*.

discordant laws and manipulating the law behind a façade of arcane mastery. Conversely there could be too few laws, and this too was a cause of arbitrary power amongst the judiciary, because the shortage of direct legal guidance would increase its capacity for stretching laws to apply to new cases. Beyond that '[t]hat law which leaves the least arbitrary power to the judge or judicatory, is the most perfect law'. That meant that laws should be relatively few, plain and brief, rather than 'perplexed, intricate, tedious and voluminous'. Some arbitrary power in the judiciary was, however, inevitable, and so it was best to ensure that there was a multitude of judges. Thus absolute monarchies did not have juries, while in a proper democracy there was in the localities always 'a jury on the bench' (not just 'at the bar' as in an aristocratical monarchy), and a clear system of appeal culminating in the sovereign (i.e. the representative of the people, in this instance) (849–51). This stress on trial by jury was, of course, a matter in which the English had long taken pride and had used to distinguish themselves from more oppressed peoples, and is indicative of the way in which Harrington was on this point perfecting traditional practices, not replacing them.

Harrington's account of a judicial system thus clearly combined features by now familiar to us, sovereign closure and the rule of law (i.e. trial by due process and not at the whim of an arbitrary power). Ultimately, the sovereign (meaning here 'the popular assembly') formed a final 'arbitrary' court of appeal to which those dissatisfied with the lesser courts could turn (850–51), thus completing the circle of sovereign closure without breaching the orderly administration of law.

Harrington contra Hobbes: a perfect politics?

Hobbes was aware that in reacting so strongly against the constitutional royalist belief in the union of sovereignty and limitation, he had instead only established the groundwork for a political system that might remain vulnerable to the destabilising actions of 'iniquitous' sovereigns. Harrington believed that he had rescued politics even from that difficulty. In several important ways Harrington took the principles of sovereign closure and order to extremes that suggested the removal of Oceana from the normal world of change and decay altogether. In Harrington the pacified polity reached utopian permanency.

Harrington's account of property and his advocacy of an agrarian law, though couched as a recognition of the natural foundations of empire, were actually attempts to show how a commonwealth could create an artificial perfection immune from natural changes. When Harrington wrote of the ways in which '[p]roperty comes to have a being before empire or government', he was not resting upon the assumption of pre-political natural property rights; but, rather, pointing out the ways in which governments had failed properly to prevent destabilising changes to the distribution of property (405–6). That problem could be overcome. The key 'order', or constitutional rule, devised by Harrington to fix the social balance of land in such a way as to prevent its accumulation in the hands of the few, was his agrarian law (231; 609–10, 664). In this way the artificial mechanisms of constitutions and politics necessarily defined property rights. Harrington stressed that any attempt to govern against the balance would inevitably result in instability. Like Hobbes, he forced his citizens to face a simple choice: '[a] people is either under a state of civil government, or in a state of civil war', or just possibly in neither condition (either of the last two alternatives, though, amount to a state 'of the privation of government'). Attempts to govern against the balance (tyranny, oligarchy, anarchy) were all forms of 'privation' and not proper civil governments at all. They were likely to be 'blown up by some tumult', unless reformed (834–7). Unless the artificial restriction of an agrarian law was employed, societies would tend to destroy the natural basis for order within themselves (i.e. by allowing the distribution of land to be altered). Disorder was, of course, fatal to property rights, so in that way landowners were advised that the maintenance of government must be in their own authority. It comes as no surprise to discover that royalists are expected to be won over to the institutions of Oceana when they realise that the only way they could 'restore the ancient government' securely would be to concentrate landownership in the hands of only three hundred men (351). Conversely, in a society with a well-framed agrarian law, there might never emerge causes of political instability.

An agrarian was a necessary but not a sufficient cause of political permanence. The one-time royalist propagandist Henry Ferne rejected Harrington's preference for a commonwealth over a monarchy with the argument that 'order is the main concernment of government, and order is more perfected by reducing to unity, or having still one chief in the order'. He reiterated, that is to say, the royalist-Hobbesian stress on *monarchical* sovereignty, and in doing so pointed out the instability of republics like that portrayed in the Old Testament. Harrington's diagnosis of the problem was different. He did not question the importance of stability, but attributed the decay of the ancient Hebrew republic into anarchy to its constitutional imperfection (it lacked a senate), and suggested 'that the unity of government consists in such a form which no man can have the will, or having the will can have the power, to disturb'. On the other hand, 'but cast all upon the unity of a person that may do what he list' and you have a recipe for chaos (376–79). Harrington thus reasserted the principle

so decisively rejected by Hobbes that laws must rule and not men
(161–62). Harrington did not mean to deny that all laws were acts of will;
but the rule of law meant that the commonwealth collectively willed the
making of laws that served the public and not private interest. '[I]s a
commonwealth to be governed in the word of a priest or a Pharisee, or by
the vote of the people and the interest of mankind?' (401–2, 404). It was
possible to devise political machinery that would ensure that laws were
always made for the public interest.

Harrington's emphasis on permanence can be approached from another
angle. How was it that a proper republican constitution would ensure
peace and obedience to the law? The answer lay in the fact that in a well-
founded republic the interests of social groups were balanced in such a
way that the laws made would serve the public good. There was in this a
tacit recognition, as there was in Hobbes, that law would be obeyed only
when it was well made (or 'necessary' in Hobbes' terms). It is therefore
possible to read Harrington as closing the gap in Hobbes' argument left by
the latter's recognition of the sovereign's capacity to make iniquitous laws,
and his equal recognition that nothing could be done about it. Harrington's
sovereign was not to be capable of 'iniquity', a term by which Hobbes
referred to the making of laws that would destroy the foundation of
sovereign authority.[83] The most remarkable expression of Harrington's
belief that an 'equal commonwealth' would be a perfect, and therefore a
permanent, political system came when he briefly spoke of it in the
language of millenarianism, admittedly with all the comfort of a tenor who
can hit but not hold his high C.[84] At a lower level Harrington's writing was
full of expressions of the enduring stability that his constitutional orders
could provide, a stability based ultimately on the simple principle that the
many would have the power but not the interest in sedition, while the one
and the few might have the interest but not the power (424–26). On that
basis Harrington could conclude that if commonwealths had been less than
perfect then it had been as a result of their particular failings, for a perfect
commonwealth like that of Oceana was a perfect government (431, 423).
The equal commonwealth was 'void of sedition, and hath attained unto
perfection, as being void of all internal causes of dissolution' (613, also
693). In contrast, even the best monarchy must be unstable, for a king will

---

[83] Perhaps particularly noteworthy in this regard is Harrington's (none too persuasive)
argument that a people trusted with power will never turn into levellers of men's estates.
The argument was crucial for the belief in the perfect stability of the equal commonwealth (428–31).

[84] See Pocock's discussion in his 'Historical introduction' to Harrington, *Political Works*, pp.
70–3; contrast J. C. Davis, 'Pocock's Harrington: grace, nature and art in the classical
republicanism of James Harrington', *Historical Journal*, 24 (1981), 683–97, esp. pp. 687–90.

be dependent either on his nobility or on his people (451). No more than Hobbes could Harrington accept a limited monarchy, for to 'undertake the binding of a prince from invading liberty, and yet not to introduce the whole orders necessary unto popular government, is to undertake a flat contradiction, or plain impossibility' (613). Only in a republic could you have the perfection of sovereign closure combined with a government that did not consume its own substance. '[A]n equal commonwealth is that only which is without flaw and containeth in it the full perfection of government' (180). In politics it was Harrington not Hobbes who squared the circle, being able to suggest that he had devised a polity that both contained an irresistible absolute sovereign (like Hobbes') and in which those with authority could not and would not act to destroy the basis of that authority itself.

Thus during the Interregnum the ancient constitutionalist ideal of a pacified polity was recast first as an absolute monarchy and then as an absolute republic.

(4) CONCLUSION

After the crisis of the common law there were two paths that could be followed. One utilised arguments based on emergency and necessity. Later these elements were to be placed into a rationalist natural-law framework, resulting in a politics reliant upon violence as the ultimate guarantor of liberties. The greatest exponent of this politics was John Locke.[85] Another, in some ways just as rationalistic, but eschewing both violence and the appeal to emergency circumstances in which normal politics might be considered dissolved, shared with the ancient constitutionalism of the early Stuart period the aim of constructing a polity in which the use of violence as a political tool would be both unnecessary and impossible. Hobbes and Harrington were key figures in this tradition. Both emphasised the illegitimacy of an appeal by citizens living within civil communities to principles and authorities lying outside the framework of civil laws and institutions, even though both, at another level, justified their political theories by appeal to principles of just that sort. For both, the art of politics involved the construction of a self-contained artificial polity, albeit on natural foundations. These men bequeathed to the Restoration world a set of values and ideas that provided very different possibilities from those to be found in Locke and other 'radical Whigs'. I would suggest that it is by

---

[85] Recent work by Jonathan Scott has done most to reconstruct this pattern of ideas for us, and to distinguish its republican adherents from Harrington. See especially Scott, 'The law of war: Grotius, Sidney, Locke and the political theory of rebellion', *History of Political Thought*, 13 (1992), 565–85, as well as his other essays cited above.

retracing these two very different paths, whose divergence dates from the 1640s and 1650s, that we can best uncover both the developmental patterns of English political thought over the years 1640–60, and the structures of later Stuart political thought. If it is true, as John Pocock has suggested,[86] that the key problem addressed in English political discourse of the later Stuart period was how to avoid any repetition of the dissolution of government experienced in the 1640s and 1650s, then attention to the development and transmission of the ideal of a pacified polity will be crucial to our full understanding of the period.

[86] J. G. A. Pocock, 'Empire, state and confederation: the War of American Independence as a crisis in multiple monarchy', in John Robertson (ed.), *A Union for Empire: Political Thought and the Union of 1707* (Cambridge, 1995), ch. XIII, pp. 320–25.

10

Equality in an unequal commonwealth: James Harrington's republicanism and the meaning of equality*

J. C. DAVIS

At the heart of James Harrington's rhetorical aspiration in framing his most famous book lay a dilemma. *Oceana* appealed to ambition in order to incite an act of consummate self-effacement. Addressed to the Lord Protector, Oliver Cromwell, as he wrestled with the prospect of kingship, it appealed to his thirst for glory only in order to persuade him to suppress his own ambition and divest himself of power.[1] Scipio was asked to become Lycurgus.

However much the difficulties of the mid-1650s, the challenges of healing and settling, might encourage Cromwell to regard any reasonable scheme with hope, this remained an over-sanguine agenda. Furthermore, as the once reluctant regicide contemplated taking the steps to the throne as a final exercise in conservative post-revolutionary reconstruction, those schemes which smacked of levelling were presumably beyond the bounds of the reasonable. The good and great interest of the nation remained the hierarchy of 'a nobleman, a gentleman and a yeoman'.[2] In the crisis of 1649 it was Cromwell who had urged the Council of State to break those who advocated legal and religious equality.[3] Yet the notion of equality was pivotal both to Harrington's republicanism and to his utopianism. Republics had failed historically precisely because they were unequal. The

---

* A version of this paper was first presented at a colloquium on 'James Harrington and the notion of commonwealth' in Montpellier, 24–25 March 1995.

[1] Cf. Paul A. Rahe, *Republics Ancient and Modern*, II, *New Modes and Orders in Early Modern Political Thought* (Chapel Hill and London, 1994) p. 187. For a recent discussion of Harrington's intention in dedicating the work to Cromwell which sees it as ironic, anti-Cromwellian and yet attempting the Machiavellian exercise of persuading the evil usurper to do good see Blair Worden, 'Harrington's *Oceana*: Origins and Aftermath, 1651–1660', in David Wootton (ed.), *Republicanism, Liberty and Commercial Society, 1649–1776* (Stanford, 1994), pp. 119–20, n. 40 p. 431.

[2] Wilbur Cortez Abbott (ed.), *The Writings and Speeches of Oliver Cromwell*, 4 vols. (Cambridge, Massachusetts, 1937–47), vol. III, p. 435.

[3] Ibid., vol. II, pp. 41–42.

republic proposed for *Oceana* in 1656 could be perfect and immortal only because it was equal.[4]

The problem of Harrington's identification of equality as the essential feature of his republicanism has two dimensions. The more general one is that of its genesis and resonance in a society permeated with ideas of natural inequality, of hierarchy as the guarantor of order, and fearful of the association between levelling and anarchy. How can Harrington's egalitarianism be reconciled to this context? More specifically there is the problem of the relationship between Harrington the rhetorician, particularly in *Oceana*, and the object of his rhetoric, Oliver Cromwell. The dedication of *Oceana* to Cromwell is no mere convention. The necessary task of persuading a powerful standing army, the New Model, to divest itself of power and agree to its own dissolution could not be achieved without him. And Olphaeus Megaletor, an idealised version of Oliver himself, is a fiction intended to persuade by showing how the statesmanship required for the establishment of a Harringtonian republic would bring Cromwell fame and glory far more lasting than anything else even he could have achieved.[5] But how could Harrington, a rhetorician advocating equality, expect to persuade Cromwell, a social conservative wedded to hierarchy and opposed to levelling, that an equal commonwealth was the solution to England's problems in 1656 and presumably for all time?[6] At first sight then, Harrington and the Lord Protector appear to be poles apart. What was Harrington doing in addressing his equal commonwealth to Cromwell? Being deliberately provocative; or simply foolish, using inappropriate language and condemning himself to rhetorical failure; or do we need to reappraise Harrington's language of equality and, if we do, does it bring him any closer to Oliver Cromwell?

We might begin by examining what equality does *not* mean in Harrington's ideal society. In the first place, it does not mean personal equality of property ownership. The 'levelling of men's estates' may be seen as 'an odious thing' but a participatory republic would not lead to this

---

[4] J. C. Davis, *Utopia and the Ideal Society: A Study of English Utopian Writing 1516–1700* (Cambridge, 1983) pp. 215–16. Oceana was unique and escaped the corruption endemic to all other republics because it was the 'first example of a commonwealth that is perfectly equal'. J. G. A. Pocock (ed.), *The Political Works of James Harrington* (Cambridge, 1977) pp. 181–82 (34). References in parentheses are to J. G. A. Pocock (ed.) *Harrington: The Commonwealth of Oceana and a System of Politics* (Cambridge, 1991).

[5] On the fame of Olphaeus Megaletor see *Political Works*, pp. 358–59 (265–66).

[6] On Cromwell's hostility to levelling and association of equality with anarchy see Barry Coward, *Oliver Cromwell* (London, 1991) p. 102. Forty years after the publication of *Oceana* an admirer could still dissociate himself from Harrington's egalitarianism: 'his Modell is meerly Democraticall: A Levelling sordid Democracy. For he chiefly aims at Equality which in plain *English* is Levelling.' Anonymous, *The Free State of Noland* (1696) p. 10.

because the people, the many, hated levelling.[7] The Agrarian Law of Oceana was a device to preserve a propertied aristocracy, as well as to prevent the balance of dominion in land tipping over into the hands of the few.[8] In addition, Harrington's commonwealth for expansion was specifically designed for the augmentation or replenishment of aristocratic fortunes.[9]

Secondly, an equal commonwealth does not embody equality of political roles. The first order of the Oceanic constitution divides the population into 'freemen or citizens, and servants', a division which Harrington believed required no further discussion 'in regard to the nature of servitude, which is inconsistent with freedom or participation of government in a commonwealth'.[10] However, important gradations, even *between* citizens, also appeared. Following Cicero and Machiavelli, Harrington believed that 'the people' left to their own devices were 'not so prone to find out the truth of themselves, as to follow custom or run into error ...'[11] They were like children who, without leaders, would be reduced to nakedness and passion, with no prospects but 'darkness, desolation and horror'.[12] Fortunately, there were natural leaders in any society. The proper function of the constitution was to make sure that the superior wisdom of this élite was recognised and given its appropriate influence. From this arose Oceana's bicameral division of legislative function, a senate debating and proposing and an Assembly resolving.[13] '... the superstructures of such a government', Harrington noted, 'they require a good aristocracy ...'[14] Characteristic of such an aristocracy was the leisure for travel and study which superior wealth alone provided. Hence the division of citizens into horse and foot. Education for 'the many, must be unto the

---

[7] Harrington, *A System of Politics*, in *Political Works*, pp. 840, 853 (277, 292).

[8] Davis, *Utopia and the Ideal Society*, pp. 231–34. See the discussion of the Agrarian Law in *Oceana*, *Political Works*, pp. 233–39 (104–11). Blair Worden's recent treatment of the Agrarian is deficient in two respects. First, it is not true that no one would be allowed to inherit land worth more than £2,000 per annum. Secondly, Harrington is inadequately described as having a preference for 'mediocrity'. Blair Worden, 'English Republicanism', in J. H. Burns with Mark Goldie (eds.), *The Cambridge History of Political Thought 1450–1700* (Cambridge, 1994), p. 464.

[9] *Political Works*, pp. 320–22 (217–20).

[10] Ibid., p. 212 (75). Harrington glances at the issue of gender equality in *Oceana* in a revealing way. Discussing the Agrarian Law, the Lord Archon repudiates the notion that 'we intended not to equal advantages in our commonwealth unto either sex'. But gender equality appears to consist of liberating women from marriages determined by property considerations. Ibid., pp. 239–40 (111–12).

[11] Ibid., p. 284.

[12] *A Discourse Showing* (1659) in *Political Works*, pp. 750–51.

[13] *Political Works*, pp. 172–73 (23–24).

[14] Ibid., p. 257 (135).

mechanics'. For the few, the élite, the universities would provide education in ancient prudence and statesmanship.[15] So, while *Oceana* provides for 'such a representative as may be equal', it is not equal in respect to the political classification and functions of either inhabitants or citizens.[16]

The rotation of elected office might ensure a wide participation in government by Oceanic citizens, but several social categories were excluded from such participation. Not only did age, gender and economic dependence exclude people from citizenship but issues of status, profession, performance and morality could exclude those otherwise qualified for citizenship from full civic participation. Bachelors were ineligible for election to the Senate or Assembly.[17] Divines, physicians and lawyers were excluded from all magistracies, offices and honours.[18] Failure in economic self-management resulted not only in loss of eligibility for office but also in loss of citizenship. Perhaps the downward mobility consequent upon extravagance was seen as disturbing to the social order. '... if a man have prodigally wasted and spent his patrimony, he is neither capable of magistracy, office nor suffrage in the commonwealth'.[19]

There are then legal distinctions between citizens and non-citizens on the basis of property and income, age, gender, profession, marital status, economic prudence and the fulfilment of military obligations. In all of these ways it might be thought that some are more equal than others in the equal commonwealth. But the truth is that, in respect to civic rights and obligations, there are also significant inequalities *between citizens*. Important features of Harrington's ideal constitution rest on the premise that there would be behavioural distinctions between citizens based on inequalities of status. All citizens in *Oceana* were independent enough to have some scope for self-rule and rule over others. In particular, they were all male heads of households. (Hence the exclusion of children, women and bachelors). They were also independent enough to enter into communal or collective self-rule without partiality. So the professions – clergy, lawyers and physicians – were excluded. Still not all those remaining in the active-citizen category were independent enough to participate in civic life without deference. Harrington was concerned to argue, in classical humanist mode, that an equal commonwealth would have social hierarchies of eminence and mediocrity but that their composition would be determined by virtue or its lack. Nevertheless, a hierarchy there would be; a nobility or gentry would be superior to the people. And such would be

---

[15] Ibid., pp. 304–6 (197–99).   [16] Ibid., p. 173 (24).   [17] Ibid., p. 227 (95).

[18] Ibid., p. 309 (203). Ministers were liable to be expelled from their parishes for meddling in politics. Ibid., p. 225 (93).

[19] Ibid., p. 213 (76). Failure to meet the requirements of military service also led to deprivation of civil rights.

the vertical integration of these social groups that, unless checked, the people would act deferentially towards their superiors. Harrington even likened this relationship (between citizens be it noted) to that between officers and soldiers in an army.[20] A republic of mechanics, he thought, would be impossibly unstable because its citizens would not have the leisure to attain civic prudence. This was why political debate was prohibited amongst the people in a well-ordered commonwealth. In normal circumstances 'the common sort' would have 'a bashfulness in the presence of the better sort or wiser men: acknowledging their abilities by attention and accounting it no mean honour to receive respect from them'.[21] For this reason, a quota of elected places were to be reserved for the foot (the poorer citizens). 'Otherwise the people, beyond all per-adventure, would elect so many of the better sort at the very first, that there would not be of the foot or of the meaner sort to supply the due number of the popular assembly ...'[22] Likewise, in matters religious, the masses would, by and large, deferentially fall in line with what was offered to them.[23] Since the people would always 'be most addicted to the better sort', the constitutional distinction between horse and foot was designed to protect the latter against their own deferential preferences.[24]

Between civic prudence, leisure and landed wealth Harrington assumed a correlation, which was the social foundation of the 'genius of a gentleman' and made the preservation of an aristocracy, *not* holding the overbalance of land, essential to the operation of a well-ordered common-wealth. In turn, that correlation is the justification for the bicameral distribution of debate/proposal and resolution in the Oceanic constitution. But it also prefigures Harrington's attempt to offset the effects of deference amongst his citizenry by apportioning representation to the foot, the status group most likely to behave deferentially. This is a far cry from Richard Overton's insistence that the good citizen should be 'no respector of persons' or from Lawrence Clarkson's impeachment of the common people of post-Civil War England for their supine deference.[25]

Harrington, then, denied equality of civic rights to those incapable of self-rule and to those incapable, as he saw it, of participation in communal self-rule without crude partiality. Yet he allowed equality of civic rights to those who, left to themselves, would act deferentially; in other words, to those whose self-ruling capacities were conditioned and constrained by a

---

[20] Ibid., pp. 182–83 (35–36). [21] Ibid., pp. 259, 268 (138, 149–50).
[22] *The Art of Lawgiving* in *Political Works*, p. 677. [23] Ibid.
[24] *Valerius and Publicola* in *Political Works*, p. 787.
[25] Richard Overton, *An Arrow Against all Tyrants* (1646; repr. The Rota, Exeter, 1976), pp. 19–20; Lawrence Clarkson, *A Generall Charge, or Impeachment of High Treason in the Name of Justice Equity, against the Commonality of England* (1647).

sense of social obligation to their superiors. Equal rights were thus granted to those who had no sense of their own social or civic equality. To manage this, Harrington introduced two compensatory devices. One was the ballot which at least freed the individual political acts of the people exercising their franchise from the scrutiny of their superiors.[26] The other was the stipulation of categories of representative to ensure adequate representation of the lower orders. Built into Harrington's constitution were unequal categories of representation to compensate for the unequal political capacities and the inequality of socio-political self-esteem of his civic actors. The culmination of this was the denial of freedom of political discussion to any but senators.[27] The equal commonwealth, therefore, assumed a society of hierarchical inequality articulated in terms of property, ability, eminence and deference. To manage and exploit these inequalities, devices were incorporated: first, to maintain hierarchy in order to benefit from the political capabilities of the republic's social élite; secondly, to limit the participation of its lower orders while protecting their decisive representation.

It is hard for us to see, in this 'equal commonwealth', an egalitarianism corresponding to anything like a post-Enlightenment meaning of the term 'equality'. Appropriately, then, we must turn to contemporary, early modern, perceptions of equality if we are properly to grasp the meaning of Harrington's equal commonwealth. But before we do so it is worth looking at Harrington's treatment of two other groups in his republic and at the language he uses, or does not use, with regard to them.

Oceana is so liberal in its treatment of royalists and the religiously heterodox that *we* might expect its provision in this respect to be described in the language of equality. After the execution of the king on 30 January 1649, almost all constitutional proposals seeking to sustain some form of republicanism excluded both ex-royalists and the religiously heterodox – of the left or right – from civic participation. Examples of the exclusion of royalists can be found in the officers' *Agreement of the People* (20 January 1649), the Levellers' third and final *Agreement of the People* (1 May 1649) and the *Instrument of Government* setting up the Protectorate on the 16 December 1653.[28] By contrast, Harrington was prepared to envisage a situation in which only royalists, 'now equal citizens', would be elected to the Senate and Assembly. Even in this extreme situation, he believed, it would not be in their interest to overthrow his perfect and immortal

[26] *Political Works*, p. 181 (33–34).   [27] Ibid., pp. 226, 297–98 (94, 187–88).

[28] *An Agreement of the People of England* (20 January 1649) in S. R. Gardiner (ed.), *The Constitutional Documents of the Puritan Revolution 1625–1660* (London, 1906), p. 364; *An Agreement of the Free People of England* (1 May 1649) in Don M. Wolfe (ed.), *Leveller Manifestoes* (London, 1967), pp. 402–3.

commonwealth.[29] This extension of civil rights to royalists appalled other republicans such as Henry Stubbe who thought that royalists, Presbyterians and Episcopalians should all be excluded and citizenship restricted to those of proven loyalty to the 'good old cause'.[30] Similarly the *Instrument of Government* and the Leveller constitutions denied civic rights to Catholics, Anglicans and antinomians.[31] Harrington had no such scruples. While we might describe his resistance to discrimination against royalists (who might after all be expected to oppose the republic) and against the religiously disaffected as equality of treatment, Harrington did not see this impartiality in their treatment as a key, or defining, feature of his equal commonwealth. In other words, equality of civic rights is not central, in either case, to his concept of equality in an equal commonwealth.

Far from equal in his treatment of the personal civil rights of citizens, as well as non-citizens, in Oceana, neither did Harrington provide for corporate equality between different status groups. On the contrary, the equal distribution of land between social groups would always lead to civil war and was therefore to be avoided.[32] Disparities of wealth between groups were translated into discriminations of function, and therefore of participation, at every level of the political and military arrangements in the commonwealth. Indeed, as we have seen, Harrington regarded this as a virtue of his complex republic. His followers were not averse to elaborating his socio-political hierarchy, adjusting it more precisely to differences of wealth.[33] One of them, William Sprigge, suggested a refinement of the Agrarian law to ensure the 'Keeping up a Gentry fit for management of the most important affairs of the Nation'.[34] It is necessary then to ask again what Harrington meant by the equality of his 'equal commonwealth' and how his usage fitted the context of contemporary perceptions of equality.

A good starting-point for considering contemporaries' perceptions of

---

[29] *Political Works*, pp. 350–51 (256).

[30] James R. Jacob, *Henry Stubbe, radical Protestantism and the early Enlightenment* (Cambridge, 1983), pp. 27–28. Jacob mistakenly believes that 'Equality of political participation was what would make it [the constitution of Oceana] work and last.' Ibid., p. 27. Also on loyalty to the good old cause as a test for eligibility for election see Gerrard Winstanley, *The Law of Freedom* in G. H. Sabine (ed.), *The Works of Gerrard Winstanley* (New York, 1941), p. 543.

[31] *Instrument of Government* in Kenyon (ed.), *Stuart Constitution* (2nd edn, Cambridge, 1986), pp. 312–13; *Foundations of Freedom; Or an Agreement of the People* (1648) in Wolfe, *Leveller Manifestoes*, p. 300.

[32] *A System of Politics* in *Political Works*, p. 853 (271).

[33] See, for example, the discussion of the anonymous *Chaos* (1659) in Davis, *Utopia and the Ideal Society*, p. 249.

[34] William Sprigge, *A Modest Plea, For an Equal Commonwealth, Against Monarchy* (1659), pp. 117–19.

equality is their use of the classical trinity of the pure forms of government: monarchy, aristocracy and democracy, with their potential for degeneration into tyranny, oligarchy and anarchy. Harrington's contemporaries saw equality as the social condition which caused the third of these declensions, the corruption of democracy into anarchy. As the Calvinist political theorist, Althusius, put it, if 'all were equal and each should wish to rule others by his own will', the consequence would be 'discord' and the 'dissolution of society'.[35] For Thomas Hobbes, likewise, it was the relative equality of men in prudence and physical capacity, in natural power, which pulled the state of nature into anarchy, a war of all against all.[36] To see this linked to the classical typologies of monarchy, aristocracy and democracy one need look no further than Charles I's answer to the Nineteen Propositions put to him by Parliament in June 1642. There the king suggested that the reduction of all to equality would license the people to 'call parity and independence liberty ... destroy all rights and properties, all distinctions of families and merit, and by this means this splendid and excellently distinguished form of government end in a dark, equal chaos of confusion ...'[37] Across the spectrum, Thomas Edwards in the preface to the third part of his *Gangraena*, which in 1646 chronicled the scandalous rise of political radicalism, linked an analysis in terms of the one, the few and the many to the emergence of anarchy on the back of democracy corrupted by equality. Having 'declared against Monarchie and Aristocracie, and for Democracie' these radicals rapidly reduced the latter to 'an Anarchie' by 'making all alike, confounding of all rancks and orders, reducing all to Adams time and condition and devolving all power upon the state Universall and promiscuous multitude ...'[38] Perhaps for these reasons, the language of Gerrard Winstanley's *Law of Freedom*, a work addressed, like *Oceana*, to Oliver Cromwell, is consistently of community, 'common preservation', rather than of equality.[39] For while Cromwell could identify liberty of conscience as 'that equality that [is] professed to be amongst us' and thought that too great disparities of wealth were not compatible with a commonwealth, he remained wedded to social hierarchy and the politics of deference. The reformation of manners for which he longed in the 1650s was necessary to 'keep up the nobility and gentry'.[40]

---

[35] Johannes Althusius, *Politica Methodice Digesta*, I, 11–12, 37, cited in Howell A. Lloyd, 'Constitutionalism', in Burns with Goldie (eds.), *Cambridge History of Political Thought 1450–1700*, p. 289.

[36] Richard Tuck (ed.), *Hobbes: Leviathan* (Cambridge, 1991) ch. XIII and pp. 107–8, 238.

[37] *The King's Answer to the Nineteen Propositions*, 18 June 1642, in Kenyon (ed.), *Stuart Constitution*, p. 20.

[38] Thomas Edwards, *The Third Part of Gangraena* (1646), Preface.

[39] Winstanley, *Law of Freedom*, passim., in Sabine (ed.), *Works of Winstanley*.

[40] Abbott (ed.), *Writings and Speeches of Oliver Cromwell*, I, p. 534; II, p. 325; IV, p. 273.

In terms of the classical taxonomy of the one, the few and the many: the rule of the one could be corrupted by the pursuit of the single ruler's self-interest; that of the few by the pursuit of the interest of the group or party; but the rule of the many (democracy) could not be corrupted by the pursuit of the interest of all. It was rendered incapable of pursuing anything at all as a collective entity by its loss of form, the incapacity for leadership arising from its condition of equality. Equality was, in mid-seventeenth-century parlance, that condition which precipitated unalloyed democracy into anarchy. It was exactly in this way that Richard Baxter read and recoiled from James Harrington's language of equality. The notion of an equal commonwealth elicited for him the horrifying prospect of a descent into anarchy. The rule of the many would be the rule of the ignorant because the many were ignorant; the rule of the many, the rule of the ungodly because the many were ungodly. In such an egalitarian nightmare representatives would be 'fetched from the Dung-cart to make us Laws, and from the Alehouse and the May-pole to dispose of our Religion, Lives and Estates ...'; '... why then,' Baxter asked Harrington, 'should we equalize unskilful Rusticks that never studied Politicks a day?'[41] He could only put the question seriously because the contemporary signification of 'equality' had led him to misread Harrington and the fear of equality, as that gravitational force which would pull democracy down into anarchy, unleashed his visceral response. Regardless of his intention, Harrington's language of equality associated him, in the minds of his contemporary readers, with anarchy.

What then does Harrington mean by equality in his equal common-wealth? The clearest and fullest definition was given in *The Art of Lawgiving*. There he wrote:

> An equal commonwealth is a government founded upon a balance which is perfectly popular and well fixed by a suitable *agrarian*, and which, from the balance, through the free suffrage of the people given by the ballot, amounteth in the superstructures unto a senate debating and proposing, a representative of the people resolving, and a magistracy executing; each of these three orders being upon courses or rotation; that is elected for certain terms, enjoining like intervals.[42]

---

[41] William Lamont (ed.), *Richard Baxter: A Holy Commonwealth* (Cambridge, 1994), pp. 136–39. *A Holy Commonwealth* (1659) was written at the invitation of James Harrington.

[42] *Political Works*, p. 613. Compare the definition given in *Oceana*: 'An equal commonwealth ... is a government established upon an equal agrarian, arising into the superstructures or three orders, the senate debating and proposing, the people resolving, and the magistracy executing by an equal rotation through the suffrage of the people given by the ballot.' At the same time, Harrington sometimes wrote as if only the agrarian and rotation were

There are then four necessary features of an equal commonwealth: an 'equal Agrarian'; the ballot; a bicameral and functionally specialised legislature with a dependent executive, and rotation of office. Only if all these institutional devices were met together would there be an equal, and therefore lasting, commonwealth. Such an institutional/constitutional framework through which the attribute of equality was given its central place is difficult to translate into our association of equality with personal and corporate rights, obligations and privileges. To overcome this sense of alienation from Harrington's language, it is useful to look at what the functions of equality are in the equal commonwealth. What does equality do in the Oceanic republic?

Three functions stand out. First, equality preserves the Oceanic status quo. '... the perfection of government lieth upon such a libration in the frame of it, that no man or men, in or under it, can have the interest or, having the interest, can have the power to disturb it with sedition'.[43] Only 'an equal commonwealth ... containeth in it the full perfection of government'.[44] The essence of equality, in this respect, is its capacity to deliver freedom from sedition; in other words, to guarantee perpetual stability. How does it do it?

To be equal a commonwealth must, according to Harrington, be equal in its foundation and its superstructures. In both dimensions, that is to say, the intention and the capacity to destabilise the commonwealth must not be allowed to come together. The agrarian, we are told, furnishes equality in the root; rotation likewise in the branch.[45] The agrarian is designed both to prevent a monarchical nobility but also to preserve a popular nobility, that is to say a nobility not overbalancing the people in property but capable of providing them with political leadership.[46] A bicameralism of specialised function – debate in the Senate, resolution in the Assembly – gives institutional expression to that relationship. Rotation prevents faction, or the putting of particular interest above the general interest in such a way as to destabilise the system.[47]

In *Oceana*, therefore, 'equality' meant those things which guarantee stability even in a commonwealth for expansion. 'Inequality' describes those attributes which were the causes of the dissolution of common-

---

essential to an equal commonwealth. Ibid., pp. 180–81 (33–34); *The Prerogative of Popular Government*, ibid., p. 473. Cf. the discussion in Davis, *Utopia and the Ideal Society*, pp. 212–16.

[43] *Oceana*, in *Political Works*, p. 179 (30–31). Cf. *The Art of Lawgiving*, ibid., p. 658.

[44] *Oceana*, in *Political Works*, p. 180 (32).   [45] Ibid., p. 231 (100–1).

[46] The fullest and clearest statement of this comes in Chapter 1 of Book III of *The Art of Lawgiving*, in *Political Works*, pp. 664–65. Cf. pp. 611, 703.

[47] 'So that if you allow not a commonwealth her rotation, in which consists her equality, you reduce her to a party ...' *Oceana*, in *Political Works*, p. 249 (123).

wealths.[48] The three causes of sedition are: desire for power, desire of riches, and desire for liberty. In an equal commonwealth people are possessed of all three – power, riches and liberty – (even if in what appear to us to be unequal ways) and are constrained by the agrarian, the ballot, the bicameral system and by rotation in such a way as to prevent the dissatisfied, envious or ambitious from obtaining the leverage to overturn the system. 'Innate sedition', otherwise known as inequality, has been eliminated.[49] Harrington's equal end (stability) was pursued by what to us might appear unequal means but Harrington drew no such distinction. More to the point is his inversion of contemporary usage. In the Oceanic lexicon 'equality' had become the guarantor of the stability of popular rule rather than the means of its subversion.

Not only did Oceanic equality maintain the correlation between the institutional structure of the commonwealth and a stabilised distribution of real power in society, it also, in its second function, engaged all appropriately qualified citizens in functionally differentiated cycles of deliberation, decision or administration. Refusal of such service could result in reduction to the status of 'helot or public servant' and heavy fiscal penalties.[50] The design was to 'take in the whole body by parts'; to ensure such a level of participation among citizens as to create a sense that the people were in possession of their own government.[51] There may be no equality between citizens in the sense of their all sharing any one of the roles set out by Harrington in his republic, or in that of enjoying equal eligibility for any of those roles. But that was not the point of Harringtonian equality which was to immunise the commonwealth against sedition by making all complicit in the operation of its constitutional systems.

The third function of Oceanic equality was to ensure the priority of the public interest over private interests. Ancient prudence, which Harrington's *Oceana* was rehabilitating, was the art of instituting civil society upon the foundation of common right or interest.[52] Replying to Hobbes, Harrington noted that 'equality of estates causeth equality of power, and equality of power is the liberty not only of the commonwealth, but of every man'.[53] This was said, however, to satirise Hobbes' views on liberty and equality. Harrington's peculiar usage was to link equality not with

---

[48] Ibid., pp. 274–76, 322 (157–60, 220).
[49] *The Art of Lawgiving*, in *Political Works*, p. 613.
[50] *Oceana*, in *Political Works*, p. 302 (195).
[51] Ibid., p. 181 (33); *The Prerogative of Popular Government*, in Ibid., pp. 424–25. If we assume an adult (over thirty) male population of one million (probably a moderately generous estimate for England and Wales in the 1650s) there would be 200,000 deputies, 50,000 of whom must have been office holders. Given the rotational cycle and vacations from office those numbers swell substantially.
[52] *Oceana*, in *Political Works*, p. 161 (8).   [53] Ibid., p. 170 (20).

liberty but with stability and the common interest, even if in ways which
seem to us emphatically unequal. Inequality led 'to strife, and strife to
ruin'.[54] It did so by facilitating the formation of parties. The consequence
was factional conflict. So commonwealths might be distinguished as equal
or unequal. '... and this', wrote Harrington, 'is the main point especially as
to domestic peace and tranquillity; for to make a commonwealth unequal
is to divide it into parties ...'[55] But equality, as a means of preventing the
rise of factionalised politics, was not a matter of equalising property or the
rights and privileges of citizenship. Rather, it was a matter of the
appropriate institutional provision. The commonwealth's *ordini* provided
thus for rotation of office, 'in which consists her equality'.[56] Similarly,
without differential bicameralism, the doors opened to sectional interest
and thereby to inequality. 'A council ... having not only the debate but the
result also, is capable of influence from without, of interest from within.
There may be a formal, a prejudicated party which will haste or cry you
from the debate unto the question, and precipitate you upon the result
...'[57] On the other hand, were the equal commonwealth to be instituted,
parties would evaporate within seven years.[58] Harrington's own ability to
devise an equal commonwealth rested, as he saw it, on his knowledge of
ancient prudence, which taught how to place common interest above
private interest, and, secondly, upon his disengagement from all parties.[59]
A principal achievement, therefore, of the institutional framework which
Harrington characterised as 'equal' was the triumph of 'common right or
interest' over 'that which sticks to every man in private'.[60]

Like John Calvin, Harrington thought it desirable to reconcile aristocratic leadership with popular control.[61] The problem was to prevent
sectional aristocratic domination, or oligarchy, on the one hand, and on the
other, the anarchy of popular rule; in other words, to preserve a balance
between aristocratic leadership and popular decision. The solutions were
to be found, he thought, in carefully crafted institutional devices: specialised bicameralism, the ballot, rotation and an agrarian law of some
considerable subtlety. To use the term 'equal commonwealth' to describe
the combination of these institutions was not simply to give the language of
equality a technical and very specific meaning, it was also to shift its

---

[54] Ibid., p. 321 (219).   [55] Ibid., p. 180 (33).   [56] Ibid., p. 249 (123).
[57] *The Art of Lawgiving*, in *Political Works*, p. 676.
[58] *A Discourse upon This Saying*, in ibid., p. 745.   [59] *Politicaster*, in ibid., p. 709.
[60] *Oceana*, in ibid., p. 172 (22). Cf. the Harringtonian Utopia of 1696, *The Free State of Noland*,
where the first day's work was the erection of 'one Common Interest'. Davis, *Utopia and
the Ideal Society*, p. 245.
[61] Cf. Sanford A. Lakoff, *Equality in Political Philosophy* (Cambridge, Massachusetts, 1964),
p. 45.

association from the contemporary context of democracy's egalitarian collapse into anarchy, to a radically different association with stability, the triumph of communal over sectional interest, and with immortality. As Jonathan Scott has observed in relation to his use of the language of classical and Machiavellian republicanism, Harrington had a predilection for inverting the languages at his disposal.[62] In this case he took what to his contemporaries – including Oliver Cromwell – would have seemed the subversive category of equality and made it the descriptor of those means conducive to order.[63] By the end of the decade in which he began his career as republican advocate, it was possible for one writer to reverse the standard associations and to link 'inequality and disorder'.[64]

The importance of this is twofold. First, we have become used to searching for the keys to the appropriate historical recovery or interpretation of texts in the linguistic context in which they were written and of which they simultaneously formed part.[65] Language is seen, just as history itself once was, to form a seamless web into which the text is woven. The semantic conventions of the context will provide the clues to interpreting, without anachronism, the usages of the text. There is no doubt that this approach has offered the opportunity to develop a genuinely historical approach to the history of political thought. But do we also need to recognise its limitations? We are beginning to recognise in Harrington, thanks primarily to the work of Jonathan Scott,[66] a subverter – rather than a transmitter – of the language of classical republicanism. In revising the signification of 'equality' in such a way as to be commonly misunderstood by his contemporary readers, Harrington was trying to wrench himself free from the linguistic conventions of his day. It is surely legitimate to ask not only why, but also what the implications of this are for the linguistic contextualist's approach to the correct and full interpretation of his

---

[62] Jonathan Scott, 'The Rapture of Motion: James Harrington's republicanism', in Nicholas Phillipson and Quentin Skinner (eds.), *Political Discourse in Early Modern England* (Cambridge, 1993), pp. 139–63.

[63] I have argued elsewhere that 'liberty' in seventeenth-century England meant appropriate subordination. Might it be that Harrington's use of equality is to suggest not equal rights or privileges but equal subordination? Davis, 'Religion and the Struggle for Freedom in the English Revolution', *The Historical Journal*, 35:3 (1992) pp. 507–30. For 'brotherly equality' as 'equal submission' see John Cotton, *The Doctrine of the Church* (1643) p. 5 and more forcefully in the manuscript version Hartlib Papers, Sheffield University Library, 40/2/42B and 46A.

[64] Peter Cornelius Plockhoy, *A Way Propounded to Make the Poor in these and other Nations happy* (1659) p. 3.

[65] See, for example, James Tully (ed.), *Meaning and Context: Quentin Skinner and his Critics* (Princeton, 1988); Conal Condren, *The Status and Appraisal of Classic Texts* (Princeton, 1985).

[66] Scott, 'The Rapture of Motion'.

thought. Secondly, and a not unrelated issue, is the role, as the exemplary republican of his generation, which has been accorded Harrington by influential interpreters like John Pocock and Blair Worden.[67] There are many reasons for questioning this – in particular Harrington's emphasis on form rather than republican spirit which sets him apart from the republicanism of Milton, Vane and Sidney[68] – but the revisionist idiosyncracies of his linguistic usage must surely be one of them.

We may end with Harrington's own tortured consciousness of these linguistic shifts. 'Equality or parity', he wrote in *A System of Politics*,

> has been represented an odious thing, and made to imply the levelling of men's estates; but if a nobility, how inequal soever in their estates or titles, yet, to come to the truth of aristocracy, must as to their votes or participation in the government be *pares regni*, that is to say peers or in parity amongst themselves; as likewise the people, to attain to the truth of democracy, may be peers or in parity among themselves, and yet not as to their estates be obliged to levelling.[69]

[67] See Worden's essays in Wootton (ed.), *Republicanism, Liberty and Commercial Society*.

[68] Jonathan Scott's review of Wootton (ed.), *Republicanism, Liberty and Commercial Society* forthcoming in *Parliamentary History*.

[69] *A System of Politics*, in *Political Works*, p. 840 (277).

John Milton and Oliver Cromwell

BLAIR WORDEN

There were two occasions when the imagination of John Milton, the supreme writer of the Puritan Revolution, focused on Oliver Cromwell, its supreme soldier and statesman. There is the sonnet 'To the Lord General Cromwell' in May 1652; and there is the passage about Cromwell in Milton's Latin prose work *Defensio Secunda*, published in May 1654, when Cromwell had been Lord Protector for six months. Both the sonnet, an exercise in verse, and the passage of prose, an exercise in eloquence, are tributes of praise. Milton honours Cromwell's stature, which elicits and affirms the poet's own. Art and power meet and pay homage to each other.

Yet after *Defensio Secunda* Milton's writings never mention Cromwell's name again. During the remaining four years of Cromwell's life they pass no explicit comment on his government.[1] Milton's pen offers no tribute to the military and naval exploits of the protectorate, no lament on Cromwell's death. His silence is loud. In August 1659, four months after the fall of Richard Cromwell and of the protectorate, the silence was broken. Now Milton described the Cromwellian regime as 'a short but scandalous night of interruption': interruption, that is, of the Long Parliament, which Cromwell had expelled by force in April 1653. The significance and bitterness of that attack have been brought out by Austin Woolrych in much the most authoritative and penetrating account of Milton's attitudes to Cromwell that we have.[2] How do we reconcile the attack with Milton's

---

[1] I concur with Martin Dzelzainis in distinguishing between Milton's own writings and the official letters he penned under the protectorate as Latin Secretary: Dzelzainis, 'Juvenal, Charles X Gustavus, and Milton's letter to Richard Jones', *The Seventeenth Century*, 9 (1994), 32.

[2] Austin Woolrych, 'Milton and Cromwell: "A Short but Scandalous Night of Interruption"?', in Michael Lieb and John T. Shawcross, eds., *Achievements of the Left Hand: Essays on the Prose of John Milton* (Amherst, Mass., 1974), pp. 208–9; and see Woolrych's Introduction to volume VII of the Yale edition of *Complete Prose Works of John Milton*, 8 vols. (New Haven, 1952–83: hereafter *CPW*), pp. 85–87. A different interpretation of Milton's words is offered in Robert T. Fallon's valuable study, *Milton in Government* (Pennsylvania, 1993);

earlier praise of Cromwell? Did Milton undergo, between 1654 and 1659, a change of heart? Or can we find, in his feelings about Cromwell, a thread of continuity? I believe we can. The praise of Cromwell in 1652 and 1654, though heartfelt, is accompanied, I shall suggest, by doubt and by warning. I shall argue that the poet's enthusiasm for his hero is conditional, and that Cromwell fails to meet the conditions. In Milton's mind the consequences of that failure were calamitous to the cause which both the poet and the hero had served. We shall look at the sonnet and *Defensio Secunda* in turn. We begin with the sonnet and with the context that produced it.

I

The sonnet was not printed at the time. It survives in the hand of an amanuensis, who headed it 'To the Lord General Cromwell, May 1652. On the proposals of certain ministers at the Committee for Propagation of the Gospel'.

> Cromwell, our chief of men, who through a cloud
>   Not of war only, but detractions rude,
>   Guided by faith and matchless fortitude
>   To peace and truth thy glorious way hast ploughed,
> And on the neck of crowned fortune proud
>   Hast reared God's trophies and his work pursued,
>   While Darwen stream with blood of Scots imbrued,
>   And Dunbar field resounds thy praises loud,
> And Worcester's laureate wreath; yet much remains
>   To conquer still; peace hath her victories
>   No less renowned than war, new foes arise
> Threatening to bind our souls with secular chains:
>   Help us to save free conscience from the paw
>   Of hireling wolves whose gospel is their maw.

The poem records Cromwell's greatest victories: at Preston in August 1648, at Dunbar in September 1650, at Worcester in September 1651. The last of those triumphs, won eight months before the composition of the sonnet, completed the conquest over royalism in the three kingdoms. That outcome transformed the political situation in England. So long as the wars had lasted, parliament had paid only intermittent attention to the

---

but I concur with the comments on Fallon's argument passed in Woolrych's review in *Albion*, 26 (1995), 136–38. Among the many opponents of the protectorate who referred to the expulsion of the Rump as an 'interruption' was Milton's hero Sir Henry Vane: see Vane's 'A Healing Question Propounded', in Sir Walter Scott, ed., *Somers Tracts*, 16 vols. (London, 1809–15), VI, 311.

demands for settlement and reform to which Cromwell's army was committed. Now he brought them to the fore.[3] He could not hope to dominate the House of Commons. In formal or constitutional terms he was but one among many members of the Rump, the remnant of the Long Parliament which had held sovereign power since Pride's Purge in December 1648. Even so, his influence, while often resisted and sometimes resented by his colleagues, was unrivalled among them. The Commonwealth, which owed its existence to his victorious army, remained dependent on it for its survival.

It was Cromwell's aim to hold parliament and army together. He sought a programme of reform that would be acceptable to both sides. On no subject was that challenge more daunting than religion, the one addressed by Milton's sonnet. MPs had wanted the revolution to puritanise the land. Instead it had produced ecclesiological and doctrinal anarchy. In the proliferation of sectarian heresies, most MPs saw an affront to God and a threat to the social order. After the king's execution, heresies became ever more shocking in content and more strident in presentation. So did anticlericalism. The very existence of the established ministry and of the parish system was denounced as Antichristian. The maintenance of the clergy by the levy of tithes came under attacks of mounting ferocity. So did the bond between church and state.

Cromwell's army was at once a source of radical demands and a stimulus to them. It called for guarantees of liberty of conscience and for an end to tithes. Hostility and mistrust characterised the relations between parliament and army over religion as over much else. Even so, Cromwell looked for common ground. Many MPs, after all, accepted the case for a degree of religious toleration; many of them disliked clerical dogmatism; many of them would have liked to find a less contentious and less inequitable system of clerical maintenance than tithes. If there were limits to parliament's conservatism, so were there to the army's radicalism. Only a minority in the army wanted anything like unlimited toleration or the separation of church from state or the disestablishment of the ministry. Most soldiers accepted that if tithes were to be abolished an alternative means of clerical maintenance, likewise supported by the state, must be found. Besides, there was one important respect in which parliament and army broadly concurred in their diagnoses of England's spiritual ills. The parish clergy, they agreed, were unequal to their tasks. Almost all MPs and at least most of the army's leaders believed that the reform of the clergy was the province and duty of the state. It was incumbent on parliament,

[3] Where I do not indicate otherwise, my account of the political history of the Rump period is substantiated in Blair Worden, *The Rump Parliament 1648–1653* (Cambridge, 1974).

they maintained, to remove profane and ignorant ministers and to install godly ones in their places.

After his victory at Worcester, Cromwell's search for a consensus on religious reform drew on all his political skills. We find him now pressing for legislative progress, now restraining it. Yet through those tactical variations his goals remained consistent. Liberty of conscience was the abiding principle of his career, the unshakeable goal to which, it can be argued, he sacrificed the possibility of durable Puritan rule. He had for long been the man to whom groups and individuals fearing persecution principally looked. Yet the toleration he sought was always a limited one. Though ready to allow a broad diversity in church-government and worship, he had a narrower conception of the permissible scope of doctrine and faith. It was the magistrate's obligation, he held, to protect those truths which might be conscionably held and which would not jeopardise a believer's salvation.[4] Cromwell never wanted to divorce church from state. He never questioned the parish system. He would have liked to see an end to tithes but not to the compulsory maintenance of the clergy.

In February 1652 Cromwell's *protégé* John Owen, who had been his chaplain on the campaigns of 1649–50 and who later in 1652 would be installed by him as Vice-Chancellor of Oxford University, submitted to parliament a scheme for 'the propagation of the gospel'. This was the plan which would be implemented, in a revised form, in 1654, and which we know, in that revised form, as the system of Triers and Ejectors. Commissions were to be established to vet candidates to livings and to remove unsatisfactory ministers from the parishes. The scheme also proposed that 'such who do not receive, but oppose, those principles of Christian religion, without the acknowledgement whereof the scriptures do clearly and plainly affirm, that salvation is not to be obtained … may not be suffered to preach or promulgate any thing in opposition to such principles'. The proposals were signed not only by Owen and other Independent divines but by two inseparable allies among the army officers, Edward Whalley and William Goffe, both of whom were invariably loyal to Cromwell.[5] If the plan succeeded, it would not only unite parliament and army in a programme of reform. It would isolate that often voluble minority which opposed all intervention by the state in the church.

Cromwell was one of the MPs appointed to the parliamentary committee which was set up to consider Owen's scheme and which became known as the Committee for the Propagation of the Gospel. The

---

[4] Blair Worden, 'Toleration and the Cromwellian Protectorate', *Studies in Church History* 21 (1984).
[5] *Journal of the House of Commons* (hereafter *CJ*) 10 February 1652, 11 February 1653.

committee adopted the scheme for its own. Yet the scheme made little headway in the House. The principal obstacle to its passage was not the programme for the purging and regeneration of the ministry but the identification of beliefs incompatible with salvation. At first it seemed that the latter initiative was directed only, or at least mainly, at one particularly shocking heresy, anti-trinitarianism. Only in the weeks ahead would the extent of Owen's ambition to suppress heresy become plain. The submission of his scheme to parliament was accompanied by a petition from him and other ministers drawing attention to a recent Latin publication which would come to be known as *The Racovian Catechism*, and which reported and endorsed the anti-trinitarian or Socinian movement in Poland. The Rump obliged the ministers by ordering the book to be publicly burned.[6]

Even among politicians and soldiers eager for a broad base of religious liberty, there was fierce opposition to anti-trinitarianism, the most insidious and most risky heresy of seventeenth-century England. In 1612 anti-trinitarianism occasioned the last public burnings for heresy. Alone of non-Roman beliefs it was excluded from the liberty granted by the Toleration Act of 1689. If anything, Puritans were still more alarmed by it than Anglicans. In 1648 a parliamentary ordinance enjoined the death penalty for it. In January 1649 the Rump, with the encouragement of John Owen, suspended one of its members, John Fry, for his anti-trinitarian beliefs. In 1651 it expelled him and ordered his writings to be publicly burned.[7] Owen had a special horror of the 'cursed Socinians', on whom he blamed the 'flood' of 'scepticism, libertinism and atheism' which had 'broken upon the world'. 'The trinity', he affirmed, was 'the great fundamental article' of Protestantism, the 'mystery the knowledge whereof is the only means to have a right apprehension of all other sacred truths'.[8]

Milton was an anti-trinitarian. Not only did he hold anti-trinitarian views, which would soon be spelled out in his manuscript treatise *De Doctrina Christiana*.[9] He took steps to promote them. Milton, it emerged, was one of the men responsible for the publication of *The Racovian Catechism*.[10] Though he was not prosecuted, he had taken a large risk. For once in his life he found himself at the centre not merely of controversy but of events. They were the events out of which the guiding ecclesiastical policies of the Interregnum grew.

[6] Ibid., 10 February, 26 March, 2 April 1652, 11 February 1653 (esp. clause 13).
[7] Worden, *Rump Parliament*, p. 241.
[8] Worden, 'Toleration', 203–5; and for hostility to anti-trinitarianism in the army see *CPW*, VII, 73.
[9] The treatise is published in an English translation in *CPW*, VI.
[10] W. R. Parker, *Milton. A Biography*, 2 vols. (Oxford, 1968), I, 394–95, II, 994.

Milton's objections to Owen's scheme would not have been confined to its proscription of anti-trinitarianism. The poet, though belonging, as far as we can tell, to no sect, agreed with that sectarian opinion which demanded the separation of church from state and the disestablishment of the ministry, whose powers and pretensions he reviled. To his mind the only proper gatherings of believers were voluntary ones, and the only proper ministers were those whom congregations chose to appoint and support. Where the state intervened or compelled in religion, he maintained, truth would always bend to it and be corrupted by it. Two enemies to truth were inseparably linked in Milton's thinking: the compulsory payment of the ministry, the instrument of 'hire'; and persecution, the instrument of 'force'. Owen's scheme did not address the issue of tithes. Yet if Milton had any doubts about parliament's intentions, they would have been resolved at the end of April 1652, when the House endorsed the principle of compulsory maintenance and ordered that tithes be duly paid until an alternative was found.[11] Meanwhile Owen and his supporters, 'in explanation' of the earlier proposal to forbid the expression of opinions incompatible with salvation, had listed fifteen 'fundamentals' of belief.[12] The 'fundamentals' were, almost certainly, those 'proposals of certain ministers' to which the heading of Milton's sonnet refers.[13]

Owen's initiative for the imposition of doctrinal orthodoxy touched a chord in the nation at large, which was displaying a mounting impatience with sectarianism, with heresy, and with the more vituperative manifestations of anticlericalism. In May, the month of the sonnet, an official newsbook indicated the regime's support for the restoration of church discipline and for the proscription of heresy. While 'all sweet liberty of conscience that might be' should be permitted 'to tender consciences, so far as the Word will warrant', it was essential 'to prevent the publishing of blasphemies, and such things as tend to the beating down of the fundamentals of religion'. It would be the task of the Committee for the Propagation of the Gospel, indicated the newsbook, to secure those 'fundamentals'.[14]

It is unlikely that Owen would have drawn up his list of 'fundamentals' without Cromwell's approval. There was nothing in them to which Cromwell would have taken theological exception. Even so, he seems to have distanced himself from them. A pamphlet published in March 1652

---

[11] *CJ*, 29 April 1652.

[12] *Proposals for the furtherance and propagation of the Gospell in this Nation* (London, 1653: [Thomason Tracts,] E683.12).

[13] On that point I concur with S. R. Gardiner, *History of the Commonwealth and Protectorate*, 4 vols. (London, 1893), II, 103n.

[14] Worden, *Rump Parliament*, pp. 296–97.

contains a report by Roger Williams, Milton's friend and fellow-advocate of the separation of church from state who was in touch with the poet at this time, that Cromwell had recently 'declared before many witnesses' that 'I shall need no revelation ... to discover unto me that man that shall endeavour to impose upon [the consciences of] his brethren.' Williams added that at a debate at the Committee for the Propagation of the Gospel, held in front of 'many auditors', Cromwell had declared that 'I had rather Mohametanism were permitted amongst us than that one of God's children should be persecuted.'[15] Those statements, if they are accurately recorded, must have made a deep impression on their hearers. Yet we should interpret them with caution. Cromwell's remark about Mohametanism, as Williams relates it, is to be understood not as a plea for the toleration of that faith but as evidence of his characteristic preoccupation with the protection of true believers. On those occasions when, as protector, Cromwell gave a measure of leeway to groups beyond the pale of salvation, it was solely in order to guard groups inside it from movements of persecution that would have crushed believer and heretic alike.[16]

In March 1652 Cromwell had good reason to make rhetorical statements that would please the sectaries. The bonds between him and them had always been important to him, politically and emotionally. In the autumn of 1651, when he offered them kind words but nothing more, the bonds came under strain. In December it was reported that 'the private churches begin to call his Excellency an apostate'. Other sectaries left London around the same time, 'much saddened' by the conduct of a leader who during his military campaigns had given hospitality and encouragement to men of their principle but who now, it was alleged, 'chose new friends'.[17] He earned mistrust on other fronts, too, by allowing himself to be publicly represented as the champion of bold measures of social and legal reform while contriving, behind the scenes, to delay if not defeat them.[18]

---

[15] *The fourth paper presented by Major Butler to the ... Committee ... for the propagating the gospel* (London, 1652: E658.9), preface; Gardiner, *Commonwealth and Protectorate*, II, 100. A pamphlet of May 1652, written either by Williams or by a close ally, resembles Milton's sonnet to Vane in urging the Rump's committee to 'distinguish between' the provinces of church and state (cf. *CPW*, VII, 243, 255) and between the magisterial and the 'spiritual' 'swords': *Ill Newes from New-England* (London, 1652: E664.5); for the authorship see David Masson, *The Life of John Milton*, 6 vols. (London, 1859–90), IV, 396n.

[16] Worden, 'Toleration'.

[17] Worden, *Rump Parliament*, pp. 278, 291; *CPW*, VII, 458 ('abandoning of all those whom they call sectaries ...').

[18] Worden, *Rump Parliament*, pp. 73–79.

II

Four years before his sonnet to Cromwell, Milton had addressed a sonnet
to Thomas Fairfax, the then Lord General. That poem, like the poem to
Cromwell, has two parts. In both cases the poem moves in its ninth line
from praise of its recipient's military exploits to counsel for the future.
Where Cromwell is urged to turn from the 'victories' of war to those of
'peace', Fairfax is directed to the challenge of reform, a 'nobler task' than
'war'.

The first eight and a half lines of the poem to Cromwell are a monument to his past. All that is good and all that is great about him is concentrated, in an astonishing feat of balance and economy, into six words:
'faith', 'matchless fortitude', 'peace', 'truth', 'glorious'. There is no missing
Milton's admiration and gratitude, and no difficulty in explaining them.
Without Cromwell's 'matchless fortitude' to sustain and rescue it, the
cause to which both men had devoted their lives would have been
shattered. Yet poetry of praise, in the Renaissance and beyond it, has to be
read with an eye to the ethical and educative purpose that was expected to
inform it. When the poet abused or bypassed that purpose, the praise
could be a mere instrument of flattery or self-seeking. But when the poet
was faithful to the purpose, the praise was an instrument of advice,
perhaps even of admonition, perhaps even of rebuke. The later lines of
Milton's sonnet are, at the least, a warning.

The standard edition of Milton's poems misses that intention. Its
commentary explains that, while Owen and his fellow ministers insisted on
the 'fundamentals', Cromwell 'was in favour of unlimited liberty of
dissent'.[19] So Milton is appealing to a fellow opponent of clerical intolerance. The sonnet acquires a different and perhaps more interesting
character when we probe behind that misconception. Cromwell was
Owen's ally, not Milton's. The 'new foes' which 'arise' derive encouragement from, indeed are embodied in, that initiative for the curtailment of
liberty of conscience which Owen has promoted and in which Cromwell is
implicated. Of course, Cromwell need not be the prisoner of that scheme.
The poem has no purpose unless Milton has some hope that Cromwell
will 'Help us'. Perhaps the speeches of Cromwell that were reported by
Roger Williams occasioned that hope. If any one person had the power 'to
save free conscience' from 'hireling wolves' it was Cromwell. Yet 'Help us'
is a plea, not an expectation. It quickens the poem with an urgency, and
troubles it with an uncertainty, which we miss if we take Cromwell's and
Milton's minds to be at one. To 'Help us', Cromwell will need to part not

---

[19] John Carey and Alastair Fowler, eds., *The Poems of John Milton* (London, 1968), p. 326.

only with Owen but with his own principles. To win the victories of peace he will need to prove himself afresh. He is on probation.

The element of doubt and admonition in the poem emerges more sharply when we set its lines beside Milton's next known poem, the sonnet he wrote to Sir Henry Vane and which he sent to Vane early in July 1652. Unlike the sonnet to Cromwell it was published in its author's lifetime: daringly and defiantly published in a laudatory biography of Vane which appeared in 1662 after Vane's execution for treason against Charles I. It was the first poem of Milton to be printed for fourteen years.

> Vane, young in years, but in sage counsel old,
>   Than whom a better senator ne'er held
>   The helm of Rome, when gowns not arms repelled
>   The fierce Epirot and the African bold.
> Whether to settle peace or to unfold
>   The drift of hollow states, hard to be spelled,
>   Then to advise how war may best, upheld,
>   Move by her two main nerves, iron and gold
> In all her equipage: besides to know
>   Both spiritual power and civil, what each means,
>   What severs each, thou hast learned, which few have done.
> The bounds of either sword to thee we owe;
>   Therefore on thy firm hand Religion leans
>   In peace, and reckons thee her eldest son.

Vane was a leading member of the Rump, a dominant figure in the formation of its policies at home and abroad. In the 1640s he and Cromwell had been close allies, Vane fixing the parliamentary support while Cromwell won the military victories. The two men had long worked together against the persecution of the godly. Yet beyond their concurrence there lay a difference. Vane was one of the very few members of parliament, and much the most influential one, to argue for the separation of church from state. He shared that view with his old friend Roger Williams, with whom, like Milton, he was in touch in the spring of 1652.[20] Vane's name was conspicuously absent from the committee for the propagation of the gospel, perhaps because MPs who were fundamentally opposed to prospective legislation were not supposed to sit on committees appointed to frame it.[21] His brother Charles was one of the signatories to a petition, supported by Williams, which told the committee that the assumption of 'a judgement in spirituals' by 'the civil power' was 'against

---

[20] Masson, *Milton*, IV, 295–96, 528–32, 549.
[21] D. H. Willson, *Privy Councillors in the English House of Commons* (Minneapolis, 1940).

the liberties given by Christ Jesus to his people'.[22] A protector of sectaries in general, Vane spoke up for anti-trinitarians in particular. In 1647 he came to the defence of the anti-trinitarian John Biddle, who would later translate *The Racovian Catechism* into English. In 1651 Vane defended the anti-trinitarian MP John Fry.[23]

The first eight and a half lines of the sonnet to Vane, like those of the sonnet to Cromwell and of the sonnet to Fairfax before it, salute its recipient's achievements in wartime. But the ninth line of the sonnet to Vane, unlike those of the earlier sonnets, brings no move from past to future. Milton sees no need to offer Vane counsel or warning. For Vane, unlike Cromwell, has nothing to learn. He has already 'learnt', 'which few have done', the 'bounds' of civil and religious liberty and 'What severs each'. So it is on Vane's 'firm hand' – not Cromwell's – that 'Religion leans'. It is Vane – not Cromwell – whom religion 'reckons ... her eldest son'.[24]

III

If Cromwell is on probation in May 1652 he remains there at the end of May 1654, when Milton publishes *Defensio Secunda*, his 'Second Defence on behalf of the English People'. His first *Defensio* was published in 1651. There Milton defended the act of regicide against the attacks of the classical scholar Claude de Saumaise, or Salmasius. The second *Defensio* was a continuation of that controversy. Like its predecessor it was written for a Continental audience but also for an English one. Yet it received a much less warm welcome from the government than its predecessor had done. The polemical triumphs of the first *Defensio* had been repeatedly trumpeted by the government's newsbook *Mercurius Politicus*. Though that journal did publish a modest advertisement for *Defensio Secunda*,[25] neither it nor any publication inspired by the government made any other mention of the work. The passage of the treatise which praises Cromwell is, as Woolrych says, 'a tremendous panegyric'.[26] It casts Cromwell in epic terms,[27] lauding his military exploits, his fortitude, his fitness to govern.

---

[22] *Fourth Paper*, title page; D. M. Wolfe, *Milton and the Puritan Revolution* (New York, 1941), pp. 93–96.

[23] Wolfe, *Milton*, p. 95; H. J. MacLachlan, *Socinianism in Seventeenth-Century England* (Oxford, 1951), p. 172n.; *CJ*, 31 January 1651.

[24] Cf. *CPW*, VII, 243. Some historians and critics have noticed contrasts between the two sonnets and have discerned some doubts about Cromwell in Milton's mind; but the extent and full significance of the contrasts and of the doubts have not, I think, been recognised.

[25] *Mercurius Politicus*, 8 June 1654.   [26] Woolrych, 'Milton and Cromwell', 191.

[27] Nicholas von Maltzahn, *Milton's History of Britain* (Oxford, 1991), p. 70.

Milton is as awed by Cromwell, and as admiring of him, in 1654 as in 1652. But the tribute of 1654, perhaps even more so than that of 1652, carries warnings. The sonnet told Cromwell that 'much remains' for him to accomplish: *Defensio Secunda* urges him to 'go on' to further exploits.[28] As in 1652, so in 1654, the policies Milton commends are not Cromwell's.

Milton's support for Cromwell's elevation to the protectorate in December 1653 is on the face of it surprising. Only men of 'envy', explains *Defensio Secunda*, oppose Cromwell's rule and fail to acknowledge his sovereign worth.[29] Yet among the bitter opponents of the protectorate there were friends of Milton whom he keenly respected and whose ideals of reform were much closer to his own than those favoured by the protector. In relating the events of 1653 *Defensio Secunda* passes rapidly over the two military coups of that year, that of April which removed the Rump and that of December which eliminated Barebone's Parliament.[30] At the first of them Sir Henry Vane had broken acrimoniously with Cromwell. So had Milton's hero and close friend John Bradshaw, to whom *Defensio Secunda* devotes so warm an eulogy. In the second coup, Milton implies, Barebone's had been dissolved for 'doing nothing'.[31] Yet Barebone's had provoked its fate not by inactivity but, on the contrary, by its readiness to consider radical proposals for ecclesiastical reform of a kind which Cromwell and the Rump had parried. A number of its members, even though not a majority of them,[32] wished to separate church from state and to end the compulsory maintenance of the clergy. They came close enough to those goals to convince Cromwell and his fellow army officers that the nation stood on the verge of anarchy. In the dramatic debates on church government that preceded the fall of Barebone's, Milton's sympathies can only have been with the radicals whom the dissolution drove from power, and who were thereafter subjected to derision from the protectorate's polemicists.

Cromwell's elevation did not alter Milton's views on the church. *Defensio Secunda* urges Cromwell to end the 'whoredom' between 'the ecclesiastical and the civil' powers, 'which are so totally distinct', and to abolish the 'hire' of the clergy.[33] Yet such a programme, which would have involved Cromwell in a sharp change of direction in 1652, would have involved him

[28] F. A. Patterson, ed., *The [Columbia edition of the] Works of John Milton*, 18 vols. (New York, 1931–38: hereafter *CM*), VIII, 225.

[29] Ibid., VIII, 223.

[30] Woolrych, 'Milton and Cromwell', 190. Here as elsewhere it is perhaps pertinent that Milton may have begun to compose *Defensio Secunda* in the autumn of 1653, when Barebone's was still in power: Parker, *Milton*, I, 434.

[31] *CM*, VIII, 221–23.

[32] Austin Woolrych, *Commonwealth to Protectorate* (Oxford, 1982), p. 339.

[33] *CM*, VIII, 235.

in a still sharper one in 1654. Milton may, it is true, have derived some
encouragement from those clauses of the new constitution, the Instrument
of Government, which contained its provisions for religion. The promise of
toleration that was held out in that 'saints' civil Magna Charta'[34] seems to
have persuaded many sectaries, including a number who were uneasy about
Cromwell's elevation, to offer him their continued loyalty. Further, the
Instrument looked forward to the removal of tithes 'as soon as may be',
though it did not say what would replace them. Shortly after his installation
as protector, Cromwell reportedly assured a group of disaffected army
officers that he would remove 'that ugly maintenance of tithes (for those
were his very words)' before 3 September 1654:[35] that is, as part of the
programme of legislation by ordinance which he was resolved to complete
before the parliament due to meet in September had assembled.

Yet by the time *Defensio Secunda* was published, the prospects of
ecclesiastical reform must have looked bleak. The wording of the Instrument's clauses on religion, which had evidently been drawn up in chaotic
haste, was loose and perplexing.[36] The new regime was embarrassed not
only by the confusion of the clauses but by their boldness. Accounts of the
new constitution in government newsbooks either omitted or played down
the provisions on toleration and tithes. In February, Marchamont Nedham's apologia for the protectorate, *A True State of the Case of the
Commonwealth*, declared that it was 'high time' for 'some Settlement in
Religious matters', in both 'discipline' and 'doctrine', which would end
'blasphemous Opinions and Practices'.[37] The conservative trend was
confirmed in March, when a government declaration denounced the more
aggressive forms of anticlericalism[38] and when a government ordinance
introduced the state-controlled system of Triers, of which Owen's initiative of 1652 had been the groundwork. Barebone's had repudiated Owen's
plan: Milton would attack it in 1659.[39] Amidst the radical excitement of
1653 the very existence of the established ministry had seemed in peril. So

---

[34] Worden, 'Toleration', 216.

[35] *A True Catalogue, or, An Account of the Several Places* (London, 1659: E999.12), p. 6. For other
versions of this episode see *The Protector (so called) in part Unvailed* (London, 1655), pp.
51–52; Bodleian Library, Rawlinson MS A21, fos. 324–25; Gardiner, *Commonwealth and
Protectorate*, III, 20n.

[36] S. R. Gardiner, *Constitutional Documents of the Puritan Revolution* (Oxford, 1958 repr.), p.
416; Worden, 'Toleration', 216. Milton may have derived encouragement from the
Instrument's insistence only upon a 'profession' of belief: cf. *To the Officers and Souldiers of
the Army* (London, 1657: E902.4), p. 2; *CPW*, VII, 323 ('all professing Scripture').

[37] Marchamont Nedham, *A True State of the Case of the Commonwealth* (London, 1654), pp.
40–43.

[38] W. C. Abbott, *Writings and Speeches of Oliver Cromwell*, 4 vols. (Cambridge, Mass., 1937–47),
III, 225–28.

[39] *CPW*, VII, 318.

had that of the universities, another target of Milton's disapproval. Yet the early months of the protectorate, and the signals they provided of the moderation of the new government's purposes, gave fresh heart to the ministry and the universities alike.

The religious group to benefit most obviously from Cromwell's elevation was the Presbyterians, Milton's *bête noire*. Cromwell had never been opposed to Presbyterianism, only to Presbyterian intolerance. In February 1654 he initiated a series of meetings at which Presbyterian and Independent divines were encouraged to work together to produce a 'fundamental confession' of faith.[40] In politics as in religion, Cromwell welcomed Presbyterians back into the fold. At the outset of the protectorate he repealed the Engagement of loyalty which the Rump had imposed on the nation and which so many Presbyterians had declined to take. The Instrument committed Cromwell to holding, in the summer of 1654, the first general parliamentary elections for fourteen years. Presbyterians could expect to do well in them, as in the event they did. *Defensio Secunda* reveals Milton's dread of the consequences of those elections and of a return to the factious and corrupt parliamentary politics of the later 1640s, which the Presbyterians had dominated.[41]

Now as then, Cromwell was the likeliest obstacle to that dominance. If from one perspective his conciliatory policies were undermining the radical cause, even betraying it, from another he was the sole instrument through which it might be preserved. If Cromwell alone could defy Presbyterianism, then he too could alone defy royalism. As Edward Hyde acknowledged, Cromwell's achievement in rescuing the nation from confusion in 1654 was a severe blow to the royalists, who had hoped to profit from the Puritan divisions of the previous year.[42] On the parliamentary side it was generally men of conservative stamp, not of Milton's radical persuasions, who in 1654 were ready to thank Cromwell for rescuing the nation from confusion. Yet *Defensio Secunda* comes close to that position: 'Cromwell, we are deserted; you alone remain.'[43]

If fears of Presbyterians and of royalists may help to explain Milton's decision to adhere to Cromwell in 1654, he may nonetheless have been troubled by Cromwell's elevation. He may have seen in it, and in the nation's acceptance of it, evidence that the reformation of the land might be long postponed. Alongside the triumphalism that characterises the successive celebrations of the English people in Milton's writings, there runs a doubt. In 1654 as at other times he asks whether the English will be

---

[40] Worden, 'Toleration', 217.   [41] *CM*, VIII, 245–49.
[42] Bodleian Library, Clarendon MS 48, fo. 44.   [43] *CM*, VIII, 223.

'fit' for the tasks of virtue with which God has entrusted them.[44] Both before and after the protectorate he indicated that only nations wanting in virtue elevate single rulers or submit themselves to them. In the first *Defensio* he explained that 'the same form of government is not equally fitting for all nations, or for the same nation at all times, but sometimes one, sometimes another, according as the diligence and valor of the people wax or wane'.[45] Does Cromwell's elevation show the diligence and valour of the English people to have waned? In 1649 and again in the spring of 1660 Milton animadverted on the 'madness' or 'idiocy' of peoples who permit themselves to 'depend' on the rule of a 'single person'. In 1660 he noted the 'unmanliness' of any nation which 'hangs all its felicitie' on 'one man'.[46] Yet *Defensio Secunda*, in addressing Cromwell, underlines England's dependence on 'you alone', 'the only hope of your country', to whose 'invincible virtue we all give place'.[47] In 1660, when he despairingly proposed the elevation of a single person on the Roundhead side so as to keep out the Stuarts, Milton acknowledged that that solution would be 'a befitting thraldom' and would signal the collapse of England's 'vertue'. The best that could be hoped from it was that 'we may chance', 'for the space of a raign or two', 'to live happily anough, or tolerably'.[48]

By 1660, admittedly, Milton's anxieties about the rule of a single person ran deeper than in 1654. It was the experience of the protectorate that had deepened them. Yet even in *Defensio Secunda* Milton did not propose Cromwell's supremacy as either a lasting or an ideal solution. Some radicals appear to have thought at first that the protectorate itself, or at least Cromwell's policy of concession to Presbyterian sentiment, might prove a temporary expedient, and to have 'waited, hoping better things'.[49] Perhaps Milton took a similar view. At all events his praise of regimes can never be taken as proof of unqualified admiration for them. In 1659, when he had restored his loyalty to the Rump, he applauded the members of that 'famous parlament', 'the authors and best patrons of religious and civil libertie, that ever these Ilands brought forth'. Yet the Rump, he conceded, was not 'blamelesse'.[50] As he had admitted in 1651 and would acknowledge again in 1660, its rule after the regicide was imperfect. The Rump was merely the best government that circumstances would permit.[51] Like Cromwell's, the parliament's religious programme was distant from Milton's own. In 1649–53 the Rump ruled out the separation of church from state, gave encouragement to the established ministry, left the system of tithes intact, declined to abolish the Presbyterian system, indeed came

---

[44] Cf. Nicholas von Maltzahn's remarks below, p. 268.   [45] *CM*, VII, 191–93.
[46] *CPW*, III, 542; VII, 361–62, 427.   [47] *CM*, VIII, 223–25.   [48] *CPW*, VII, 482.
[49] *The Cause of God* (London, 1659: E968.11), p. 22.
[50] *CPW*, VII, 274, 324–25.   [51] *CM*, VII, 29; *CPW*, VII, 430.

close to endorsing it. If in 1659 the restored rulers are the 'best patrons ... of libertie', in *Defensio Secunda* Cromwell is the 'patron ... of liberty'.[52] In both cases that patronage has been limited and flawed.

All the 'well-affected ... will confesse', wrote Milton of the members of the restored Rump in 1659, that 'they have deserved much more of these nations, then they have undeserved'.[53] In 1654, Cromwell, who has deserved so much, has undeserved too, not only in religion but in politics. To follow the political advice of the second *Defensio* we must look back to the first, of 1651. There, praising the 'matchless' and 'heroic deed' of regicide, he had written ostensibly for the Commonwealth regime, in reality for a party within it.[54] The Rump was divided, from its early stages, between those who had favoured the regicide and those who declined to endorse it. The latter, for the most part, had conservative motives for retaining their seats. They aimed to restrain the course of the revolution and to return power from military to civilian hands. They wanted, not to recall or celebrate the revolutionary actions which the first *Defensio* celebrates, but to dull the memory of them.

Having written for the radical cause in 1651, Milton writes for it again in 1654. His choice of title, 'A Second Defence on behalf of the English People', and his opening salvo in praise of that people, affirm a continuity not only with the first *Defensio* but with the revolutionary purpose hailed by that earlier work. Milton had written his first 'Defence on behalf of the English People' as the servant of a regime which had ruled in the name of the people of England. The protectorate dropped the language of popular sovereignty. *Defensio Secunda* preserved it. The first *Defensio* had lauded the Rump as 'the supreme council of the nation'. *Defensio Secunda* uses the same phrase of the Rump, thus reminding its readers of that legitimate exercise of sovereignty of which, in the minds of the commonwealthmen, Cromwell's coup of April 1653 has deprived it. Milton was to adopt a similar tactic in his *A Treatise of Civil Power* in February 1659 (six months before indicating that the dissolution of the Rump had been a 'scandalous ... interruption'). By dedicating that tract to parliament as the 'Supream Council', he indicated what the government would have firmly denied, that Richard Cromwell's executive was the constitutional subordinate of the Commons.[55]

Still less than the moderate party in the Rump in 1651 was the protector eager in 1654 to remind the nation of the execution of the king.

[52] *CM*, VIII, 227.   [53] *CM*, VII, 324–25.

[54] Blair Worden, 'Milton and Marchamont Nedham', in David Armitage *et al.*, eds., *Milton and Republicanism* (Cambridge, 1995), p. 164.

[55] *CM*, VII, 459; VIII, 151; *CPW*, VII, 242. (In the instances of 1654 and 1659 Milton takes advantage of an ambiguity in the word 'supreme'.)

Cromwell's whole policy of 'healing and settling' depended on the distancing of the memory of regicide. His friendship towards the Presbyterians was at the centre of that policy. Yet *Defensio Secunda* describes the Presbyterians as Cromwell's 'enemies'.[56] Who then are, or should be, his friends? Milton's answer is clear: the hard-line supporters of regicide and revolution. The second *Defensio*, like the first, commends those civilian members of the Rump who remained firm for the godly cause during that crisis. Again like the first *Defensio*, it commends still more warmly the soldiers whose heroism was proved in that hour. In 1654 Cromwell was anxious both to bring moderates into his government and to conceal its military origins. Milton warns him against both courses: 'I see not in what men we can at last rest and confide, if we are not to have confidence' in the soldiers who carried through the regicide, and we should 'not suffer ourselves to think that there are any who can preserve it with better diligence'.[57]

Those were bold words. Cromwell's elevation had caused widespread resentment and discontent in the army, especially among men who saw themselves as guardians of the 'good old cause'.[58] *Defensio Secunda* pays a glowing tribute to Milton's close friend Colonel Robert Overton,[59] who had been dismayed by Cromwell's installation as protector and who would soon join the movement of military resistance to the regime. He endured a harsh imprisonment from which he would be released only after the fall of the protectorate. John Bradshaw, whom *Defensio Secunda* praises still more fulsomely, would soon join the movement of military resistance too.[60] He had presided over the regicide court and was, in Milton's mind, the principal hero of that event.[61] If Cromwell would have been unlikely to welcome the allusions made by *Defensio Secunda* to the events of 1649, he would have found still less cause for pleasure in its thinly veiled allusions to his conduct in 1653, which had antagonised republicans and commonwealthmen. Cromwell, Milton warns him, must not 'forcibly seize upon the liberty of others', must not 'offer violence' to the 'liberty' won by the regicide or 'suffer' it 'to be violated by yourself'.[62]

Panegyric can be a two-edged instrument. The panegyrist, celebrating an ideal, is uniquely positioned to register departures from it. The

---

[56] *CM*, VIII, 207.
[57] Worden, 'Milton and Marchamont Nedham', p. 165; *CM*, VIII, 231–35.
[58] Barbara Taft, '*The Humble Petition of Several Colonels of the Army.* Causes, Character, and Results of Military Opposition to Cromwell's Protectorate', *Huntington Library Quarterly*, 42 (1978).
[59] *CM*, VIII, 233–35; Worden, 'Milton and Marchamont Nedham', p. 178.
[60] Taft, '*Humble Petition*', 20, 36–38.
[61] Worden, 'Milton and Marchamont Nedham', 161–63.   [62] *CM*, VIII, 227.

protector showed no appetite for panegyric. His government knew how easily a cult of personality might rebound. A week before *Defensio Secunda* praised Cromwell as 'our Camillus', there had been published an attack on him as England's Julius Caesar, the tyrant who had usurped Rome's liberties.[63] The propaganda sponsored by the regime concentrated mainly on the office, not the person, of the protector. The nearest the government came to an official definition of its aims and character, Nedham's *A True State* published in February 1654, emphasised the checks and balances through which the new constitution, the Instrument of Government, would curb the protector's power.[64] Though Nedham and others in government circles were keen, in the initial stages of the protectorate, to dwell on Cromwell's virtues and his fitness to rule,[65] and although an appetite for hero-worship of him occasionally surfaces in the press during the first half of 1654, such sentiments were generally shunned.[66] *A True State* barely refers to Cromwell and never mentions his name.

Milton's publication, by contrast, does not mention the Instrument. It does allude to some of its provisions, but only fleetingly and vaguely. Cromwell's claim to eminence, as Milton describes it, is not constitutional. It is purely personal. Constitutional formulae, in Milton's account, exist at that level of 'expedience' to which greatness of spirit is obliged to descend but which cannot measure or bound it. Cromwell rules by virtue of the Aristotelian principle of distributive justice, which awards power proportionately to merit. As a man of supreme worth he is entitled to supreme power.[67] Yet both before and after the protectorate Milton deployed Aristotle's principle to an opposite end. At those times he detected an equality of merit among the nation's Puritan leaders, and called for, or vindicated, the sharing of power among them.[68] He did concede, in the first *Defensio*, that monarchy may be the appropriate form of government 'if the monarch be very excellent and best deserve to reign'. Yet 'without such supposition, no other form of government so easily slips into the worst sort of tyranny'.[69] In 1654 there were friends of Milton to whom Cromwell seemed the worst sort of tyrant.

To Milton the Puritan Revolution was a decisive stage in the divine scheme of history. In the events of 1641 he had detected the prelude to the

[63] Ibid., VIII, 211; *A Politick Commentary on the Life of Caius Julius Caesar* (London, 1654: E735.17); cf. G. K. Fortescue, *Catalogue of the Thomason Tracts*, 2 vols. (London, 1908), II, 66.

[64] Woolrych, 'Milton and Cromwell', 192.

[65] Longleat House, Whitelocke MS. xv, fo. 1; British Library, Additional MS. 32093, fo. 317.

[66] Cf. Gardiner, *Commonwealth and Protectorate*, III, 14.

[67] *CM*, VIII, 223–25.   [68] Ibid., VII, 127 (cf. 379); *CPW*, VII, 364.

[69] *CM*, VII, 279 (with which cf. *CPW*, V, 366).

deliverance of the world from spiritual and political tyranny, perhaps to
the reversal of the Fall. Since that time, hope had mingled or alternated
with despair. By 1654 the whole destiny of the cause had come, in Milton's
judgement, to rest on Cromwell's combat with adversity and temptation.
Temptation, the great theme of Milton's greatest poems, was a force which
even a persistent admirer and close observer of the protector saw at work
in him.[70] The Cromwell portrayed in *Defensio Secunda* confronts the
temptation of personal aggrandisement,[71] the very temptation to which his
enemies during the protectorate believed him to have succumbed. *Defensio
Secunda* dwells on that 'heaviest burden' of responsibility which Cromwell
carries. The burden is the measure of the man's greatness, but also of his
vulnerability. His response to it, Milton tells Cromwell,

> will show what is the predominant disposition of your nature, what is your
> strength, what is your weight; whether there is indeed in you that living
> piety, that faith, justice, and moderation of mind, for which we have thought
> that you above all others deserved, by the will of God, to be elevated to this
> sovereign dignity.[72]

By 1659 the answers to those questions would be grimly clear.

IV

There is room for a sceptical explanation of Milton's conduct in 1654. He
has it both ways, advertising his support and admiration for the ruler
whose government has retained his services, while signalling his continuing radical credentials to his radical friends. Only in 1659, when
Cromwell was safely dead and his regime had fallen, did Milton declare
openly against his rule. Can he have then responded without discomfort to
the dry remark to him of the commonwealthman Moses Wall, who
recalled wondering whether the poet's 'Relation to the Court' had dimmed
his ideals?[73]

Scepticism could explain only so much. In May 1654 even Robert
Overton, though dismayed by the protectorate, had yet to turn against it.
He retained his command and, around the time when *Defensio Secunda* was
published, promised Cromwell to let him know 'when I could serve him
no longer; adding, that when I perceived his lordship did only design the
setting up of himself, and not the good of those nations, I could not set one
foot before another to serve him'.[74] *Defensio Secunda*, though posing no
threat of opposition on its author's part, does indicate, in a spirit perhaps

---

[70] Thomas Birch, ed., *Thurloe State Papers*, 7 vols. (London, 1742), I, 766.
[71] *CM*, VIII, 223–25.   [72] Ibid., VIII, 227–29.   [73] *CPW*, VII, 510.
[74] Birch, *Thurloe State Papers*, III, 110.

close to that of Overton's statement, the conditional nature of Milton's commitment. A week after its publication there appeared a pamphlet in praise of Cromwell by John Price, the ally of the radical minister John Goodwin, whose own decision to support Cromwell's elevation gave the new regime a propaganda coup.[75] Yet Goodwin indicated that his support was tentative.[76] Price, more subtly, registered his own anxieties. His tract, which is often close to *Defensio Secunda* in sentiment, draws a series of distinctions between a protectorate and a tyranny. The dividing line between those two forms of rule is explained in terms which at once vindicate Cromwell and warn him to remember it.[77]

When did Milton's hopes of Cromwell end? Not many of them are likely to have survived September 1654, when the protector forcibly expelled the commonwealthmen from parliament, declared his resolve to suppress heresies and blasphemies, and publicly scorned critics of the established ministry.[78] Within months Overton was in gaol. Milton did remain at his post. He continued to produce state papers at the government's behest.[79] Yet, as the behaviour of Milton's friend Marchamont Nedham illustrates, service of the protectorate was no guarantee of enthusiasm for it.[80] The likelihood of enthusiasm on Milton's part faded as the failures of the protectorate became more transparent. *Defensio Secunda* urged Cromwell to end the censorship of the press, but in 1655 the protector reinforced it.[81] *Defensio Secunda* warned him to 'shun the pomp of wealth and of power',[82] but the monarchical trappings of the regime, which had already caused some offence in radical circles by the time Milton wrote,[83] would arouse much more, especially after Cromwell's reinstallation as protector under the Humble Petition and Advice in 1657. In welcoming that constitution Cromwell implicitly accepted the principle, alien to Milton's sympathies,[84] of hereditary rule. There was one respect, admittedly, in which Cromwell made progress of a kind recommended in *Defensio Secunda*: the reform of the law.[85] The protector gave strenuous and well-publicised support to initiatives for law reform and steered through the reform of Chancery. Yet the issue does not seem to

---

[75] Ibid., II, 164; *Mercurius Politicus* 23 February 1654.

[76] John Goodwin, *Peace Protected* (London, 1654: E732.27).

[77] John Price, *Tyrants and Protectors set forth in their Colours* (London, 1654: E738.18).

[78] *CPW*, VII, 32; Abbott, *Writings and Speeches*, III, 436.

[79] For his public service see Fallon, *Milton in Government*.

[80] Blair Worden, 'Marchamont Nedham and the beginnings of English Republicanism', in David Wootton, ed., *Republicanism, Liberty, and Commercial Society 1649–1776* (Stanford, 1994), 74–81.

[81] Woolrych, 'Milton and Cromwell', 195.   [82] *CM*, VIII, 229.

[83] Taft, '*Humble Petition*', 16.   [84] Woolrych, 'Milton and Cromwell', 186.

[85] *CM*, VIII, 237.

have been high among Milton's priorities;[86] the reforms, the drafting of which Cromwell confined to lawyers,[87] were probably less far-reaching than Milton would have liked; and by 1656, in any case, the regime's commitment to significant legal reform was effectively dead. So was any chance of fundamental ecclesiastical reform or of an extension of religious toleration.

Milton's distress at the developments of the protectorate is visible in a substantial piece of writing which he seems to have composed in or from 1655.[88] This was the completion of his manuscript work on pre-Norman history, the 'History of Britain', the first part of which had been written in 1649. The new material offers unmistakable parallels to the present. Its opening passage relates the disappointment of the hopes raised by the elevation of King Egbert, when 'the best part' of 'this island' was 'reduc't ... under the power of one man; and him one of the worthiest'.[89] Subsequent passages correspond to attacks made by commonwealthmen on the protectorate. Milton meditates on the baneful influence of 'Court-Parasites' and 'Court Flatterers'. He reflects on the evil consequences of 'ambition', the characteristic to which, together with hypocrisy and dissimulation, Cromwell's enemies had generally come to attribute his conduct. Milton observes the 'fond conceit in many great ones, and pernicious in the end, to cease from no violence till they have attain'd the utmost of their ambitions and desires'.[90] His remarks on ambition look forward to 1659–60, when he aimed a series of hits at the 'close' or 'secret' 'ambition' of Cromwell and his fellow officers, whose 'hypocritical pretences' had brought them to power and kept them there.[91]

Once the protectorate had fallen, open attacks on the dead protector became frequent. Earlier, critics of the regime who wished to avoid confrontation with it had indicated their discontent between the lines of their prose.[92] No one deployed interlinear criticism more dextrously than Milton's friend Marchamont Nedham, his regular visitor during the protectorate. In 1656 Nedham republished propaganda which he had written for the Rump in 1651–52, when, like Milton, he had spoken for the radical party in parliament and army. Material which had then been aimed at the tyrant Charles I would now have read as a criticism of the tyrant Cromwell, the usurper of that authority which the Rump had rightly

---

[86] *CPW*, vii, 332.   [87] Longleat, Whitelocke MS. xv, fo. 117.

[88] Von Maltzahn, *Milton's History of Britain*, pp. 168–76.

[89] *CPW*, v, 257; H. R. Trevor-Roper, *Catholics, Anglicans, and Puritans* (London, 1987), p. 272.

[90] *CPW*, v, 365, 366, 394.   [91] Ibid., vii, 120, 328–9, 337, 365, 380, 458.

[92] Blair Worden, 'Harrington's "Oceana": Origins and Aftermath, 1651–1660', in Wootton, *Republicanism*, 113–26.

claimed from the king.[93] In 1658 Milton republished a work which *he* had written in 1651 for the Rump and the radical party, the first *Defensio*.[94] Passages of that work which had been aimed at Charles I would now have read as comparisons between Cromwell and the usurpers who had ended the Roman republic, or as invitations to the English to exercise their right to depose their new ruler.[95] It was in 1658, too, that Milton brought into print another treatise which attacked the protectorate through oblique means. This was a manuscript collection of maxims which he (erroneously) ascribed to Sir Walter Raleigh and which he published as *The Cabinet-Council*. In a remarkable essay Martin Dzelzainis has shown the publication to have been an exercise aimed by Milton at Cromwell's Machiavellian statecraft.[96]

So while Milton would not, before 1659, have publicly described the protectorate as a 'scandalous night of interruption', the dislike he voiced against the regime in that year was not new. It seems to have been in or around 1657 that Milton, who had suspended his major poetic ambitions for nearly two decades, returned to them and began to compose *Paradise Lost*. Critics have often discerned reflections of Cromwell in Milton's Satan. Does Satan's invocation of 'necessity, the tyrant's plea' point to Cromwell, who held that 'providence and necessity' had justified the regicide and, in turn, his own elevation? We should no doubt hesitate to explain too much in Milton's masterpiece in strictly analogical terms or in local political ones. Yet if we ask what made the Fall so compelling a subject for Milton, may not a part of the answer lie in the fall of the Puritan Revolution and in the failure, at Cromwell's hands, of the momentous destiny which the poet had expected for it? The English people, in submitting to the great dissimulator Cromwell, have been fatally beguiled, as are Adam and Eve in submitting to Satan. Perhaps Milton has been beguiled too. At all events, by 1657 his role as the monitor of the Puritan Revolution seems to have failed and to be over.

If the outcome of the revolution is the tragedy of the nation and of the poet, is it not also, when viewed from another angle, the tragedy of the figure whom, in *Defensio Secunda*, Milton portrayed in epic terms? The test of Adam, as Milton had explained in *Areopagitica*, was the 'triall' of his 'vertue', and 'triall is by what is contrary'.[97] *Defensio Secunda*, where

---

[93] Worden, 'Marchamont Nedham and the beginnings of English Republicanism', 74–81.

[94] Martin Dzelzainis, 'Milton and the Protectorate in 1658', in Armitage, *Milton and Republicanism*.

[95] *CM*, VII, 47–49, 107–9, 265, 315, 321, 337, 359, 363. Cf. Dzelzainis, 'Milton and the Protectorate', 205; Dzelzainis, 'Juvenal, Charles X Gustavus, and Milton's Letter to Richard Jones'.

[96] Dzelzainis, 'Milton and the Protectorate'.   [97] *CPW*, II, 515.

Cromwell confronts so much that is contrary, explains to him that the challenge before him will 'try you thoroughly', and that failure would be 'destructive and deadly ... to the very cause of all virtue'. The Puritan cause, like the fate of mankind in Paradise, is won and lost in a single spiritual struggle: in Cromwell's case, amidst pressures which, as Milton tells him, 'will search you through and through, and lay open your inmost soul'.[98]

[98] *CM*, VIII, 227.

From pillar to post: Milton and the attack on republican humanism at the Restoration

NICHOLAS VON MALTZAHN

Austin Woolrych's introduction to volume VII of the *Complete Prose Works of John Milton* provided an exemplary contribution to Milton studies.[1] By describing the historical context in which Milton wrote at the Restoration, Woolrych gave signal assistance to literary scholars working on the writings, published and unpublished, in which Milton responded to the turbulent events of 1658–60. Subsequent scholarship has been much in his debt. The present argument returns to Milton in this connection, and especially to responses in 1660 to Milton's pamphleteering. The emphasis here will be not on Milton's achievement but on the tactics his three main opponents chose in writing against him in March–April 1660. Their varied responses to the republicanism especially of *The Readie and Easie Way* (1660) were often couched as attacks not just on Milton's politics, but also on the very idiom in which Milton had proposed political change. His republican invocation of Ciceronian ideals of public service could be made to appear outmoded by pamphlets that instead dramatised arguments from interest, the political currency of an increasingly commercial society. In particular, the rhetorical splendour of Milton's prose made him vulnerable to the coffee-house style of his antagonists. The imperious claim to objectivity in Milton's grand style might be brought low by their studied assumption that he wrote for personal advantage, and their sharp questioning of his prescriptions for the public good. The aggressive subjectivity of such pamphleteering, especially in the hands of Roger L'Estrange and Samuel Butler, may be read as anti-humanist as well as anti-republican. Those writers deploy humanism against itself, a versatility in polemic that will here be compared with the oratorical ambitions of the third opponent, George Starkey, who sought with a style more in keeping with 'Ciceronian'

---

[1] *Complete Prose Works of John Milton* [hereafter *CPW*], gen. ed. D. Wolfe, 8 vols. (New Haven, 1953–82), VII, 1–228.

rhetoric to vanquish his republican opponent and to celebrate his own service as a royal subject.

I

The historical and biographical circumstances of Milton's writing *The Readie and Easie Way* have often been rehearsed: Masson's compelling account was successively supplemented in a number of useful studies, and then most notably superseded in Woolrych's magisterial survey.[2] I shall not, in Monck's words, 'now trouble you with large Narratives',[3] whether of Monck's arrival in London in early February 1660, or of his ending the political impasse worsened by the diminished authority of the remnant of the Rump, or of the return of the secluded Members and the attendant celebrations in London on 21 February, probably the same day that Milton hastened to finish a first version of *The Readie and Easie Way*. It may be recalled that Milton needed to refinish that work before its publication: he had now to acknowledge the recent re-admission of the secluded Members, the Presbyterians who were ready to assert their recovered franchise in favour of some royal settlement. But except for some revealing prefatory comment, Milton did not acknowledge the fuller political import of this development.

Thus the delay in the appearance of *The Readie and Easie Way*, for at least a week after its first composition and perhaps as late as the first days of March, further exposed Milton to the anti-republican resentments of monarchists who sensed that their time had again come.[4] Against impending change, only independents such as Milton were proclaiming the extremes to which a cavalier parliament might go in seeking to reconstruct the old regime. That his suspicions sharpened his advocacy of a republican settlement, and lent a hortatory note to his publications, has too often been mistaken either for some inability on Milton's part to read the drift of contemporary events or for a final heroic stand against the public tide. On the latter point, it was Masson who did most to shape the romantic

---

[2] Don M. Wolfe, *Milton in the Puritan Revolution* (London, 1941), pp. 288–310; Arthur E. Barker, *Milton and the Puritan Dilemma* (Toronto, 1942), pp. 260–90; Godfrey Davies, 'Milton in 1660', *Huntington Library Quarterly* 18 (1955), 351–63; Barbara Lewalski, 'Milton: political beliefs and polemical methods, 1659–60', *Publications of the Modern Language Association* 74 (1959), 191–202; W. R. Parker, *Milton: A Biography*, 2 vols. (Oxford, 1968), pp. 518–82, 1067–94.

[3] *The Lord General Monk his speech delivered by him in parliament on Munday, Feb. 6. 1659* (London, 1660), p. 1.

[4] *The Readie and Easie Way* appeared in the last days of February or first days of March, 1659/60 (*CPW*, vii, 343–45); the errata for the first edition are published in *Mercurius Politicus*, No. 610 (1–8 March 1660).

construction of Milton's career on the eve of the Restoration.[5] If Milton wrote for a losing cause, however, there is much to suggest that he did not view a losing cause as a lost one. 'It was received by many with Applause', a contemporary could claim of *The Readie and Easie Way*, 'and stumbled severall whom it could not seduce, if not to reject, yet to suspect and be jealous of Monarchy, or at least to lay aside your Majesty, as an unsafe person, and set up another'.[6] Even if we do not take this polemicist quite at his word – as Woolrych observed, this author has reasons to dignify Milton even as he impugns him[7] – his claim indicates that Milton's strictures carried weight among moderates, and that hindsight has too much obscured the effectiveness of this publication. Moreover, if the growing chorus in favour of a 'free parliament' soon became bolder in its appeal for the king, the constitutional settlement that might emerge was by no means clear, and the terms of reconciliation had yet to be established. Milton's warnings against the abuses of royal power might still be heeded in some part, since the contending parties had much to decide about what limitations should be imposed on the Crown.[8] Only with the second edition of *The Readie and Easie Way*, a fugitive duodecimo from which the bookseller and printer removed their names, had Milton entirely lost his audience.[9]

Woolrych has shown how the first edition of *The Readie and Easie Way* is not just a constitutionalist tilt at political windmills, but one of the many efforts to secure commitments from politicians, and Monck in particular, in February 1660. Woolrych does much to address the underlying quest for stability that is characteristic of so many political proposals from this period, whether in the republican vision of a changeless balance or in a monarchist affection for the historical restoration of feudal tenures, or in the appeals from various perspectives to the wisdom of the ancient constitution. The title of Milton's tract immediately places it in a tradition emphasising stability among the ready benefits of truly republican rule;

---

[5] 'There is no grander exhibition of dying resistance, of solitary and useless fighting for a lost cause, than in his conduct through April 1660. Alone he then stood ...' David Masson, *The Life of Milton*, 7 vols. (London, 1881–94), v, 674, 643–703.

[6] G. S., *The Dignity of Kingship Asserted* (London, 1660), sig. a2v.   [7] *CPW*, vii, 200–1.

[8] N. von Maltzahn, 'Republication in the Restoration: some trimming pleas for limited monarchy, 1660/1680', *Huntington Library Quarterly*, 56 (1993), 281–91.

[9] It may be said with the imprint that this was indeed a work 'Printed for the Author', since the publication of the much-revised second edition of *The Readie and Easie Way* seems to have been much less bold than its composition. It has no known printer or bookseller (Milton's recent bookseller, Livewell Chapman, having now been cited for arrest, had had to disappear); Milton's contemporaries make no note of it; and even his friend Thomason does not have a copy in his collection. It remains an unusually rare tract (Parker, *Milton*, 1074, 1212). The work may have appeared later in April than has been supposed (even after Milton's *Brief Notes*). Evert M. Clark, ed. *The Readie and Easie Way* (New Haven, 1915), pp. xiv–xvii (cf. *CPW*, vii, 399–400, 408).

Milton's title was designed to comment on James Harrington's recent *The wayes and meanes whereby an equal & lasting commonwealth may be suddenly introduced and perfectly founded with the free consent and actual confirmation of the whole people of England* (c. 6–8 February), with 'readie and easie' improving on Harrington's mysterious 'suddenly'. The ecclesiastical dangers to be feared in compromises with any new regime made such political proposals all the more urgent.

But the crises of 1659–60 also forced a more open expression of long-standing doubts on Milton's part about the English. His earlier pessimism about his countrymen may be glimpsed behind the rhetoric of *Eikonoklastes* and the *Defensio*, and is writ large in the two editions of *The Tenure of Kings and Magistrates*, in his *History of Britain*, in the conversations recorded by Hermann Mylius, and in the stern injunction to his compatriots in the conclusion to *Defensio secunda*. How civic duties should be fulfilled with Ciceronian fortitude had long been Milton's concern;[10] his awareness that they were not being thus fulfilled in England finds plainer expression on the eve of the Restoration. Milton obviously distrusts his countrymen in his constitutional proposals of 1659–60, especially in his desire 'that the Grand or General Councel being well chosen, should sit perpetual', and that its members should not be exposed to 'the noise and shouting of a rude multitude', or any popular voice that might make of the state 'a licentious and unbridl'd democratie'.[11]

The Readie and Easie Way stands out among contemporary pamphlets for what students of Milton's poetry might with Christopher Ricks call its 'grand style'.[12] But what was the relation of such eloquence to virtue? Milton could be suspicious of eloquence, but his impulse was often less cautious, or more exalting of what true eloquence might be.[13] In earlier controversy, he had allowed that he was not 'utterly untrain'd in those rules which best Rhetoricians have giv'n, or unacquainted with those examples which the prime authors of eloquence have written in any learned tongue'. More truly, however, eloquence was 'none, but the serious and hearty love of truth':

> And whose mind so ever is fully possest with a fervent desire to know good
> things, and with the dearest charity to infuse the knowledge of them into

---

[10] Martin Dzelzainis, 'Milton's classical republicanism', in *Milton and Republicanism*, ed. D. Armitage, A. Himy and Q. Skinner (Cambridge, 1995), 10–15.

[11] *CPW*, vii, 369 (433), 442, 438. See also his hopes elsewhere 'that they and all henceforth to be chosen into the parlament do retain their places during life', and that 'we shall have little cause to fear the perpetuity of our general Senat' (*CPW*, vii, 336, 394).

[12] Christopher Ricks, *Milton's Grand Style* (Oxford, 1963).

[13] Nicholas von Maltzahn, *Milton's History of Britain: Republican Historiography in the English Revolution* (Oxford, 1991), pp. 65–69.

others, when such a man would speak, his word (by what I can expresse) like so many nimble and airy servitors trip about him at command, and in well order'd files, as he would wish, fall aptly into their own places.[14]

Again Woolrych has supplied an appropriate comment: 'It is no derogation to say that he was a rhetorician rather than a political philosopher, for rhetoric can be a worthy servant of great causes, and Milton's at its best is supremely noble.'[15] But 'noble' in what sense? The contest has sometimes seemed unequal between the blunt violence of royalist satire at the Restoration and the highly wrought subtleties of Milton's prose. Against the crudity of the former, Miltonists and long tradition have much extolled the latter, a preference often strengthened by admiration for the perceived nobility of Milton's person and by sympathy for his difficult position on the eve of the Restoration. Milton, who in Macaulay's words ever 'pressed into the forlorn hope', was now beset by antagonists, of whom the most vociferous was that bitter pamphleteer Roger L'Estrange, whose attack Macaulay would revile as 'coarse, and disfigured by a mean and flippant jargon'.[16] The cruelty of the Restoration verdict has gained Milton still further defenders. How with this rage should beauty hold a plea?

But the beauty of Milton's rhetoric had coercive designs of its own, in keeping with humanist tradition, especially in 'its ideal of the *vir civilis* and hence the theory of citizenship associated with the classical art of eloquence'.[17] Requiring disciplined self-knowledge, such republican humanism resented the claims of interest, and asked for citizens who were 'men more then vulgar, bred up ... in the knowledge of Antient and illustrious deeds, invincible against money, and vaine titles, impartial to friendships and relations'.[18] Critics seized on the discrepancies between this exalted ideal and the conduct of republicans. The stylistic exaggerations of a Harrington or Milton thus came into discredit, as anti-republican writers sought ways to disarm humanist rhetoric in its service to classical republicanism, the political dimension of what Milton styled 'true eloquence'. For Milton in every sphere the establishment of ethos is central to his civic and religious commitments and to the obligation of others to like responsibilities. His presentations of the excellence of his own character are a recurring feature of his work in prose and poetry, in which he follows

---

[14] *CPW*, I, 949.

[15] 'Political theory and political practice', in *The Age of Milton*, ed. C. A. Patrides and Raymond B. Waddington (Manchester, 1980), p. 65.

[16] Macaulay, *Literary Essays from the Edinburgh Review* (London, 1932), p. 48; *History of England*, ed. C. Firth, 6 vols. (London, 1913–15), I, 382.

[17] Quentin Skinner, *Reason and Rhetoric in the Philosophy of Hobbes* (Cambridge, 1996), pp. 257, 284–93.

[18] *CPW*, v, 451; von Maltzahn, *Milton's History*, p. 191.

humanist advice in fostering such means of persuasion.[19] His vulnerability
to the anti-humanist critique has long been noted with reference to
Hobbes's gibe against Milton and Salmasius.[20] For Hobbes, Quentin
Skinner has observed, 'the establishment of ethos is an irrelevance', even in
the moral sciences.[21] In demonstrating the anti-humanist turn in Hobbes's
career after the mid-1630s, Skinner has shown that his suspicions of
humanism are couched first in the scientific inheritance of reductive anti-
humanism, but then in a further polemical strategy, which pits humanism
against itself. The potential for abuse of argument *in utramque partem*
sharpens Hobbes' hostility to rhetoric, and he therefore adapts humanist
methods of expressing scorn to discredit humanist eloquence itself.[22] What
Hobbes was presenting in terms of more fully reasoned arguments, many
of his contemporaries, driven by present polemical opportunity, were
attempting in a more *ad hoc* way. In the spring of 1660, Milton the
pamphleteer encounters some debate but more mockery, and the mockery
was sharply reactive against the rhetorical sophistication as well as the
political burden of *The Readie and Easie Way*.

II

It was against political solutions that would limit monarchy too much that
a succession of monarchist writers directed their polemics in the late
winter and spring of 1660. Perhaps the most *ad hominem* of the responses to
Milton's republican position appear in the frequent and vehement contributions to the press of Roger L'Estrange.[23] He intermittently seizes on
Milton as a peculiarly vulnerable defender of the Good Old Cause, and
vulnerable because not sufficiently adaptable to present political debate.
And yet an overview of L'Estrange's responses shows that the rebuttal of
arguments by the Good-Old-Cause men was not his chief objective. The
gathered pamphlets that L'Estrange publishes as *L'Estrange His Apology*
(London, 1660) do include a number of the sallies against the 'Commonwealthmen', but his larger agenda had only begun to emerge. Milton
provided a stalking-horse as L'Estrange approached his real target, the
compromised Presbyterians. Winning over the Presbyterians was of course
necessary for the Restoration, and with each pamphlet by Milton,

---

[19] Skinner, *Reason and Rhetoric*, pp. 128–33.

[20] See now especially Dzelzainis, 'Milton's classical republicanism', 3–7; Hobbes, [*Behemoth
       or*] *the History of the Civil Wars of England* (London, 1679), pp. 229–30.

[21] Skinner, *Reason and Rhetoric*, p. 258.   [22] Ibid., pp. 256–89.

[23] On this subject I am much indebted to discussions with Dorothy Turner and to her study
       of 'Roger L'Estrange and the print culture of the Restoration' (University of Ottawa PhD
       dissertation, 1996).

L'Estrange could further impugn the independent and republican politics from which Presbyterians might at first be excused. After the Restoration, having earlier sharpened this distinction between Presbyterian and independent, L'Estrange soon turns to blurring the lines between Presbyterian, resistance theorist, republican, and sectarian, even as he urges their collective exclusion from the government of state and church alike. As Marchamont Needham would put it, in impersonating such a duplicitous cavalier, 'Hug them you cannot hang, at least until you can.'[24]

The core of L'Estrange's political argument is that republicanism is finally about personal power and individual interest, whatever its misleading claims about the public good. His was the common royalist claim that republicanism encouraged the interminable turmoil of popular faction and competing interests, with no recourse available to the overarching sovereignty of the crown. The republican dishonesty in response to such disorder exasperated royalists. In part, their anger followed from present political opportunity: L'Estrange's first response to Milton, his anonymous *Be Merry and Wise*, is quick to spot the last-minute additions to *The Readie and Easie Way*, and he fulminates against such republican efforts to control the fluid political situation.[25] Recalling the re-emergence of 'the Good-Old-Cause men' the previous December, and their reluctance to re-admit the secluded members to the parliament under their control, L'Estrange scorns their attempt narrowly to qualify the electorate, and recalls the longer pedigree of the beneficiaries of the Purge: 'We do remember, who they were who ruled in 48 and we are sensible, what they would do still, if they had Power.'[26] But this was just an example of the permanent crisis that republicanism, in royalist eyes, must induce in a nation denied the better permanence of the crown and ancient constitution.

Where Milton saw his contemporaries as blinded by a mistaken conception of their interest, L'Estrange, with a sharper imputation also against Milton's disability, claimed that the blindness lay another way, in the republicans' inability to recognise the degree to which the pressure of events made a mockery of their rhetoric of stability and balance. Milton's concessions to the changing political situation responded to just the element of contingency that his political proposals were intended to master, or deny. The difficulty went to the heart of Milton's later republicanism, in which he was led to propose a static polity in which a stabilised central government controls a confederation of local subgovern-

---

[24] *Newes from Brussels* (London, 1660), p. 4.

[25] Both title page and Thomason give the date as 13 March 1659/60. The tract is later claimed by L'Estrange as his own in *L'Estrange His Apology* (London, 1660), pp. 78–86, and its presentation is visibly in his style.

[26] L'Estrange, *Be Merry and Wise*, pp. 1, 4, 6.

ments, as in a classical hegemony, with the state made especially unresponsive to the shifting political will of the wider population. Monck had already made the move that Milton sought to forestall ('I could only wish his Excellency had been a little civiller to Mr. Milton'). Where Milton, with the return of the secluded members, proposed a perpetual 'Grand, or generall Counsell' governing a populace free of 'that fond Opinion of successive Parliaments', L'Estrange simply answers that elections are now imminent for a 'full and free' parliament.[27]

Owing to the rigidities of Milton's system, and the pessimism about his countrymen that these reflect, his quest for settlement was now vulnerable to the claims for liberty that he himself made elsewhere in *The Readie and Easie Way*, and would seek further to recover for his purposes in the second edition of that tract. L'Estrange, in keeping with the populism of his own work that winter and spring, dwells on the limitation of the franchise by Milton and other proponents of the politics of seclusion: 'One Man of Forty shall be allowed to Vote, or sit, and the other 39 must call That a Free-Parliament, and swear, it Represents the People.'[28] Ever skilful in quoting his adversaries to their disadvantage, L'Estrange appropriates Milton's terms to deride Milton's cause. In seeking stability, Milton had gone too far. But the search for stability animated many tracts, republican and royalist, that appeared in these revolutionary months. Republican claims for 'free states' had long been founded in the supposed merits of these systems in preserving themselves against corruption. It is these claims to stability that royalist writers questioned, rejecting the possibility of integrating conflict into the status quo, and instead seeing only the turbulence of faction where republicans proposed a stabilising competition.

Milton's republican proposals still speak an uncompromising language of liberty, sterner in prescribing the obligations of discipline, and cold to personal advantage. To write of the public interest as if it were just a sum of private interests is foreign to Milton's Stoic rhetoric, which is addressed still to a governing body deemed capable of implementing political reform without reference to popular demands. It has been observed that Milton himself sought to adapt his work to the emerging terms of political discussion, and that in 1660 he 'employs arguments from interest, not typical of Milton's writings'.[29] But the adaptation did not reach very far, and it is Milton's suspicions of trade that rightly have been seen as more characteristic of his republicanism. As claim and counter-claim are made in 1659–60, the language of interest is everywhere. Public interest

---

[27] Ibid., p. 6.   [28] Ibid., p. 6.
[29] Joad Raymond, 'The Cracking of the Republican Spokes', *Prose Studies*, 19 (1996), 262.

continues to be honoured in comparison with private 'vile and ugly interest and ends', but in contrast to the exalted conceptions of a Milton or Sir Henry Vane, it is increasingly conceived of as economic health. Some commercial renewal was widely sought as a means of repairing 'Trade being dead and decayed'.[30] More visible and personal declarations of interest, and the evolving commonplace that *Interest will not lie* (to cite the title of Marchamont Nedham's tract of 1659), made plain the indifference to such considerations of Milton's humanist rhetoric. Moreover, the acts of writing and more especially publishing might themselves increasingly be seen as an expression of private interest, a possibility often spoken to in seventeenth-century English publications, but which now became a special source of concern.

The voice of *The Readie and Easie Way* seeks to propose a coherent solution to the political complexities that many other voices were addressing at the same time, but to do so in terms that failed to admit to particular private interest. This omission Milton's antagonists were quick to make good by allying his claims to those of others who had benefited from the interregnum regimes. Milton's stance of disinterest stands out amid the competing strategies for self-presentation at the time: his magisterial prose implies a comprehensive recognition of the political situation and its consequences, and the aspiration to control competing interests rather than to compete among them. In answer to such rhetorical claims, hostile writers (of any stripe) could represent such political proposals as having a quality of fantasy, which the impoverished nation was unlikely to indulge.[31] Ambition and fantasy were thought to be closely linked – we may recall the example of *Macbeth* – and so the excesses of personal interest and the extravagance of imagined schemes could be condemned together.

Thus L'Estrange's colloquial and disparaging voice in *Be Merry and Wise* conveys a message too. This joco-serious mode was one that he made his own in the winter–spring of 1660 (and again in the Restoration crisis of 1679–83), with his hortatory emphases underscored by the printers' use of different fonts to make his works still more vivid. The scope for the joco-serious in journalism had been explored by Nedham and others in the partisan publications of the 1640s and since. In a way that Nedham's

---

[30] *CPW*, VII, 105; *Englands Monarchy Asserted* (London, 1660), p. 2; *No Droll, but a Rational Account* (London, 1660), p. 6; *A Short Discourse upon the Desires of a Friend* (London, 1660), p. 9; *A Declaration of the Parliament assembled at Westminster* (London, 23 January 1660), pp. 5, 7–9. Nedham's tract responded to John Fell's royalist *The Interest of England Stated* (London, 1659).

[31] E.g. *A Short Discourse upon the Desires of a Friend*, p. 10; *England's Monarchy Asserted*, p. 1; N. D. Gent, *A Letter Intercepted Printed* (London, 1660), p. 1.

extraordinary career may be thought to dramatise, an evolving 'coffee-house' style increasingly acknowledged competing interests debated in a public sphere broader than the forum that Milton prefers, that parliament, 'Areopagus', or senate he variously addresses in his tracts, where his humanist counsel might sway senators on matters of public interest. The strength of L'Estrange's work remains its insistent identification of public forms of address with private motivations, in a way calculated to diminish the authority of Milton's less obviously personal voice. When 'men are grown so wise in this Coffee Age',[32] the political writer has to entertain them as much as educate them. Against Milton's 'Pedantique, and Envenom'd scorn', too 'Peremptory, and Magisterial', a more supple and spoken style proves to be the answer.[33]

It is to another royalist writer against Milton that we should turn for a fuller expression of the ridicule that was humanism's great weapon against itself, that friend of Hobbes and remarkable satirist, the poet Samuel Butler.[34] How many pamphlets Butler contributed to the press in the spring of 1660 remains unclear. The recent re-attribution to him of several pamphlets indicates that there may well be other works that went to press that are likewise not included in his *Genuine Remains*.[35] The Butler who published *The Character of the Rump* and *The Censure of the Rota* (17 and 30 March) is as likely to have published more, and his flair for impersonating his satirical targets can lead us to suspect his hand in a number of contemporary tracts that depend on this device. As Joad Raymond has observed, another burlesque impersonation published in April – a funeral sermon for the Rump that much recalls the *Character* – may well be from that author's hand, since he directs his reader to 'our Treatise called the Rumps Character'.[36] The same invented author, a canting sectarian named John Feak (so as to recall Christopher Feake the fifth monarchist), publishes another funeral sermon that autumn lamenting the death of General Harrison, and this satirical effusion looks entirely Butlerian as well.[37] Such impersonations were not uncommon in the pamphlet litera-ture of the time, and there is a rash of them in March–April 1660. What of the satirical method itself?

---

[32] *Sir Arthur Hesilrigs Lamentation, and Confession* (London, 1660), p. 4.

[33] *Treason Arraign'd* (London, 1660), p. 1; L'Estrange, *No Blinde Guides* (London, 1660), p. 3.

[34] John Aubrey, *Brief Lives*, ed. A. Clark, 2 vols. (Oxford, 1898), I, 342.

[35] R. Thyer, ed., *The Genuine Remains in Verse and Prose of Mr. Samuel Butler*, 2 vols. (London, 1759). The following paragraph draws on my fuller discussion of Butler's authorship of *The Character of the Rump* and *The Censure of the Rota* in 'Samuel Butler's Milton', *Studies in Philology*, 92 (1995), pp. 482–95.

[36] *A Word for All: or, the Rumps Funerall Sermon* (London, 1660), p. 24 (= 2); Raymond, 'The cracking of the republican spokes', 257, 271.

[37] *A Funeral Sermon Thundred Forth* (London, 1660).

The Censure of the Rota is an inspired improvisation, of 'more wit and substance', as Woolrych has observed, than *The Character of the Rump*.[38] Purporting to be the verdict of the Rota on *The Readie and Easie Way*, as reported by a rueful Harrington, reluctant to impart bad news to a fellow republican, the *Censure* has without too much exaggeration been called 'the cleverest and most penetrating of all the criticism ever levelled at [Milton] by his contemporaries'.[39] Butler's resentment of Milton the orator had already surfaced in *The Character of the Rump*, where he impugns 'their Goosquill Champion', who has 'a Ramshead, and is good only at Batteries': 'an old Heretick both in Religion and Manners, that by his will would shake off his Governours as he doth his Wives, foure in a Fortnight'.[40] In the *Censure*, Butler returns to this view of republican discussion as 'knocking Argument against Argument, and tilting at one another with our heads (as Rams fight) untill we are out of breath'. He was happy to recall the peculiarity of Milton the divorcer, and thus to impugn Milton's 'Liberty of Conscience, and Christian Liberty'; he was also alert to Milton's long suspicions of the Rump, which might be thought to compromise his present service to it. The scale of his response, in two sheets quarto, reflects the level of his exasperation, and the degree to which Milton's position seemed formed of 'perpetuall falshoods and mistakes'. In the 'windy foppery' of this 'Retorician' lay the fundamental error of humanist oratory, against which Butler (like Hobbes) proposed stricter, more specific requirements for knowledge:

> You trade altogether in universals the Region of deceits and falacie, but never come so near particulars, as to let us know which among diverse things of the same kind you would be at ... Besides this, as all you politiques reach but the outside and circumstances of things and never touch at realties, so you are very solicitous about weeds as if they were charmes, or had more in them then what they signifie: For no Conjurer's Devill is more concerned in a spell, then you are in a meer word, but never regard the things which it serves to expresse.[41]

'All the liberty you talk so much of consists in nothing else but meer words': to this danger Butler, himself a very learned poet, was especially attuned.[42] His special talent was to use learning against learning, if more in ridicule than debate. His complaint against Milton might in part have been turned on himself: 'you fight alwayes with the flat of your hand like

---

[38] *CPW*, VII, 199.   [39] Parker, *Milton*, 558–9.
[40] Butler, *Character of the Rump*, pp. 2–3.   [41] Butler, *Censure*, pp. 3, 4, 5, 11–14.
[42] Butler's varied and curious learning appears at every turn in his works, and no less an authority than Selden 'much esteemed him for his partes, and would sometimes employ him to write letters for him beyond sea, and to translate for him'. Aubrey, *Brief Lives*, ed. Clark, I, 137.

Retorician, and never Contract the Logical fist'.[43] His lengthy verse satire on 'The abuse of learning'[44] addresses a frequent target in his work, which finds its best-known expression in the wide vein of false or confused learning throughout *Hudibras*. It is the fantastic quality of such error that Butler's satire defines as so destructive in its consequences. In his view republicans and fanatics were all too alike in this respect, whether in 'Mr. Harrington's Romantick Commonwealth' or the impulses of inner light. It was their very excesses of language that signalled the discrepancy between professed intention and the active interest of the individual, to which the national interest was being sacrificed. The humanist contribution to such excess required an anti-humanist corrective, so that 'Orators Poets, and Fanatiques' – and Milton was all three – might be brought to reason.[45]

III

In their attacks on Milton the orator, L'Estrange and Butler variously repudiated his Ciceronian emphasis on classical eloquence, and did so by defining his very oratory as a signal that private interests were being promoted without being announced. The purpose was to set the style against the ethos, and to redescribe the eloquence that Milton offered as an expression of virtue as instead an expression of fantasy and personal ambition. But not all of his antagonists were so suspicious, or capable of so disregarding his ethos and devaluing his rhetoric, even if they disagreed with him. The seductions of Milton's humanism are writ large in the lengthy response to *The Readie and Easie Way* by G[eorge] S[tarkey], in *The Dignity of Kingship Asserted*, written in March 1660.[46] Starkey conceived of himself as an 'Orator', and repeatedly subscribes himself as such, however 'unworthy' or 'humble' in his loyalty to the crown;[47] he styles himself and Milton as champions in the oratorical lists;[48] and his tract ends with an extended 'Peroration' to Monck, and his officers, and to the parliament about to meet. Born and raised in Bermuda, and then a

---

[43] Butler, *Censure*, p. 13.

[44] Butler, *Satires and Miscellaneous Poetry and Prose*, ed. R. Lamar (Cambridge, 1928), pp. 68–81.

[45] Butler, *Character of the Rump*, p. 4, and *Prose Observations*, ed. H. de Quehen (Oxford, 1979), p. 187.

[46] Errata dated March 29. The work was '"intended to be published before" the fateful meeting of the Convention Parliament on April 25 ... (although the Thomason copy is dated "May")'. G. S. *The Dignity of Kingship Asserted*, ed. William R. Parker (New York, 1942), pp. vi–vii. Cf. Raymond, 'Cracking of the republican spokes', 264–65.

[47] Starkey, *Dignity Asserted*, pp. a4r, 208, 221; he subscribes himself similarly in George Starkey, *Royal and Other Innocent Bloud Crying Aloud to Heaven for Due Vengeance* (London, 1660), pp. A2v, 43.

[48] Starkey, *Dignity Asserted*, sig. A2v, a2r.

graduate of Harvard (1643–46), this 'alchemically inclined *enfant terrible*' had been part of the Hartlib circle in the early 1650s, when he also advised Robert Boyle, before losing their confidence and returning to obscurity and to a need for patronage in any quarter to sustain his alchemical experiments and iatrochemical cures.[49]

Starkey's support for the Presbyterian position carried much further than did L'Estrange's feigned assurances. Like L'Estrange he seeks to distinguish independency from Presbyterianism, but not just for present political purposes. In 1650 he was reported 'a Presbyterian and of Scots-parents borne',[50] and he seems to have taken an Ussherian view of the scope for combining 'Episcopacy, and a Godly moderate Presbytery ... only nominally differing, but really the same' (he thought the lords spiritual would never regain their place in parliament).[51] That Starkey's Presbyterian sympathies would encounter Anglican resentment may be guessed, and appears in some manuscript comment found in the Library of Congress copy of the 1661 reissue of *Dignity Asserted*. It was not just that Starkey 'nibbles at Loyalty so cautiously, as if he were afraid to provoke the Faction'. The Anglican was suspicious chiefly of two Presbyterian motives:

> 1. To be revenged on the Independents who had run down and baffled Presbytery all over the nation. 2. To destroy the Ch: of England by the Kings Authority, for they alwaise resolvd to restore him on Conditions, whereof the cheif should be That he would suffer himself to be Gagg'd with the scotch Covenant.[52]

'But Risit Deus in excelsis.' Events would leave such Presbyterian temporising – which might have seemed finely judged in March 1660 – vulnerable to accusations that this had indeed been too cautious a loyalty, or, worse, a Presbyterian attempt to preempt the truer restoration of the crown and episcopacy.

Starkey's respect for Milton stems for his regard for 'the ability of the Author' as a humanist persuader. The effects of 'fair pretenses and Sophisticate Arguments' compel Starkey's attention (these had, *mutatis mutandis*, been his stock in trade as an alchemist); he is fascinated by Milton's possible success with the moderate or incautious ('inconsiderate' but also 'otherwise Judicious') reader, who seems close to the 'impartial' and 'judicious Reader' whom Starkey too is addressing.[53] He acknowledges

---

[49] William R. Newman, *Gehennical Fire: the Lives of George Starkey, an American Alchemist in the Scientific Revolution* (Cambridge, Mass., 1994), pp. 57, 204–5, 15–83, 170–208.

[50] Newman, *Gehennical Fire*, p. 191.   [51] Starkey, *Dignity Asserted*, pp. 142–44.

[52] Starkey, *Dignity Asserted*, ed. Parker, p. xiv.

[53] Starkey, *Dignity Asserted*, pp. a1r, a2r, a3v, 9.

Milton's 'Language to be smooth and tempting, the Expressions pathetical, and apt to move the Affections', and that the rhetorical manipulation ('unawares to insnare') has left readers 'staggered' or 'unsetled' or 'stumbled'.[54] Nor is this just true of *The Readie and Easie Way*. Milton's 'satyricall pen' had not been without effect against the 'most Solid Arguments; and Patheticall Expressions' of 'the most learned Salmasius', 'in all which he expressed, as his inveterate, and causeless malice, so a great deal of wicked desperate wit and learning, most unworthily misbestowed'. Milton's was a 'dangerous wit and wicked Learning, which together with Elegance in expression is alwaies, (in some measure at least) perswasive with some'. Even this reserve Starkey sometimes abandons, as when he allows that Milton answered Salmasius' success 'with as much Learning and Performance as could be expected from the most able and acute Scholar living', and that Milton is indeed 'acute and universally owned a learned man'.[55]

Starkey's acknowledgement of Milton's gifts does not just glorify his own attempted triumph over them. He would like to oppose the private virtue of a subject against claims for the public virtue of the citizen. When he pleads himself not 'a competent Champion, to mannage [the crown's] most just, and Princely quarrel', he is plainly using the rhetorical figure of parrhesia, contriving 'a tone of "humble submission and modest insinuation", thereby forestalling any displeasure and offence at our speech'.[56] A 'competent Champion' is just what he aims to be. When generating an ethos of his own with which to confront Milton's reputation, this 'G. S.' excuses his relative anonymity ('I question not but my person will be enquired after') by allying his prudent modesty to a higher ideal of disinterested service. He forswears the 'itch or ambition of appearing in publique'; nor is politics his 'Sphere'. In listing Milton's humanist skills – 'acute wit, ready invention, much reading, and copious expression' – Starkey makes the familiar claim that such rhetorical sophistication does not address his own concernments 'as a man, and as a Christian'.[57] This is the critique of eloquence without wisdom, as when Sallust warns against the danger of Catiline. And yet as an orator against oratory, Starkey cannot find the needed distance from his target, which L'Estrange and Butler achieve through more vigorous scorn and mockery. He is much influenced by Milton's example, even as he seeks to counter the republican champion with a high style of his own, and never more so than in his 'Conclusion, to His Royall, most Excellent, Sacred Majesty':

> Thus having, most judicious, truly pious, and most accomplished Prince, performed this defense of Regall Government and Authority, against an

---

[54] Ibid., sig. a2r–a3v.   [55] Ibid., pp. A4v–A6r, 5–6. Parker, *Milton*, 560–1.
[56] Skinner, *Thomas Hobbes*, p. 133.   [57] Starkey, *Dignity Asserted*, pp. A2v–A3r, 1–7.

acute, although scurrilous Antagonist, whose Reproaches of, and impious falshoods concerning your Majesties most glorious Predecessor, and Royall Father, I have wiped off, and discovered the Impiety therein, of him who cast them.[58]

The philippic note, also of self-congratulation, recalls Milton's in the *Defensio,* although here it is a subject- rather than a citizen-orator who has vanquished the ambition of a corrupt antagonist. Starkey's use of the word 'subject' reveals some concerns about how palatable monarchy will prove to moderates: it is at this date not simply a royalist commonplace to assert that kingship is most desirable because 'suited to a Nation really free, and yet truly Subject, where Majesty and subjection ma[k]e a true harmony'. Starkey is otherwise chary in his use of 'subject', reserving it chiefly for his present dedication to Charles [II], or to heighten indignation at the betrayal of Charles I by his 'subjects'.[59]

Starkey employs an unusually oratorical style even as he questions the instabilities of republican discourse. His argument finally reverts to some familiar royalist themes, but he does not use a clash of styles to question the humanist sophistications of Milton's republican arguments. Thus he revives the old gibe against Milton the divorcer in order to liken domestic to political loyalty (there is in each case 'a much greater liberty, being engaged in an inviolable bond'), and to add the royalist commonplace that patriarchal sovereignty in the family must also extend to the state. In describing Milton as 'one of those Christian Libertines' who 'throw off all externall coercive, or binding lawes, and desire only to be governed by the Law within them', Starkey denies the civic thrust of Milton's humanism, and sees it instead as betraying the extravagance of private interest. The same point sharpens the accusation that republican proposals are 'fantastically absurd' (Harrington's *Oceana*) or just 'fanatique State-whymsis' (Milton's proposed decentralisation of government and education in *The Readie and Easie Way*).[60] But against such unnatural projections, born of eloquence rather than wisdom, Starkey will not mount an anti-humanist argument, deploy scorn or mockery, or much investigate questions of private versus public interest.

In view of the issues at his disposal, Starkey is hampered in argument by the ethos he has adopted. He will not much disturb his oration with any particular animus against Milton. Even when touching on Milton's blindness – 'Surely Sir, the Proverb is in you veryfied, None so blind as he that will not see' – he insists that he speaks 'not this of your Corporall blindnesse', 'for that, (God is my Judge) I pity, but of your better eyes,

---

[58] Ibid., p. 219.   [59] Ibid., pp. A2r, a3v, 2, 35, 57–58, 64.
[60] Ibid., pp. 12, 65–66, 70–71, 109–10.

(viz.) the understanding, which (methinks) cannot be so palpably blinded, as you would make appear it is'. This may not be disingenuous: although Starkey hopes that the parliament will not attempt 'a generall Act of Amnesty', especially for those guilty of the regicide, he does not cite Milton as an object of resentment, even when the opportunity arises (he may have been hindered in this respect since he himself had dedicated an alchemical treatise to the regicide Robert Tichborne).[61] Nor after the Restoration, when he calls for justice on the regicides, and also on those who 'had as deep hand in that Crimson fact, as any who were present at sentence, or confirmed it under hand and Seal', does he make much of Milton's possible guilt, which he mentions more incidentally elsewhere.[62]

Moreover, Starkey writes as a royal subject and not as one expressing any strong private interest. The constraint is particularly notable on the issue of trade, a prime motivation for political change in the winter of 1660. Starkey can decry Milton's indifference to trade, especially when Milton had likened the return to kingship to the Jews' return 'into Egypt, for the sake of Onyons, Garlick and Flesh-pots, (trading to wit, which by our casting off Kingship, hath been decayed).'[63] Impugning the rule of 'Liberty', Starkey can cite the 'impoverishment of the Nation, losse of Trade, decay of Ingenious Arts, and manufactures, the ecclipsing of our former credit, esteeme, and reputation in the eys of our neighbouring Nations', by contrast with its previously flourishing condition, when the gentry was freer of taxation and 'our Citizens had a rich Trade, and for wealth, London could compare with any Metropolis in Europe'. But in this promotion of the national interest he achieves only a generalising description of national civility, reputation and credit, whereas his critique of republican regimes can elaborate on the turbulence of classical examples, the primitive life of the Swiss, and especially the mercenary lack of quality in the Dutch. He is especially sharp about the latter, those 'Common Pedlars of Europe', whose dishonest pursuit of monetary advantage is all-consuming: 'What have they so sacred that they will not prostitute for Profit sake?'[64] By contrast, the dignity Starkey asserts asks a rhetorical extravagance that, as Butler might have observed, largely sets words against words. But Starkey's interest lay another way. Such Presbyterian oratory shows chiefly the desire to distinguish the Presbyterian role from that of the independents, and to clear the former of Milton's imputation that they too were irredeemably implicated in the execution of Charles I.

---

[61] *CPW*, vii, 200–1; *Dignity Asserted*, ed. Parker. p. xx.
[62] Starkey, *Dignity Asserted*, pp. 87, 201, 204; *Royal and Other Innocent Bloud*, pp. 15, 18.
[63] Starkey, *Dignity Asserted*, p. 26; cf. *CPW*, vii, 462–63.
[64] Starkey, *Dignity Asserted*, pp. 43, 116, 96–119, 130.

IV

At issue was the first step in that great betrayal of the Presbyterians which marks the history of the early 1660s, and which so colours the politics of the ensuing decades. This turned on the Presbyterian role in restoring kingship, and the terms on which such a restoration might be based. Underlying these negotiations were long-standing royalist misgivings about the Presbyterians' part in bringing down Charles I in the 1640s. True, they had balked at radical measures in 1647 and 1648, and numbers of them had been purged from parliament in the events leading to the crisis of the revolution in 1648/49. But an amnesty based on such nice considerations was easily discarded by the cavalier interest once the Presbyterians had played their part in restoring Charles II. Here L'Estrange again proves his agility as a polemicist. In March and April 1660, he is in the forefront of pamphleteers who reassure Presbyterians that they could not be mistaken for the guilty party. Such reassurance was needed because republican writers were reminding Presbyterians of their stake in the earlier revolution, which Nedham had been doing since the previous year (*Interest will not lie*) and was now doing more dramatically in his *Newes from Brussels*, where he had created a fierce cavalier with whom to frighten Presbyterians with presage of royalist revenge. Within a year, however, L'Estrange would be in the forefront as cavalier turned on Presbyterian. Now he could draw on exactly the examples of Presbyterian sedition to which the republican writers had earlier drawn attention. If L'Estrange formerly cried down republicans who sought to worry Presbyterians about their part in the rebellion, he could now quote the republicans' accusations as he worried the Presbyterians himself.

L'Estrange therefore returns to the attack on Milton as opportunity affords that spring. Indeed, the incentive to impugn independency leads him to draw Milton into the fray even when there is little other cause, as with two anonymous tracts aimed at disuniting Presbyterian and royalist, *Plain English* (22 March 1660) and *An Alarum to the Officers and Souldiers of the Armies* (late March 1660). He was eager to misattribute such works as they served his turn, and when he then professes his error in citing the twin republicans as the source of these 'Two sharper Pamphlets ... Printed by Livewell Chapman', the admission just lets him repeat the names 'Milton' and 'Nedham' as a way of once more representing the faction; the tracts 'are Twinns; the issue of the same Brayne, as they are related to the same maine end'.[65] The connection with the bookseller Chapman and one

---

[65] *Double Your Guards* (London, 4 April 1660), p. 3; nor, when he learns that the tracts were written by 'a Renegado Parson', does he bother to name him (*L'Estrange His Apology*, p. 113).

shrewdly chosen sentence[66] lead L'Estrange to the unlikely proposition that Milton might have written in the style of *Plain English*, or still less likely the *Alarum*, which presents itself as written from a soldier to soldiers (a subterfuge most unlike Milton). L'Estrange was pleased to ignore the evident differences between Nedham's and Milton's works, since it was more advantageous to identify the two as almost interchangeable, 'a Couple of Currs of the same Pack'.[67] 'Say, – MILTON; NEDHAM; either, or both, of you, (or whosoever else)': L'Estrange just names these republicans as representative of those now attempting 'an Alarm to all the Phanatiques in England', and recalls the cursed name of Milton's *Eikonoklastes* in order to sharpen his point.[68] The benefit in developing the association led other royalist writers to the same practice: thus Butler commands Milton to 'stand close and draw in your Elbows, that Nedham the Commonwealths Didapper may have room to stand by you' – this to fit them both under the Tyburn gallows – and another tract notes 'all the Indignities and Disgraces, that Milton, and Nedham, with the help of Jack Hall' have heaped on the royal family.[69]

Some recent articles have explored the affinities between Milton and Nedham,[70] and Joad Raymond has seen their works on the eve of the Restoration as sharing much, including a final daring of the worst as the return of the king impended. Raymond allows that 'on the surface, *Newes from Brussels* is written in a mode very different from *The Readie & Easie Way*',[71] but seeks to show the common ground between their works, or more especially Milton's debt at this juncture to Nedham's work of a few years before, in particular *The Excellencie of a Free State*. Their association appears to be confirmed by their being named together by L'Estrange and Butler, although this should be viewed with more suspicion given the polemical advantage in yoking the two as a common target. Nedham has changed his tactics much more than Milton had, and the resulting vulnerability of Milton's work to pamphlet attack gave his and Nedham's antagonists good cause to wish them still a team. Milton's contribution is a

---

[66] 'We cannot yet be persuaded, though our fears and jealousies are strong, and the grounds of them many, that you can so lull asleep your Consciences, or forget the publick Interest, and your own, as to be returning back with the multitude to Egypt, or that you should with them be hankering after the Leeks and Onyons of our old bondage.' *Plain English* (London, 1660), p. 1; L'Estrange, *Treason Arraigned*, p. 1. For this commonplace in Milton's works, see *CPW*, vii, 325, 463, 511 (Moses Wall's letter to Milton, 26 May 1659).

[67] *L'Estrange His Apology*, p. 113.   [68] L'Estrange, *Treason Arraigned*, p. 5.

[69] Butler, *Character of the Rump*, p. 3; *A Third Conference between O. Cromwell and Hugh Peters in Saint James's Park* (London, 1660), p. 8.

[70] See especially Blair Worden, 'Milton and Marchamont Needham', in *Milton and Republicanism*, ed. Armitage, 158–80.

[71] Raymond, 'Cracking of the republican spokes', 262–3, 269.

far cry from Nedham's brilliant intervention in *Newes from Brussels*, and the stylistic differences point to political differences. If Milton's tract seems 'defiantly impractical', in Raymond's words, this is worth contrasting with the defiantly practical turn of Nedham's satire, which is better adapted to present requirements. Other republicans too were pouring old wine into new bottles; Harrington and Neville,[72] for example, can be found adapting their work to current needs in these months.

This pairing of names reflects the increasing frequency with which the roll-call of those who were associated with the regicide was being recited as the Restoration approached. Increasingly, the catalogue expanded to include many other figures prominent in the Interregnum, in the earlier history of opposition to the King, and sometimes just in the politics of 1659–60. With intermittent reference to *Eikonoklastes* and the *Defensio* in particular, these lists came often to cite Milton as one of the bogies from the past, as Presbyterian and royalist alike advanced more personal attacks on the supposed proponents of parliamentary rule.[73] Listing figures in order to define an opposition would become a frequent feature also of L'Estrange's pamphlets. Thus Milton may now be found on L'Estrange's lengthening list of commonwealthsmen ('Rebellious Devils') in *Treason Arraigned*: 'Oh for Tom Scot's sake; for Haslerig's; for Robinson, Holland, Mildmay, Mounson, Corbet, Atkins, Vane, Livesay, Skippon, Milton, Tichbourn, Ireton, Gourdon, Lechmore, Blagrave, Barebones, Nedham's sake ...'[74] Here republicans and regicides stand side by side. It was not yet clear how far republicanism might be confused with regicide in future judgement. After the Restoration the list would come to include further Presbyterian figures, such as Richard Baxter, and a generation later L'Estrange could still cite these with animus in his tracts in the Exclusion Crisis.

Fiercer still would be L'Estrange's response to Milton's *Brief Notes Upon a Late Sermon* (c. 10–15 April 1660).[75] Two months later he would remember Milton's as 'a bawling piece against Dr. Griffith' to which he had been urged to reply although already 'the heart of the design was almost broken'.[76] His response came soon enough in *No Blinde Guides* (20 April

---

[72] *CPW*, VII, 103–4; N. von Maltzahn, 'Henry Neville and the art of the possible: a republican *Letter Sent to General Monk* (1660)', *The Seventeenth Century*, 7 (1992), pp. 41–52.

[73] Thus the *Defensio* joins company, in William Prynne's overwritten margins, with 'Godwins Obstructors of Justice, Cooks & Bradshawes Speeches', and elsewhere Prynne lists Milton the apologist for regicide with 'John Goodwin, Markham, Needham', Prynne, *The Re-publicans and others spurious Good Old Cause* (London, 1659), p. 10; *A true and perfect narrative* (London, 1659), p. 50.

[74] L'Estrange, *Treason Arraigned*, [30]; here quoted in the text from *L'Estrange His Apology*, p. 143.

[75] *CPW*, VII, 464–65.   [76] *L'Estrange His Apology*, p. 157.

1660). In *Brief Notes*, Milton had responded to a vehement and premature sermon, *The Fear of God and the King*, by Dr Matthew Griffith, a royalist in favour of episcopacy, who sought a little too soon to identify the Presbyterians and independents as birds of a feather. As early as the end of March 1660, Griffith had cheered Monck's work towards the restoration of Charles II; he was sent to Newgate for writing and publishing the 'seditious and libellous book', to which Milton responded first by jeering at the imprisoned minister and by impugning his arguments.[77] Next came the more difficult task of upholding his own republican principles while conceding the demand for the present rule of a single person. He settled on the expedient that his countrymen choose 'out of our own number one who hath best aided the people, and best merited against tyrannie', so that they might hope to live 'the space of a raign or two ... happily anough, or tolerably', until the corruption endemic to unelected kings closed in again.[78]

When L'Estrange responds to *Brief Notes* in late April 1660, the Presbyterian question still governs his argument with Milton. He claims, for example, that Milton's other 'Factious Labours' need not be addressed in the present context, but before he can turn to *Brief Notes* he finds himself compelled by way of introduction to recall Milton's previous outrages as author of the *Defensio* and *Eikonoklastes*. Inveighing against the *Defensio* for its addressing a wider European audience, and thus blasting 'the English Nation to the Universe', L'Estrange is still more exasperated by *Eikonoklastes*. Revealingly, he focuses on a stylistic point: Milton's use of the omniscient narrator, which he treats as if it were the worst violation of royal prestige. L'Estrange's lasting grievance on this point suggests the original force of Milton's iconoclastic historiography and his republican transgression of degree, since a special affront lay in Milton's demystification of the King:

> There, not content to see that Sacred Head divided from the Body; your piercing Malice enters into the private Agonies of his struggling Soul; with a Blasphemous Insolence, invading the Prerogative of God himself: (Omniscience) and by Deductions most Unchristian, and Illogical, aspersing his Last Pieties (the almost certain Inspirations of the Holy Spirit) with Juggle, and Prevarication.[79]

But Milton's insolent familiarity with the figure of the king and martyr causes a more present concern. Republicans were now comparably 'invading' the thoughts of the 'king' in prospect in order to aggravate the intense unease among Presbyterians about possible royal misconstructions of their part in the earlier Revolution. All the more reason then for

[77] *CPW*, vii, 465, 485. [78] *CPW*, vii, 481–2. [79] L'Estrange, *No Blinde Guides*, p. 2.

L'Estrange to rail against 'the bold censure' of the king's 'secret thoughts', when republican tracts were reminding Presbyterians that they should 'accuse themselves' and that the king would accuse them too.[80]

The crime of the regicide pamphlets soon came to outweigh that of Milton's republican writings at the Restoration. L'Estrange can in late April taunt Milton with the recent developments in Parliament; can mock his being 'for divorce, I see, as well as Governours, as wives'; and can laugh at the abbreviation of *Plain English* and *An Alarum* in a 'lewd Pamphlet titled, – EYE-SALVE for the English Army, &c', since 'This Eye-Salve, Gentlemen, which our pretending Oculist presents you with, is a medicine of the same Composition, which (by general report) strook Milton blind.'[81] But the dangers of having written the republican pamphlets at the Restoration derived chiefly from the degree to which they might recall Milton's earlier, and much graver, assaults on kingship, in his celebrations of the execution of Charles I, that ineradicable crime. Milton's tracts of 1660 scarcely feature in the censure to which he was exposed after the Restoration, and such late political contributions seem to have meant little after the end of the interregnum. Punishment in 1660 and after attached chiefly to the crime of regicide, rather than to works of political theory: notably *Eikonoklastes* and the *Defensio* were dangerous to Milton, but the much more radical political theory of the *Tenure* hardly draws comment until the Exclusion Crisis, except briefly from L'Estrange. Milton was famous first and last for *Eikonoklastes* and *Defensio*, his two great humanist commissions. These transgressed, of course, not only in their shocking treatment of Charles I, especially in *Eikonoklastes*, but also in their wide availability, especially the much-published *Defensio*.[82] The anti-humanist thrust of L'Estrange and Butler, all the plainer in comparison with Starkey's more compromised work, would have an enduring influence on Milton's reputation in the years following the Restoration. Their derision, *ad hominem* attacks, and coffee-house impatience with the grand style left a legacy of scepticism to later writers; indeed so much so that only at the Revolution of 1688–89 would Milton's tracts of 1660 again be prepared for the press, not to appear until a decade later when the collections of Milton's prose of 1697 and 1698 gave them a new currency, in the time of another generation of political discontent.

---

[80] L'Estrange, *Double Your Guards*, p. 3.

[81] L'Estrange, *No Blinde Guides*, pp. 3, 8–9, 10; L'Estrange, *Physician Cure Thy Self* (London, 1660), p. 2.

[82] These conclusions are based on the evidence of J. T. Shawcross, *Milton: A Bibliography for the Years 1624–1700* (Binghamton, NY, 1984), on my own survey of Restoration materials, and on the census of extant copies of Milton's works reported in Parker, *Biography*, Appendices 1 and 2, (1206–7, 1209–12).

13

'They* that pursew perfaction on earth ...'
The Political Progress of Robert Overton

BARBARA TAFT

During the last years of Robert Overton's life, which were marked by nine years in prison (1663–71), he compiled a 360 page manuscript of prose and verse. 'Goverments gaine & goodnesse &c' (pp. 34–40), the segment that is edited here,[1] is a treatise of advice to political malcontents. Overton was a deeply religious parliamentary officer who fought with dedication throughout the Civil War and was concerned with the successive governments established during the decade of revolutionary polity. The conclusions about government that he recorded after the restoration are the fruit of his experience and are foreshadowed in his writings and conduct during the interregnum. Overton is frequently mentioned by historians; he has been less than correctly described. His learning and moral rectitude are unquestioned, but he has been too easily tagged as fifth monarchist, leveller and uncertain ally. An examination of his manuscript and a review of his actions and observations before the restoration raise questions about the accuracy of these attributions as they reveal an increasingly realistic idealist who is credible and consistent.

Before turning to 'Goverments gaine & goodnesse &c' pertinent aspects of Overton's life will be considered: relations with his family, friends and other contemporaries, his political experiences and his published writings. He was the son and heir of John Overton of Easington, a gentleman of landed estates in south-eastern Yorkshire where Overtons had lived for generations. Robert matriculated at St John's College, Cambridge, in 1627,

---

*I am indebted to Linda Levy Peck and Lois Schwoerer for perceptive advice about organisation, to Ian Gentles for apposite suggestions and references, and to Blair Worden for his careful critique. I thank all of them for assisting me toward a number of improvements.

[1] Published with permission of the Manuscripts Division, Department of Rare Books and Special Collections, Princeton University Libraries. I am indebted to Caroline Robbins for calling my attention to the Overton manuscript many years ago.

entered Gray's Inn four years later, and married Ann Gardiner in 1632.[2] The manuscript illuminates his enduring devotion to his wife and reveals a little about their children. Transcripts of letters that Robert wrote after Ann's death include letters to three daughters and three sons. Five of the six are notably gentle. The sixth, to his heir, John Overton, begins: 'Son. And therein (by reason of sin) my sorrow, my shame.' Throughout more than four closely written pages he bitterly reproaches John for apostasy and 'sinful defilements', urges profound repentance, and recalls that, 'your dear Mother sayd youe had been a sonn of sorrow to her soule' (pp. 130–34; cf. p. 86). Ann Overton was a formidable woman. A petition addressed to the protector in 1658 requests clemency for Colonel Overton, contending that he 'had never continued soe obstinate if it had not been for the imperious spirrit of his wife'. A decade before, Ann's audacity is evident in a letter to Lord Fairfax asking that Robert's rank be advanced to colonel.[3] The many religious passages in the letter reveal Ann's piety, and in 1665 her confident anticipation of a celestial heaven is vividly recorded by her daughter A.B. in a letter to Robert describing the days before her mother's death.[4] A.B.'s letter also discloses Ann's courage and her contentment that Robert – 'soe tender a spirit' – not witness her suffering (p. 87). 'Poore heart', she said another day, 'he's noe self seeker; he hath sought Christ, & kept him, ever since he had him, blessed be God' (p. 83).

Overton's qualities are attested by his contemporaries. A royalist held prisoner by Overton in 1648–49 recalls him as 'a great independent ... ane enemie to monarchie, whatever name it had ... a schollar, bot a litle pedantick', who treated his prisoners well.[5] In 1651 Sir John Danvers proposed Overton for appointment to the Hale commission on law reform, describing him as 'both rational and learned, and of good estate ... whose

[2] *Alumni Cantabrigiensis*, ed. John Venn and J. A. Venn, Part I, 4 vols. (Cambridge, 1922–27), III, 289. Except where otherwise noted, the facts of Overton's life are from C. H. Firth's article in the *Dictionary of National Biography* and J. F. McGregor's account in *Biographical Dictionary of British Radicals in the Seventeenth Century*, ed. Richard L. Greaves and Robert Zaller, 3 vols. (Brighton, 1982–84), II, 279–81. For details of his military career see Charles Firth and Godfrey Davies, *The Regimental History of Cromwell's Army*, 2 vols. (Oxford, 1940), esp. II, 546–61.

[3] Petition of John Shaw (?), 1658, 'Two letters addressed to Cromwell', ed. C. H. Firth, *English Historical Review*, 22 (1907), 308–15, esp. p. 313. Ann Overton to Ferdinando, Lord Fairfax, 28 July 1647, British Library, Add. Mss. 18979, fos. 251–61, esp. fo. 252; I owe this reference to Ian Gentles.

[4] For suggestions that Ann Overton may have been close to the fifth monarchists, see David Norbrook, '"This blushing tribute of a borrowed muse": Robert Overton and his over-turning of the poetic canon', *English Manuscript Studies, 1100–1700*, 4 (1993), pp. 220–66, esp. pp. 227–31. I am grateful to Dr Norbrook, whose article is largely concerned with the elegies, for generously sharing his unpublished comments about Overton.

[5] Sir James Turner, *Memoirs of his own Life and Times* (Edinburgh, 1829), pp. 78–79.

forward zeal to justice and right made the Levellers assume to own him ...
but remaining trusty to the public interest'.[6] In 1654 Overton was among
the men whom John Milton hoped would be close to Cromwell in the
protectorate. 'You, Overton', wrote Milton, 'for many years have been
linked to me with a more than fraternal harmony, by reason of the likeness
of our tastes and the sweetness of your disposition'. Milton also praises
Overton's military skills and notes that the Scots regard him as 'a most
humane foe, and ... a merciful conqueror'.[7] Oliver Cromwell valued
Overton's abilities as an army commander, and in May 1654 General
Monck welcomed his appointment as second in command in Scotland.[8]
Soon thereafter, Overton raised his concerns about the protectorate, and
Andrew Marvell, poet, politician and Yorkshireman, wrote to Milton of his
own 'affectionate Curiosity to know what becomes of Colonel Overtons
businesse'.[9] Clearly, Overton inspired respect and affection, but as the
complications of revolutionary politics intensified he acquired opponents
who doubted and feared him.

During the first war, Overton served in the northern army under
Ferdinando, Lord Fairfax, and his son, Sir Thomas. Both Fairfaxes thought
well of Overton, and in the summer of 1647 Sir Thomas – by then
commander-in-chief of the New Model – secured him a commission as
colonel of foot. He was named to committees during meetings of the
general council of the army at Reading in July and at Putney three months
later.[10] There is no record of his participation in the debates at either
place, and by March 1648 he was in Hull as Fairfax's deputy governor.
Prominent townsmen and corporation officials considered Overton a
religious radical and asked that he be replaced, but no particular charges
were cited, the garrison and Fairfax supported Overton unreservedly, and
he held the post for many years.[11]

---

[6] Danvers to Bulstrode Whitelock, 26 December 1651, quoted by Blair Worden, *The Rump Parliament, 1648–1653* (Cambridge, 1974), p. 272.

[7] John Milton, *A Second Defence of the English People* ([30 May] 1654), as in *Complete Prose Works of John Milton*, ed. Don M. Wolfe *et al.*, 8 vols. (New Haven, 1953–82), IV (Pt 1), 676.

[8] Cromwell to Sir Thomas Fairfax, 11 March and 22 October 1647, *The Writings and Speeches of Oliver Cromwell*, ed. W. C. Abbott, 4 vols. (Cambridge, Mass., 1937–47), I, 430, 513–14. Monck to the Protector, 6 May 1954, *Scotland and the Protectorate ... 1653 to 1659*, ed. C. H. Firth, Scottish Historical Society, 31 (Edinburgh, 1899), pp. 101–2.

[9] Marvell to Milton, 2 June 1654, *The Poems and Letters of Andrew Marvell*, ed. H. M. Margoliouth, 3rd edn, revised by Pierre Legouis, 2 vols. (Oxford, 1971), II, 306. For the 'businesse', below, pp. 291–92.

[10] *The Clarke Papers* (hereafter *CP*), ed. C. H. Firth, 4 vols. (Camden New Series, xlix, liv, lxi, lxii, 1891–1901), I, 183, 279, 415.

[11] Inhabitants of Hull to Fairfax, 4 March 1648, and Fairfax's response – as in John Rushworth, *Historical Collections*, 8 vols. (London, 1721–22), VII, 1020–21. Letters from

Before the defeat of the king in 1648, Overton made only one known comment about his revolutionary objective: in February 1648, in a letter to Fairfax's secretary, Overton expresses pleasure that the king's servants have been removed and suggests that it would 'prove a happy privation if the Father would please to dispossess him of three transitory kingdoms to infeoff him in an eternal one'.[12] There is no reason to infer that Overton's comment is a covert plea for regicide. Eleven months later, when he was named a commissioner for the trial of the king, Overton remained in Hull, apparently believing that it was more important to be with the garrison at a critical time.

Three weeks before the king's execution, Overton addressed a letter to Fairfax that accompanied an eloquent *Declaration* from the officers of the garrison. The first nine pages are rife with Latin phrases and historical references that suggest Overton's complicity, and both *Declaration* and Overton's accompanying letter are marked by the compelling style and vivid analogies that are found throughout Overton's writings. Responding to the army's November *Remonstrance* – 'with every tittle whereof we totally comply' – the *Declaration* reviews grievances, notes the promises of the previous six years, and condemns the 'corrupted party' in the Commons. The final six pages delineate a settlement similar to proposals in the *Remonstrance*: a speedy end to the present parliament; a succession of free biennial parliaments with an equitable distribution of seats; future kings elected by the people's representatives and having no negative voice; a 'universal and mutual Agreement' asserting the power of parliament inferior only to that of the people. Overton's letter reflects his belief that there is little likelihood that the 'corrupt Commons' will effect these reforms. He asks that, 'in this last Act of our Age', Fairfax lead the army, resolved 'rather to perish with your honest Officers and soldiers, then otherwise to enjoy the Genius of a temporall happinesse'. It is Overton's only known proposal for military action to secure 'the accomplishment of those remonstrated principle[s]'.[13]

Five months later, in June 1649, Overton's regiment at Hull issued a *Remonstrance* denying any association with recent Leveller uprisings led by William Thompson. Overton appended a letter to Fairfax pledging

Hull, June 1648 – as in Historical Manuscripts Commission (hereafter HMC), *Portland*, 1, 468; Fairfax letters, 2 and 8 July 1648 – ibid., pp. 471, 478. See also *Calendar of State Papers Domestic* (hereafter *CSPD*), 1648–49, pp. 137–38, 226 (20 June, 21 July 1648).

[12] Overton to William Clarke, 11 February 1648, *Memorials of the Civil War … Correspondence of the Fairfax Family*, ed. Robert Bell, 2 vols. (London, 1849), II, 10–12.

[13] *A Remonstrance Of … the Generall Concell of Officers … 16. November, 1648* ([22 November] 1648); *The Declaration Of the Officers of The Garrison of Hull* (1 March 1649), esp. pp. 4, 6–10, 15–20. Overton's letter, dated 9 January 1649, ibid., pp. 1–3; cf. Milton, *On the Lord General Fairfax* (Sonnet xv, August 1648).

obedience to parliament and the army – 'yet ever with such due Reservations as tended to the keeping sacred and inviolable my particular and private Trust, which ... I purpose never to part withall'. Overton deplores divisions and distractions which but for the goodness of God would have destroyed England and which did prevent more timely assistance in Ireland 'whilst we go about to raise structures of brain-sick and Eutopian Governments after our own inventions, striving like giddy Copernicusses ... to turn all things topsy turvy, as if we meant to call the universe into its former Chaos'.[14] The letter displays Overton's acceptance of the Rump's existing government, his commitment to his own vision, his disapproval of current policies – and his liking for an arresting metaphor.

There is no other known account of Overton's opinion of the 1649 republic, but he concurred with the widespread approval of Cromwell's forcible dismissal of the Rump in April 1653. Saints in the gathered churches and the army hailed Cromwell as a new Moses who would bring about a godly reformation. Among the wilder pamphleteers was John Canne, chaplain to Overton's regiment in Hull from the spring of 1650 until April 1653. During most of Canne's chaplaincy Overton was in Scotland (July 1650 to February 1653), but Canne's *Voice from the Temple* includes an address to Overton 'and his Religious Lady'. Cromwell is urged to search the prophecies and prepare for God's rule: the 1,260 years of Revelation expired in 1648; the 'Antichristian Kingdome shall not passe the yeare 1660'; in 1665 – 6,000 years after the creation – the Lord will overthrow earthly thrones everywhere in Europe.[15]

Canne's apocalyptic prophecies are a far cry from Overton's thoughtful response to the dissolution. On 6 June, six days before George Thomason dated Canne's *Voice*, he secured *More Hearts and Hands Appearing for the Work*, a short pamphlet consisting of a letter from Overton to Cromwell and a second letter from Overton and his officers to the council of officers. Both letters are notably dispassionate in word and tone. The second letter expresses 'free and hearty Concurrence with the Reason given' for the dissolution, declines any 'meddling with State matters', and asks Cromwell to employ 'religion, reason, and resolution ... that all your attempts may end in such attainments ... that so all our hearts and hands may be tied unto you'. Overton's short letter is equally restrained: the Lord is blessed for inspiring the dissolution and has given Cromwell power which, if he 'wisely & worthily dispose thereof ... I doubt not but Religion and Liberty shall againe flourish, whilest Tyranny and Oppression, like a desolate

---

[14] *The Humble Remonstrance and Resolves of Col. Overtons Regiment ... Together with Colonel Overton's Letter to the General* ([5 June] 1649), esp. pp. 6–8.

[15] John Canne, *A Voice From the Temple to the Higher Powers* ([13 June] 1653), Dedication, Epistle and pp. 14, 22, 29–30.

woman, shall dye Childlesse'.[16] It would not be easy to cite a roundhead tract that contrasts more sharply with the effusions of enthusiasts like Canne. At the same time, while no known evidence associates Overton with any prophetic revelations, he was undoubtedly pleased with Cromwell's decision to entrust the state to 144 godly men empowered to establish a moral reformation.

If the dissolution of the fractious assembly known as Barebone's Parliament was regretted only by fanatical saints, the protectorate established in December 1653 soon raised serious concerns among thoughtful officers. Within a few weeks an Address of allegiance was sent to outlying regiments for subscription. The Address includes a pledge of obedience and service to 'your Highnesse' in 'the station God hath placed you'.[17] The implication of divine authority is subtle, but when the proposed Address arrived in Hull Overton rejected it as 'oppugnant', contrary to the designs of the war and to previous engagements. In the spring Overton saw the protector in London and told him of his concerns. After some discussion, Overton accepted another commission for service in Scotland to oppose the 'Common Enemy'. He promised that as long as Cromwell pursued the good of the nation he would 'serve him with his life and fortune', but if it should appear that Cromwell designed his own interests Overton would not 'put one foot before another to serve him'. The protector 'told him, he was a Knave if he did otherwise'. Overton repeated his pledge to Monck when he arrived in Scotland in September.[18]

By the end of 1654 concerns about protectoral government emerged in regiments commanded by Overton. Before leaving London, Overton had met with John Wildman, who was conspiring with dissident colonels preparing an attack on the foundation of the protectorate.[19] Notes by John Thurloe, the intelligence chief of the protectorate, state that Overton and Wildman discussed 'their dislik of things', and although Thurloe did not believe that any plan was laid at the meeting, he reported that when Overton reached Scotland he sent word 'that there was a party which would stand right for a commonwealth'. Thurloe gives no sources for his notes, but in December officers in Overton's Aberdeen headquarters drafted a circular announcing a meeting to consider whether the army had

---

[16] *More Hearts and Hands Appearing for the Work* ([7 June] 1653), pp. 1–6, passim.

[17] For Address, January 1654, see *Scotland and the Protectorate*, pp. 10–11.

[18] *The sad Suffering Case of Major-General Rob. Overton ...*, by J.R. ([3 March] 1659), pp. 4–5; the account of the discussion evidently was taken from an intercepted letter from Overton, published in 1655 (below, n. 21). Monck to the Protector, 28 September 1654, *Scotland and the Protectorate*, p. 193.

[19] For this and related plots, see Barbara Taft, '*The Humble Petition of Several Colonels of the Army*: causes, character, and results of military opposition to Cromwell's protectorate', *The Huntington Library Quarterly*, 42 (1978), 15–41.

been faithful to its duty 'to assert the freedomes of the people in the priviledges of parliament'. Overton's sympathy with such a concern is not surprising. It is a corollary to his rejection of monarchy in any form and reflects reservations that he had expressed to Cromwell. One of the signatories to the circular declared that nothing had been done without Overton's 'privity and concession' and all participants were innocent of hostile intentions toward the protectorate. Monck and Cromwell thought otherwise. Overton was sent by frigate to London and imprisoned in the Tower. He steadfastly denied any wrongdoing and no proof of guilt was ever presented against him.[20]

Intercepted letters from Overton to a friend reveal his state of mind at this time. A letter from Aberdeen dated 26 December professes his innocence, his hope that God will not forsake him, and declares that if he is called 'to seal the cause of God and my country ... by suffering death, or by bearing any testimony to the interest of my nation and the despised truths of these times, he is able to support and save me'. Overton 'trusts' that he need not fear punishment for any action since coming to Scotland, but his tone is less than confident. A longer letter, written in the Tower on 17 January 1655, professes his loyalty and counters specific accusations with accounts of his conduct and judgement. 'If a leveller', he states, 'be one, who bears affection to anarchy, destroying property or government, then I am none. But if ... for the setling of well grounded government, redress of grievances ... or inflicting condign punishment upon capital offenders, &c. if this be levelling, I was and am a leveller.' Acknowledging 'dissatisfaction' when some of his junior colonels were preferred over him, he denies that that or 'any other neglect' hindered him from doing his duty faithfully and effectually. He has been true to his pledge to the protector and had warned his officers that if they intended anything 'unwarrantable' he would report it. He did not 'ever go about to divide the army, promise to head any party, or intend to joyn the cavileers'. An experienced officer, he would never be guilty of 'dividing and marching a part of the army into England', well knowing that such action would be 'most unlikely to end in any thing but division and destruction ... therefore as far from my purpose, as in itself impracticable'. Conjoining pragmatic argument with faith in Christ's promise, Overton concludes: 'I trust I shall not be condemned, before I be convicted.'[21]

His trust was not rewarded. While it is not possible to absolve Overton of doubts about the protectorate or of his failure to inform Monck of

---

[20] Ibid., pp. 37–38. For Thurloe's Notes, *A Collection of the State Papers of John Thurloe*, ed. T. Birch, 7 vols. (London, 1742), III, 148.

[21] Intercepted letters, ibid., III, 47, 110–12; the letters were published by the recipient, 'J.H.', *Two Letters from Major-General Overton ...* (1655), Postscript.

political dissension among his officers, no evidence of his participation in any conspiracy was ever forthcoming. Nevertheless, he was imprisoned for more than four years without charge, trial, or, after transfer to Jersey, right of habeas corpus. The severity of the punishment strongly suggests the protector's fear of Overton, and it is probable that respect for his military skill and concern about his appeal as an opposition leader[22] were more responsible for all his imprisonments than any specific offence.

In February 1659 Commonwealthsmen in Richard Cromwell's parliament responded to a petition from Overton's sister by demanding his appearance for a hearing. Within a month one tract detailed his unjust suffering, at least one other noted it, and when Overton arrived in London by frigate he received a triumphal welcome that was a striking contrast to his arrival from Scotland in 1655. On 15 March Overton spoke briefly to the Commons, declaring that he had been true to principles for which he had first engaged and confidently submitted his cause to the House – which ordered his release the same day.[23] The Rump, which returned in May, indemnified Overton and restored his commands, including his post as governor of Hull. As the commander of a major garrison, recently acclaimed as a martyr to protectorate injustice, Overton would reach the crest of his political involvement during the successive crises that marked the last months of revolution.

Overton supported the restored republic as the most expedient settlement, but as the Rump's divisions and weaknesses became ever more apparent he again envisioned a government by godly men. His name is among the twenty signatures to *An Essay toward Settlement*, a petition published by 19 September 1659. A number of the signatories have been styled fifth-monarchy men,[24] but the appeal is devoid of millenarian prophecy and reflects the aspirations of many moderate theocrats. Like other proposals at this time, *An Essay* begins by asking that there be no single person or house of lords. Further requests include: no protectorate supporters in positions of authority; reform of the ministry and the law in

---

[22] Respect for Overton's abilities was widespread. In April 1654 the King wrote to Overton offering a pardon in exchange for support – *Calendar of the Clarendon State Papers*, ed. O. Ogle *et al.*, 4 vols. (Oxford, 1869–1932), II, 344. Whether Overton received the letter is not known. A year later, 20 March 1655, a protectorate agent warned that Charles and Overton 'were agreed before he was a prisoner' – *State Papers of Thurloe*, III, 280; the report is not plausible.

[23] *Diary of Thomas Burton, Esq.*, ed. John T. Rutt, 4 vols. (London, 1828), III, 45–48 (3 February), IV, 150–61 (16 March). *The sad Suffering Case of ... Overton*, [John Rogers], *The Plain Case of the Common-weal Neer the Desperate Gulf of the Common-Woe* ([3 March] 1659), p. 15. Newsletter [12 March?], *CP*, III, 184–85.

[24] Overton is among the twelve identified as fifth-monarchy men by B. S. Capp, *The Fifth Monarchy Men* (London, 1972), p. 126 and App. 1.

accordance with scripture; true liberty of conscience and no state church. The petition also asks for a government by 'men of courage, God fearing, and hating Covetousnesse' who will rule the nation 'as part of Christs universall Kingdome'.

In early October, regiments outside London received letters asking them to subscribe a petition submitted to parliament by the council of officers. The petition included the untenable demand that, except in cases of disbandment, no officer or soldier be dismissed except by court martial.[25] Overton and his officers replied that it would be improper to subscribe to a petition that had already been submitted. At the same time they qualify support for the Rump by stating that they are obliged to support parliament 'in all their Just and Equitable determinations'.[26] On 12 October, parliament cashiered the nine officers who signed the letter asking for support for the petition and placed command of the army in the hands of seven commissioners, one of whom was Overton. His tenure was brief. The next day troops of the dismissed officers obstructed all entrances to the House.[27] Once again the army would try – and fail – to establish a government.

Monck, like Overton, had rejected the officers' petition[28] and was one of the seven commissioners named to govern the army. When he learned of the lock-out of the members, he immediately declared for the parliament and prepared to march south. On 20 October he wrote to Overton and others asking for their support.[29] No reply from Overton has been found, but in early November he published a six-page tract, *The Humble and Healing Advice ... to Charles Lord Fleetwood, And General Monck.*[30] His chagrin at yet another dismissal of government is evident in the first paragraph: 'Babel-like, our buildings are accompanied by nothing but confusion and contempt, which makes the Nations abroad to scoff and scorn, and our enemies at home to rejoyce in hopes of our ruine.'[31] However dismayed,

---

[25] See, e.g., *A Letter from the Lord Lambert And other Officers to General Monck, Inviting the Officers under his Command to subscribe the Representation ... presented to the Parliament the day before. With ... Answer thereunto by General Monck,* ([22 October] 1659). *The Humble Representation and Petition,* reprinted, Richard Baker, *A Chronicle of the Kings of England,* 4th edn (London, 1665), pp. 714–16, was presented to parliament 5 October (*Commons' Journals* (*CJ*), VII, 792).

[26] *A Letter from Ma. Gen. Overton, Governour of Hull, And the Officers under his Command* (11 October 1659).

[27] Newsletter, 13 October 1659, *CP*, IV, 60–61.   [28] Above, n. 25.

[29] Monck to Ludlow with notation: 'The like to M.G. Overton' – *The Memoirs of Edmund Ludlow,* ed. C. H. Firth, 2 vols. (Oxford, 1894), II, 449.

[30] For probable date, see Godfrey Davies, *The Restoration of Charles II, 1658–1660* (Oxford, 1955), p. 161, n. 56.

[31] Norbrook, '"Blushing tribute"', p. 226, points out that Milton expresses similar chagrin in *The Readie and Easie Way to Restore a Free Commonwealth* (March 1660).

Overton contends that the Lord has been forced to 'overturn and overturn' because no foundation has conformed with 'what we professe' – not even Barebone's Parliament, which was 'mischievously mixed for other ends'.

After reviewing a decade of disappointment, Overton turns to his immediate concern: the danger of bloodshed between the armies in England and Scotland. The council of officers in England are warned not to take advantage of their power to aggrandise themselves. Monck is beseeched to 'drive not so furiously against the dispensation of God, though it be clouded with the weaknesse and failings of the instruments'. Both councils are reminded that they are brethren who must bind up their breach, otherwise 'another overturne will suddenly overtake you'. As for himself, Overton will endeavor to secure the peace of Hull and stand ready to support the settlement that 'hath the most of the ... superscription of Christ upon it'. In his last published tract, Overton recognises that government by godly men is a remote ideal.

The return of the Rump on 26 December ended ten weeks of military government and the danger of anarchy and violence receded. Monck's forces crossed the Tweed on 1 January and as he led them south his welcome overwhelmed resistance. In York, Monck was told that Overton was preparing to defend Hull against a siege. He sent a message asking for 'a full and free declaration' of Overton's adherence to the restored parliament. Overton replied the next day, 13 January, expressing satisfaction that Monck stood against the readmission of the members secluded in 1648, explaining that he had been 'necessitated' to 'walke soe warily' lest he lose his command. With his reply Overton enclosed a copy of his letter of 11 October rejecting the council of officers' petition to parliament. Monck accepted Overton's explanation, emphasising their mutual concern to thwart those 'whose designs itt is to bring in the Common Enimie'.[32]

Monck's intentions remained obscure for more than a month, but on 21 February, when he directed the seating of the secluded members, the return of the 'Common Enimie' became a certainty. A week later Overton and the Hull garrison addressed a letter to Monck in which they declare their 'disconcurrence' with proceedings that confirm their worst fears and assure him of their determination to live and die for the cause that he has hitherto 'publicly owned with us'. Copies of the letter – which may never have been sent to Monck – were widely circulated among troops in Yorkshire who are urged to concur for the good old cause against the king or single person. When Monck received a copy, sent by Colonels Bethell

---

[32] The three letters, 12, 13, 14 January, are printed in *CP*, IV, 244–47. The first two were published in *The Publick Intelligencer*, 23–30 January 1660, pp. 1037–39, and as a pamphlet, *A Letter from ... Monck, to ... Overton ...* (January 1660). For 11 October letter, above, n. 26.

and Charles Fairfax, he named Fairfax governor of Hull and sent Overton a stiff letter in which he denies any diminution of his own devotion to parliament, states that Overton's actions put the nation at risk of war, and orders him to leave for London within six hours.[33] If Monck received a rambling letter sent by Overton on 6 March, he did not mention it, and when Overton received Monck's order he recognised that surrender was inescapable: cavalier interests were rapidly gaining support in Hull and the garrison's soldiers were divided. He left immediately, reaching London on 18 March.[34] His military career was over.

He soon lost his freedom as well. The king returned in May, and although Overton had taken no part in the trial of Charles I and was not excluded from the act of pardon, in December he was seized in a series of arrests said to forestall a 'horrid contrivance' against the 'peace of the Nation'. Overton denied participation in any plot and when accused of bringing arms to London he said that he would prove by oath that it was to sell them. He was never permitted a trial, and there is no hard evidence that the 'horrid contrivance' existed. Nevertheless, the following November, amid reports of another amorphous plot, Overton was moved from the Tower to Chepstow where he was held a close prisoner. At some point in the next eighteen months he gained his freedom, for in May 1663 he was again arrested, 'suspected of seditious practices, and refusing to take the oaths or give security'.[35] In 1663/64 he was again sent to Jersey, where it is probable that he had reasonable freedom on the island and evident that he was well supplied with books. Yet island winters were bleak and the isolation away from family and friends a severe deprivation. His health probably suffered, and this may have been a factor in his release to his brother-in-law, Thomas Gardiner, in 1671.[36] Nothing has been discovered about his subsequent life or his death.

---

[33] Hull garrison to Monck, 28 February, HMC, *Leyborne Popham Mss.*, p. 163. Bethell and Charles Fairfax to Monck, 2 March, *CP*, IV, 264–65. Monck's letter to Overton is printed without date in Baker, *Chronicles*, pp. 753–54; on 4 March the council of state ordered Overton to obey Monck (*CSPD*, 1659–60, p. 381).

[34] Overton to Monck, 6 March, HMC, *Leyborne Popham Mss.*, pp. 170–71. Letters from Hull, 7 March, *Mercurius Politicus*, 8–15 March, pp. 1163–65; ibid., 15–22 March, p. 1190; *Memoirs of Ludlow*, II, 246–47. John Price, in *The Mystery and Method of His Majesty's happy Restauration* (1680), pp. 125–6, states that Major Jeremiah Smith, sent to Hull with Colonel Alured, 'bought off the Souldiers' with money'. Price was one of Monck's chaplains.

[35] *Mercurius Publicus*, 13–20 December, pp. 810–11; *The Diary of Samuel Pepys*, ed. Robert Latham and William Matthews, 11 vols. (London, 1970–83), I, 318–19. *CSPD*, 1661–62, p. 141 (9 November). HMC, *Eleventh Report*, App., Pt vii, pp. 3, 6 (8 November 1661, 26 May 1663).

[36] *CSPD*, 1663–64, p. 461 (30 January 1664). Ibid., 1671–72, p. 13 (6 December 1671).

THE MANUSCRIPT

Overton's manuscript, which is catalogued with the title of the first section, 'Gospell Observations & Religious Manifestations, &c.', is a quarto volume of 360 pages bound in undressed calf; the page size is 15.8 × 22.7 cm (c. 6½ × 9 inches). Each of the fourteen sections has a title and running heads, and the volume concludes with a three-page index.[37] The writing is small, neat and legible, and is Overton's hand throughout. A poetic dedication on the flyleaf and the prose preface 'To the Reder' (pp. 151–52), which precedes many poetic and prose tributes to Ann Overton, indicate that Overton considered his work a memorial to his wife, who died in 1665. The opening lines of one poem – ''Tis now since I began to die, / six yeares …' (p. 183) – reveal that the poem was written in 1671, the last year of Overton's imprisonment.[38] How much of the manuscript was composed before or after this date is unknown. The tone and content of the first section suggests that all but the last entry (pp. 71–77), which was dated 4 June 1665, was written before Ann Overton's death.[39] Much of the verse in subsequent sections includes unattributed excerpts from other authors; the evidence of Overton's earlier writings leaves no reasonable doubt that the political segment published here is his alone.

'Goverments gaine & goodnesse &c' (pp. 34–40) is addressed to potential rebels whom Overton would deter. Overton was among the revolutionaries who believed that the Civil War was the beginning of a unique moment in England's history.[40] Throughout the wars he fought with confidence that God had decreed the military successes of parliament's forces and would guide them on the path of righteousness to a moral and peaceful state. Disillusioned when the Rump continued to govern after the abolition of monarchy, he took his stand in June 1649, pledging acceptance of an unsatisfactory settlement while keeping inviolable his 'private Trust'.[41] Overton maintained this position throughout the interregnum, supporting successive settlements as the available obstacles to the return of the king. Occasionally, he stated his concerns – which may have caused his critics to infer that he was an uncertain ally, vacillating

---

[37] Catalogue entry: Overton, Robert: 'Gospell Observations and Religious Manifestations, &c', Ms. CO 199. For a detailed description of the manuscript see Norbrook, '"Blushing tribute"', App., pp. 246–63.

[38] 'Gospell Observations', p. 214, dates Ann Overton's death, '12 Janu: 1665'; ibid., p. 92, indicates that the date is new style.

[39] The pagination in section one skips from p. 60 to p. 70. Norbrook, '"Blushing tribute"', p. 224, states: 'the later part of the manuscript, and probably the whole of it, thus dates from his last year on Jersey or from the obscure final period of his life'.

[40] Cf. John Milton, *Areopagitica* (1644), as in *Complete Prose*, II, 552–3.

[41] Above, pp. 289–90.

between obedience and resistance.[42] With the possible exception of the few weeks in 1660 when he briefly opposed Monck's moves toward restoration of the monarchy, examples of Overton's vacillation are nowhere evident while his surrender to Monck's insuperable position is another example of his realism. He was a thinking man who responded rationally to existing situations while never abandoning his vision of government by godly men.

'Religious advertisements &c' (pp. 40–44), which succeeds 'Goverments gaine & goodnesse' in Overton's manuscript, reveals that he was also religiously reasonable and unusually tolerant. Many historians (including the present writer) have stated that Overton was a fifth-monarchy man.[43] In fact, there is no evidence that Overton subscribed to tenets that set fifth monarchists apart and there is clear evidence that he rejected concepts that distinguished fifth-monarchy men from the many revolutionaries who hoped for government by godly men. Except for a brief moment in January 1649 – three weeks before the execution of the king and more than two years before the fifth-monarchy movement emerged – Overton never suggested that any polity be established by armed force and at no time did he concur with the radical social changes associated with fifth-monarchy men. There is no suggestion in Overton's known writings that he expected a literal Second Coming, let alone by a date certain. To the contrary, Overton states that 'high and sundry assertions often end in shismes & many mistakes', notes the miscalculations of the time of the pope's fall and Rome's ruin (p. 40), and concludes that 'the 5th Monarchy Millinaryes are men of a comfortable creed, were it not for the many incongruetyes & contradictions they encounter' (p. 42). Despite incongruities, Overton asks that no profession of piety be despised (p. 40). It was, he wrote, 'well sayde that a good religion might be composed oute of the Papists charity, the Protestants profession, the Puritans prayers & (I may ad) the Quakers piety & spirituality in theire active and passive practices' (p. 42).

The overarching theme of Overton's political treatise is acceptance of existing authority. From the opening sentence – 'Itch not after any untried goverment, chainge is often a cheat' – to the concluding paragraph – 'live not theirfore licorish after chainge, for feare (as formerly) of being cheated' (p. 39) – Overton repeatedly advises quiet obedience 'to any power which providence appointes to sit in the sadle of soveraighnity' (p. 35). Avoid 'commotions', he cautions, 'be not the pen or mouth of the multitude' (p. 34), but do not hesitate to 'give honor to fresh families whoe have ascended' (p. 36), and 'dispise meaneness of blood in none' (p. 37).

[42] See, e.g.: Maurice Ashley, 'The vacillations of Major-General Robert Overton', Ashley, *Cromwell's Generals* (London, 1954), pp. 137–49; McGregor, above, n. 2.

[43] From Firth to McGregor, above n. 2.

Throughout 'Goverments gaine & goodnesse' Overton's magnanimity and charity are evident. Despite the failure of the revolution and his own maltreatment, the fairness and humanity attested by wartime foes as well as friends were conjoined with an uncommon 'sweetness of disposition'[44] that saved him from a bitterness that would be understandable in one who suffered years of imprisonment that few could consider just. In his published writings Overton's concerns are strongly stated and frequently enhanced with engaging metaphors. His political manuscript is quieter, almost contemplative, and his points are often accentuated with biblical references. No longer working amid the political turmoil of the interregnum, Overton wrote calmly and confidently. The mood of the maxims is philosophical, but there is no lack of vitality. Critical recollection of the duplicities of Cromwell and Monck, who 'foole and unman', reveals that Overton was not devoid of asperity, and he clearly condemns the empowerment of soldiers in a state established by armed forces (p. 39).[45]

More significant is the absence of any comment about the Stuart restoration and the dispassionate observations about monarchy (pp. 38–39). Possibly, Overton said no more because he wrote in prison. It is more probable that, even as he admires the fate of those who struggle for 'publick liberty', he advises submission to any expedient power (pp. 36–37) because he believed that godly government is the province of God. In accordance with his conclusion in 1659 – 'the Lord himself ... is forced to shake and shake, overturn and overturn' the defective governments of the 1650s – Overton may well have regarded the restored monarchy as one more flawed settlement in the 'overturning' that must continue until a foundation is laid that will 'answer the end of God'.[46] It is a short step from *The Humble and Healing Advice* to Overton's admission in 'Goverments gaine & goodnesse' that a godly state is beyond the reach of mortal men: 'They that pursew perfaction on earth will leave nothinge for saintes to finde in heaven, for while men teach theire will be mistakes & errors in both church and state' (p. 39).

GOVERMENTS GAINE & GOODNESSE &C[47]

Itch not after any untried government, chainge is often a cheat. The die of warre seldome consortes his commodity that first cast it. Goverment is

---

[44] Above, p. 288.
[45] Cf. 'Gospell Observations', p. 166, where 'C & M' are again denigrated; I owe this reference to Norbrook, ' "Blushing tribute" ', p. 237.
[46] *The Humble and Healing Advice*, pp. 1–2; above, p. 294.
[47] Abbreviations have been extended or standardised in modern form. Spelling is as in the original, except for 'i' to 'j' and 'u' to 'v' when appropriate. Missing letters have been

Gods gift but mens commotions are not commodius, advanceinge little more then our owne miseries, beinge often maimed but at best layd by withoute rewarde soe soon as the state returnes to its prestine splendor, common soldiers resemblinge cocks that feighte for the benifit & ambition of others more then theire owne. Theirfore rather stay within doores then step into the distempers of superior plannets. In civill commotions money & men muste communicate quiet. In this respect be not the pen or the mouth of the multitude, least upon a pardon or complyance thou be left in the lurch to the punishment of an exasperated power. Rather have patience & see the tree sufficiently shaken before youe fetch the fallen fruite since the zeale of the rable is not soe soone heated by the oppression of theire princes or rulers but may be more quickly cooled & conquered by their specious promises & plausable respects, brought forth by the breath of authority. Nurce not ambition by thine owne blood nor beleive a blast of honor big enough to blow away the buble of a buried valour. Parties possesst with a religious pretence are (as exasperated beares) not opposed withoute prejudice. The rude rable (like Moses rod) denounces all for diabolicall that opposes their proceedings with the swine in the Gospell, [34] beinge agitated more by others furious spirits then theire owne, to sinke or swim in a sea of blood.

In bad times, the example of Brutis rather than Cato is by many commended. Its safer (in this respect) to be a patient foole then an active mad malcontent. Our Saviour himselfes not heard to inveigh against that present power which had made John Baptists heade the frollick of a feast. Ile owne the magistrates power but not his evel practises. Ahab might better have committed murther then to reach Naboths vineyard under the forme of a religious fast, to have made soe many accessories & instruments in those impieties whereof hee himselfe was principall. Beinge fixt, forsake not your side for any ill successe. The irresolution of a Jack on both sides is seldome worth the owneinge by any interest. Hee thats inconstant to one side is never in earnest for another. Fidelity is seldom frounde on & as seldome failes of forgivenesse from a noable enemy whoe cannot but honor him whome he founde faithfull & honest in armes against him. Wee may prudently & piously purchase our preservation but he that prolonges his life by the forfiture of his faith husbands it worse then if he had buried it in the bed of honor or feild of fortitude – trators to trust beinge in all ages equally detested by both sides. Submit peaceably to any power which

supplied when needed. Capitals have been lower cased in modern style. Paragraphing has occasionally been altered and punctuation has been revised to assist understanding without destroying the rhythm. Page numbers of the manuscript have been inserted in the text in square brackets. I am indebted to Laetitia Yeandle of the Folger Shakespeare Library for advice in transcribing the manuscript.

providence appointes to sit in the sadle of soveraighnity withoute inquireinge (for conscience sake) into residentiall right. The many headed multitude is as often gulled by the new as the olde sadle of riders. When the game proves good what care I what cardes turned trump. Henceforward, theirfore, holde it a high frenzy to dispute a setled perceptive power. If it be no folly to submit to theeves into whose fiste youe are fallen, let not the example [35] of a few fooles whoe (like poore lice thrive noe where soe well as in prison) tempt youe to oppose your peace against the imperative power of youre person.

Theirfore, if youe may enjoy the liberty of your carcasse, conscience & estate, question not the desert or right of those by whome youe doe it. Upon this accounte he cracks his credit that is overawed by the errors of his conscience. Be not offended to give honor to fresh families whoe have ascended theireunto by some stares of honor as our forefathers did: what was new is now olde, & what now new will be olde hereafter. Pull noe unnecessary sufferinges upon your selfe, wee see none more grounde to powder in this mill of vicissitudes then those that obstinately glory in the repute of sufferinge as state martyrs after they are dead, of which they shall be noe more sensible then was Busephelus of his maister Alexanders indulgence or universall soveraighnity. Theirfore let nobody begg to be buried in the ruines of publick liberty, but yet hees brave who that way sinkes where sicophants swim, for the former shall be justified while the latter is moste deserveingely traduste by the letter. Affect not false fame nor follow her trumpit which for the moste part congrigates more enemies then friends. Consider the inconstancy of common applause, how many have had theire reputations rackt or ruined upon that which rayzed it? This renders it the poorist purillity, to be leased with reportes or applause, for good is quickened or evell quenched in nothing more then the neglect of that gaudy goddess, the peoples prayses, whose soome of false fame hath foundered more then ever grace or goodnesse glorified. Prudent persons ever passe over ostentations brought forth from birth or breedinge whereby the very foundations of honor suffer shakeinges. Be not abused by bustlinge for the uper end of the borde. [36] This pulls back in others repute what thoue promotes in thine owne opinion &c.

Dispise meanenesse of blood in none; to make inferior parsons (clarified with parts) your companions is noe disparagement. Upon an uncertaine publick pursewance of power postepone not thy owne private preservation. What signifies such superiors to us as seame unable (though by our assistance) to supporte themeselves? Powers are to protect us, whoe are to live happy under them, not miserable for or by them (if possible to be prevented). In this sense all goverments pass amongst the rest of Gods plagues, poured down upon our primitive parents & us for oure disobedience. This makes our wills (like Eves) subject to others. No goverment can be safely engaged by a single parson above or beyond requitall. Kinges deem it a deminution of honour and republicks repute it a perrillus step to popularrity. Upon this accounte consider the care of circumspection, perceiveinge it possible for virtue to forme a ponyeard for its owne prejudice. If it be daingerus to ore oblige a Kinge, its mortall to a free state whose ingratitude & forgetfullnesse is manifested to soe many as they are scarce capable of shame, or thankes to such servants as have sided with or soally served themselves. The history of great Warwick and Stanly tells us that a power may sometimes be as safely puled downe as set up. Commonwealths are in nothinge greater then ingratitude, either goverment findeinge it greater husbandry to free enemies then favour friends with rewards. Its unsafe to trust a reconciled foe, yet (if any) a great one, [37] it being easier for such to manifest their mallice then conceale it. Hee is no better to be trusted whome youe have by brides or bounty obliged.

Nothinge beinge more manifest then to see ill natures quit such scores with hatred or treachery as care & kindenesse hath conferd. How many milions of heartes have been empty of pitty to oppressed princes, whose hands have formerly been filled with their favours, whoe are now neglected & offended with theire frounes? In this regarde charrity seldome goes to the gate but it meetes with ingratitude. Thus they (for the moste part) prove the greatest enemies that have been bought or purchast at the highest price of respect. This proceedes from the high pride of humanity. Be theirfore as little flatterd to doe good (upon accounte of requitall) as I woulde have you terified for feare of its contrary. Crasse providence hath appointed us all partes of perplexinge calamities; its folly theirfore to make after markits of misfortunes as they doe that contract forraigne infelicities, consumeinge themselves for the miscarriage of the Prince of Cunde [sic] in France, the death of the Kinge of Sweden in Germany, or of Kinge Charles the first in England. In this respect is not Tophet prepared as wel to perplex unquiet spirits of pevish subjects as of proudest princes? High degrees of honor are easilyer attained to under monarchy then theires room for in a republick, as may be founde in favorites that have had the full administration of all affaires. Yet some suppose that the people suffer in not subjectinge themselves to the passions of a single person. Republicks lye most obnoxious to popular pettishnesse. Monarchies stand most lyable to clandestine attempts. [38] In the first its unsafe to be founde, except soe epidemicall as they may safely assure successe.

In the latter its most loathesome (thoughe seconded by security), noe hands beinge more base and hatefull then those that are tainted by blood and treachery. But where a golden tongue falls under a furnisht head it shall soone influence & soe safely sway a whole senate. They that pursew perfaction on earth leave nothinge for saintes to finde in heaven, for while men teach theire will be mistakes & errors both in church & state. Live not theirfore licorish after chainge, for feare (as formerly) of beinge cheated. Why may not future ages (as well as former) finde a Crumwell or a Munke to foole & unman them? Its policy to make men of parsons or partes state friends by preferment. The complyance of an eloquent pen or tongue is of publick as of politick improvement either in peace or war to prevent conspiracies, as to promote pius or publick pursewances, especially beinge imbarked in religious bottomes under the semblance of safety, setlement, & sanctity. I commend not the punishinge of children for their fathers crimes or offenses. To rooke their families whoe have participated (upon specious pretenses) with the promoters of publick oppression is more Romish then religious & as daingerus as to be detested, for riged security is seldome seasonable or free from a rude & rash revenge. I conceive it unsafe for any state founded by blood to conceed or place too great a power in soldiers for their satisfaction, seeinge they (like the spirits of conjurers) many times teare & pul their maisters in peices (as was witnessed in Crumwell and his creatures) [39] for want of a more profitable imployment. Theirfore, seinge it passes the plenty of any prince, or state, to proportion a payment to the price they put upon theire owne perrils or performances, it behoves a supreme power to bury theire ambition in the feildes of a forraign warfaire, yet with as little discontent as can be denoted, never grudgeinge them the gratitude of good servants, soe they scilently imagin & beleve them bad maisters, ever rememberinge that the cause for which they were first raysed is not so deeply buried but that it may rise againe to the terror of all those that woulde withstand it. &c. [40]

14

Locke no Leveller

G. E. AYLMER

The political philosophy of John Locke continues to arouse controversy. This in itself is testimony to the interest both of the man and of his writings. The most ambitious attempt of recent years to set Locke's political ideas in a detailed biographical and historical context is to be found in the work of the late Richard Ashcraft.[1] To quote his words:

> What I have attempted, therefore, is a marriage of Locke's ideas with the actions and objectives of a political movement in which Locke was a participant and for which his ideas served as an articulate expression of the meaning of those actions and goals.[2]

His location of Locke in the radical (and not merely Whiggish) politics of the 1670s and 1680s led Ashcraft in a very specific direction: 'I have throughout this work placed Locke in much closer proximity to the Levellers and to the radical political theory they developed than has previously been supposed.'[3] While this interpretation has been severely criticised by some historians and social scientists,[4] Ashcraft's work has been sufficiently influential to merit further scrutiny. Needless to say, it is a matter of much regret that he can no longer himself join in this discussion.

There is more than one way of approaching the possible connections

---

[1] Richard Ashcraft, *Revolutionary Politics and Locke's Two Treatises of Government* (Princeton, 1986).

[2] Ibid., Preface, p. xi.   [3] Ibid., ch. 4, pp. 164–65.

[4] Gordon J. Schochet, 'Radical Politics and Ashcraft's Treatise on Locke', *Journal of the History of Ideas*, 50 (1989), 491–510, is much more critical than I am but concentrates on different aspects of Ashcraft's book; both seem to me to underrate, even to neglect, J. Tully, *A Discourse on Property: John Locke and his Adversaries* (Cambridge, 1980). More recently *The History of Political Thought* devoted a whole issue, vol. 13, no. 4 (1992) to John Locke, a large proportion of it being taken up with criticisms of Ashcraft and his lengthy defence against these. My only qualification for adding to this debate is that I have previously written on the Levellers and that I am currently working on royal office-holders under Charles II (1660–85).

between Locke and the Levellers. It is possible to argue that those who were called Levellers (of whom John Lilburne, Richard Overton, William Walwyn and John Wildman were the most important, together with Thomas Rainsborough and Edward Sexby for their part in the Army debates) were more interested in preserving individual property rights than they were in complete democracy, even if the right to vote in parliamentary elections was limited to adult males. This was more or less the position of the late C. B. Macpherson in his work on what he called 'possessive individualism'.[5] By thus making the Levellers less populist, and so as democratic theorists less revolutionary, than used to be supposed, it is possible to see Locke as having followed in their ideological footsteps without needing to make him democratic or revolutionary. This, however, was far from being Ashcraft's view; indeed he devoted considerable energy to refuting it. Alternatively it may be argued, and for most historians today with a good deal more plausibility, that the Levellers were not a homogeneous group, let alone a monolithic party; and that some of them, such as Maximilian Petty at Putney, did indeed adopt a position consonant with 'possessive individualism', while others were nearer to being 'true Levellers', as the Diggers sometimes styled themselves. The thesis that some Levellers became persuaded that true democracy was incompatible with unfettered private ownership of land and capital is strengthened if we accept the proposition (advanced by Olivier Lutaud, and perhaps also believed by H. N. Brailsford) that Walwyn was the author of the anonymous *Tyranipocrit* of August 1649.[6] This emphasis on Leveller heterogeneity, taking into account the supposed contrast, indeed disagreement between possessive individualists and true Levellers, was the interpretation adopted by the Russian scholar, M. Barg, which has been accepted by Christopher Hill in his later writings.[7] On this view the traditional Locke would not be so different from the more conservative Levellers, or perhaps we should say from the more conservative elements in Leveller thought, in particular that of Lilburne and the authors of the

---

[5] C. B. Macpherson, *The Political Theory of Possessive Individualism* (Oxford, 1962). See also Brian Manning, *The English People and the English Revolution* (London, 1976), and *The Crisis of the English Revolution* (London, 1992) for the best re-statements of a broadly similar position.

[6] O. Lutaud, *Cromwell, les Niveleurs et la République* (Paris, 1978), pp. 79–81; *Winstanley: socialisme et Christianisme sous Cromwell* (Paris, 1976), pp. 183, 437; H. N. Brailsford, *The Levellers and the English Revolution* (London, 1961), p. 71, n. 1. This is not accepted by Barbara Taft in *The Writings of William Walwyn*, ed. Jack R. McMichael and Barbara Taft (Athens, Georgia, 1989), pp. 532–35, 564–65. For a modern edition of the text, see *Tyranipocrit Discovered*, ed. Andrew Hopton (London, [1990]).

[7] C. Hill, *The World Turned Upside Down* (London, 1972).

compromise clauses on the franchise in the Second and Third *Agreements of the People.*[8]

But this is not the way in which the matter has been approached by those who can see Locke as having been influenced by Levellerism. Rather it is argued that he was some kind of political 'Nicodemean', whose real convictions were more radical, not to say revolutionary, than he allowed to appear, except by reading between the lines of his writings. There is certainly not unanimity about this among scholars of Locke's life and works. In his Introduction to the classic modern edition of the *Two Treatises on Government* Peter Laslett overturned all previous interpretations by arguing, with great persuasiveness and precision, that their composition dated, not from the immediate aftermath of the Revolution of 1688–89, but from the beginning of that decade or even earlier; in brief most of the *Second Treatise* was first written during the winter of 1679–80, and the *First Treatise* in 1680, with additions to the former being made in 1681 and continued alterations and amendments into 1682 and 1683, followed by final revisions in 1689.[9] Ashcraft by contrast believed that the *First* and *Second Treatises* were written in that order during 1681–82; that is, not while the Exclusion, or (as Jonathan Scott and others now prefer to call it) the Restoration Crisis was still in progress, or at least only in its latter stages, after Shaftesbury and his allies had been defeated and had turned from political opposition to plans for armed rebellion. So the *Second Treatise* was in no way an Exclusionist tract against James Duke of York but a revolutionary manifesto against Charles II, and one so potentially dangerous to its author that it could not be published until after the death of that King and the overthrow of his brother.[10] The disagreement about dating between Laslett and Ashcraft is not central to the present argument; even if the *Treatises* were written when and for the purposes proposed by Ashcraft, it would not prove his case about Leveller influence. In order to reach a balanced answer to this question we need to compare the Levellers and Locke over the widest possible range of issues, involving both beliefs and actions. We might be persuaded that Locke was more subversive, in the sense that he was helping Shaftesbury to try to engineer a revolution,

---

[8] For the full texts of all the *Agreements*, see Don M. Wolfe (ed.), *Leveller Manifestoes* (New York, 1944, and later reprints); for the first and third Leveller *Agreements*, G. E. Aylmer (ed.), *The Levellers in the English Revolution* (London, 1975).

[9] P. Laslett (ed.), *Locke's Treatises on Government* (Cambridge, 1960), Introduction, s. iii, esp. p. 65; reprint edn (Cambridge, 1988), pp. 123–26, Addendum to Introduction.

[10] The clearest statement of his preferred dating is in R. Ashcraft, *Locke's Two Treatises of Government* (London, 1987), Appendix, pp. 286–97, rather than in his *Revolutionary Politics* where it is implicit in much of the argument, but not explicitly stated. Laslett's response is in his Addendum of 1988, giving ground only as to the date by which Locke could have read Filmer's *Patriarcha* and thus have begun to write the *First Treatise*.

without necessarily having to agree that he was more populist, democratic or 'Levellerist' than the received view has generally held him to have been. This in turn hinges almost as much on Shaftesbury and his intentions as on Locke. The Earl was associated with some undoubtedly radical figures, including a few ex-Levellers and more ex-republicans from the 1640s and 1650s, but it does not follow that he shared their beliefs. His relationship with them might have been comparable to that of the opposition leaders in the Long Parliament with the militant Londoners, including some future Levellers, during 1640–42: ready to use them as an instrument by means of which to put pressure on the King without sharing their programme or aspirations.[11]

The theory of convergence, that the Levellers and Locke were more alike than has generally been supposed, may be supported on varying grounds, not all of them compatible with each other. On one view the Levellers were so socially conservative, so limited in their democratic desires, that they differed little if at all from the later seventeenth-century 'Commonwealthmen' and the more radical of the early Whigs. Their contemporaries misunderstood them, or to put it another way they appeared to be more radical than they really were, partly through inadvertence, partly due to their tactical ineptitude. The criticisms of Macpherson's interpretation of the Levellers and the franchise, made some years ago by Sir Keith Thomas, Ian Hampsher-Monk and others, have made such a strong case against it that this scarcely needs further rebuttal.[12] Nonetheless, as already noted, we have to be careful to see precisely which interpretation is being rebutted by whom. Thus a slightly different and certainly more sophisticated version appears in some of Mark Kishlansky's writings: that the practical grievances of the Army were more important than radical political or religious ideas in the crisis of spring and early summer 1647, and that consensus not confrontation was the objective of all parties in the Putney Debates; the Agitators were not Levellers and a Leveller movement scarcely existed.[13] Austin Woolrych has himself discussed this very fully, and I certainly cannot improve on his account. In his most recent treatment he has portrayed the Leveller leaders, especially Lilburne, as tactically inept politicians, but he hardly

[11] K. Haley, *The First Earl of Shaftesbury* (Oxford, 1968).

[12] K. Thomas, 'The Levellers and the Franchise', in G. E. Aylmer (ed.), *The Interregnum. The Quest for Settlement 1646–1660* (Basingstoke, 1972), pp. 57–78, 207–8, 219–22; Ian Hampsher-Monk, 'The Political Theory of the Levellers: Putney, Property and Professor Macpherson', *Political Studies*, 24 (1976), 397–422. For Macpherson's reply to his critics see his *Democratic Theory: Essays in Retrieval* (Oxford, 1973), ch. xii.

[13] M. Kishlansky, *The Rise of the New Model Army* (N.Y. and Cambridge, 1979); 'The Army and the Levellers: the roads to Putney', *Historical Journal*, 22 (1978), 777–824; 'Consensus politics and the structure of debate at Putney', *Journal of British Studies*, 20 (1981), 50–69.

carries this to the length of suggesting that they pretended to be more radical than they were, although to appear so might have been one (unintended) result of their ineptitude.[14] In some of the earliest attacks made on them by the Presbyterian minister Thomas Edwards, in his *Gangraena* of 1646, and from some of the things which were said by Cromwell and Ireton at Putney, we can see that those who were given the name Levellers by their enemies were open to portrayal as dangerous extremists, whether in good faith – whatever his other failings, Edwards was surely sincere – or disingenuously in order to discredit them – and there might be room for disagreement here both about Ireton in the debates and about some of the later anti-Leveller pamphleteers in 1649. The generalised Anglican-Cavalier stereotype after 1660, describing all radicals loosely as 'fanatics', deliberately lumped together millenarian Puritans, secular republicans and Commonwealthmen and surviving ex-Levellers, without any attempt to discriminate between them or to analyse their very real and substantial differences and disagreements. In the last-named category John Wildman was potentially the most dangerous not only on account of his undoubted talents but because of his connection with that archetypal aristocratic *frondeur*, the second Duke of Buckingham. But although Buckingham and Lord Ashley (later Earl of Shaftesbury) were to be political allies on and off, both in government and in opposition, during the later 1660s and the 1670s, it is quite untenable to elide the political attitudes of their respective clients, Wildman and Locke. More-over it is open to debate whether Wildman still was a Leveller, in the 1647–53 sense of the term, after the Restoration. Even his pamphlet of 1659, called *The Leveller*, could be seen as misleading in this respect. Only the choice of political colours – the sea-green Leveller badges and ribbons of 1647–49 and the Green Ribbon club of 1678–80 – provides an element in common, assuming that it was the same shade of green.

There is always a risk of ascribing hidden motives and concealed views on the basis of people's silence, or by reading into what they said or wrote a startlingly different message from what the texts appear to tell. It is usually more sensible for the historian to assume that people meant what they said, and – more cautiously – to suppose that they did not mean what they did not say. This is subject to an obvious and very important qualification: at different times in different places, some beliefs – and disbeliefs – have been too dangerous for public expression, and risky enough even in private letters, diaries or conversations. Not the least remarkable feature of the 1640s and 1650s, by contrast with both earlier

[14] See *The Historian*, 34 (Spring 1992), 3–8; and in greater detail his classic study *Soldiers and Statesmen: The General Council of the Army and its Debates 1647–1648* (Oxford, 1987).

and later times, is the extent to which radical ideas about politics, religion and society were openly expressed. The Treason and Blasphemy laws were invoked variously against Levellers, Unitarians, Ranters and Quakers; Winstanley and the Diggers were the victims of harassment and persecution for their actions rather than prosecution for their writings; the early Quakers, before they embraced pacifism and non-violence, suffered on both counts. The best-known case of a Leveller concealing the radicalism of his views depends on the hypothesis (already mentioned) that Walwyn wrote the *Tyranipocrit*: for what it is worth, near the beginning of that extraordinary work the author tells his readers that he is concealing his identity, not to protect himself but to prevent the ideas which he is expressing from being discredited – an unusual, though not unique, form of avoiding 'guilt by association'. But the usual reason for anonymity was of course to protect the writer, as with other Interregnum pamphlets and post-Restoration publications; and, in the case of Locke's *Two Treatises*, even with a book published after the Revolution.

None of this seems to take us any nearer to validating a Locke–Leveller convergence. One superficially more relevant piece of evidence is provided by the part played during the Popish Plot years and in the Rye House assassination plot by some ex-Agitators and other one-time Army radicals from thirty years before. Whether Locke or Wildman or Sidney at any time favoured and worked to bring about an armed uprising against Charles II and his regime is naturally of much historical interest; but whatever the answer to this may be, it leaves the matter of 'Levellerism' untouched. Except for the May 1649 army mutiny (when the Leveller leaders were already either dispersed or in the Tower), and Sexby's assassination plots against Cromwell in 1656–58, the so-called Levellers had conspicuously not advocated or practised terrorism and violence as means to their ideological ends. So we must bear in mind that in the mid- and later seventeenth century, as much as in the twentieth, belief in and support for the use of armed force to bring about political change is not the same as support for democracy, or vice versa. Levellerism, if we can define it at all, was a specifically seventeenth-century phenomenon, even if the terms leveller and levelling are still in political currency today.

We are therefore driven back to Locke's views as expressed in his writings, in order to test them for Leveller influences. These comprise his youthful *Treatises*, so admirably edited by Philip Abrams in the 1960s,[15] the 'Fundamental constitutions of Carolina' (by all accounts a truly joint production with his patron, then Lord Ashley),[16] and above all the *Two*

---

[15] John Locke, *Two Tracts on Government*, ed. P. Abrams (Cambridge, 1967).

[16] Haley, *Shaftesbury*, pp. 242–48.

Treatises of Government (first published in 1689–90). No doubt account should also be taken of possibly relevant passages in his other published works on *Education, Toleration* and *Human Understanding,* his occasional writings such as those connected with his views on currency and trade, besides his voluminous correspondence, now available in a definitive edition, the final achievement of the late E. S. de Beer.[17] But it is the *Two Treatises* and in particular the *Second* on which Professor Ashcraft rested his case, as he was surely right to do. What can these texts tell us that bears on the issue?

Whether or not Locke's 'industrious and rational' people, to whom God gave the earth for them to develop it as private property, are to be equated with the Levellers' designation of those 'not dependent upon the wills of other men', and therefore qualified to have the vote, might indeed affect where we thought the two parties stood on the franchise question. There are, however, other aspects of Leveller democracy for which it is harder to find any possible Lockean echoes or parallels. The authors of the Second and Third *Agreement of the People* (of December 1648 and May 1649, respectively) wanted frequent – annual or biennial – elections, not just regular annual sessions of parliament; members were to be subject to what we should now call mandation and recall; above all the unicameral legislature to which they looked forward was to be bound by fundamental laws, where statute was most emphatically not an omnicompetent sovereign. Locke, however, was a client and personal friend of a great radical aristocrat. If an Interregnum precedent or parallel is to be sought, the relationship of Henry Parker to Viscount Saye and Sele is more apposite.[18] Wildman's connection with Buckingham after 1659–60 is less to the point here, since (as has already been suggested) it is unclear in what sense he was still a Leveller, at least as understood in 1647–49. Furthermore, and one might think decisively, although an executive council is grudgingly allowed in the second and third *Agreements,* there is no evidence whatsoever of an upper house or bicameral legislature.

Locke might be held to have followed the Levellers in accepting the case for parliamentary reform, in the sense of redistributing seats and re-drawing constituency boundaries. But in fact this had been a consistent concern of the Independents from the summer of 1647 on, culminating – via the Rump's constitutional bill of 1650–53 – in the Instrument of Government and the Cromwellian parliaments elected in 1654 and 1656. Even Clarendon thought that the re-apportionment of seats was 'fit to be

---

[17] *The Correspondence of John Locke,* 8 vols. (Oxford, 1976–89).
[18] See M. Mendle, *Henry Parker and the English Civil War: The People's 'Privado'* (Cambridge, 1995).

more warrantably made and in a better time'.[19] Redistribution of seats and changes in the franchise could go together, as was the case for the counties but not for the boroughs in the constitution of 1653–57, but this was not necessarily so; the preference of the Independents was clearly for redistribution being related to taxable wealth, of the Leveller for its being based on the numbers of people, whether of all male inhabitants or of non-pauper, tax-paying householders. The question here is with which of these preferences Locke's remarks on redistribution are more consonant, and whether he is more likely to have arrived at this position through Leveller or Independent influences from the Interregnum, or through his own reasoning unaided by either of them. Thus he tells us that the Executive can and should regulate the proportions of representation by applying right reason, which would or might lead to the creation of new constituencies and the abolition of others. However nothing specific is said about who should vote; in that respect Locke's silence is comparable to (though not of course identical with) the imprecision of the Levellers in clause 1 of the first *Agreement of the People*,[20] which was so notoriously seized upon by Ireton at Putney, whereas the General Council in its *Representation of the Army* of 14 June 1647 (generally agreed to have been drafted by Ireton) is more specific, calling for redistribution between counties and towns 'proportionable to the respective rates they bear in the common charges and burdens of the kingdom'.[21] We cannot be certain whether this meant equal electoral districts according to the number of tax-paying inhabitants, or according to the taxable wealth of those inhabitants. The former would not have been so different from what was in fact to be agreed and became common ground between Independents and Levellers in 1648–49; the latter would have been highly inegalitarian in numerical terms. In theory a single street or row of houses occupied by the richest men in London would have been entitled to return more members than the whole tax-paying electorate of Wales or the far north of England. It seems more plausible that even Ireton at his hypothetically most conservative would have meant something nearer to the first alternative.

Another way of approaching this problem in Locke's case is to look outside his own text and to consider how far his own preferences can be

---

[19] Clarendon, *History of the Rebellion*, ed. W. D. Macray, 6 vols. (Oxford, 1888; reprinted 1988); v, 299 (Book xiv, para. 43). I am grateful to Blair Worden for this reference, as for much other help in preparing this essay.

[20] Text available in S. R. Gardiner (ed.), *Constitutional Documents of the Puritan Revolution 1625–1660* (Oxford, 1889; many later editions and reprints), Wolfe, *Leveller Manifestoes*, Aylmer, *Levellers*, and other collections.

[21] Full text in Wolfe, *Leveller Manifestoes*, extracts in W. Haller and G. Davies, *Leveller Tracts 1647–1653* (New York, 1944), A. S. P. Woodhouse (ed.), *Puritanism and Liberty: being the Army Debates ... [of 1647–9]* (London, 1938, and later reprints).

inferred from his close relationship with Shaftesbury between 1667 and 1682. But on closer investigation this does not prove very fruitful. Whereas Kenneth Haley regards the *Fundamental Constitutions of Carolina* and *A Letter from a Person of Quality* (1675) as authentic works of joint authorship, he dismisses *Some Observations concerning the regulating of Elections* (published 1689) from the Shaftesburian canon, and this would seem by implication to absolve Locke from having had any hand in it.[22]

Excessive concentration on parliamentary issues and preoccupation with definitions of 'the people' in relation to property, important as these are, may cause other aspects to be neglected. Locke's argument for the right of resistance, for the dissolution of government by the action of the people, is indeed a powerful justification for violent revolution in extreme circumstances. But it is far removed from the Leveller notion of fundamentals, or what might nowadays be called reserved powers, things which the Representative (the Levellers' preferred name for the legislature, or Locke's 'Legislative') cannot do without itself dissolving the Agreement and thus committing the equivalent of High Treason. For Locke the legislative is the supreme arm of government; it might be uni- or bicameral or tripartite, as where he envisaged it including the executive. Not only because of his close connection with Shaftesbury, common sense suggests that he assumed the existence of the House of Lords as well as the Commons. The nearest point of contact here is that the Levellers wanted a single chamber parliament of 300 or 400 members, and that Sir Anthony Ashley Cooper (as he then was) served in the first Protectorate council of state at a time when the constitution provided for just such a parliament (plus Irish and Scottish members, but that is hardly to the point here); this remained the form of the Cromwellian legislature until the Instrument of Government was discarded in favour of the Humble Petition and Advice in 1657–58. Moreover Ashley Cooper was a member of the two parliaments elected on this basis, although he only sat in the first of them, being excluded from the second by the executive (his own erstwhile colleagues on the council of state). It would, however, be absurd to infer from this that he actually preferred a unicameral legislature. And it is worth remembering that, until the final lurch towards revolution in the winter of 1648–49, the Independents had consistently made a stronger showing in

---

[22] *Two Treatises*, II, ch. XIII, paras. 157–58; compare *A Letter from a Person of Quality to his Friend in the Country* ... (Wing, *STC*, S2897; reprinted in *Cobbett's Parliamentary History of England*, IV (1808), Appendix V, pp. xxxviii–lxviii, but *not* with *Some Observations concerning the regulating of Elections for Parliament* ... (Wing, S4534; reprinted in *Somers Tracts* (1st edn, 1748), I, i, 63–72. For the acceptance of the one and rejection of the other, see Haley, *Shaftesbury*, pp. 390–93, 739–40.

the Lords than in the Commons.[23] In that way too Shaftesbury's alliance with other opposition peers in 1675–80 was in the tradition of Lord Saye in the 1640s, different as the historical context was in other, vital respects.

For Locke, 'in all cases whilst the Government subsists, the Legislative is the Supream Power', even though 'the Legislative being only a Fiduciary Power to act for certain ends, there remains still in the People a Supreme Power to remove or alter the Legislative', when they find it acting 'contrary to the trust reposed in them'.[24] To offer a specific parallel, a Representative introducing military or naval conscription would be acting beyond its powers under the successive Leveller *Agreements of the People*, and would thus be dissolving the Agreement itself. In Locke's case we have to exercise our imagination to work out what would justify the People becoming persuaded that the Legislative was acting contrary to the trust reposed in them: suspending future elections and declaring themselves perpetual legislators might be one such case, surrendering to the Executive the right to levy taxes or abolishing trial by jury would be others. But this is nowhere spelled out and has to be inferred; the *Second Treatise* is not a blueprint for a written constitution, or even for a future Bill of Rights. The examples which Locke does give relate almost exclusively to misuse of its powers by the Executive and the consequent justification for its removal by force. Whether it is to be seen as a manifesto for the last Exclusion Parliament, Rye House, the Monmouth rising or the Dutch invasion, the *Second Treatise* made the case for acting against an executive, namely the monarch, who had either suspended or emasculated the legislative. In Leveller writings, on the contrary, the executive is so feeble a thing, so shadowy an entity, that the people scarcely need protecting against it; that is, once the Agreement has been implemented and become operative. In the actual circumstances of 1647–49 their attitudes towards the king and then the Council of State under the Commonwealth were of course very different.

As to Leveller demands for reform and decentralisation of the law, more prominent in some of the tracts than in the *Agreements* themselves, there is no real equivalent in Locke's writings. He certainly appreciated that the executive had to have 'discretion', or 'Prerogative', notably when the legislative is not in session, and one of the ways in which this could be abused is by the misuse of judicial power; but that is hardly a call for reform of the law or the legal system.

The case for a transmission of Leveller ideas from the mid- to the later

---

[23] See J. S. A. Adamson, 'The English nobility and the projected settlement of 1647', *Historical Journal*, 30 (1987), 567–602.

[24] *Second Treatise*, ch. XIII, paras. 150, 149.

seventeenth century must rest either on the written word (in print and manuscript), or on the role of surviving individuals, or on a more generalised oral tradition. In practice these three modes might well have overlapped, and it does not seem sensible to examine each separately in isolation from the other two. The use of 'levelling' as a general term of abuse by their enemies against non-conforming sectaries, republicans and later even radical Whigs certainly reveals continuity, and Ashcraft's quotations are to the point here. But that in itself tells us little, if anything, about actual Leveller influence. How much weight is to be put on the survival of Wildman himself and various other ex-officers and ex-soldiers from the 1640s and 1650s, who had been active political radicals? Major (finally 'Colonel') Abraham Holmes was certainly a radical puritan and republican; the evidence for his ever having been a Leveller is distinctly thin.[25] John Breman and Richard Rumbold seem to be the only two conspirators or rebels of the 1680s, apart from Wildman, who can definitely be identified as Levellers in earlier times.[26] It may of course be objected that, just as Wildman had acted in concert with a range of other republicans in opposition to the Protectorate in 1654–55 and with other varied supporters of the restored Commonwealth in 1659, so in the later years of crisis (1678–89) the distinction between ex-Levellers and ex-republicans is not of great moment – and did not have much contemporary significance. I have a good deal of sympathy with this point of view, but it can be seen to cut both ways as regards any specific Leveller influence on Locke.

Another contributor to this volume has seen religious toleration as the Levellers' fundamental objective, to which all their other policies were subsidiary means.[27] Without going so far as this (preferring myself to believe that they had a plurality rather than a hierarchy of values), its importance for them is beyond dispute. That remains true even if the nature and the boundaries of such freedom of worship and expression were a matter of disagreement among those who may all loosely be called Levellers. Similarly, whatever Locke's priorities at different times and in

[25] *Dictionary of National Biography* (*DNB*); *The Clarke Papers*, ed. C. H. Firth, 4 vols. (Camden New Series, xlix, liv, lxi, lxii, 1891–1901), I, 161, 436; C. H. Firth and G. Davies, *The Regimental History of Cromwell's Army*, 2 vols. (Oxford, 1940), pp. 438, 456, 459, 479–80, 535–36, 539, 540–41.

[26] For Breman (spelt in several different ways) see *Clarke Papers*, I, 790, 161; Firth and Davies, *Cromwell's Army*, pp. 144, 151, 154–57, 162–63. For Rumbold, *DNB*; *Clarke Papers*, II, 194; Firth and Davies, *Cromwell's Army*, pp. 75, 80. For Wildman see also M. Ashley, *John Wildman, Plotter and Postmaster* (London, 1947), an excellent biography but now in need of revision or updating.

[27] J. C. Davis, 'The Levellers and Christianity', in B. S. Manning (ed.), *Politics, Religion and the English Civil War* (London, 1973), pp. 225–50.

different contexts, there can be no doubt that he held consistently to a doctrine of toleration, at least from 1667 to the end of his life.[28] Whatever the formative influence of Lord Ashley (as he then was) on Locke's ideas about religion and the state, no one to my knowledge has seriously suggested that Ashley arrived at a tolerationist position because of Leveller influence. Not that Richard Ashcraft argued for this; it is, however, another reminder that sharing beliefs does not necessarily indicate, let alone prove, any influence in either direction.

Ashcraft may, however, seem to have been on stronger ground when he argued that in Locke's dissolution of government, which is equivalent to a revolution, 'the people' at large are entitled to participate. And the question is whether, from Locke's wording, we can infer that he meant the entire adult male population, all property-holders, or simply the existing electorate. His text strongly suggests that he used 'the people' in a deliberately loose, undefined way.[29] Even if 'the Property of the People' includes their 'Lives, Liberties and Estates', their right to act in such an extreme situation is much more to restore the proper, that is the previously existing, rights of the electors, not to change the electorate, by for example including all adult males in its ranks. If this makes a famous philosopher seem vague and indecisive, we may rather believe that Locke saw the potential inconsistency opening up as his argument proceeded, and left the issue deliberately imprecise. Even if we were to accept that his 'industrious and rational', those to whom he ascribed such a key role in developing the earth's riches, were substantially the same as the Levellers' 'not subject to the will of others' (that is, more or less the suffrage agreed between them and the Independents in 1648–49), which itself involves some daring conceptual acrobatics, this really does not prove the influence of the one upon the other. Were John Lilburne's 'laborious and industrious people', for whom he claimed to speak and for whose enfranchisement he called,[30] really the same as Locke's 'industrious and rational', to whose use 'God gave the World ... in Common'? Or the same as 'the People', who 'are at liberty to provide for themselves by erecting a new Legislative'? Locke was confident that the legislative would remain, as it had since time immemorial, vested in a hereditary single person, an assembly of hereditary nobles (he might well have wished to do without bishops, but that is hardly a central point here), and an assembly of representatives chosen, *pro*

---

[28] This is explained convincingly and in detail by John Marshall in his *John Locke: Resistance, Religion and Responsibility* (Cambridge, 1994), esp. pp. 62–72.

[29] *Second Treatise*, ch. XIX, paras. 221–22.

[30] Quoted by David Wootton in his 'Leveller Democracy and the Puritan Revolution', ch. 14, p. 413, in *The Cambridge History of Political Thought 1450–1700*, ed. J. H. Burns and M. Goldie (Cambridge, 1991).

tempore, by the People. He saw successive revolutions as merely having moved the crown from the head of one prince to that of another within the same family or dynasty; such passages were clearly intended to place 1688–89 firmly in the tradition of 1327, 1399, 1461 and 1485, possibly also of 1660 and conceivably even of 1066. They seem likely to have been added to his text in 1689, and are categorically not any kind of revived call for a Leveller-style new constitution, such as has been demanded back in 1647–49.[31]

A further point of difference is that the Levellers nowhere discussed or drew the distinction between society and government in the way that Locke did.[32] James Tully's argument that Locke's theory of property was not substantially different from that of Lilburne and Overton has to be taken in the context of his case against C. B. Macpherson, and is not intended to suggest that he was influenced by them.[33] And even if we accept that Locke's social and economic ideal was a society dominated by small independent owner-occupiers and self-employed craftsmen and tradesmen, unlike the Levellers he nowhere proposed a political programme designed to bring this about. While acknowledging the delicacy of selective quotation, it may also be worth citing the post-Tully but pre-Ashcraft approach followed by Neal Wood: 'taking the radical levelling slogan of liberty and equality against tyranny, Locke transformed it into a more conservative justification of inequality in landed property against absolutism, a position bound to have an irresistible appeal to Whig husbandmen of upper and middle rank'.[34] Although this goes a good deal further towards economic reductionism than my own doubts about Ashcraft's thesis, it is worth putting in the balance along with Tully, since both of them by implication contradict Ashcraft.[35]

The conservative Whig, William Atwood, is said to have had Locke in mind, rather than the lesser radical and republican pamphleteers of 1689, when he complained of the danger of anarchy if everybody were entitled to share in making a new government following the flight of James II.[36] By his own standards Atwood was correct to be worried about the potential effect which the *Second Treatise* might have had, if it fell into the wrong hands in a popularised form (reminiscent of the argument that a pornographic novel is dangerous in a cheap paperback but not in an expensive

---

[31] *Second Treatise*, ch. xix, paras. 213, 223.
[32] Ibid., ch. xix, *passim*.   [33] Tully, *Discourse on Property*, p. 169.
[34] Neal Wood, *John Locke and Agrarian Capitalism* (Berkeley, CA, 1984), p. 70.
[35] A further historiographical complication is that Tully, apparently persuaded by Ashcraft, has changed his views about Locke since then: see *Cambridge History of Political Thought*, IV, ch. 21, pp. 616–52.
[36] See ibid., p. 639 and compare Ashcraft, *Revolutionary Politics*, pp. 585–59.

limited edition). We may grant too that by 1690 Locke might well have been disappointed with the course of political developments since the Revolution, but he would have had to have been so by August 1689 at the very latest for this to have influenced anything in the text of the *Two Treatises*. Nor has enough evidence yet been adduced that between the autumn of 1688 and the summer of 1689 he was other than a more or less orthodox Orangist, with his Shaftesburyite and thus by implication Monmouthite past to be lived down.

Locke's views on taxation have rightly been seen as anticipating, and subsequently helping to justify the later eighteenth-century American and British radical slogan of 'No taxation without representation'. What Locke wrote about this could be taken to mean that everyone who pays taxes should be represented in the sense of having the right to vote as a parliamentary elector. It could have the slightly but significant different meaning that only those who pay taxes need or should be represented. The question partly turns on the meaning of paying taxes; Locke might well have wished to distinguish between direct taxation levied on individuals – landowners, householders, merchants and tradesmen (down to the cut-off level of exemption from subsidies, hearth tax or poll taxes) – and indirect taxation in the form of higher prices being paid by retailers and consumers because of the levying of customs and excise duties, which were actually paid by merchants and wholesalers. The doctrine of majority rule through a tax-paying electorate is overridden by gender; otherwise there would be a shocking inconsistency in Locke's case due to propertied widows and spinsters not having the vote. While married women and daughters could be regarded as being virtually represented by their husbands and fathers or brothers, respectively, in a society with as high a death rate as late seventeenth-century England, there must always at any given time have been quite a number of women without these male adjuncts and yet possessing property on which taxes were to be paid. All that can be said is that Locke's assumption that gender overrode all claims except those of queens regnant affected fewer individuals in the population than the Leveller denial of votes to women in their proposed franchise. With this exception, it is possible to argue that Locke was consistent in maintaining that taxation required consent, and consent representation.[37]

Ashcraft also argued that Locke and the Levellers shared a common dislike of primogeniture. Both believed in the equal inheritance of landed property by all the sons in a family (if not also the daughters). However Locke's main concern in the relevant sections of the *First Treatise* was of course to deny that the first-born had any prescriptive right to rule or to

---

[37] *Second Treatise*, ch. XI, paras. 140, 142.

transmit such a right to their posterity. He may have shared James Harrington's belief in the desirability of an agrarian law, to prevent land from falling into the hands of too few people by limiting the size of landed estates, and he may possibly have favoured partible inheritance; but to make this into any part of Locke's political programme is to strain the evidence excessively.[38]

Locke could be said to have upheld the principle of equality before the law much as it had been expressed by the Levellers in the first (1647) *Agreement of the People*. But he clearly took for granted the existence of a society where wealth was very unequally distributed; whatever his theories about the origins of society, he offers absolutely nothing by way of a programme to reduce such inequalities, and certainly nothing remotely comparable to the third (1649) *Agreement to the People*'s insistence on the abolition of all customs as well as excise duties and their replacement by 'an equal rate in the pound upon every reall and personall estate in the Nation' – whether we are to take this as a call for a flat-rate income tax or for a levy on capital.[39] So, apart from the principle of representation, which would take us back to the question of who was to be represented and how, there is nothing here to suggest any specifically Leveller influence.

Much has been made by recent commentators of Locke's interesting and important letter to his good friend Edward Clarke, written a week after the opening of the Convention but before Locke had himself arrived in London. The letter stands out because it is such a rare instance among his surviving letters in being overtly political in content. From what he had already heard of its opening proceedings, he was critical of the Convention for behaving like a normal parliament, that is to say for wasting time on trivial and routine matters instead of getting on with the really important business of 'restoring our ancient government, the best possibly that ever was if taken and put together all of a piece in its originall constitution'; the members should be dealing with 'the great frame of government' and should then address the urgent, pressing problems of foreign affairs and Ireland.[40] So far from offering any conceivable sort of parallel with Leveller demands for an Agreement of the People, to be universally subscribed by the entire electorate, it seems more instructive to compare this with the remarkable 'Paper of Instructions for the Parliament Meeting

---

[38] Ashcraft, *Revolutionary Politics*, p. 283, enlisting the support of Tully (see *Discourse on Property*, pp. 134, 146, 169); both rely heavily on Locke, *First Treatise*, paras. 90–97, 111–12, 119. The anti-Filmerian purport of Locke's argument is abundantly clear.

[39] Wolfe, *Leveller Manifestoes*, p. 407; Haller and Davies, *Leveller Tracts*, p. 325; Aylmer, *Levellers*, p. 165.

[40] *Locke Correspondence*, III, (1978), 545–47, letter no. 1102, 29 January/8 February 1688/89.

after the revolution', written by the Dorset Whig Thomas Erle and recently published in *Parliamentary History* with a valuable brief introduction by Mark Goldie. Being so easily accessible a full summary is hardly in order. Erle's paper is a perhaps predictable mixture of detail and generality, but his theory of contract is much to the point:

> The obligation between the King and the people seem to me to be mutual, the King binding himself first, by his coronation oath, to govern according to law ... The subjects have taken an oath not to take arms against the King upon any pretence what soever ... The King first breaking his oath with his subjects, they are no longer bound by their oath of allegiance to him.[41]

Goldie properly distinguishes Erle's proposals from those of the neo-Harringtonian *Some remarks upon Government*, which he ascribes (in all probability) to John Wildman; he identifies Wildman correctly as 'an old leveller', but does not describe him as a Leveller in any meaningful sense by 1689. Not, as has already been suggested here, that too much should be made of any such possible links. Wildman was a reluctant Monmouthite, having been prepared to try to start a rising in London if the pretender's cause looked like triumphing, but of course prudently getting out when it was patently failing to do so. Locke's Monmouthism was through association with his friend and patron Shaftesbury; his views on the abortive 1685 invasion as seen from his exile in Holland remain a matter of surmise. Both of them in different ways had pasts to live down. How far this explains Locke's persistent refusal to declare his authorship of the *Two Treatises* until he came to make his will in 1704 is conjecture likewise; fear of a successful Jacobite restoration would seem at least as valid a reason for anonymity after 1688–89 as for non-publication before then.

As for levelling in the social sense, Lord Beloff demonstrated in his first published book many years ago that there was no lack of popular disturbances, in addition to the more politically motivated plots and conspiracies, during these years. But of actual 'levelling' there is little evidence, though the name was allegedly adopted by agrarian rioters (or criminals) in Worcestershire at the end of 1670. Their aims and objectives, if any, remain obscure.[42]

To argue that because a few one-time Agitators from the 1640s were involved in the projected uprisings and assassination plots of the early 1680s, therefore the clients and agents of these undertakings' aristocratic fellow-travellers were under Leveller influence, is to verge on the fanciful. Moreover, if we do think back to the Interregnum, none of the Levellers

---

[41] *Parliamentary History*, 14, Pt 3 (1995), quotation from p. 347.

[42] M. Beloff, *Public Order and Popular Disturbances, 1660–1714* (Oxford, 1938), p. 23 and n. 1. The original state papers (PRO, SP29) add nothing to the *Calendar*.

except for Edward Sexby (who had been dead for twenty years by the time of the Popish Plot) had advocated 'lopping', as the proposed killing of the King and the Duke was apparently called (the arboreal metaphor perhaps being designed to soften the brutal reality), while the only person to have attempted the assassination of the Protector was Miles Sindercombe in 1657. The evidence that Locke took part in planning the Rye House or any other murder scheme against Charles and James is nonexistent; but even if he were drawn into discussions of armed insurrection after the Oxford Parliament and the reaction which followed its dissolution, it would by no means prove that either his actions or his political thinking were Leveller-influenced. The same might be said in the case of Algernon Sidney, but that is another story.[43]

Since no manuscript versions of the *Two Treatises* are known to survive, it remains a possibility that Locke did consult the Leveller tracts in the possession of his friend and host in exile, Benjamin Furley, and that he then revised parts of the *Second Treatise* with the effect of making it more democratic, sometime during the mid- or later 1680s. This cannot be proved or disproved. Nor did Ashcraft rest his case on it, preferring instead a similar argument to that adduced by Peter Laslett in 1960: 'It was from this source [the general climate of ideas], from conversation and casual contact, not from documentary acquaintance, that Locke inherited the fruit of the radical writings of the Civil War.'[44] But I cannot find that Ashcraft anywhere cited the more specific, and it might be thought more relevant, passage earlier in the same text: 'The fact is that as far as we know Locke never read Lilburne and the other Levellers, then [i.e. in 1659–60] or afterwards. He was brought back to the tradition which they began by an unexpected turn in his personal life.'[45] I take Laslett's last phrase here to refer to the connection with Shaftesbury. There remains a further possibility: that Locke did indeed browse in Furley's library, but did not significantly alter anything in the text of the *Treatises* because of anything which he lighted upon there. Locke himself possessed the following works published between 1640 and 1660 which might have

---

[43] Jonathan Scott, in his *Algernon Sidney and the English Revolution 1623–1677* (Cambridge, 1988) and more particularly *Algernon Sidney and the Restoration Crisis 1677–1683* (Cambridge, 1991), appears to see Sidney favouring some kind of 'tribunitian' military democracy. Compare Blair Worden's considered judgement that: 'His [Sidney's] clear preference is for a mixed government in which aristocracy is the predominant form ...' (A. B. Worden, 'English Republicanism', *Cambridge History of Political Thought*, IV, pp. 460–61.)

[44] Ashcraft, *Revolutionary Politics*, p. 165, n. 145; Laslett, *Locke's Two Treatises*, Introduction, p. 75.

[45] Ibid., p. 22.

helped in different ways to shape his own views in relation to the later events of 1678–89.

The *Grand Remonstrance* (1641);
Henry Parker's *Free Trade* (1648);
The *Remonstrance of the Army* (November 1648);
The *Proclamation for the Trial of the King* (January 1648/9);
The *Eikon Basilike* (1649);
William Lilly, *Monarchy or no monarchy* (1651);
Hobbes, *Leviathan* (1651);
George Lawson, *An Examination of Hobbes* (1657);
Harrington, *The Art of Lawgiving* (1659);
P. C. Zuriksee, *alias* Plockhoy, *A Way propounded to make the poor ... happy* (1659);
Rushworth's *Historical Collections*, vol. 1 (1659);
Lawson's *Politica sacra et civilis* (1660).[46]

It would of course be absurd to suggest that Locke's reading was confined to items which he himself owned, either in Oxford or later; too much therefore should not be made of this. John Marshall has pointed out that Locke's recommended authors on history and politics, for an English gentleman, were William Atwood, William Petyt, John Sadler and James Tyrrell.[47] All four were proponents of the 'ancient constitution' rather than of natural rights, while Sadler was a millenarian Puritan to boot. Again it would be wrong to make too much of this, but it cannot be totally swept aside.

It now seems to be agreed by most historians of Charles II's reign that there were two conspiracies in 1681–83. One was to promote an insurrection in Scotland as well as in England, in order to force the King to change his ministers and his policies, in effect to surrender his powers as his father had had to do in 1640–41; in various ways Shaftesbury, Essex, Russell and Sidney were implicated in this, and were thus guilty of conspiring to bring about a rebellion tantamount to high treason; if this is correct, Locke should presumably be included among those involved. Secondly there was a plot, perhaps more than one, to murder the King and his brother; this was to be followed either by the setting up of a puppet king (Monmouth) or by the restoration of a republic. How many people were privy to both projects is unknown and likely to remain so: too much of the evidence is tainted, coming from terrified informers seeking to save their own lives, or from double agents, or else was extorted under torture. Ironically John Wildman, who died in his bed a knight and alderman of the City ten years

---

[46] J. Harrison and P. Laslett, *The Library of John Locke* (2nd edn, Oxford, 1971), nos. 2465a, 2197, 1091, 598, 596, 1753, 1465, 1695, 1387, 3196, 2514, 1695a.
[47] *John Locke*, pp. 278, 318.

later, may possibly have been one of the very few who were fully aware of both undertakings. That Locke knew of the plan to kill Charles and James is not logically impossible, but on the evidence available seems very unlikely. That of course does not lessen his intellectual commitment to the right of resistance and hence his support for a possible armed uprising in extreme circumstances. The alternative to all this, once more fashionable than it is today, is to regard the whole thing, or to be precise both things, as a frame-up; to hold that the alleged conspirators of 1681–83 – implicated at most by the wild talk of drunks and desperadoes – were no more guilty than the five Catholic peers and the other victims of the opposite ideological paranoia in 1679–80. Although something like the issue of Essex's death – suicide or murder? – can still excite disagreement between serious scholars, the general burden of evidence seems to point away from the frame-up theory, in which case Locke's vulnerability was not due simply to the vindictiveness of those involved in the court-Tory reaction of the 1680s.

Granted all the anachronisms in the use of such labels, John Locke may reasonably be thought of as an individualist liberal,[48] a constitutionalist and (in language nearer to his own) a Whig and a believer in the right and duty of resistance to tyrants, even to the point of violent revolution. It remains to be demonstrated that he owed much to the ideas or the example of the mid-century Levellers.

---

[48] This is to go against the interpretation advanced with force and elegance by John Dunn in his *The Political Thought of John Locke. An Historical Account of the Argument of the 'Two Treatises of Government'* (Cambridge, 1969). Compare his *Locke* (Pastmasters series, Oxford, 1984; reprinted 1996).

A bibliography of the writings of Austin Woolrych, 1955–95

COMPILED BY SARA COOMBS

1955

Penruddock's Rising, 1655 (London: Historical Association General Pamphlet Series, no. 29, 1955).

1956

'Yorkshire's Treaty of Neutrality', *History Today*, 6 (1956), pp. 696–704.

1957

'The Good Old Cause and the Fall of the Protectorate', *Cambridge Historical Journal*, 13 (1957), pp. 133–61.

Reviews:

D. H. Pennington and I. A. Roots, eds., *The Committee at Stafford, 1643–1645* (Manchester University Press and Staffordshire Record Society, 1957); A. M. Everitt, *The County Committee of Kent in the Civil War* (University of Leicester Press, 1957), in *History*, 42 (1957), pp. 240–41.

1958

'The collapse of the Great Rebellion', *History Today*, 8 (1958), pp. 606–15.
'Yorkshire and the Restoration', *Yorkshire Archaeological Journal*, 39 (1958), pp. 483–507.

1959

'Our liberties as Men and Christians', *The Listener*, 61 (1555), 15 January 1959, pp. 102–4. Text of a talk on Oliver Cromwell, broadcast by *Third Programme* in a series entitled 'Revolutionaries and their Principles'.

Reviews:

Maurice Ashley, *Oliver Cromwell and the Puritan Revolution* (London: English Universities Press, 1958), in *History*, 44 (1959), p. 162.

Alfred H. Burne and Peter Young, *The Great Civil War* (London: Eyre and Spottiswoode, 1959), in 'Civil War Battle-Pieces', *The Listener*, 61 (1563), 12 March 1959, p. 473.

Ernest John Knapton, *Europe, 1450–1815* (London: John Murray, 1959), in *The Listener*, 62 (1579), 2 July 1959, pp. 29–31.

1960

Reviews:

C. V. Wedgwood, *The King's War, 1641–1647* (London: Collins, 1958), in *English Historical Review*, 75 (1960), p. 163.

Christopher Hill, *Puritanism and Revolution* (London: Secker and Warburg, 1958), in *English Historical Review*, 75 (1960), p. 164.

Hugh F. Kearney, *Strafford in Ireland, 1633–41: A Study in Absolutism* (Manchester: Manchester University Press, 1959), in *History*, 45 (1960), pp. 56–57.

Hesketh Pearson, *Charles II: His Life and Likeness* (London: Heinemann, 1960), in *The Listener*, 63 (1624), 12 May 1960, pp. 854–55.

1961

Battles of the English Civil War: Marston Moor, Naseby, Preston (London: B. T. Batsford, 1961). Also, Pan Books edition, 1966; Pimlico edition, with new Preface, 1991.

Reviews:

Leo F. Solt, *Saints in Arms: Puritanism and Democracy in Cromwell's Army* (Stanford University Press; London: Oxford University Press, 1959), in *English Historical Review*, 76 (1961), p. 155.

David Underdown, *Royalist Conspiracy in England, 1649–1660* (New Haven: Yale University Press, 1960), in *History*, 46 (1961), pp. 145–46.

D. L. Hobman, *Cromwell's Master Spy: A Study of John Thurloe* (London: Chapman and Hall, 1961), in *History*, 46 (1961), pp. 251–52.

G. E. Aylmer, *The King's Servants: The Civil Service of Charles I, 1625–1642* (London: Routledge and Kegan Paul, 1961), in *The Listener*, 65 (1666), 2 March 1961, pp. 401–2.

Christopher Hill, *The Century of Revolution, 1602–1714* (Edinburgh: Thomas Nelson, 1961), in *The Listener*, 65 (1682), 22 June 1961, p. 1102.

H. N. Brailsford, *The Levellers and the English Revolution*, ed. Christopher Hill (London: Cresset Press, 1961), in *The Listener*, 66 (1688), 3 August 1961, p. 179.

1962

Reviews:

Valerie Pearl, *London and the Outbreak of the Puritan Revolution* (London: Oxford University Press, 1961), in *English Historical Review*, 77 (1962), pp. 773–74.

Alan Everitt, ed., *Suffolk and the Great Rebellion, 1640–1660* (Ipswich: Suffolk Records Society, 1961), in *English Historical Review*, 77 (1962), pp. 775–76.

Helen A. Kaufman, *Conscientious Cavalier* (London: Jonathan Cape, 1962), in *The Listener*, 68 (1750), 11 October 1962, pp. 576–77.

Carola Oman, *Mary of Modena* (Hodder and Stoughton, 1962), in *The Listener*, 68 (1760), 20 December 1962, pp. 1058–60.

1964

Oliver Cromwell (Oxford: Oxford University Press, Clarendon Biographies Series, 1964).

Reviews:

William M. Lamont, *Marginal Prynne 1600–1669* (London: Routledge and Kegan Paul, 1963), in *History*, 49 (1964), pp. 74–75.

H. G. Tibbutt, ed., *The Letter Books of Sir Samuel Luke 1644–45* (London: HMSO, 1963), in *History*, 49 (1964), pp. 226–27.

1965

'The Calling of Barebone's Parliament', *English Historical Review*, 80 (1965), pp. 492–513.

1966

Reviews:

Maurice Ashley, *The Glorious Revolution of 1688* (London: Hodder and Stoughton, 1966); Richard Oller, *The Escape of Charles II after the Battle of Worcester* (London: Hodder and Stoughton, 1966); Elizabeth Read Foster, ed., *Proceedings in Parliament, 1610*. Volume I: *House of Lords*; Volume II: *The House of Commons* (New Haven: Yale University Press, 1966), in 'A diversity', *The Listener*, 76 (1958), 6 October 1966, p. 512.

1967

'Puritanism, democracy and the English Revolution', in *Inaugural Lectures, 1965–1967* (Lancaster University, 1967), pp. 99–114.

'The collapse of the Great Rebellion', in Ivan Roots, ed., *Conflicts in Tudor and*

Stuart England: Selections from History Today (Edinburgh and London: Oliver and Boyd, 1967), pp. 82–101. Article originally published 1958.

Reviews:

Andrew G. Watson, *The Library of Sir Simonds D'Ewes* (London: Trustees of the British Museum, 1966), in *English Historical Review*, 82 (1967), pp. 836–37.

Clayton Roberts, *The Growth of Responsible Government in Stuart England* (Cambridge University Press, 1966), in *History*, 52 (1967), pp. 201–4.

Ivan Roots, *The Great Rebellion, 1642–1660* (London: B. T. Batsford, 1966), in *History*, 52 (1967), pp. 330–31.

1968

'The English Revolution: An Introduction', in E. W. Ives, ed., *The English Revolution, 1600–1660* (London: Edward Arnold, 1968), pp. 1–33.

'Puritanism, Politics and Society', in E. W. Ives, ed., *The English Revolution, 1600–1660* (London: Edward Arnold, 1968), pp. 87–100. Revised edition of a broadcast for the BBC, as part of their series entitled 'The English Revolution', in 1966.

Reviews:

Roger Howell, Jr, *Newcastle-upon-Tyne and the Puritan Revolution: A Study of the Civil War in North England* (Oxford: Clarendon Press, 1967), in *History*, 53 (1968), p. 113.

1970

'Early Modern History', in Harold Perkin, ed., *History: An Introduction for the Intending Student* (London: Routledge and Kegan Paul, 1970), pp. 57–70.

'Oliver Cromwell and the Rule of the Saints', in R. H. Parry, ed., *The English Civil War and After, 1642–1658* (Basingstoke and London: Macmillan, 1970), pp. 59–77.

Reviews:

J. T. Cliffe, *The Yorkshire Gentry from the Reformation to the Civil War* (London: Athlone Press, 1969), in *Northern History*, 5 (1970), pp. 229–31.

1971

Reviews:

Donald Veall, *The Popular Movement for Law Reform, 1640–1660* (Oxford: Oxford University Press, 1970); Michael Landon, *The Triumph of the Lawyers: Their Role in English Politics, 1678–1689* (University of Alabama Press, 1970), in *History*, 56 (1971), pp. 269–70.

Alan MacFarlane, *The Family Life of Ralph Josselin, a Seventeenth Century Clergyman* (Cambridge University Press, 1970), in *English Historical Review*, 86 (1971), pp. 412–13.

1972

'Last Quests for a Settlement, 1657–1660', in G. E. Aylmer, ed., *The Interregnum: The Quest for Settlement, 1646–1660* (Basingstoke and London: Macmillan, 1972, revised edn 1974), pp. 183–204, pp. 232–34.

'Milton's left hand', *Cromwelliana* (1972), pp. 1–5. Based on a Radio 3 lecture of 3 March 1971.

Reviews:

Vernon F. Snow, *Essex the Rebel: The Life of Robert Devereux, the Third Earl of Essex, 1591–1646* (Lincoln: University of Nebraska Press, 1970), in *English Historical Review*, 87 (1972), pp. 624–25.

Clive Holmes, ed., *The Suffolk Committees for Scandalous Ministers* (Ipswich: Suffolk Records Society, 1970), in *English Historical Review*, 87 (1972), pp. 626–27.

David Underdown, *Pride's Purge: Politics in the Puritan Revolution* (Oxford: Clarendon Press, 1971), in *English Historical Review*, 87 (1972), pp. 825–86.

A. L. Morton, *The World of the Ranters: Religious Radicalism in the English Revolution* (London: Lawrence and Wishart, 1970), in *History*, 57 (1972), pp. 128–29.

1973

'Oliver Cromwell and the Rule of the Saints', in Ivan Roots, ed., *Cromwell: A Profile* (Basingstoke and London: Macmillan, 1973), pp. 50–71. Revised edition of a paper of the same title, originally published 1970.

'Penruddock's Rising', in K. H. D. Haley, ed., *The Historical Association Book of the Stuarts* (London: Sidgwick and Jackson, 1973), pp. 104–32. Originally published 1955, Historical Association Pamphlets, General Series, no. 29.

'The English Revolution: An Introduction', in Charles D. Hamilton, ed., *Western Civilisations: Recent Interpretations*. Volume I: *Earliest Times to 1715* (New York: Thomas Y. Crowell Co., 1973), pp. 508–32. Article originally published 1968.

'The English Revolution: An Introduction', in L. Kaplan, ed., *Revolutions: A Comparative Study* (New York: Vintage Books, 1973), pp. 77–111. Revised edition of a paper of the same title, originally published 1968.

Reviews:

Wilfred R. Prest, *The Inns of Court under Elizabeth I and the Early Stuarts, 1590–1640* (London: Longman, 1972), in *English Historical Review*, 88 (1973), pp. 628–29.

Christopher Hill, *Antichrist in Seventeenth Century England* (London: Oxford University Press, 1971), in *English Historical Review*, 88 (1973), p. 899.

B. S. Capp, *The Fifth Monarchy Men: A Study in Seventeenth Century English Millenarianism* (London: Faber and Faber, 1972); Christopher Hill, *The World Turned Upside Down: Radical Ideas during the English Revolution* (London: Temple Smith, 1972), in *History*, 58 (1973), pp. 289–91.

1974

'Historical Introduction (1659–1660)', in Robert W. Ayers and Austin Woolrych, eds., *Complete Prose Works of Milton*. Volume VII: *1659–1660* (New Haven and London: Yale University Press, 1974), pp. 1–228.

'The Meeting of the Long Parliament', in Christopher Hibbert, ed., *Milestones of History: 6. The Pen and the Sword* (George Weidenfeld and Nicolson Ltd. for Readers Digest, 1970; revised and expanded, 1974), pp. 64–69.

'Milton and Cromwell: "A Short but Scandalous Night of Interruption"?' in Michael Lieb and John T. Shawcross, eds., *Achievements of the Left Hand: Essays on the Prose of Milton* (Amherst: University of Massachusetts Press, 1974), pp. 185–218.

'Milton and Richard Heath', *Philological Quarterly*, 53 (1974), pp. 132–35.

'Milton's political commitment: the interplay of Puritan and classical ideals', *Wascana Review*, 9 (1974), pp. 166–68.

Reviews:

Peter Clark and Paul Slack, eds., *Crisis and Order in English Towns, 1500–1700* (London: Routledge and Kegan Paul, 1972), in *English Historical Review*, 89 (1974), pp. 172–73.

1975

Reviews:

Antonia Fraser, *Cromwell, Our Chief of Men* (London: Weidenfeld and Nicolson, 1973), in *English Historical Review*, 90 (1975), pp. 194–95.

J. S. Morrill, *Cheshire, 1630–1660: County Government and Society during the English Revolution* (London: Oxford University Press, 1974), in *English Historical Review*, 90 (1975), pp. 369–71.

David Stevenson, *The Scottish Revolution, 1637–1644: The Triumph of the Covenanters* (Newton Abbot: David and Charles, 1973), in *English Historical Review*, 90 (1975), p. 648.

G. E. Aylmer, *The State's Servants: The Civil Service of the English Republic, 1649–1660* (London: Routledge and Kegan Paul, 1973), in *History*, 60 (1975), pp. 123–25.

John Adair, *Cheriton 1644: The Campaign and the Battle* (Kineton: The Roundhead Press, 1973), in *History*, 60 (1975), p. 299.

Blair Worden, *The Rump Parliament* (Cambridge University Press, 1974), in *History*, 60 (1975), pp. 299–301.

Miscellany:

Ivan Roots, *Oliver Cromwell: His Rise to Greatness* and *Oliver Cromwell: the Lord Protector* (London and New York: Audio Learning Ltd; Harper and Row, 1975). Audiotape discussion between Roots and Woolrych.

Ivan Roots, *The General Crisis of the Seventeenth Century* and *The Thirty Years War* (London: Audio Learning Ltd, 1975). Audiotape discussion between Roots and Woolrych.

1976

Reviews:

David G. Hey, *An English Rural Community: Myddle under the Tudors and Stuarts* (Leicester: Leicester University Press, 1974), in *English Historical Review*, 91 (1976), pp. 198–99.

Christopher Hill, *Change and Continuity in Seventeenth Century England* (London: Weidenfeld and Nicolson, 1975), in *History*, 61 (1976), pp. 113–14.

Ruth Spalding, *The Improbable Puritan: A Life of Bulstrode Whitelocke, 1605–1675* (London: Faber and Faber, 1975), in *History*, 61 (1976), p. 114.

Lois G. Schwoerer, *'No Standing Armies!': The Anti-Army Ideology in Seventeenth Century England* (London: Johns Hopkins University Press, 1975), in *History*, 61 (1976), pp. 284–85.

Derek Hirst, *The Representative of the People?: Voters and Voting Behaviour in England under the Early Stuarts* (Cambridge: Cambridge University Press, 1975), in *History*, 61 (1976), pp. 285–86.

Charles P. Korr, *Cromwell and the New Model Foreign Policy: England's Policy towards France, 1649–1658* (London: University of California Press, 1975), in *History*, 61 (1976), pp. 450–51.

1977

Reviews:

Brian Manning, *The English People and the English Revolution, 1640–1649* (London: Heinemann, 1976), in *History*, 62 (1977), pp. 120–21.

Christopher Hill, *Milton and the English Revolution* (London: Faber, 1977), in 'John Milton, revolutionary', *The Listener*, 98 (2529), 6 October 1977, pp. 451–52. Text of a Radio 3 broadcast.

1978

'Oliver Cromwell', vol. II (1978), pp. 95–97, 'Richard Cromwell', vol. II (1978), pp. 97–98, 'Thomas Fairfax', vol. III (1978), pp. 87–88, 'Charles Fleetwood', vol. III (1978), pp. 104–5, in William B. Hunter, Jr, ed., *A Milton Encyclopaedia*

(Lewisburg: Bucknell University Press; London: Associated University Presses Ltd, 8 vols., 1978–1980).

Reviews:

Maurice Ashley, *General Monck* (London: Jonathan Cape, 1977), in *History*, 63 (1978), pp. 126–27.

R. C. Richardson, *The Debate on the English Revolution* (London: Methuen, 1977), in *History*, 63 (1977), p. 306.

J. G. A. Pocock, *The Political Works of James Harrington* (Cambridge University Press, 1977), in *History*, 63 (1978), pp. 458–59.

1979

Reviews:

J. P. Kenyon, *Stuart England* (London: Allen Lane, 1978); Robert Ashton, *The English Civil War: Conservatism and Revolution, 1603–1649* (London: Weidenfeld and Nicholson, 1978); J. R. Jones, *Country and Court: England 1658–1714* (London: Edward Arnold, the New History of England Series, no. 5, 1978), in *History*, 64 (1979), pp. 288–90.

B. G. Blackwood, *The Lancashire Gentry and the Great Rebellion, 1640–1660* (Manchester University Press for the Chetham Society, 1978), in *History*, 64 (1979), pp. 453–54.

Donald Pennington and Keith Thomas, eds., *Puritans and Revolutionaries: Essays in Seventeenth Century History presented to Christopher Hill* (Oxford: Clarendon Press, 1978), in *Times Literary Supplement*, 4001, 23 November 1979, p. 32.

1980

'Historical Introduction (1659–1660)', in Robert W. Ayers and Austin Woolrych, eds., *Complete Prose Works of Milton*. Volume VII: *1659–1660* (revised edn, New Haven and London: Yale University Press, 1980), pp. 1–228.

'Political Theory and Political Practice', in C. A. Patrides and Raymond B. Waddington, eds., *The Age of Milton: Backgrounds to Seventeenth Century Literature* (Manchester: Manchester University Press, 1980), pp. 34–71.

'Sir Henry Vane the Younger', vol. VIII (1980), pp. 116–18, in William B. Hunter, Jr, ed., *A Milton Encyclopaedia* (Lewisburg: Bucknell University Press; London: Associated University Presses Ltd, 8 vols., 1978–1980).

'Court, Country and City Revisited', *History*, 65 (1980), pp. 236–45. Review Article for Robert Ashton, *The City and the Court* (Cambridge University Press, 1979); Peter Clark, Alan G. R. Smith and Nicholas Tyacke, eds., *The English Commonwealth, 1547–1640: Essays in Politics and Society Presented to Joel Hurstfield* (Leicester University Press, 1979); Conrad Russell, *Parliaments and English*

Politics (Oxford University Press, 1979); Stephen D. White, *Sir Edward Coke and the Grievances of the Commonwealth* (Manchester University Press, 1979).

Reviews:

F. D. Dow, *Cromwellian Scotland, 1651–1660* (Edinburgh: John Donald, 1979), in *Times Higher Education Supplement*, 386, 14 March 1980, p. 16.

1981

Reviews:

Margaret A. Judson, *From Traditional to Political Reality: A Study of the Ideas set forth in support of the Commonwealth Government in England, 1649–1653* (Hamden, Connecticut: Archon Books for the Conference in British Studies and Wittenberg University, 1980), in *History*, 66 (1981), pp. 303–4.

Marie Gimelfarb-Brack, *Liberté, Egalité, Fraternité, Justice!: La Vie et L'Oeuvre de Richard Overton, Niveleur* (Berne: Peter Lang, 1979), in *History*, 66 (1981), pp. 515–16.

1982

Commonwealth to Protectorate (Oxford: Clarendon Press, 1982). Reprinted, 1986.

'Milton and the Good Old Cause', in R. G. Shafer, ed., *Ringing the Bell Backward: The Proceedings of the First International Milton Symposium* (University of Pennsylvania Press, 1982), pp. 135–50.

Reviews:

Patricia Crawford, *Denzil Holles, 1598–1680: A Study of his Political Career* (London: Swift Printers (Publishers) Ltd for the Royal Historical Society, Studies in History Series, no. 16, 1979), in *Parliamentary History*, 1 (1982), pp. 247–48.

1983

England without a King, 1649–1660 (London and New York: Methuen, Lancaster Pamphlets series, 1983).

Reviews:

Willson H. Coates, Anne Steele Young and Vernon F. Snow, eds., *The Private Journals of the Long Parliament, 3 January to 5 March 1642* (London: Yale University Press, 1982), in *History*, 68 (1983), p. 331.

Miscellany:

Letter re: 'Charles and Cromwell' in response to an article (28 January 1983) by Paul Pickering on Charles I in *The Times*, 4 February 1983, p. 13.

1985

Reviews:

Roger Howell, *Puritans and Radicals in North England: Essays on the English Revolution* (London: University Press of America, 1984), in *History*, 70 (1985), p. 517.

Nancy L. Matthews, *William Sheppard: Cromwell's Law Reformer* (Cambridge: Cambridge University Press, 1984), in 'Other men's grievances', *Times Literary Supplement*, 4275, 8 March 1985, p. 252.

1986

'Putney Revisited: Political Debate in the New Model Army in 1647', in Colin Jones, Malyn Newitt and Stephen Robert, eds., *Politics and People in Revolutionary England: Essays in Honour of Ivan Roots* (Oxford: Basil Blackwell, 1986), pp. 95–116.

'The Civil Wars, 1640–1649' in Blair Worden, ed., *Stuart England* (Oxford: Phaidon Press, 1986), pp. 93–119.

'The Date of the Digression in Milton's *History of Britain*', in Richard Ollard and Pamela Tudor-Craig, eds., *For Veronica Wedgwood These: Studies in Seventeenth Century History* (London: Collins, 1986), pp. 217–46.

Reviews:

Peter Newman, *Atlas of the English Civil War* (London: Croom Helm, 1985), in *History*, 71 (1986), pp. 523–24.

John Wilson, *Fairfax* (London: John Murray, 1985); Peter Young, *Naseby 1645: The Campaign and the Battle* (London: Century Publishing Co., 1985), in *History*, 71 (1986), pp. 524–25.

Maija Jansson, *Two Diaries of the Long Parliament* (Gloucester: Alan Sutton, 1984), in *Parliamentary History*, 5 (1986), pp. 155–56.

Christopher Hill, *Collected Essays*. Volume I: *Writing and Revolution in Seventeenth Century England*; Volume II: *Religion and Politics in Seventeenth Century England* (Brighton: Harvester, 1986); Paul S. Seaver, *Wallington's World: A Puritan Artisan in Seventeenth Century London* (London: Methuen, 1985), in 'Radicalism, enduring and resisted', *Times Literary Supplement*, 4332, 11 April 1986, p. 380.

C. W. Brooks, *Pettyfoggers and Vipers of the Commonwealth: The Lower Branch of the Legal Profession in Early Modern England* (Cambridge: Cambridge University Press), in 'Legal Labyrinth', *Times Literary Supplement*, 4362, 7 November 1986, p. 1258.

1987

Soldiers and Statesmen: The General Council of the Army and its Debates, 1647–1648 (Oxford: Clarendon Press, 1987).

1988

'Revising Stuart Britain: Towards a New Synthesis?', *Historical Journal*, 31 (1988), pp. 443–52. Review Article for Anthony Fletcher, *Reform in the Provinces: The Government of Stuart England* (New Haven and London: Yale University Press, 1986); Derek Hirst, *Authority and Conflict: England 1603–1658* (London: Edward Arnold, 1986); Esther S. Cope, *Politics without Parliaments, 1629–1640* (London: Allen and Unwin, 1987); Maurice Lee, Jr, *The Road to Revolution: Scotland under Charles I, 1625–1637* (Urbana and Chicago: University of Illinois Press, 1985); R. C. Richardson and G. M. Ridden, eds., *Freedom and the English Revolution: Essays in History and Literature* (Manchester: Manchester University Press, 1986); Peter Gaunt, *The Cromwellian Gazetteer: An Illustrated Guide to Britain in the Civil War and Commonwealth* (Gloucester: Alan Sutton and the Cromwell Association, 1987).

Reviews:

V. F. Snow and A. S. Young, eds., *The Private Journals of the Long Parliament, 7 March–1 June 1642* (New Haven and London: Yale University Press, 1987), in *History*, 73 (1988), p. 501.

C. V. Wedgwood, *History and Hope: The Collected Essays* (London: Collins, 1987); Lawrence Stone, *The Past and the Present Revisited* (London: Routledge and Kegan Paul, 1987), in 'Two artists of explanation', *Times Literary Supplement*, 4429, 19–25 February 1988, p. 194.

Christopher Hill, *A Turbulent, Seditious and Factious People: John Bunyan and his Church* (Oxford: Clarendon Press, 1989); Geoff Eley and William Hunt, eds., *Reviving the English Revolution: Reflections and Elaborations on the Work of Christopher Hill* (London: Verso, 1988); J. T. Cliffe, *Puritans in Conflict* (Routledge, 1988); Pauline Gregg, *Oliver Cromwell* (Dent, 1988), in 'On the side of the poor', *Times Literary Supplement*, 4474, 30 December 1988–5 January 1989, p. 1436.

Miscellany:

Letter re: 'Unfair to Charles Rigg' in *Times Education Supplement, Scotland*, 19 February 1988, p. 7.

Letter re: 'The John Rylands Library' in *Times Literary Supplement*, 4438, 22–28 April 1988, p. 449.

1989

'The role of the army in the English Revolution', in J. F. Wang, ed., *Proceedings of a Symposium on British History and the Modernisation of China* (Nanjing University, 1989), pp. 115–41.

1990

'Cromwell as a Soldier', in John Morrill, ed., *Oliver Cromwell and the English Revolution* (Harlow: Longman, 1990), pp. 93–118.

'The Cromwellian Protectorate: A Military Dictatorship?', *History*, 75 (1990), pp. 207–31.

Reviews:

Nigel Smith, *Perfection Proclaimed: Language and Literature in English Radical Religion, 1640–1660* (Oxford: Clarendon Press, 1989), in *History*, 75 (1990), pp. 323–24.

1991

Battles of the English Civil War (Revised edition, London: Pimlico, 1991).

1992

'Historiographical Preface', in *The Clarke Papers: Selections from the Papers of William Clarke, Secretary to the Council of the Army, 1647–1649, and to General Monck and the Commanders of the Army in Scotland, 1651–1660* (London: Woodbridge, for the Royal Historical Society, 1992).

'Oliver Cromwell and the people of God', *Cromwelliana* (1992), pp. 2–8. Based on a Cromwell Day address of the same title given in London on September 3 1991.

'Looking Back on the Levellers', *The Historian*, 34 (1992), pp. 3–8.

Reviews:

Jack R. McMichael and Barbara Taft, eds., *The Writings of William Walwyn* (Athens, Georgia and London: University of Georgia Press, 1989), in *Parliamentary History*, 11 (1992), pp. 164–65.

Nicholas von Maltzahn, *Milton's History of Britain: Republican Historiography in the English Revolution* (Oxford: Clarendon Press, 1991), in 'Recycling the past', *Times Literary Supplement*, 4643, 27 March 1992, p. 7.

Barry Coward, *Oliver Cromwell* (Harlow and London: Longman, 1991), in 'Between God and Parliament', *Times Literary Supplement*, 4659, 17 July 1992, p. 23.

1993

'Gerald Aylmer as a Scholar', in John Morrill, Paul Slack and Daniel Woolf, eds., *Public Duty and Private Conscience in Seventeenth Century England: Essays presented to G. E. Aylmer* (Oxford: Clarendon Press, 1993), pp. 19–28.

'Dating Milton's *History of Britain*', *Historical Journal*, 36 (1993), pp. 929–43. Part of a debate with Nicholas von Maltzahn, 'Dating the Digression in Milton's *History of England*', *Historical Journal*, 36 (1993), pp. 945–56. See also the review of von Maltzahn's book in *Times Literary Supplement*, 4643, 27 March 1992, p. 7.

1994

Reviews:

Robert Thomas Fallon, *Milton in Government* (Pennsylvania State Press), in *Albion*, 26 (1994), pp. 136–38.

P. R. Newman, *The Old Service: Royalist Regimental Colonels and the Civil War, 1642–46* (Manchester: Manchester University Press, 1993), in *Albion*, 26 (1994), pp. 508–9.

Perez Zagorin, *Milton, Aristocrat and Rebel: The Poet and his Politics* (New York: D. S. Brewer, 1992), in *History of Political Thought*, 15 (1994), pp. 306–8.

J. T. Cliffe, *The Puritan Gentry Besieged, 1650–1700* (London: Routledge, 1993), in 'Keeping the faith alive', *Times Literary Supplement*, 4739, 28 January 1994, p. 24.

Mark Charles Fissel, *The Bishops Wars: Charles I's Campaigns against Scotland, 1638–1640* (Cambridge: Cambridge University Press, 1994), in 'Where it all started', *Times Literary Supplement*, 4787, 30 December 1994, p. 25.

Miscellany:

'Obituary: Maurice Ashley', *Independent*, 4 October 1994, p. 32.

1995

Reviews:

Robert Ashton, *Counter Revolution: The Second Civil War and its Origins, 1646–48* (New Haven and London: Yale University Press, 1994); David L. Smith, *Constitutional Royalism and the Search for Settlement, 1640–1649* (Cambridge: Cambridge University Press, 1994), in 'The King's mistake', *Times Literary Supplement*, 4797, 10 March 1995, p. 9.

Index